THE LETTERS OF MARGARET FULLER

Margaret Fuller. Daguerreotype, 1846. Courtesy of the Metropolitan Museum of Art, gift of I. N. Phelps Stokes, Edward S. Hawes, Alice Mary Hawes, Marion Augusta Hawes, 1937; and the Schlesinger Library, Radcliffe College.

THE LETTERS OF
Margaret Fuller, *1810-1850*

Edited by

ROBERT N. HUDSPETH

VOLUME I · 1817–38

Cornell University Press

ITHACA AND LONDON

PUBLICATION OF THIS BOOK WAS ASSISTED BY A GRANT
FROM THE PUBLICATIONS PROGRAM OF THE NATIONAL ENDOWMENT
FOR THE HUMANITIES, AN INDEPENDENT FEDERAL AGENCY.

First published 1983 by Cornell University Press.
Published in the United Kingdom by Cornell University Press Ltd.,
Ely House, 37 Dover Street, London W1X 4HQ.

International Standard Book Number 0-8014-1386-9
Library of Congress Catalog Card Number 82-22098

Printed in the United States of America

*Librarians: Library of Congress cataloging information appears
on the last page of the book.*

*The paper in this book is acid-free, and meets
the guidelines for permanence and durability
of the Committee on Production Guidelines for
Book Longevity of the Council on Library Resources.*

To the memory of my son
ROBERT NEAL HUDSPETH, JR.

PREFACE

A woman of many accomplishments, Margaret Fuller drew to her the most serious writers and thinkers of the mid-nineteenth century. She was brilliant, witty, imperious, demanding, abrasive, and charming. Ralph Waldo Emerson rightly thought her the most talented woman of their day; Horace Greeley made her one of the first professional book reviewers in America; Thomas Carlyle thought she talked too much; Giuseppe Mazzini guided her to an involvement in the Italian revolution of 1848–49. No matter where she was or what she was doing, she was the center of attention, thanks to the sharpness of her mind and the openness with which she responded to people. Though she lived but forty years, no antebellum American save Edgar Allan Poe wrote so much serious literary criticism. Not only a founder and editor of the *Dial*, she was an early and important critic and translator of Goethe; she wrote an influential feminist book; she reviewed books and wrote travel letters for the *New-York Daily Tribune*, and she served the Republicans in the Italian revolution. Her admirers included many of the most famous literary names in antebellum America: Emerson, Henry David Thoreau, Bronson Alcott, George Bancroft. Even those who took a more reserved position toward her recognized her talent.

Despite her fame in her lifetime, Fuller's writings are now scattered; her works have never been completely edited, nor have her private papers been published before. The principal document on which later readers have relied is the two-volume *Memoirs of Margaret Fuller Ossoli*, edited by Emerson, James Clarke, and William Henry Channing in 1852. For several reasons (explored fully in the section headed "The Sources"), that work is unreliable: it is factually incorrect, highly selective in its materials, and misleading in its conclusions. Yet to this day

7

it has remained the most important source for biographers and critics who have sought to understand Fuller and her work. Scattered letters appear in anthologies and biographies; portions of her journals have been edited by individual scholars; but until now no complete, fully annotated collection of her personal papers has been published.

This first volume begins with the letters of a seven-year-old child and ends with those of a young woman who was an apprentice writer ready for a larger challenge than schoolteaching offered her. Fuller's early letters to her parents provide a detailed record of life in Cambridgeport and in the schools she attended. We get family portraits and descriptions of her friends mixed with reports of her reading. This small world grew larger when Fuller began to read German literature and discuss books with James Freeman Clarke. She began her writing career with a brief essay in the *Boston Daily Advertiser*, then followed that with essays in the *American Monthly Magazine* and the *Western Messenger*.

During these years her personal life was beset by frustrations. Her father moved the family from Cambridgeport to Groton in 1833, separating his daughter from the young intellectuals at Harvard; she fell in love with George T. Davis and was rebuffed; her father died in 1835, and Fuller had to abandon her plans to visit Europe. Finally, her biography of Goethe withered for lack of information.

Fuller briefly held a position in Bronson Alcott's Temple School, but she left when Alcott was unable to pay her. She then became a teacher at the Greene-Street School in Providence. Although the position was well paid, Fuller came to see in 1838 that she was not temperamentally suited to teaching, and she resolved to go back to Boston and concentrate on her writing.

The reader finds in this volume of letters the sources of her emotional and intellectual life. The letters include characterizations of her many friends—both accomplished and obscure—and her correspondence traces her growth as a writer.

The immediate reward offered by her letters is obvious: Fuller tells her own story in her own words; the letters become an autobiography written on the spot, more complete and more trustworthy than the account of her life she wrote as an adult. Like many of her contemporaries, she was intensely self-conscious, always on the watch, scrutinizing and judging her emotions, responding to her friends and to their attitudes toward her. Fuller was equally intent on developing her mind, on plunging ever further into history, literature, and social reform. No one correspondent ever had the chance to understand the range of her mind, for she always kept a part of her personality to herself. In gaining access to Fuller's many self-definitions, to the diversity of her ideas and passions, the reader discovers what it was to be an American intellectual in the first half of the nineteenth century.

ROBERT N. HUDSPETH

State College, Pennsylvania

Contents

Contents

1819

1820

1821

1822

Contents

Contents

1828

1829

1830

1831

1832

Contents

1833

1834

1835

Contents

1838

Contents

ILLUSTRATIONS

ACKNOWLEDGMENTS

I am grateful to John C. Fuller, Willard P. Fuller, Elizabeth Channing Fuller, and Richard E. Fuller for permission to publish Margaret
Fuller's letters. I also thank the following institutions and individuals
for permission to publish the Fuller letters in their possession which
appear in this volume: the Trustees of the Boston Public Library;
the Brown University Library; Margery L. Chandler, for permission
to publish the Fuller letters she deposited in the Andover-Harvard
Theological Library and for permission to quote from the letters
of Henry Hedge to Margaret Fuller; the Chicago Historical Society;
the Cornell University Libraries; the Fruitlands Museums, Harvard,
Massachusetts; the Trustees of the Ralph Waldo Emerson Memorial
Association, the Harvard College Library, and the Houghton Library,
Harvard University; the Andover-Harvard Theological Library of
Harvard Divinity School; the Massachusetts Historical Society; the
Miscellaneous Papers Collections of the Manuscripts and Archives
Division of the New York Public Library, Astor, Lenox, and Tilden
Foundations; the Pennsylvania State University Library; the Rhode
Island Historical Society; the Humanities Research Center, University
of Texas; the University of Virginia Library; and the Yale University
Library.

The following librarians have been generous with their time and
attention: John Alden of the Boston Public Library; Edmund Berkeley, Jr., and Barbara C. Bettcher of the University of Virginia Library; Patricia Bodak of the Yale University Library; W. H. Bond,
director of the Houghton Library, Harvard University, and of the
Ralph Waldo Emerson Memorial Association; Dorothy W. Budgwaler
of the Yale University Library; Martha Crowe of the Cornell Univer-

sity Libraries; Rodney Dennis of the Houghton Library, Harvard University; Ellen S. Dunlap of the Humanities Research Center, University of Texas; Donald D. Eddy of the Cornell University Libraries; W. H. Harrison of the Fruitlands Museums; Christine D. Hathaway of the Brown University Library; Carolyn Jackeman of the Houghton Library, Harvard University; Clifton Jones of the Brown University Library; John D. Kilbourne of the Historical Society of Pennsylvania; James Lawton of the Boston Public Library; Jean R. McNiece of the Manuscripts and Archives Division of the New York Public Library; David Martz of the Brown University Library; June Moll of the Humanities Research Center, University of Texas; Archie Motley of the Chicago Historical Society; Jeanne Newlin, curator of the Theatre Collection of the Houghton Library, Harvard University; Martha Ramsey of the Houghton Library, Harvard University; Richard Reed of the Fruitlands Museums; Concetta N. Sacco of the Yale University Library; Alan Seaburg of the Andover-Harvard Theological Library, Harvard Divinity School; Marte Shaw of the Houghton Library, Harvard University; Nathaniel Shipton of the Rhode Island Historical Society; Faye Simkin of the Manuscripts and Archives Division of the New York Public Library; Louis L. Tucker of the Massachusetts Historical Society; and Jane E. Woolston of the Cornell University Libraries. The staff of the reading room at the library of the New England Historic Genealogical Society greatly assisted my use of that splendid collection.

Among the scholars who have helped me locate letters, solve textual puzzles, and identify mysterious references are Patricia Barber, Charles Blackburn, Paula Blanchard, Arthur W. Brown, Lynn Cadwallader, Joseph Jay Deiss, Russell E. Durning, Alfred R. Ferguson, Elizabeth Maxfield-Miller, Howard N. Meyer, Margaret Neussendorfer, Alice deV. Perry, Bruce A. Ronda, Fred Shapiro, Madeleine B. Stern, Carl F. Strauch, Eleanor M. Tilton, Barbara M. Ward, and Richard P. Wunder. Kathy Fuller of the Division of Research Programs at the National Endowment for the Humanities was generous with her help; Karen Szymanski alerted me to the existence of several Fuller letters; Stephen Riley of the Massachusetts Historical Society very kindly helped me gain access to several uncatalogued collections in that library. My departmental chairmen have been patient, full of support, and generous to me in my research: Robert B. Heilman and Robert D. Stevick of the University of Washington, and David Stewart, Arthur O. Lewis, Robert Worth Frank, Jr., and Wendell V. Harris of the Pennsylvania State University. I am especially pleased to be able to acknowledge the assistance given me by my colleagues Andrew Hilen,

Roger B. Stein, Robert Shulman, and particularly Richard E. Baldwin in Seattle and Robert D. Hume, Robert Lougy, John Moore, James Rambeau, and Ernst Schürer of the Pennsylvania State University. Wilma R. Ebbitt has given her time and wisdom far beyond the call of friendship, and Charles Mann, the Rare Books and Manuscripts Librarian of the Pennsylvania State University, has acquired Fuller material for this edition. For years I have profited from the advice, learning, and industry of Joel Myerson of the University of South Carolina, whose scholarship has been useful beyond description.

This edition has been furthered at many points by very able research assistants: Iris Malveau, who helped me with my original calendar of the Fuller letters; Carolyn Kephart, who read manuscripts and tracked down many a literary reference; Charles Hackenberry, who spent many hours reading manuscript letters to me; Larry Carlson, who ferreted out annotation material with patience and industry; Anne Hostetler, who helped with the annotations; and Robert D. Habich, who worked longest and often under the most difficult circumstances to wrest information from a recalcitrant past, to read my prose with a judicious and severe eye, and to check and recheck my facts. Barbara Salazar, senior manuscript editor of Cornell University Press, has helped make this a better edition by her careful attention to detail and her judicious suggestions for revisions. Once again Kay Hudspeth has given unfailingly of her time and energy to help me with countless details, to read the most illegible manuscripts, and to encourage me during the years this work has taken.

This edition of Fuller letters has received financial support from the University of Washington Graduate School Research Fund, the Pennsylvania State University College of Liberal Arts Research Fund, administered by Thomas Magner, and the Pennsylvania State University Institute for the Arts and Humanistic Studies, administered by Stanley Weintraub. I am grateful for this support. The preparation of all the volumes of this edition was made possible in part by grants from the Program for Editions of the National Endowment for the Humanities, an independent federal agency.

R. N. H.

INTRODUCTION

I

During her lifetime Margaret Fuller commanded attention for what she wrote and said and for her presence at the center of a lively intellectual circle. Born to controversy, for the Fuller family had a tradition of rebelliousness—one ancestor had Tory sympathies during the Revolution, and her father was a Republican from Federalist Massachusetts—Fuller continued the family tradition. She championed Goethe and George Sand despite their scandalous lives; she wrote a feminist book that openly criticized the place America created for women; she had a marriage shrouded in secrecy, one that created endless gossip; finally, she served a republican army fighting the combined powers of the papacy, Austria, and France. To call her a Transcendentalist, as many literary historians do, is to limit her presence. Important though she was to that influential group of writers, Fuller moved far beyond their ken to make herself felt in a bigger world. To many people her name was anathema; to many more it was the name of our most accomplished woman of letters.

Though her public life spanned only fifteen years, Fuller made a lasting impact on our literature. Alone with Poe, she raised literary criticism from a dreary, carping level to an intellectually diverse and provocative form of analysis. She was well read, full of insight, quick-witted, and articulate. In a series of essays and books Fuller pursued two aims, one symbolic, one practical. Symbolically she played an audience to Genius. Always ready to praise new and bold efforts, she wanted to be the eclectic, well-read, and sympathetic person an artist needed. Closely tied to this vision of her role was her practical idea that she could teach others how to be better readers. If she was the representative reader, she also did her best to make her audience more skilled and receptive.

Fuller made herself into a gifted conversationalist. In person she was dramatic and commanding. She radiated self-confidence; she assumed her right to an equal place in the circle of writers. There seemed to be no moderate response to her. Many people loved her deeply; many feared and despised her independence and her bold radicalism. Yet from 1835 to 1850, Margaret Fuller was a presence to be reckoned with. Whether she spoke in print or in person, she challenged the minds of her audience.

Her letters are the best means we have of capturing the whole of her diverse personality. We have, of course, her published writings, but these are productions for specific, well-defined ends. The letters give us an immediate knowledge of the range and quickness of her mind. In them we find displayed the intensity and variety of emotions that animated her friendships. While a large number of her friends and acquaintances wrote sketches of her, these studies naturally are filtered by the writers' memories and by their conscious and unconscious definitions of her. What her letters give in detail is her own vision of herself. Here, through her letters, the voice that entranced so many of her friends speaks for itself.

Fuller often viewed letter writing as an unwelcome intrusion on her time, but she was ungenerous to herself in her impatience, for it was in her letters that she tried out ideas, expressed her frustrations, and practiced, even if unconsciously, a variety of roles. She was often so harried and ill that her correspondence carried more obligations than rewards. Yet she was devoted to her letters, and she spent hours at her writing desk attending to them. We know that for her and for her friends, letters were a forum for intellectual exchange that filled the gap between private journals and published books. Fuller often shared a bundle of letters with her friends, and she knew that her letters would frequently be read by more than one person. Thus despite her grumbling, her letter writing was neither trivial nor unrewarding. She had good reason to be a faithful correspondent, if sometimes a begrudging one. She learned to write letters early in her life by writing to her father, a stern and demanding man who corrected her phrasing and her penmanship. She learned to be interesting, to be careful, and to be punctual.

Her habits as a letter writer were consistent throughout her life: she appears never to have written drafts, and only seldom did she keep copies of her own letters. Even when a letter was to have a calculated effect, it was written at one sitting, for Fuller had a keen ability to compose quickly and to connect her thoughts on the spot. Even when openly displaying her haste and impatience, she was lucid and to the point. Because enough of her letters survive to form a coherent autobiography and because the letters were written to a variety of recipients, we can see that Fuller was free to express a range of emotions and attitudes in her letters. She scolds her brothers and sister, makes detailed criticisms of Emerson's prose, and grows giddy with love for James Nathan. These letters give what we need—a full account of the writer's interior life. They amply document the personality that made her both loved and feared. Though she protected the very private center of her personality, Fuller did admit friends into her confidence to a surprising degree. We will never know that inner life in its entirety, but through her letters we can extend our knowledge.

The reader pauses over what Fuller omitted. For example, she never mentions the severe economic depression of 1837 or a single presidential campaign after John Quincy Adams' election in 1824. Because she ignores the storms created by Emerson at the Harvard Divinity School and by Theodore Parker among the Unitarian clergy, one would never imagine the excitement and bad feeling generated by her close friends. The Dorr Rebellion, one of the most remarkable events of our internal political life before the Civil War, gets only a passing, disdainful mention, despite Fuller's knowledge of Providence and Rhode Island. In short, until she went to Europe she ignored the world of politics in those letters that survive.

But still she was involved with her culture, looking deeply into the personalities she met. Her letters give us Bronson Alcott in moments of remorse; they show us Ellery Channing in black moods; they show us Emerson's aloofness and Elizabeth Peabody's ineptitude in business. Fuller's letters are central to our understanding of the *Dial,* and they give a sustained account of how German Romanticism affected a very bright young mind. If she sometimes left out the political life, Fuller more than adequately compensated for the omission through her record of the life of the mind and emotions.

"Whatever is truly felt has some precious meaning," she said in an 1844 letter. Perhaps this unguarded comment most clearly says what she had in mind when she sat down to write letters. First she had to report some "true" feeling; then she had to arrive at the "precious meaning." If this meaning was not to be gotten immediately, at least she had recorded the feeling so that its meaning could be seen later. Such a large number of her letters reveal her feelings that the reader must conclude that she was not only a literary critic, but a critic of the emotional life as well. For her, a cold life was a dead life, and letters were one important way of judging and recording the liveliness of her existence.

Of her close contemporaries, only Emerson has left us such a life-long record. Thoreau's letters begin in 1835, when he was at Harvard; of Alcott's, only six written before he was twenty-one have survived. Because her family was unusually careful with their family records, Fuller's early letters survive, followed by those saved by her friends as she entered adulthood. With but one significant chronological gap, this collection of letters shows us Fuller from childhood to her death in all of her occupations, in her many moods, and in her sustained friendships. Even with the inevitable lacunae of lost letters and with the unfortunate ambiguities created by incomplete or copied ones, the reader enters Fuller's world as she lived it. One of the clear habits of her mind was to create a "Margaret Fuller" for the world; she was given to self-dramatization and to a consciousness of the singular impact she made. These letters let us see how she did it, for they record the keenness of her intellect, the intensity of her emotion, and the ease with which she moved among diverse classes and kinds of people. She can range from playfulness with Almira Barlow ("My dear Simplicetta why don't you get well?") to rapture with Nathan ("You shall upbear me up to the stars, where your energies overflow"). She confesses her trouble to Costanza Arconati ("I am suffering as never before from the horrors of indecision"), but she was stern and commanding with her brother Richard ("I grieve to see how great the chance is of your making the miserable mistake that has wrecked so many of my best friends in marriage. I conjure you not to be so rash and impetuous").

The friends who knew her best tried to do justice to her personality after her death, but they could not comprehend her many complexities. Their creation, represented by the *Memoirs of Margaret Fuller Ossoli,* has created a literary, queenly Fuller, while hiding both the mundane and the radical parts of her character. Thus readers of her letters will find other embodiments of her personality. Competent in business, she was engaged in the affairs of the world, handling adversity as it came. She did have bursts of emotional intensity bordering on incoherence; she, the model of intellectual curiosity, fell for James Nathan and got singed emotionally. Despite her considerable accomplishments, there was always an incompleteness, a frustration, and a waste to her professional life. She wrote too hurriedly, for she was on the move too much.

But to confront these realities raises rather than diminishes our opinion of Margaret Fuller. She emerges richer and more intriguing when we reduce her from the too-large proportions created by the *Memoirs*. She made her life into art, accomplishing what Thoreau claimed for himself: "My life has been the poem I would have writ, / But I could not both live and utter it."[1] Her letters sustain a judgment Emerson wrote to himself at her death: "Her love of art, like that of many, was only a confession of sympathy with the artist in the mute condemnation which his work gave to the deformity of our daily life; her co-perception with him of the eloquence of Form; her aspiration with him to a life altogether beautiful."[2] Emerson names here the traits that often mark Fuller's responses: confession, condemnation, co-perception, and aspiration. At war with complacency, she felt herself alienated, but she found in art the records of loneliness and striving with which she could sympathize. Especially in the Germans she found echoes of her distress and restlessness. In part her emotional life propelled her toward criticism because in literature she found a world to share—vicariously with the author, more directly with her own audience. When Fuller urged James Clarke to read Franz Reinhard, she was confessing her sympathy. "Admire," she said, "those habits of patient investigation, that freedom of spirit joined with candour and humility— See how beautifully his life passed, spirit constantly victorious over the rebellion of matter." Even more to the point is her sally to Henry Hedge when the *Dial* was being created. "I really hope you will make this the occasion for assailing the public ear with such a succession of melodies that all the stones will advance to form a city of refuge for the just." Instinctively she moves from "assail" to "refuge," for, combative though she was, Fuller strove for a "justice" more broad and more humane than that she found in the *Boston Daily Advertiser* or the *Christian Examiner*. Fuller was willing to acknowledge the complexity and richness of a literary text or of a life. Like Carlyle, she refused to dismiss a work that placed demands on a reader. As a result, her letters reveal her scolding and pleading, soothing and encouraging her friends to work harder.

While the letters are monologues by their nature, they are of course but one half of a dialogue. She wrote because she responded; others wrote to her to get that response. In her public writing Fuller was

1. Henry D. Thoreau, *The Collected Poems of Henry Thoreau*, enl. ed., ed. Carl Bode (Baltimore: Johns Hopkins Press, 1964), p. 85.

2. Ralph Waldo Emerson, *The Journals and Miscellaneous Notebooks of Ralph Waldo Emerson*, ed. William H. Gilman et al. (Cambridge: Belknap Press of Harvard University Press, 1961–), vol. 11, *1848–1851*, ed. A. W. Plumstead, W. H. Gilman, and Ruth H. Bennett (1975), p. 257. Hereafter abbreviated *JMN*.

herself a professional audience, a voice giving back the response an artist needed, especially in a nation with too few thoughtful voices. In the letters she is the private audience—the other half of the miracle of aesthetic and intellectual creation. Both in print and in her letters, Fuller taught her readers how to respond. Emerson spoke precisely when he lamented at her death: "I have lost in her my audience."[3] For her time, and for ours, it was an irreparable loss, one that may be measured through her letters.

II

Sarah Margaret Fuller was born on 23 May 1810, the first of Timothy and Margarett Crane Fuller's nine children. Timothy was a Harvard-educated lawyer (class of 1801), son of a minister whose American ancestry went back well into the seventeenth century. He was a self-confident young man, sober, and overbearing in his earnestness. Like Fullers before and after him, he had a rebelliously independent streak. So when he turned to politics, he became a Republican in the heart of New England Federalism. It was no easy thing to be a Jeffersonian in the years when the troubles with England and the embargo had brought New England, and especially Boston, to the edge of ruin. Fuller, however, persisted in his principles and ran for Congress. In 1817 his Cambridge townsmen sent him to Washington.

He served eight years, making yearly trips down to the capital, where he spent a lonely but industrious six months each session. He did his share of the work by serving on the Naval Affairs Committee, but he never rose to any prominence in the House. Despite his Jeffersonianism, he was a staunch supporter of John Quincy Adams and worked hard for his election in 1824. Thanks more to Henry Clay than to Fuller, Adams won, and Timothy could indulge himself in hopes of his reward. The family tradition had it that he expected an ambassadorship and that he told his daughter to prepare for a trip abroad. But fate never quite cooperated with any of the Fullers, and the reward never came. Long since weary of the burdens of election, travel, and loneliness, Fuller decided to retire from Congress (a notion he had entertained even before the election of 1824) to return to his law practice in Massachusetts.

In 1809 he had married Margarett Crane, the daughter of Peter and Elizabeth Crane of Canton, Massachusetts. His bride was an at-

3. Emerson, *JMN*, 11:258.

tractive, quiet young woman who had taught school in her native town. Her family was part of the area's largest clan, one that ranged from wealthy to poor, from influential to obscure. Her father had served in the Continental Army and was called by the honorific title of major, even though he took no significant part in the drama of the Revolution. A gunsmith by trade, he had three daughters, and a son who ran away from home and disappeared. With her marriage to Timothy Fuller, Margarett rose a notch in society and took on the duties and satisfactions that could be expected in the household of a successful professional man.

The Fullers settled in Cambridgeport, the developing part of Cambridge between Harvard College and the new bridge to Boston. The construction of the first access from Cambridge to the city had opened the area to speculation, and Timothy Fuller bought a house and lot on Cherry Street. There he and Margarett raised a family and made a place in the society of a rather unusual community. Cambridge was quite rural, small, and drowsy, but it was the home of Harvard College, the center for theology, belles lettres, and the rudimentary sciences of that time. The Fullers took part in the social life of dances, visits, and teas. Margarett and her daughter thoroughly enjoyed dancing with the young college men, and Timothy himself was sociable. They moved easily among both the faculty and the professional families of lawyers and clergy, making friends, for instance, with the Samuel Fay family (he was later judge of the Middlesex Probate Court), with the Danas, and with the Holmeses. In every way the Fullers had a secure and comfortable place among their neighbors.

This was the world Margaret Fuller knew as a girl. Though Timothy was by no means wealthy, he had an adequate income and was a careful manager. His daughter had the advantages a child of her class would expect: books, dances, and education in the available schools. It was this last that immediately concerned her father, for he was determined that his eldest child should receive a genuine education, even though girls were not normally expected to have one.

The way she got this education and the problems it created for her have fascinated her biographers. First she studied under her father's care; then she had tutors from the college; after that she attended private grammar schools in Boston, Cambridgeport, and Groton. Even a casual reader of her letters realizes that Margaret Fuller had an unusual power of concentration and memory, that she learned languages with facility, and that she read widely. Later in her life she singled out her early years as a period of trauma and emotional confusion caused by her father's demands. No doubt she was right, for he was stern and lacked perception when it came to his daughter's emotions. He expected precise Latin translations; he set a high standard of reading (Shakespeare was too light for Sunday), and he was impatient. Ever striving to please, Margaret drove herself at an early age to earn his approval and to be the serious, high-minded person he wanted her to be. So she learned Latin, French, and a little Greek. She studied rhetoric and logic, dabbled in mathematics, and devoured history. Responding to the pressures of her father's demands, Fuller exhausted herself during the day and then had nightmares at night. Little wonder that she recalled the time with horror. We need to remember, however, the observation that Henry Hedge made many years later: Margaret Fuller, he said, had a normal education. She had what most boys of any promise had, and pretty much under the same grueling conditions. New England was never easy on its bright children. They learned to parse and spell in English, Latin, and Greek, and they learned to be diligent no matter what the subject. So while Fuller undoubtedly did have frustrations, they were not unique to her. Still, the autobiographical memoir she wrote in the 1840s focuses not on the achievement but on the remembered pain of her childhood.

On this topic the *Memoirs* has given us a half-light that obscures more than it illuminates, because it gives us nothing beyond Fuller's later recollection. Her letters, as well as the ones that her parents wrote each other, amply demonstrate her place in the social life of Cambridge and Boston. She was neither a recluse nor an outcast, for she had friends, she had relatives, and she had parties aplenty. Fuller did indeed feel driven in her lessons, but she had frequent dances and social calls. The nightmares were undoubtedly real, but so were the friendships with Harriet Fay in Cambridge and her cousins in Boston. From her childhood on, Fuller was fond of dramatizing her life, and it is not too much to say that she lived with an eye to heightening the drama. She was psychologically astute and full of insight into herself and into others. Understandably, her complex adult mind found it necessary to recall her childhood in its pain and torment, but a more complete record seen in the letters makes us read the dramatized fiction in a new way. Fuller caught the meaning of her father's attitudes: his sternness gave her discipline, but it robbed her of a child's delight. In the end, however, she absorbed his will power and his fortitude without falling prey to his limitations, for she had the ability to empathize with her friends.

Yet despite this extensive combination of work and play, Fuller was, in her own way, isolated in the family. Beginning in 1817, her father was gone for six months each year, and her mother was frequently caring for a new child. As the oldest daughter, Margaret was expected to help, to be a nurse and companion to her brothers, and to make do for herself when her mother was occupied. This set of circumstances combined with her early bookishness to lead her ever more deeply into romances and histories and encouraged her fantasies of escape and transformation. Her earliest letters show a consistently developing intensity, suggesting both a power of concentration and a use for nervous tension. She early learned to inhabit a world of books and an increasingly rich parallel world of her own imaginative fancy.

Fuller had a stroke of good fortune in 1821, when her father decided to send her to Boston to study with Dr. John Park, a man who had had careers in medicine and newspaper publishing before opening a school for young ladies of Boston's middle class. He offered a curriculum devoted to books rather than to sewing and singing, and he emphasized languages. Although Margaret entered the school with reluctance, she quickly responded to Dr. Park and to her fellow pupils. With the background her father had given her, she progressed rapidly and swept up the honors and recognition she so coveted.

In 1824, when she had gotten all she could from Dr. Park, Margaret thought she would go on to a school conducted by William and Ralph Waldo Emerson, where she could keep up her friendships among the Boston girls she liked so much. But Timothy had other ideas. He much preferred the isolation of a Groton school conducted by Susan Prescott, the daughter of a friend in the Middlesex bar. Ignoring his daughter's preference, he sent Margaret to the Young Ladies Seminary of Groton. Though she was disappointed and resentful, she quickly got over her hard feelings, found congenial friends among the other children, and even came to adore Susan Prescott and her sisters.

While the *Memoirs* leads us to think of these years as only traumatic, the letters show another side of the Prescott school. Fuller kept up her work in languages, read widely in poetry, and seems to have been encouraged in her intellectual life. Undoubtedly at this time she passed through a crisis of adolescence and came to be at odds with many of the other girls. But a significant part of her time in Groton appears to have been satisfying, socially as well as intellectually. We best understand the meaning of her adolescence if we see both the zest with which she worked and the tensions created by her need to be the center of attention.

By now an increasingly familiar pattern emerges in her experience.

She was pressured first by her father, then by the competition with her schoolmates. These pressures led to nightmares, physical exhaustion, and collapse. Yet coinciding with this pain was a steadily increasing mastery of books and ideas. Neither Timothy Fuller nor the girls at Groton could ruin Fuller's education. Though she paid a frightening price for her effort, she was learning to create out of emotional tumult, to bring order in one realm when disorder was blighting the other. Throughout her life, her letters are full of her pain—her head hurt insufferably; her eyes betrayed her; she had to stop work because of nervous tension. Still, out of these crippling times Fuller emerged with a lucid mind and an inquiring spirit.

By the time she came home in 1826, Fuller was a young woman of accomplishments, but now she faced difficult decisions. She had the education and the intellect of an unusually bright young person, but she had nowhere to go. A boy would be enrolling in Harvard with a clear path to the ministry or to the bar. The knowledge gained from all those books would culminate in a vocation. For Fuller it was purely a personal pleasure, for society decreed marriage to be the vocation of young women, no matter how well educated.

III

The meaning of her frustration can only be inferred, for, just as she came to the end of her adolescence and to a crisis involving her sense of herself and her relationships with her contemporaries, the details of her life almost vanish from us. While we have an extensive record in her letters and in those of her parents between 1815 and 1825, for the years from 1826 to 1830 we have little more than a blank page. Just at the time when we need insight, we are turned away. After this period we do know of two major events: she immersed herself in German literature, and in 1833 Timothy Fuller quit the law, moved to Groton, and became a farmer.

His decision was that of a frustrated man who had not met his high expectations for himself. It was also the action of a man who sought fulfillment in a pastoral dream, who wanted to find his place on his own land in the quiet of an isolated Massachusetts countryside. Like so many of the father's dreams, this one was not the daughter's. Unlike Emerson and Thoreau, with whose names hers has always been linked, Margaret Fuller found little of value in rural Massachusetts. On occasion the countryside was a refreshing tonic, but only as a respite from serious work in the town. Fuller needed people, talk, and ideas to stimulate and satisfy her many interests, and none of them was to be found in Groton. Little wonder she resented the move, for she was increasingly secure in the life of Cambridge in the early 1830s. There she had shown herself to be the equal of her male contemporaries—James Clarke, Henry Hedge, Wendell Holmes. Her interest in German language and literature found its complement in Clarke and his friends; Fuller had books to read and men to talk to about them. But this joyous time was brought to a crashing end with Timothy's demand that the family pick up and move to Groton.

As she always did, she compensated for her loneliness by turning to her books. Responding to the most modern thought available to her, Goethe especially, she found the enthusiasm and daring of the Germans to be exactly what she needed. The fragments of her letters preserved by James Clarke express the delight she found in the Germans. Though her future was unclear, her intellectual life was finding its own destiny. In reading Goethe, Fuller had learned that her restlessness was a badge of courage. Moreover, she had gained a focus, for from this reading she grew more and more interested in writing a life of Goethe.

In 1835 Fuller was offered a chance to gather material on Goethe and to experience Europe at firsthand. John Farrar, a Harvard mathematician, and his wife, Eliza, who had become especially friendly with Fuller, invited her to accompany them on a trip abroad. She was prepared to accept the invitation, but just at that moment the first real calamity of her life struck. On 30 September 1835, Timothy Fuller, exhausted by draining a meadow, suddenly fell sick, developed a high fever, and died of cholera within twenty-four hours. Stunned by his death, the family found itself on the verge of ruin, for he had tied up most of their money in land that yielded very little revenue. Fuller died intestate, so his affairs fell to the care of his brother, Abraham, a Boston lawyer, who was unsympathetic to Margaret and her ambitions. The estate of some $21,000 was divided into a widow's share and seven children's shares. Not only did the family have current expenses, but there were young sons to educate, and no one was readily available to provide a steady income. Neither of the two older brothers, Eugene and William Henry, was able then (or ever) to support the family.

Of course the European trip was off for Fuller, faced as she was with responsibility for the family's management. They had enough cash to survive at Groton for a time, so Margaret took on the task of teaching the younger children—Arthur, Ellen, and Richard. Though she assumed the responsibility willingly, she felt the painful frustration of seeing her own study superseded by her duties to the family.

35

This was the first of a notable series of deflections that shaped Fuller's career. She failed to get to Europe when she was intellectually most ready; the men she was to love early in her life failed to return her emotion; she was to leave the *New-York Daily Tribune* at the height of her professional success; and the revolution to which she devoted herself was crushed. She was, however, educated in Timothy Fuller's sense of responsibility, and so she endured the pain and frustration.

In 1836 an opportunity to earn some money suddenly appeared. Bronson Alcott, who was then making a reputation as an innovator and as an intellectual radical, needed a teacher of languages and an assistant to record the "conversations" he held with the pupils at his Temple School. Elizabeth Peabody had resigned the position, and Fuller happened to meet him just as the vacancy occurred, so she left Groton to work with the most daring teacher in Boston. Fuller came to admire Alcott's ways and his attitude toward his students, but as much as she liked the situation, she could not continue, for, to her dismay, Alcott was unable to pay her. With the responsibility for the family lying heavily on her, she was forced within a few months to look elsewhere. When a disciple of Alcott's opened the Greene-Street School in Providence and made an offer to Fuller, she accepted. Hiram Fuller (no kin), who had vowed to emulate Alcott's intellectual freedom, offered Fuller $1,000 a year to teach languages and to be his assistant. In many ways it was an extremely good position for Fuller. The salary was handsome, and most of the pupils came from families in which learning was a tradition. The income was large enough to enable her to support herself, to add to the family's fund, and even to save some. The move to Providence let her escape the isolation of Groton, and it gave her the opportunity to join a circle of Rhode Island intellectuals, among them the writers Albert G. Greene, Francis Wayland, and Sarah Helen Power Whitman.

During the two years she spent there, Fuller made her place in the literary life of the town, but she never liked Providence or the school very much, for she resented the time that teaching took from her writing. Fuller gave private lessons in German language and literature, and she attended private and public discussions of poetry and philosophy, but she never found in her Providence friends the intelligence or the vitality of the people she had left behind in Cambridge and Boston. In part the Providence intellectuals were too political for her tastes. While she was amused to hear Tristam Burges at a Whig caucus, Fuller was simply uninterested in serious political questions, let alone partisan jostling.

So in 1838, after spending less than two years in Providence, Fuller made the first of many restless changes: never in her life was she to stay put. The move from Alcott's school was forced, but the departure from Greene-Street was voluntary. She resigned from the school and went back to Groton to collect herself. She spent the winter with her family before moving to Jamaica Plain, a Boston suburb, where she began to write and to teach a few private pupils.

Fuller had developed a career as a writer with the help of James Freeman Clarke, who had published several of her essays and poems in the *Western Messenger*. This was apprentice work for Fuller. She devoted the early part of 1839 to her translation of *Eckermann's Conversations with Goethe*, which was published in May as part of George Ripley's series, Specimens of Foreign Standard Literature. Her work on the *Messenger* and the translation show the shape her career was taking—an introduction of contemporary European thought to Americans and an evaluation of that literature.

At the same time that her writing prospered, she fell in love with Samuel Gray Ward, a young Harvard graduate who was toying with a career as an artist. They had met during his college days when he boarded with the Farrars (who invited him as well as Fuller to accompany them to Europe in 1836). Fuller and Ward had since met often, shared a deep interest in art and in Germany, and found themselves increasingly drawn to each other. Although much of their correspondence during this period has been lost, enough of her letters remain to show clearly that in 1839 she was in love with Ward and that she thought he loved her. Like so many of her expectations, however, the romance dissolved. Ward turned from Fuller to her friend Anna Barker, and decided to follow his father into banking with Baring Brothers.

Fuller was in despair. Her letters to Ward at this time are records of anguish and bitterness, for she was facing failure on several levels. Ward's actions betrayed her deeply held aesthetic and cultural ideals. Rightly or not, she thought he had talent as an artist, and she knew that in America no aesthetic talent, even a modest one, could afford to be discarded. Further, even in her twenties Fuller was aware of life's impermanence. Friends and loved ones could vanish all too easily; the security of home and of love, the promise of hopes and dreams—all were at the mercy of sudden change. If there was genuine permanence, it lay in art, in the physical record of an inner life. For this reason, the symbolism of a painter turned banker was grotesque to Fuller. Finally, she lost Ward to a close friend. Throughout her life Fuller was deeply attracted to a number of women, and she had the gift of drawing them to her. Fuller was so close to Anna

Barker that Ward's presence complicated the strong feelings the two women shared.

Most important, however, Ward had simply rejected Fuller. It must have seemed to her in the late summer of 1839 that her lifelong fate was to be balked: she had missed at least two trips to Europe; her father had died early; she could not get the material she needed for a long-planned life of Goethe; she had fallen in love with George Davis years before, only to be thwarted; now her beloved "Raphael" (as she called Ward) rejected her for Anna Barker. From our perspective we can see a different pattern—her father's death released her from his demand for obedience; her failure to complete her *Goethe* was compensated for by her seminal work on the *Dial*—but for Fuller it was still a bleak time.

Outwardly she bore her disappointment very well, and fortunately her intellectual life was expanding to fill the void created by Ward's departure. Her earlier essays and the Goethe translation shaped Fuller's sense of vocation, and Emerson was regularly praising her writing. An essay on "jejune France" that she wrote just as Ward broke with her was especially rewarding, for it was an exploration of significant modern writers—George Sand, Alfred de Vigny, and Pierre de Béranger. Even if the essay had no immediate prospect of publication, it gave her a chance to expand her ideas for a circle of friends who read the manuscript. Finally, just when she needed them, Fuller found two public outlets for her intellectual life: her "conversations" and the *Dial*.

IV

Each fall and spring from 1839 to 1844, Fuller organized a series of weekly meetings with women who wanted to participate in discussions of art, literature, mythology, and education. Fuller opened each meeting with a brief statement about the week's topic and then drew in members of the group. As much as anything else she did, the conversations gave her an identity in Boston. Neither exclusively lectures nor merely social events, these meetings combined both into an intellectual activity that was special to the time and place. Fuller probably got the immediate idea for them from Alcott, who had been using the format for some time. Her boldest act was to hold her meetings for women, for she was convinced that women needed a public forum and some practice in thinking together. From these meetings several themes emerge: Fuller was still teaching, but she was doing so in her own way; she was discovering an outlet for her interest in developing women's intellectual opportunities; and she was thoroughly enjoying her position as a center of intellectual activity. Naturally, Fuller led the discussion, but she was extraordinarily successful in drawing out her audience. The women were sometimes halting in their responses, but Fuller's prodding and her own intellectual insight into the topics combined to make her a brilliant leader. She was the focus, but she never overwhelmed her fellow seekers.

In the fall of 1839 Fuller received $10 each from the twenty-five women who attended the course of conversations. To supplement this income she gave private classes in German and Italian, and she took a few young women as private pupils. Now that her brothers were growing up and going out on their own, she was able to improve her financial situation. It was fortunate that her conversations were even modestly profitable, because her other new venture was not. That same fall, the members of the Symposium (or "Hedge's club," as Emerson called it, or the Transcendental Club, as it is now known) had finally decided to start a new magazine to rival *The North American Review* and *The Christian Examiner,* both of which were much too narrow for the tastes of Ripley, Emerson, and Fuller. Fuller was the logical choice for the editorship, for Emerson refused to be drawn into the tangle of affairs that inevitably would go with the position, and none of the others who were available had the talents needed for the work.

Fuller edited the *Dial* from its first issue until March 1842, when in exhaustion she turned the journal over to Emerson. During this period she was responsible not only for her own writing but for getting material from others, editing the copy, and dealing with the printers. While her work took its toll in headaches and nervous exhaustion, the journal gave her a place for her writing just at a time when she had become confident of her powers as a critic. Her "Short Essay on Critics," written for the first issue, was a point of reference that shaped her writing for the next several years. While some of her work for the *Dial* was routine, much of it was ambitious criticism, unsurpassed by the work of any contemporary. Her writing for the journal marks a significant turning point in Fuller's style. More comfortable in conversation than in writing, she had sometimes been too abstract and impressionistic in her essays before 1840. She was having trouble finding the right voice. Emerson's quip earlier in their friendship hit the mark exactly. "If I write too many aphorisms," he said, "I think you write too few."[4] During the *Dial* years her writing became concrete and pungent.

4. Ralph Waldo Emerson, *The Letters of Ralph Waldo Emerson*, ed. Ralph L. Rusk (New York: Columbia University Press, 1939), 2:142.

Fuller's impact through the *Dial* came in two ways, for she was both the editor and a major contributor. From the start she had an exact idea of what the magazine was to be—an open forum for many talents and many points of view. After Emerson took the editorship, she sadly remarked to him that his was to be a different and to her a diminished journal. Energetic and insistent during her editorship, she solicited essays and poems, criticized manuscripts before she returned them to the authors, and kept trying to improve the quality of each issue. Moreover, with the forty-six pieces she published in the magazine, Fuller made the *Dial* into her forum of instruction. She showed her audience how to read the Germans, how to evaluate their American contemporaries, and how to formulate more subtle questions than those normally asked about books. Beginning in the *Western Messenger* as an apprentice critic without a clear sense of direction, Margaret Fuller ended her writing for the *Dial* as a woman of letters.

v

After she left the *Dial*'s management to Emerson, Fuller took an opportunity for travel. With James Clarke's sister Sarah, Fuller went to Niagara Falls and then on to the Middle West in the summer of 1843. They joined Sarah's brother Samuel, a Chicago businessman, and took a wagon tour of parts of Illinois and Wisconsin. Here Fuller was in prairie country, on the edge of a frontier of sorts. Chicago was a new world. Fuller got to see the sad remnants of some of the midwestern Indian tribes, and she got a firsthand look at some of the European émigrés who had taken refuge in the American heartland. She absorbed all she saw. Though the dirt and noise of Chicago did not repel her, the squalor of the Indians struck her as a national shame.

Her trip to the Midwest reveals a deep need in Fuller, for throughout her life she was on the move. Without a permanent home in her adult life, she interrupted her writing for periodic vacations and journeys. In important ways she was a typical restless American. Travel offered a way to find new experiences. The romances of Goethe and Schiller had caught her up in the vague notion of "seeking," and here in the Midwest Fuller was acting out her own form of that quest. Instead of the foreign mysteries of Germany, she was finding concrete facts of settlers' cabins, of Indian burial grounds, of campfires on the open prairie, of raw, muddy streets in a new metropolis. She surrendered the comfort and familiarity of her New England life to find the stimulation of new places. While she never consciously articulated her need, she clearly *had* to be on the move, to be a seeker. From Boston to Providence to Boston, from New England to New York, from America to Italy, Fuller moved onward, convinced that rest meant failure.

When she returned home in September 1843, Fuller began to organize her thoughts about the journey. By early 1844 she had completed a book-length manuscript. It was published in May as *Summer on the Lakes*. While her travel book was neither a critical nor a financial success, it was a transition for Fuller, for it turned her attention from Germany to America and from literary criticism to cultural analysis. The book gave her the chance to try some nonliterary observations. As she meditated on the fate of the Indians who both drew and repelled her, she voiced her feelings about a countryside that was novel to her. Both the rawness of Chicago and the surprising variety of the prairie gave her an opportunity to see new qualities in American landscapes. Without knowing it, Fuller was training herself to evaluate fresh impressions as a traveler, making herself ready for the later journey to Europe. In *Summer on the Lakes* she developed her habit of looking beyond the obvious.

VI

Summer on the Lakes provided Fuller with the opportunity to make another major change in her life, for Horace Greeley, the editor of the *New-York Daily Tribune*, read and liked the book and offered her a job on his paper. If she would leave New England, she could become his book reviewer. Though the change was drastic, the opportunity was large, for the *Tribune* was a major paper, her audience would immediately jump into the hundreds of thousands, and Greeley paid a steady salary. Before making the move she took a long vacation with her close friend Caroline Sturgis in the Hudson Valley. There she completed *Woman in the Nineteenth Century*, an expansion of a two-part essay she had written for the *Dial*.

Woman in the Nineteenth Century was in many ways the culmination of several of Fuller's intellectual interests. Drawing on her knowledge of history, myth, and literature, she demonstrated her power to observe and interpret human lives. The book clearly shows Fuller to be an intrepid critic: she wrote on sexual topics; she described lonely and oppressed wives; she repeatedly drew painfully accurate conclusions: "The life of woman must be outwardly a well-intentioned, cheerful dissimulation of her real life."[5] *Woman in the Nineteenth Century* had no real precedent in America (and few in Europe), so Fuller found herself where she was by now accustomed to be: by herself. No other woman edited a magazine like the *Dial,* and none reviewed for a major urban newspaper. Certainly few had either the education, critical acumen, or willingness to judge and find wanting a whole society's treatment of women. *Woman in the Nineteenth Century* was a bold book, boldly conceived and boldly written. Not unexpectedly, it was abused by many reviewers. A few defended it, and it was read more widely than any of her other books. For her effort, Fuller earned herself a place of honor in the history of American feminism.

VII

The interlude in the New York mountains with Sturgis was the most peaceful and productive time in Fuller's life. She had leisure to think, to write, and to relax. The book was all but done by late November, when she left Sturgis and went to Manhattan. Wasting no time when she got to the city, Fuller produced reviews at a steady pace, and almost immediately she went with William Henry Channing to Sing Sing prison to hold conversations with the female prisoners. Over the next fifteen months Fuller enjoyed her greatest professional success, publishing 250 articles in the *Tribune*—literary criticism, music reviews, and social analysis. She reviewed Melville's *Typee,* Philharmonic concerts, and Robert Browning's poetry. She did theater reviews of *Antigone* and social reports on prisons; she reviewed children's books, books on travel, and Emerson's second book of essays. This clearly was congenial work to Fuller's inquisitive mind. Covering a variety of topics, she could "teach" her newly enlarged audience. Her many interests were nourished by the stream of new books to be reviewed. From the variety emerged a direction: she became more and more involved in social issues. For the first time she spoke up for benevolent societies and for changes in a social system that tolerated slavery and bred poverty.

In New York, as in Cambridge, Providence, and Boston, Fuller was drawn into a lively social and intellectual circle. A woman with such a magnetic personality and with such strongly held and well-articulated ideas was bound to be visible in a city's salons. Fuller renewed her friendship with Lydia Maria Child, met Poe, and became an occasional member of Anne Lynch's literary salon. She met reformers (Isaac

5. S. Margaret Fuller, *Woman in the Nineteenth Century,* ed. Joel Myerson (Columbia: University of South Carolina Press, 1980), p. 145.

Hopper and Lucretia Mott), writers (William Gilmore Simms and Cornelius Mathews), and literary entrepreneurs (Evert and George Duyckinck). While she was more on the periphery than she had been in the smaller world of Boston, she made her mark.

Only the Greeleys, however, were aware of another, more intense friendship. In February 1845 Fuller met James Nathan, a German businessman from Hamburg. She immediately fell in love and spent the spring meeting with him, thinking about him, and writing long letters to him. During this time she was as passionately devoted to Nathan as she was to her writing. The secrecy of her involvement with Nathan reminds us of Fuller's ability to wall off parts of her experience so that one set of friends might be wholly apart from and even ignorant of other sets. Her capacity for new experience was matched by her ability to keep quiet about it.

But she had not known Nathan long before he announced his intention of returning to Europe. His impending departure both frustrated her and led her to record her feelings in letters to him. She did not immediately see his growing coolness toward her, however, or his inability to share her passion. We can infer from her letters that he was backing away from her, and we know that at the end he came to use her business connections for his own advantage. After he left, he wrote seldom, and he gave clear signals that she should not continue to expend her passion on him.

As she had done with George Davis and Sam Ward, Fuller had committed herself to a man and had been rebuffed. Again she was alone, and again she had to hide her wounds. She took her disappointment as well as she could and kept busy. The only interruption in her steady work for the paper came in October 1845, when she took a brief vacation in New England. She renewed old friendships but found Emerson distant and intellectually unapproachable.

The importance of Emerson to her in the late 1830s and during their work on the *Dial* sometimes obscures the fact that they were close to each other only from 1836 to 1844—not even a decade. After she left New England, Fuller steadily grew away from Emerson, though she kept her affection for him. In part she needed the face-to-face confrontation of good talk to stimulate her intellect. But more important, she was changing: her concern now was increasingly in social reform, an interest Emerson shared only mildly if at all. By 1845 Emerson was established as the sage of Concord, a man who clearly knew his strengths and his weaknesses. In the 1830s Fuller had met those strengths, for she shared his passion for the life of the spirit and for writing that made the spirit live in words. But her move

43

to New York coincided with her growing need to help make the world a better place in which to live, and this was Emerson's admitted weakness. While his ethical sense was finely etched, he would not move to collective action. The physical distance between the two cities both objectified the emotional and intellectual distance that had sprung up between the two writers and guaranteed the permanence of their separation.

By the first of November, Fuller was back to her writing and to life in New York. In February 1846 she met Evert Duyckinck, who encouraged her to publish an edition of her essays. She worked quickly— too quickly, she later thought—to get together a pair of volumes published as *Papers on Literature and Art.* Combining her work from the *Dial* and the *Tribune,* the book gave little attention to her new interests in reform. Although she published no new essays, the book kept her in the minds of other writers and won her a small but highly appreciative audience in England. Like all her commercial venture, *Papers on Literature and Art* brought her little money, but she was building a fund of goodwill and critical interest that could have been turned to good account had she not died so young.

As she was collecting the essays, Fuller was thinking again about Europe. Marcus and Rebecca Spring, wealthy friends who were ardent reformers, invited her to go with them on a tour of England and the Continent in the fall of 1846. They even offered to advance some of the money she would need. Fuller accepted and scraped up the remainder of the money from Boston friends, from her family, and from Greeley, who promised to pay her $10 each for travel letters from Europe.

Finally, in August 1846, Margaret Fuller realized her long-standing dream of heading for the Old World. She was acutely, even bitterly aware of how much more the trip would have meant to her a decade earlier. She was no longer devoted to German literature, nor had she pursued her interest in biography and philosophy. Overtly she was taking just another of her extended vacations, but Fuller could never keep up a routine for long; she was so intense in everything she did that she wore out her enthusiasms. Though the job with the *Tribune* satisfied many of her needs—psychological, professional, intellectual, and financial—she took the first opportunity to move on. It was to be a limited trip, but none of her surviving letters speaks of any possibility of returning to Greeley's paper. A small but significant mystery remains—why Fuller should so abruptly have made what looks to be an absolute break from the *Tribune.* While she and Greeley were often brusque with each other, they were on quite good terms, both professionally and personally, in 1846. Whatever her motives,

Fuller left. The journey from New York to Europe was an extension of her move from Boston to New York. Her shift from the New World to the Old opened a life that was less secure but richer in possibilities.

VIII

After a visit home for hasty farewells to her family, Caroline Sturgis, and Emerson, Fuller and the Springs sailed on the *Cambria* in August. The crossing took just ten days—a new record. Arriving in Liverpool with the usual letters of introduction, they spent some time examining the Mechanical Institute before going on to Manchester, to Westmorland, and on into Scotland. Fuller got a firsthand look at the factories and workers' schools in Manchester. She made the obligatory stop to visit the elderly Wordsworth in Cumbria, but she seemed more gratified to see Harriet Martineau, whom she had known years earlier and with whom she had corresponded. The party visited Ben Lomond, where Margaret climbed the mountain late in the afternoon, got lost, and frightened the Springs by spending the night on the hillside. She made light of her adventure, but it was an uncomfortable experience for her. That episode and several sorties into coal mines and factories were duly reported in her long travel letters for the *Tribune*. With her good eye for the details of people and habits, she filled her letters with evaluations of English life and letters.

The party stayed in London for six weeks. Fuller called anxiously at the bank for letters from Nathan, only to be disappointed. His silence by now confirmed what she had hated to admit: he had dismissed her. But she had little time to fret, for her schedule was full of visits and sightseeing. Emerson had given her a letter of introduction to Thomas Carlyle, thus bringing together two of the great talkers of the time. Carlyle's response to Emerson was more than cordial. "A high-soaring, clear, enthusiast soul," he called her, "in whose speech there is much of all that one wants to find in speech. A sharp subtle intellect too; and less of that shoreless Asiatic dreaminess than I have sometimes met with in her writings. We liked one another very well."[6] Fuller found in Carlyle the grace, wit, and force she had always admired in his writing. He was, after all, the outstanding critic of her generation. His essays and translations had introduced her to Germany; his wit and criticism in *Sartor Resartus* had shown her the possibilities of a new literature and a new life.

6. *The Correspondence of Emerson and Carlyle*, ed. Joseph Slater (New York: Columbia University Press, 1964), p. 410.

But she and Carlyle could never have coexisted, for each had to have center stage, and Carlyle had the energy to outtalk her.

Fuller also met the Italian revolutionary Giuseppe Mazzini, who combined political enthusiasm with a foreign sort of mysticism of just the kind to appeal to her. The quickness and completeness with which Mazzini displaced both Carlyle and Emerson in her life emphasize the distance Fuller had put between herself and her earlier life. In Mazzini she found politics, religion, and aesthetics merged. He was one more in the series of men who played necessary symbolic roles for Fuller. First Goethe, then Emerson, then Mazzini came to have special and extensive meaning for her. Different though each was from the others, each shared a vision of a better world. Though it is convenient to talk of a "progression" in Fuller's career, in fact she made modifications of a point of view that remained remarkably constant. For her, life was a series of possibilities; one lived with an enthusiasm for fulfilling those possibilities or one died—aesthetically, spiritually, or politically.

In November, Fuller and the Springs moved on to Paris, where she met almost all of the significant literary figures: Lamennais, Béranger, and, most important, George Sand, whose novels Fuller had been reviewing and defending for years. At a time when Sand was scandalous to an American audience, Fuller was calling her one of the few vital novelists of their day. Those of Fuller's friends who were later confused by her marriage should have read her defense of Sand with more care, for though Fuller was overtly conventional about marriage and sexuality, she was equally willing to be independent, as any attentive reader of *Woman in the Nineteenth Century* could have seen.

Her schedule was more rushed yet more satisfying in Paris than it had been in London: she took lessons in French to improve her pronunciation; she went to the theater, to museums, to charitable organizations, and to the Chamber of Deputies. Not the least of her discoveries was Adam Mickiewicz, the Polish poet-statesman, whose intensity powerfully attracted her. In a series of letters to her, he urged her to indulge her emotions, to exercise her femininity, and to relax her intellect. While none of her replies to him survives, his letters to her show that he was urging her to think of herself in new terms.

IX

In late April 1847 Fuller and the Springs left Paris for the south of France on their way to Genoa. There they boarded a packet bound for Naples. As the ship left the harbor, it hit a mail boat. Fuller was unhurt but badly frightened, for she had a deep fear of death by water. A second try brought an easy passage to Naples, where she arrived in a world so old as to be totally new. Italy was a unique combination of art, architecture, literary splendor, and sculpture; but it also had a new dimension, one she was ready for: this was a land of growing revolution. She arrived on the peninsula just as Pope Pius IX was liberalizing the papal government and just as the Republicans were gaining a following in the north. Naples itself existed in horrendous squalor under a tyrannical king, but the other Italian states showed signs of increasing ferment and even of some Republican successes. So Fuller found herself in a heady atmosphere when she traveled on to Rome. There she saw the sights, visited the American artist colony, quickly got a grasp of the political situation, and continued to write long letters back to the *Tribune*. After a short stay in Rome the party went to Florence, where Fuller met Horatio Greenough and Hiram Powers and saw their newest sculptures. She toured the churches and the museums, taking in all that she could in a short time. Then she and the Springs were off to Bologna, Ravenna, and Venice, where they spent a fortnight.

It was in Milan, their next stop, that Fuller got her real education in Italian politics, for the coming crisis was most visible there. She probably met some of Mazzini's supporters, and she made a close and lasting friend in the marchesa di Arconati Visconti, a young noblewoman sympathetic to the Republicans. The beautiful marchesa was to be a touchstone for Fuller during the next two turbulent years. Whenever she felt herself on the brink of despair, Fuller knew she could find comfort and good sense in her friend.

In northern Italy she parted company with the Springs, who were going on to Switzerland and Germany. Nothing more clearly marks the difference between the Margaret Fuller of the 1830s and the woman of the 1840s than this decision. Her earlier passion for the Germans had all but disappeared; she was increasingly a social reformer to whom literature was important but less immediately interesting. So she set out alone with her slim finances and an untrustworthy servant to go back to central Italy. Early in her journey she came down with a severe, almost fatal case of cholera. She arrived in Rome in the middle of October, weak but in good spirits.

A century of scholarship, speculation, and gossip has never been wholly able to untangle the events that followed. During her first stay in Rome, Fuller had become acquainted with Giovanni Angelo Ossoli, a younger son of a noble Roman family well connected with the papal service. A handsome young man ten years her junior, Ossoli had only the rudiments of an education and no profession. His strong Republican sentiments put him at odds with his family. The only thing we know with certainty about the beginnings of their life together is that early in 1848 Margaret Fuller was pregnant with Ossoli's child. Whether or not they were then married, or indeed whether they ever married, is not known. The best circumstantial evidence we have suggests a marriage in 1849, some months after the birth of the child. After her death, the Fuller family, with the help of her close friends, created and kept alive a tradition of a marriage late in 1847.

X

As her private life took on awesome complications, the political life in Italy became dramatically more turbulent. Early in 1848, insurrections occurred in Sicily, and news of further troubles on the peninsula could be heard almost daily. Riots broke out in Palermo on 12 January as the Sicilians revolted against the Bourbon rule of King Ferdinand. In February he was forced to grant a constitution for the kingdom of the Two Sicilies. Cautious as this move was, it was followed in March by the granting of constitutions in Tuscany, Piedmont, and even the Papal States.

The rebellion that deposed Louis-Philippe of France in February spread to Austria, and Metternich fell in the middle of March. With Austria in disarray, Lombardy became inflamed, and Milan went through five days of revolutionary furor. By the end of March the Republicans throughout the Italian states could take hope in the extent and the intensity of political upheaval. Much of the activity was parochial, for the Sicilians were more interested in freeing themselves from Naples than they were in promoting Italian independence, and Charles Albert in Piedmont, intent on expanding his influence at the expense of the Austrians, was hardly liberal. Still, rebellion was the first step toward independence, national identity as Italians, and political reforms.

Through the thirteenth of May, Fuller kept her *Tribune* readers informed of these events, so important to her personally and to Italy's future. She gave vivid accounts of political demonstrations in Rome and of the increasing defection of Pius IX as he drew back from the forces he had inadvertently set in motion. A reader can imagine the complexity of her emotions as she bore the secret of her pregnancy with its ominous implications just at the time when the political life of the Italian states became heavy with possibility.

By the end of the spring the rebellions had quieted and the pope refused to go further toward reform, so Fuller's departure for the mountains came in a lull of the political activity. In late May she left for the Abruzzi Mountains, leaving Ossoli behind in Rome. She went first to Perugia and then on to Rieti, a village in the mountains northeast of Rome. There she was cut off from public life, and from her lover. She was writing a history of the political upheaval of the rebellions, but she was far from the books and people she needed to consult, and her pregnancy drained her strength.

On 5 September her son, Angelo Eugene, was born. She apparently had a reasonably easy labor, for she was able to dictate a letter to Ossoli a few hours afterward. The father came from Rome as quickly as he could, but he could not be absent for long, and Fuller was forced to stay alone in the mountains during the autumn rain and gloom. Finally she was well enough to leave the child with a nurse and go back to Rome. She had to fight her way through a flood to get to the city, but by mid-November she was once again writing from Rome. She resumed her letters to the *Tribune* and began to see her Roman friends socially. She kept her motherhood secret.

In the winter and spring of 1849 the political situation in Italy was rapidly reaching a crisis. In December 1848 Pius IX had fled Rome for Gaeta, in the kingdom of Naples, where he joined the exiled grand duke of Tuscany. The Republicans gained control of Rome, and in March Mazzini entered the city in triumph. He became one of the triumvirs who led the Constitutional Assembly toward a genuine republic. But the conservative, Catholic powers of Europe were not about to let a republic grow up in the city of Saint Peter. After a short period of quiet, the French led an attack against the Romans, and the Austrians moved down from the north. In May, Rome was a city under siege.

Fuller had taken a brief trip to Rieti in March to see her son, whom she found half dead from neglect. When she had nursed him back to health she returned to Rome, for she knew that events there were reaching a climax. She was appointed head of a hospital and served there throughout the siege. Ossoli was a member of the Civic Guard, the citizen army on which Mazzini was relying. For many days she and Ossoli served the Republican cause at great personal risk. He was in the middle of the fighting; she was working daily at the hospital, as separated from him as she was from her son. Finally, in June, the French under Oudinot crushed the Romans, Mazzini and Garibaldi were forced to flee, and the Republic collapsed. The first stage of the Risorgimento ended in what appeared to be abject failure. One by one, the conservative monarchical governments resumed control over the Italian states from Naples to Piedmont.

XI

The Ossolis were in a precarious position: he was a rebel nobleman, at odds with his family and the papal authorities; she was a foreigner as well as a Republican. So in July they left for Rieti, where they were finally united with their son. They spent the rest of the summer in the mountains recovering from the war, but at the beginning of September they moved on to Florence, where the political life was more moderate and there was a sizable colony of American and English artists and writers, most notably William and Emelyn Story and Robert and Elizabeth Browning.

The whole of 1849 had been a continuous trauma for Fuller—separation, physical pain, ruined political hopes—but the move to Florence brought a special kind of problem. She now introduced Ossoli as her husband and revealed the existence of their child. The reaction was muted but tense. The child was a year old, and no one had suspected that she was married, let alone a mother. She wrote to a few American friends and to her mother announcing the fact of her new life, but she let William Story learn of it secondhand, wounding one of her staunchest friends in Italy.

Exhausted as she was, Fuller had a moment of calm in Florence between two storms. She saw the Brownings often, the Horatio Greenoughs were good company, but mostly she enjoyed being with Ossoli and Angelo. After the tumult, the quiet of a home steadied her as she contemplated the future. Then in 1850 Fuller had to make a decision. Her book on the Italian revolution was almost finished, but she was unsure how to publish it. One query to a London publisher brought mild encouragement without an offer to publish the work. Lacking money or means of support, she and Ossoli were in a desperate position. The only alternative was to go to America, publish the book there, and try to revive her profession as a writer. Even though she faced a hostile reception in New England, or at best a condescending and inquisitive one, Fuller resolved to leave Italy. If her friends would only accept her as she was, the other people were not worth troubling about.

The Ossolis spent the spring in Florence making plans for their trip. She wanted to go by one of the safer, newer steamers, but the cost made such a trip out of the question, so she booked passage on the *Elizabeth*, a sailing schooner under Captain Seth Hasty of Maine.

In May the Ossolis sailed from Leghorn, bound for New York. Early in the trip Captain Hasty fell sick with a fever and grew increasingly ill with smallpox. Shortly after the *Elizabeth* arrived at Gibraltar, he died. Because the port authorities immediately quarantined the ship, the captain was buried by his men at sea; the Atlantic voyage fell to his first mate, Henry P. Bangs.

The crossing took almost six weeks. All went well enough until the trip arrived off the American coast. There the weather worsened. Although Bangs seemed to know where he was, he had miscalculated his position and let the *Elizabeth* come too close to Fire Island. During the early morning of 19 July the ship hit a sand bar within a half mile of the island. Though they were in sight of shore, the seas were high, and the passengers and crew were in mortal danger. As the day wore on, the ship gradually broke up. Around noon several of the passengers and crew tried to swim to shore or to float in on debris. Some survived, but the Ossoli family was swept off the hulk and drowned. Toward evening Angelo's body floated to shore; those of his parents were never recovered.

Emerson and the stunned Fuller family dispatched Thoreau to New York to see whether the bodies or any of the baggage could be recovered. He was joined by Ellery and William Henry Channing. Together the three talked to survivors and to witnesses, but little was to be done. Thoreau did recover a large leather trunk containing a quantity of books and manuscripts, but the history of the Italian revolution was lost.

XII

And so, a few months past her fortieth birthday, America's most accomplished woman of letters fulfilled her own worst dreams of death at sea. Like Poe, Thoreau, and Stephen Crane, she died so early as to make evaluation difficult for the people who knew her best. For those of us who come later, the task of interpretation is easier, but still her life was so incomplete as to challenge our best efforts. Fuller left no masterpiece, as the others did; she wrote in no established genre, for criticism was (and is still) a troubling form. Fuller was captivated by personality, by the play of psyche both in print and in life. An actress who wrote her own scripts, she knew how to be commanding and interesting; she asked for intellectual and emotional enthusiasm from her friends, and she gave as good as she got. While Margaret Fuller offended some powerfully imaginative minds (Hawthorne and Carlyle, for instance), she helped to mature the efforts of other, equally imaginative people. She was true to her own inner promptings, and she braved the scorn of conventional people. Because she was not easy to know, many people mistook her for a caricature of herself, but she was capable of fidelity that braved the troubles the world brought. She knew the perils of daily life even before the sudden, shocking death of her father, and so she resolved to live deeply while she could. Like all good teachers, Fuller was an adept student. From Carlyle she learned to read the Germans; Emerson taught her to accept idealism; Greeley showed her the humanity of reform movements; Mazzini led her to revolution. But like all superior students, Fuller remained independent of her teachers, accepting what each offered without being limited by his point of view. Wholly confident in her ability, she was keenly receptive to the talents of her contemporaries.

In part her enduring interest for later readers springs from that breadth of her life. She did so much, covered so much territory, and made so many acute observations that we cannot ignore her. But beyond this interest lies the possibility of interpretation, of our seeing how both her life and her work yield a knowledge of our cultural yearnings and accomplishments, our failures and our triumphs.

Let us begin with the fact that she died in passage from one home to another. Throughout her life she was restlessly on the move. The Cambridge of her youth was the nearest thing she ever knew to a permanent home. Each of her well-known contemporaries had a specific place with which he was associated, literally and symbolically: Emerson had Concord, Hawthorne the Manse, Thoreau his pond. Giving latitude to the imagination, the place could be transformed into a concrete embodiment of ideas. A fixed residence was a sign of emotional maturity and stability; it provided circumference and protection against the claims of intruders. Even Brook Farm, the experimental community that fired the enthusiasm of her Transcendentalist friends, provided its residents with an identity and kept the world at bay for a time.

But Fuller was placeless. The psychic and imaginative rewards granted to Thoreau and Hawthorne were never hers. Without a center, she had no controlling symbol to help her define herself and her place. In part she was too restless to be satisfied with a single definition; in part she kept fleeing from her own incompleteness. But we should not forget that she often chose isolation: she refused strong inducements to join Brook Farm; she considered, but then rejected, the possibility of moving to Concord; she chose the uncertainty of Europe over the more secure position with Greeley.

In common with many writers whom we call Romantic, Margaret
Fuller feared stasis above all else. Better to seek and fail than merely
to be safe. The very intellectual premises of creativity that she most
admired called for action, for a "coming into being." Therefore, those
few times when she was most settled were the very times she most
scorned: girlhood, her years as a teacher, her later years as editor
of the *Dial* and writer for Greeley. In part she was caught in the
worship of experience, of finding the new sensation and perspective.
Thus she was an eager and observant traveler, for she was always on
duty. Even routine vacations were occasions for meditation and interpretation. It seems clear that the symbolic nature of having a place
was for Fuller too close to a failure of perception. Having a home
meant having a life that lacked renewal. She rather too literally played
out her role of seeker, but that is the irony all American Romantics
faced: the nature of their most significant insights often plagued their
personal lives. Hawthorne's profound concern with guilt nearly par-
alyzed him early in his career; Emerson's ideal of friendship made
friendship all but impossible.

At its best, however, Fuller's energetic comings and goings stimulated her criticism. The ability to judge and strengthen her sensibility
required both physical and psychic journeys. Her readiness to entertain new experiences was intertwined with criticism, and criticism was
the ability to be an audience, to be the necessary participant in an
aesthetic performance. Some critics berate Emerson for his failure to
understand Fuller when, immediately after her death, he wrote in
his journal: "I have lost in her my audience."[7] This lament sounds
cold and self-centered, but it is just the tribute that he should have
paid her. To misread Emerson here is to miss the significance of
Fuller's presence, both professionally and personally, in his life. To
be an audience was to complete a sacred bond with the artist. For
what else had she labored? It was neither vanity in him nor sub-
servience in her that led Fuller to her role. Her greatest danger lay
in her necessary self-scrutiny. To be a critic demanded an eternal
questioning of her responses, for to know what she felt and why she
felt it was central to Fuller's being. Similarly, she kept a close eye
on her emotional involvements with her friends. This scrutiny pleased
her but led her to the dangers of introspection. She had a habit,
for example, of keeping one friend walled off from others, thus
making the friendship more private and more nearly an object of
observation for herself alone but also making it dangerously intense,

7. Emerson, *JMN*, 11:258.

with too little latitude for differences of opinion. Thus life became a stage; individuals played parts in long-running dramas of the soul. Over and over she emphasized the idea that the total effect of a life was really what mattered. This attitude converts persons into mental visions; actions become ideas; the world is internalized as life becomes an art, and all individuals must be critics.

Fuller's surest protection against narrowness was her lifelong reading in history and languages. Knowing as she did the vitality of other thinkers, she avoided a psychological and intellectual parochialism. While this point of view deflected her from social criticism early in her career, it gave her the room to take the psyche seriously. In the 1830s she needed ways to explore and to champion an antisocial self, one cut off from material standards of achievement. As she moved on through the 1840s, Fuller shifted to social criticism, to the union of thought and action devoted to improving social life, but this shift could come only after she had worked out her ideas about literature.

Fuller was reacting to felt perceptions of our national suspicion of emotion, ideas, and art. Though she wrote often about foreign literature and used foreign models to judge the nineteenth century, it was America that she was criticizing. The problems she addressed—of creating an audience, of having standards, of pushing life beyond mercantilism—were specifically American problems, ones a European critic did not have to face. Neither here nor abroad did she find models of criticism that wholly satisfied her. She once tartly observed of the English that "there is very little valuable criticism extant . . . in proportion to the number of attempts."[8] From her earliest writing, Fuller championed an intellectual activity America had never acknowledged to be of value.

Emerson had voiced her fears as well as his own when he deplored that "rigor of our conventions of religion and education which is turning us to stone, which renounces hope, which looks only backward, which asks only such a future as the past, which suspects improvements, and holds nothing so much in horror as new views and the dreams of youth."[9] We had to have a new literature to escape this mistrust, and Fuller was committed to the idea that a genuine act of criticism helped create the possibility for that literature. "What tongue could speak," she asked, "but to an intelligent ear."[10] Judged in the light of Emerson's comment, Fuller's takes on immediacy. Were

8. *New-York Daily Tribune*, 21 January 1845.
9. [Ralph Waldo Emerson], "The Editors to the Reader," *Dial* 1 (1840):1–2.
10. [Margaret Fuller], "A Short Essay on Critics," *Dial* 1 (1840):7.

life to be improved, literature had to come to terms with the state of our dullness, and active criticism had to offer encouragement, interpretation, and judgment. If life was as threatened as Emerson held, then someone had to challenge false assumptions and to commend to us a better vision.

In her critical essays Margaret Fuller created a personality for her readers that represented the best a critic might offer—judgment and the power of interpretation. She was always ready to risk offending popular taste by taking up the cause of a neglected or maligned writer (Shelley, Sand) or of deflating an unearned reputation (Longfellow). Her standard was straightforward: "True criticism, as distinguished from petty cavil and presumptuous measurement, on the one hand, and encomiums, based merely on personal sympathy, on the other, supposes a range and equipoise of faculties, and a generosity of soul. . . . The great Critic is not merely the surveyor, but the interpreter of what other minds possess."[11] Although not many had that "range and equipoise," Fuller knew that she did, and she was intent on being an interpreter.

This need was a consistent theme in her writing, because individuals, works of art, historical facts, and natural phenomena were all objects to provoke her analysis. Quite literally, nothing was wholly what it seemed, or rather, everything was much more than it seemed. Her most natural role was that of sibyl. Fuller might well have been describing herself when she observed: "The muses only sang the praises of Apollo; the Sibyls interpreted his will." The sibylline power, she said, lay in the "passionate enthusiasm of her nature, rather than in the ideal perfection of any faculty."[12]

We should remember that interpretation for her was not necessarily an attempt to understand causes or to produce technical discussions of the sort so fascinating to Poe. To Fuller, interpretation was fundamental to knowing, and the worst blight on life was ignorance. In many ways her habit of placelessness and her willful self-scrutiny came from her search for knowledge. Her times of mystical elevation and her interest in mesmerism were as valuable to her as her intellectual training, for they were all a part of the larger problem of interpretation. To interpret was to know, to know was to live. Because the power of interpretation was so central to her life, her most poignant and revealing cry was "Cheat me on by no illusion."[13] Aware

11. *New-York Daily Tribune*, 21 January 1845.
12. *Memoirs of Margaret Fuller Ossoli*, ed. R. W. Emerson, W. H. Channing, and J. F. Clarke, 2 vols. (Boston: Phillips, Sampson, 1852), 1:190.
13. Emerson, *JMN*, 11:486.

as she was of the fact of painful misperceptions, she was equally aware of healing insight.

Margaret Fuller is our Romantic critic: devoted to the self, to quests, to transcendence. Her natural gesture was one of extravagance. If any one trait unites all the American Romantics, it is their commitment to hyperbole, to "speak somewhere *without* bounds," as Thoreau put it.[14] For Fuller, the validity of criticism came from the capacity to see finally beyond the form to pure idea. Consequently, what she achieved was a series of integrations. Self and society coexisted on terms satisfactory to the soul; nature and the soul were not ultimately antagonists. Despite an increasingly industrialized society with all its confusions, a spiritual life might still be found. In this century we may not share her faith, but it would be wrong to dismiss it lightly.

Fuller's life was an American phenomenon in its contradictions. She was an exotic immersed in the literature of Europe and in the reality of a far-distant past, yet she was a child of Cambridge. She was an aristocrat by choice: learned, imperious, cosmopolitan, given to wearing a fresh flower every day. Yet she visited the female felons in Sing Sing and found in them a genuine audience. She became the marchesa d'Ossoli, but she wanted most of all only a chance to love her husband and child. She was a sensitive register of her time and place: as a young woman she found Goethe's writing; she heard Emerson preach, and she listened to Hawthorne tell stories in Sleepy Hollow Cemetery; she visited Mazzini in the last hours of the Roman Republic and mourned with him the end of their dreams. The woman who moved among American Whigs became a revolutionary: she was a truly native daughter.

We should end by returning to the beginning and remembering her early life. Fuller was a contemporary of Oliver Wendell Holmes and Richard Henry Dana, Jr. James Russell Lowell was only slightly her junior. She went to school with them, and often talked to Richard Henry Dana, Sr., one of the few New England poets with a reputation in the 1820s. Holmes, Dana, and Lowell: the triumvirate of native Cambridge men who made the village famous. They fashioned a world of tradition, turning their wit and charm into a modest literature. Margaret Fuller had every reason to be one of them, for she grew up among them and took part in the same culture. But she learned to live in a larger world, to respond to the vitality of the new challenges of Romanticism. She never had the wide acceptance

14. Henry D. Thoreau, *Walden*, ed. J. Lyndon Shanley (Princeton: Princeton University Press, 1971), p. 324.

enjoyed by Holmes and Lowell, but in the end she left us more. The past was real to her, even more so than to the Cambridge men, but she knew history to use it, not to be its prisoner. Her seeking took the form of a risky commitment to the new, to the self, to the possibilities of growth. Fuller left an uneven record, fragmentary and dispersed, but her life, especially as we find it recorded in her letters, dramatizes the perils and accomplishments of an American life well lived.

THE SOURCES

Memoirs of Margaret Fuller Ossoli

The reaction of Fuller's friends to her death shaped our view of her for nearly a century. Almost immediately they made plans for a memorial volume to be called "Margaret and her Friends." William H. Channing wrote Emerson suggesting the book; Greeley wrote from New York, not only urging the writing but insisting that the publication take place within a couple of months. On 2 August, exactly two weeks after Fuller's death, Emerson wrote Sam Ward about the plans. Her friends had immediately found the right tribute, for Fuller had made herself into an intellectual who took pride in both her public life as a critic and in friendships. A book, and especially one devoted to "Margaret and her friends," was a memorial that made sense.

Emerson was the obvious choice to edit the book, but he had little enthusiasm for tasks that deflected him from his vocation. He did, of course, agree to contribute to the memorial, but he refused to write the entire book. From the first, William Henry Channing was included in the plans, though Greeley accurately predicted the limitations that marred Channing's part of the project. Emerson sought and got the collaboration of Sam Ward, who accepted the responsibility reluctantly.

By November 1850 Emerson, Channing, and the Fuller family were collecting the letters and manuscripts Fuller had left behind when she went to Europe. The editors had many of the letters she had written to each of them over the course of their friendship; Caroline Sturgis, Charles Newcomb, Elizabeth Hoar, and Madame Arconati all contributed bundles of material, as did Ellen, Richard, and Mrs. Fuller. Ellen took charge of the family's portion and got together a sizable quantity of her sister's papers. Not surprisingly, there were large gaps: Greeley, despite his early voluble enthusiasm, either contributed nothing or sent material the editors chose not to use; early women friends—Almira Penniman, Amelia Greenwood, Belinda Randall—were absent, as were George Davis, Mary Soley DeWolfe, and a host of newer friends, including the Howitts in England, Mickiewicz in France, and Mazzini in his London exile.

Several people wrote reminiscences of their friendships with Fuller. The Storys sent a long account of their days with her in Italy; both Mazzini and Browning claimed to have written their recollections and to have sent them to William Story, but any narratives they wrote have disappeared. Emerson repeatedly sent requests to Europe but never received a reply.

From the start there were obvious problems, the most conspicuous of which was the secrecy surrounding Fuller's marriage and the timing of Angelo's birth. Each of the editors was expected to help clarify this ambiguous and embarrassing situation. Beyond this problem lay Fuller's history as a confidante. Almost immediately after he got word of her death, Emerson wrote in his journal: "When I heard that a trunk of her correspondence had been found & opened, I felt what a panic would strike all her friends, for it was as if a clever reporter had got underneath a confessional & agreed to report all that transpired there in Wall street."[1] Thus the editors proceeded cautiously; they presented little personal about Margaret Fuller's friends, and included only the part of her life that was seemly. The book would name few names, indulge in no gossip, include no trivia of daily life.

For his part, Emerson created a "Margaret Fuller Ossoli" journal, a separate notebook in which he copied extracts from the manuscript letters and journals that passed through his hands and wrote out drafts of his part of the biography. The family, meanwhile, hired a copyist to transcribe much of the material in Ellen Channing's possession. Madame Arconati's letters were copied and returned to her; the Springs and Storys sent copies they had made of Fuller's letters but kept the originals. By the middle of 1851 a stream of paper about Fuller was coming into and going out of Concord. Nor did Emerson or the family keep it all straight. Charles Newcomb complained for a year that he never got his letters back, and when Emerson finally sent them, they went astray.

---

1. Ralph Waldo Emerson, *The Journals and Miscellaneous Notebooks of Ralph Waldo Emerson*, ed. William H. Gilman et al. (Cambridge: Belknap Press of Harvard University Press, 1961–), vol. 11, *1848–1851*, ed. A. W. Plumstead, W. H. Gilman, and Ruth H. Bennett (1975), p. 258.

By midsummer 1851 the book was taking shape. On 8 August, Emerson acknowledged receipt of a portion of Ward's manuscript and urged him to send more, despite the banker's reluctance to continue. Then, on 10 September, Emerson wrote James Clarke not as to a friend who had manuscripts but as to a coeditor. Between 8 August and 10 September, Ward dropped out and was replaced by Clarke, who brought with him both a friendship with Fuller longer than Emerson's and a very large cache of Fuller's letters and journals. Ward apparently took his material with him when he left, for nothing remains in the published volume that can be identified as having been in his possession or having come from his pen. No trace of his motive for withdrawing remains. Once the man she loved, Sam Ward simply trailed out of Fuller's life and work.

Finally, eighteen months after her death, Fuller got her memorial: *Memoirs of Margaret Fuller Ossoli* was published in two volumes by Phillips, Sampson and Company of Boston in February 1852. In many ways the book was a notable success, for her biographers were talented men. Choosing from a wealth of sources, they picked informative letters, lively passages from journals, and solid essays. They knew exactly what they were doing, and they did it well. No one, then or now, has been in a position to match their selection. They were interested in showing Fuller's mind, and so they printed her remarks on books; they wanted to capture her personality as they experienced it, so they let her speak for herself, which is exactly what she would have wanted.

But Channing, Clarke, and Emerson so bowdlerized and manipulated their evidence as to ruin a splendid book. The *Memoirs of Margaret Fuller Ossoli* is a mess. Given their complex set of motives, the editors created a version of Margaret Fuller that is distorted by their own points of view. They had to repress her sexuality, her quarrelsomeness, her brooding sense of incompleteness, and her increasingly radical political point of view. On the one hand, they did what any biographer must do: they created a personality they understood. On the other, they did not have a complete record to work with, for they knew nothing about the Nathan episode and little about her European life. Finally, the mid-nineteenth century did not share our insistence on the sanctity of texts. For them, private writing was just that: private. No one saw a problem in excising paragraphs written in haste or sickness, in pique or passion; no one doubted the need to protect the reputations of surviving friends and acquaintances. The evidence, though, suggests another level of creation, an attempt to make Fuller intellectually safer and sexually acceptable, her marriage normal, her son legitimate.

One can hardly overemphasize the effects of that memorial both in its accomplishment and in its harm. Because it was constructed from manuscripts, many of which were later lost or destroyed, and because it was written by three close friends, each of whom understood a part of Fuller's personality, the book cannot be ignored. No later work save Thomas Wentworth Higginson's *Margaret Fuller Ossoli* has been based so exclusively on primary material, yet the *Memoirs* has crippled our responses as much as it has enlightened us. *Memoirs of Margaret Fuller Ossoli* went beyond its function as a memorial to a dead friend: it created a mythic Margaret Fuller.

Emerson and his friends recognized the value and richness of her letters, for a predominant portion of what they used comes from them. Unfortunately, they often did not like (consciously or not) what they found, and so they set about "improving" upon the situation. What they did varied from editor to editor. Clarke played a smaller part than the other two, probably because of his late arrival on the scene. Most of his section is based on Fuller's letters to him and on her autobiographical account of her childhood. Few of the original letters he presented survive, so it is difficult to assess his editing.

Emerson, like his coeditors, omitted almost all names, failed to distinguish between passages of letters and journals, and used snippets taken completely out of context, but he does appear to have quoted accurately, if we can generalize from the few comparisons we can make between surviving holographs and his copies or his published versions. He routinely altered punctuation and slightly modified wording, but otherwise remained reasonably faithful to the text. Channing created the most serious problems for his readers. He had the troublesome last half decade of Fuller's life to cover, and he seems to have been most willfully capricious in handling the manuscripts. His section of the *Memoirs* is a briar patch. People are misidentified; separate letters are silently joined together; letters are joined to *Tribune* essays; and Fuller's language is often drastically changed.

We can make these observations on the book: (1) Almost no letters are intact. As a result, Fuller sounds tiresomely serious; her voice is habitually literary and self-searching. A reader of her letters as they were written quickly sees that she mixed her criticism and her Romantic self-scrutiny with family matters, gossip, and business details. The whole tone changes if she is presented through nothing but excerpts. (2) She appears in the *Memoirs* to be consistent in her attitudes, but in fact she could be quite one woman to one correspondent and another to a second. Without knowing to whom the letters were addressed, a reader cannot know which Fuller is speaking. (3) The promiscuous mixing of letters and essays obliterates the rhetorical situation that prompted the writing. The public and private voices merge into one continually public Margaret Fuller. (4) The shattered chronology in the *Memoirs* (misdatings are common; much of the material is undated) obscures the growth of Fuller's mind and personality. (5) The necessary gaps created by the limited number of sources created large blind spots in the *Memoirs*: no hint, for instance, of her love for Davis, Ward, or Nathan. (6) Fuller's childhood letters were not used in the *Memoirs*, so her early life is recreated only by her adult autobiography, which, while revealing, is an *ex post facto* account that tells us more about Fuller's adulthood than about her childhood.

Thus the very format of the *Memoirs* created limitations about which we can do little, for many of the original documents were destroyed. The editors often scissored a passage from a letter and then pasted it onto a sheet at the appropriate spot in their text. Emerson ruefully said later that these sheets came back from the typesetter so soiled as to be ruined. A portion of the manuscripts in Channing's possession was later given to Higginson for his biography. He, in turn, left most of them to the Boston Public Library. The sad evidence of the physical abuse still exists: letters have whole paragraphs blotted by gobs of purple ink; other letters are cut into halves or quarters; editorial changes are written over Fuller's writing.

One paragraph from Volume 1 will illustrate the damage the *Memoirs* has done to Fuller's presence in our minds. At a time when she was struggling with major questions about Christianity, she wrote (in the *Memoirs* version) to a friend:

> My object is to examine thoroughly, as far as my time and abilities will permit, the evidences of the Christian Religion. I have endeavored to get rid of this task as much and as long as possible; to be content with superficial notions, and, if I may so express it, to adopt religion as a matter of taste. But I meet with infidels very often; two or three of my particular friends are deists; and their arguments, with distressing sceptical notions of my own, are haunting me forever. I must satisfy myself; and having once begun, I shall go on as far as I can.
>
> My mind often swells with thoughts on these subjects, which I long to pour out on some person of superior calmness and strength, and fortunate in more accurate knowledge. I should feel such a quieting reaction. But, generally, it seems best that I should go through these conflicts alone. The process will be slower, more irksome, more distressing, but the results will be my own, and I shall feel greater confidence in them.[2]

2. *Memoirs of Margaret Fuller Ossoli*, ed. R. W. Emerson, W. H. Channing, and J. F. Clarke, 2 vols. (Boston: Phillips, Sampson, 1852), 1:151.

Undated, unidentified, these paragraphs appear to be excerpted from a letter; the section of this chapter in the *Memoirs* was designed, Clarke said, to show "how stern was her schooling" in doubt and yet how solid her faith in a divine Providence. The two paragraphs are in fact from separate letters (which survive) to Frederic Henry Hedge—the first dated 30 November 1834, the second 1 February 1835. Clarke reproduced the first paragraph pretty much as Fuller wrote it (except for the punctuation, which bears little resemblance to Fuller's eccentric habits), though he did change the second clause of the second sentence. He substituted "to be content with superficial notions" for Fuller's "to content myself with superficial notions." The shift from her active, reflexive form to a neutral "to be" is, if minor, still a telling change. Similarly, Fuller italicized her imperative "I *must* satisfy myself" at the end of the passage, but Clarke omitted the emphasis.

More troublesome is the handling of the second paragraph (which in the holograph is not a paragraph at all but part of a longer and quite complex discussion). Clarke has Fuller say: "My mind often swells with thoughts on these subjects, which I long to pour out on some person of superior calmness and strength, and fortunate in more accurate knowledge." Fuller herself had written: "My mind often burns with thoughts on these subjects and I long to pour out my soul to some person of superior calmness and strength." The substitution of "swells" for "burns" is unfortunate, for it dampens her intensity. Then, where she made "soul" be the object of "pour," Clarke substituted a clumsy relative clause modifying "subjects," which is both misleading and stylistically awkward.

The editing deliberately changes Fuller's ideas as much as it changes her style. Clarke's second paragraph takes for its topics "these subjects," the "evidences of Christianity," the Deistical arguments, and Fuller's doubts—a mélange of notions. The paragraphs are presented as if they were a coherent, though vague, response by Fuller. "These subjects," however, were in fact specifically named earlier in an omitted sentence. Fuller had said to Hedge, "I have no confidence in God as a Father, if I could believe in Revelation and consequently in an over-ruling Providence many things which seem dark and hateful to me now would be made clear or I could wait." Her "burning" was more specific, more radical, and more unsettling than Clarke could let her admit in print.

To review for a minute: the two passages come from letters written two months apart (she was engaged in a running, though written, conversation), to Hedge (a minister, theologian-to-be, and so a man to whom she would naturally raise these questions), and in the context of other topics (the local but mediocre preaching; her desire to meet Emerson, whom she did not yet know; Hedge's article on phrenology; Carlyle; her Tasso translation; Eichhorn's limitations; gossip about the Channing family). Hedge and Fuller had exchanged other letters between the two passages. She was, of course, intense about her religious doubt, but that doubt shared space with other passionately held ideas, all of which disappear from the *Memoirs*. Clarke's version of Fuller is narrow, inaccurate, and badly written.

Troublesome as the *Memoirs* may be, the volumes remain a source of information. In this edition of Fuller's collected letters, the *Memoirs* material is used only when no better text survives. Insofar as possible, the letters are dated, recipients identified, and the contents annotated. While we can reduce if not correct the damage, the reader should constantly remember that the editor cannot vouch for the accuracy of texts whose only authority is the *Memoirs*.

Other Publications

In 1884 Higginson drew on the *Memoirs* manuscripts given him by Channing as well as on the Fuller family's collection. Again several of the letters from which he quoted have subsequently disappeared, and we are left with only a printed record. A comparison of the surviving manuscripts with his published versions, however, shows him to be more scrupulous in his handling of the originals than his predecessors were.

In 1903 *Love-Letters of Margaret Fuller* appeared, revealing for the first time her "affair" with James Nathan, who had offered the letters for sale to the family. Higginson, however, persuaded the Boston Public Library to buy them. The 1903 edition, with a preface by Julia Ward Howe and reminiscences by Emerson and Greeley, is unannotated, and it presents incomplete versions of some of the letters. Several of the holographs have cancellations added by a later, unknown hand. The deleted portions do not appear in the *Love-Letters*, though they are still legible in the manuscripts. The texts have been restored in this edition of Fuller's letters.

Since 1903 only a scattering of Fuller letters has come into print. Mason Wade published several in *The Writings of Margaret Fuller*. A few have appeared in scholarly journals; Bell Gale Chevigny in 1976 published *The Woman and the Myth*, which uses several previously unpublished letters. Volume 11 of *The Journals and Miscellaneous Notebooks of Ralph Waldo Emerson* includes the "Ossoli" notebook Emerson created as he worked on the *Memoirs*.

The Manuscripts

Between them the Fuller family and Higginson preserved a large quantity of Fuller's letters. Partly as a family habit and partly from the impetus of the *Memoirs*, the family gathered a large group of Fuller's papers—letters, journals, and notebooks. These papers, together with a very large collection of other Fuller family material, were given to the Houghton Library at Harvard University. The family papers contain some copies of Margaret Fuller letters. Made by unknown hands, these copies are, in part, spread through the binders containing the holographs. The remainder of the copies were written directly into three large notebooks (labeled "Works").

Higginson added to the Boston Public Library collection by donating his Fuller manuscripts. This collection, too, contains both copies and holographs. Here the problem is more difficult, however, for many of the copies were made for the *Memoirs*, and they are mostly fragments. Often it is impossible to determine with certainty whether the manuscripts are pieces of letters or parts of Fuller's journal. In one instance, fragments from several folders can be reassembled into a more complete copy by matching the edges of the paper. Beyond these two quite large collections, other family papers contain Fuller manuscripts: the Emerson, Tappan, Clarke, and Ward family papers at the Houghton Library are rich in letters to and from Margaret Fuller; the Peabody and Duyckinck collections in the Berg Collection and the Manuscripts and Archives Division of the New York Public Library also have Fuller letters.

EDITORIAL METHOD

This edition brings together for the first time all the known extant letters written by Margaret Fuller. The texts are presented in their entirety in chronological order. Only conservative emendations, as outlined below under "Text," have been incorporated in the text; all others are recorded in textual notes. The text has been prepared from holographs whenever possible. When a holograph is lacking, the text is based on a manuscript copy of the lost holograph. When two manuscript copies of the same letter survive in the absence of a holograph, the more nearly complete version has been chosen. If both are of the same length, I have chosen the copy prepared by the Fuller family, because a spot comparison of other family copies with their surviving holographs shows them to be more nearly accurate than copies by other hands, if not exact. Only those letters with no manuscript authority have been taken from printed sources. Those letters dated by year only appear at the head of the year; those dated only by month, at the head of the month; undated letters come at the end of the edition, arranged alphabetically by recipient when known.

To establish the text, I first gathered microfilm or Xerox copies of all the manuscript letters and then made typed copies of these photoreproductions. I also typed versions of all the letters that now exist only in printed versions. I then corrected the typescript twice: first an assistant read aloud to me all the photoreproductions and the printed versions of the letters; later, two other assistants (working with me at different times) accompanied me to the libraries that hold the original manuscripts and read those manuscripts aloud to me as I again corrected the typescript. (There is one exception to this second check, for I was unable to visit one library.)

The final text derives from the corrected typescript, and proof was read aloud at two stages.

Format

The letters are numbered chronologically and the recipients identified in uniform headings. All dates, locations, salutations, and signatures are regularized in the following manner: dates and locations are set flush against the right margin, salutations flush against the left margin; signatures are set in large and small capitals and indented from the right margin at the bottom of the letter; when two or more initials are used in a signature, they are regularized with a space between each pair.

Text

The text is presented as faithfully as possible with conservative emendations. Fuller's spelling, capitalization, and punctuation are retained, as are her occasional slips of the pen (e.g., *and and*). Her end punctuation is often ambiguous, for her period resembles a comma. In all instances this mark is preserved as a period. Punctuation is supplied in brackets only when its absence leads to confusion. A paragraph is often indicated in the holographs only by a space at the end of the preceding line. In all such instances the following paragraph is silently indented. Fuller used the dash as an all-purpose mark of punctuation; her dashes are consistently retained. Abbreviations are not expanded save in those instances where ambiguities might otherwise result. When expanded, the additions are enclosed in square brackets. Cancellations are omitted from the text, and superscriptions and interlined additions are lowered; all such emendations are reported in the textual notes. Cross-hatching (Fuller occasionally turned the sheet and wrote at a right angle across her letter) and all symbols, notes, and marks added by later hands are emended and unreported. The German ß is set as "ss"; "&" becomes "and." Unless otherwise noted, the matter canceled by a later hand in the collection of the Boston Public Library has been recovered. All the letters and fragments taken from Emerson's "Ossoli" journal (MH: bMS Am 1280 [111]) are in his hand.

Annotation and Index

The text of each letter is followed by a provenance note that indicates the source of the text, any surviving manuscript copies, any previous publishing history, the name and address of the recipient as written by Fuller, the postmark, and the recipient's endorsement, if any. A brief biography of the recipient follows the provenance note to the first surviving letter to him or her, unless the recipient has already been identified. Then come textual notes listing editorial emendations and variants among manuscript copies, Fuller's cancellations, and her interlined insertions. Fuller's words here are set in roman type; editorial interpolations are set in italics. The numbered annotations that follow the textual notes identify all people mentioned in the letter except those well known to readers (for example, Dante, Shakespeare, Milton) and those previously identified, and all books, literary and historical allusions, and quotations that can be established. Brief biographies of well-known individuals who are not identified in the notes can be found in *Webster's Biographical Dictionary.*

Citations to the Massachusetts vital records office take two forms. Citations to nineteenth-century records refer only to volume and page numbers. Thus "MVR 331:102" cites page 102 of volume 331 of the death record. Beginning in this century, the reference has a preceding date. Thus "MVR 1906, 36:120" cites the death record for 1906, volume 36, page 120. Unless otherwise noted, all citations are to death records.

Publication data come from the *National Union Catalogue* of the Library of Congress or, when otherwise necessary, from the *British Museum General Catalogue of Printed Books.* Occasional notes explain ambiguities in the text, summarize events in Fuller's life, or refer the reader to other letters. The surviving letters written to Fuller have provided explanatory material for many of the annotations. Unidentified items are usually silently passed over.

An appendix in the final volume lists chronologically the letters Fuller is known to have written but which have not survived.

Each volume of the letters has a separate index. A comprehensive index appears in the final volume.

Editorial Apparatus

Textual Devices

The following devices are used in the text:

[Square brackets] enclose editorial additions.
[*Italics*] indicate editorial comments.
[   ] marks matter missing from the text.
Superscript^n refers the reader to a textual note.
Superscript^1 refers the reader to an explanatory note.

The following devices are used in the textual notes:

⟨Angle brackets⟩ identify recovered cancellations.
⟨?⟩ identifies unrecovered cancellations.
↑ Opposed arrows ↓ indicate interlined insertions.
Italics indicate editorial comments.

Descriptive Symbols

AL   Autograph letter, unsigned
ALfr   Autograph letter fragment, unsigned
ALfrS   Autograph letter fragment, signed with name or initial(s)
ALS   Autograph letter, signed with name or initial(s)
AMsfr   Autograph manuscript fragment; may not be a letter for the reason
            stated
EL   Edited letter, as previously published; holograph now lost
ELfr   Edited letter fragment, as previously published; holograph now lost
MsC   Manuscript copy of a Fuller letter in a hand other than Fuller's;
            unless otherwise indicated, the holograph has not been recovered
MsCfr   Manuscript copy of a fragment of a Fuller letter in a hand other

71

than Fuller's; unless otherwise indicated, the holograph has not been recovered

TC   Typed copy; holograph now lost

Location Symbols

CtY   Yale University Library
ICHi   Chicago Historical Society
MB   Boston Public Library, Department of Rare Books and Manuscripts
MH   Harvard University, Houghton Library
MH-AH   Harvard Divinity School, Andover-Harvard Theological Library
MHarF   Fruitlands Museums, Harvard, Massachusetts
MHi   Massachusetts Historical Society
NIC   Cornell University Libraries
NN-M   New York Public Library, Manuscripts and Archives Division
NcU   University of North Carolina, Chapel Hill, Wilson Library
PHi   Historical Society of Pennsylvania
PSt   Pennsylvania State University Library
RHi   Rhode Island Historical Society
RPB   Brown University Library
TxU   University of Texas, Humanities Research Center
ViU   University of Virginia Library

Short Titles and Abbreviations

ABD: *Allgemeine Deutsche Biographie*, 56 vols. (Leipzig: Duncker & Humblot, 1875–1912).

Barker Genealogy: Elizabeth F. Barker, *Barker Genealogy* (New York: Frye, 1927).

Biographical Directory: *Biographical Directory of the American Congress, 1774–1971* (Washington, D.C.: Government Printing Office, 1971).

Boston Births: *A Report of the Record Commissioners of the City of Boston: Boston Births, A.D. 1700 to A.D. 1800* (Boston: Rockwell & Churchill, 1894).

Bowen, *Woodstock Families*: Clarence Winthrop Bowen, *The History of Woodstock, Connecticut: Genealogies of Woodstock Families*, 8 vols. (Norwood, Mass.: Privately published by Plimpton Press, 1935–43).

Brown, *American Stage*: T. Allston Brown, *History of the American Stage* (New York: Dick & Fitzgerald, 1870).

Brown Historical Catalogue: *The Historical Catalogue of Brown University, 1764–1934* (Providence, R.I., 1936).

Bullard, *Rotches*: John M. Bullard, *The Rotches* (New Bedford, Mass.: Privately published, 1947).

Butler, *Town of Groton*: Caleb Butler, *History of the Town of Groton* (Boston: T. R. Marvin, 1848).

Carlson, "Alcott's Journal": Larry A. Carlson, "Bronson Alcott's Journal for 1837: An Edition, with Notes and an Introduction," Ph.D. dissertation, Pennsylvania State University, 1979.

CC: *Columbian Centinel* (Boston).

Chevigny: Bell Gale Chevigny, *The Woman and the Myth: Margaret Fuller's Life and Writings* (Old Westbury, N.Y.: Feminist Press, 1976).

Clarke, *Greenes*: Louise B. Clarke, comp., *The Greenes of Rhode Island* (New York: Knickerbocker Press, 1903).

Clarke, *Richard Hull*: Samuel C. Clarke, *Records of some of the Descendants of Richard Hull, New Haven* (Boston: D. Clapp & Son, 1869).

Cleveland and Cleaveland: Edmund J. Cleveland and Horace G. Cleveland, *The Genealogy of the Cleveland and Cleaveland Families*, 3 vols. (Hartford, Conn.: Case, Lockwood & Brainard, 1899).

CVR: *Vital Records of Cambridge, Massachusetts, to the Year 1850*, 2 vols. (Boston: Wright & Potter, 1914–15).

DAB: *Dictionary of American Biography*, ed. Allen Johnson and Dumas Malone, 20 vols. (New York: Scribner's, 1928–36).

Dana Family: Elizabeth Ellery Dana, *The Dana Family in America* (Cambridge, Mass.: Privately published, 1956).

Davis, *Ancient Landmarks*: William T. Davis, *Ancient Landmarks of Plymouth*, 2d ed. (Boston: Damrell & Upham, 1899).

Davis, *Suffolk County*: William T. Davis, *Professional and Industrial History of Suffolk County*, 3 vols. (Boston: Boston History Co., 1894).

Descendants of John Dwight: Benjamin W. Dwight, *The History of the Descendants of John Dwight, of Dedham, Mass.*, 2 vols. (New York: J. F. Trow & Son, 1874).

Dexter, "BVR": John H. Dexter, "Boston: Vital Records," 3 vols. NEHGS.

DivCat: *General Catalogue of the Divinity School of Harvard University, 1901* (Cambridge, Mass., 1901).

Dwight, *Select Minor Poems*: John Sullivan Dwight, *Select Minor Poems, Translated from the German of Goethe and Schiller*, vol. 3 of *Specimens of Foreign Standard Literature*, ed. George Ripley (Boston: Hilliard, Gray, 1839).

Emerson–Carlyle Correspondence: *The Correspondence of Emerson and Carlyle*, ed. Joseph Slater (New York: Columbia University Press, 1964).

Emerson Lectures: *The Early Lectures of Ralph Waldo Emerson*, ed. Stephen E. Whicher, Robert E. Spiller, and Wallace E. Williams, 3 vols. (Cambridge: Belknap Press of Harvard University Press, 1961–72).

Endicott, *BMD*: Frederic Endicott, ed., *The Record of Births, Marriages and Deaths . . . in the Town of Canton from 1797–1845* (Canton, Mass.: W. Bense, 1896).

Fay Genealogy: Orlin P. Fay, *Fay Genealogy: John Fay of Marlborough and His Descendants* (Cleveland: J. B. Savage, 1898).

Gannett Descendants: Michael R. Gannett, *Gannett Descendants of Matthew and Hannah Gannett of Scituate, Massachusetts* (Chevy Chase, Md.: Privately published, 1976).

Goethe, *Gedenkausgabe*: Johann Wolfgang Goethe, *Gedenkausgabe der Werke, Briefe und Gespräche*, ed. Ernst Beutler, 24 vols. (Zurich: Artemis Verlag, 1948–54).

Gray, *Poems of Goethe*: Ronald Gray, ed. *Poems of Goethe* (Cambridge: At the University Press, 1966).

Green, *Historical Sketch*: Samuel Abbott Green, *An Historical Sketch of Groton, Massachusetts, 1655–1890* (Groton, Mass.: n.p., 1894).

"Greene-St. School": Henry L. Greene, "The Greene-St. School, of Providence, and Its Teachers," *Publications of the Rhode Island Historical Society*, n.s. 6 (January 1899):199–219.

Grove's Dictionary: *Grove's Dictionary of Music and Musicians*, ed. H. C. Colles, 3d ed., 6 vols. (New York: Macmillan, 1927–34).

GVR: *Vital Records of Groton, Massachusetts, to the End of the Year 1849*, 2 vols. (Salem, Mass.: Essex Institute, 1926).

Habich, "JFC's 1833 Letter-journal": Robert D. Habich, "James Freeman Clarke's 1833 Letter-journal for Margaret Fuller," *ESQ* 27(1981):47–56.

Hall, "Dr. John Park": Edward H. Hall, "Reminiscences of Dr. John Park," *Proceedings of the American Antiquarian Society*, n.s. 7 (October 1890):69–93.

Heralds: Samuel A. Eliot, *Heralds of a Liberal Faith*, 3 vols. (Boston: American Unitarian Association, 1910).

Higginson, *MFO*: Thomas Wentworth Higginson, *Margaret Fuller Ossoli* (Boston: Houghton Mifflin, 1884).

Higginson, *Reverend Francis Higginson*: Thomas Wentworth Higginson, *Descendants of the Reverend Francis Higginson* ([Cambridge?, Mass.]: Privately published, 1910).

History of Lynn: Alonzo Lewis and James R. Newhall, *History of Lynn, Essex County, Massachusetts* (Boston: John L. Shorey, 1865).

"Hollis Street Church": "Hollis Street Church, Boston: Records of Admissions, Baptisms, Marriages and Deaths, 1732–1887," NEHGS.

Holman, *John Coney*: Mary L. Holman, *Ancestors and Descendants of John Coney of Boston* (Concord, N.H.: Rumford Press, 1928).

Hunnewell, *Town Life*: James F. Hunnewell, *A Century of Town Life: A History of Charlestown, Massachusetts* (Boston: Little, Brown, 1888).

Huntoon, *Town of Canton*: Daniel T. Huntoon, *History of the Town of Canton* (Cambridge, Mass.: J. Wilson & Son, 1893).

Ipswich Emersons: Benjamin Kendall Emerson, *The Ipswich Emersons* (Boston: D. Clapp & Son, 1900).

Jacobus, *Descendants of Robert Waterman*: Donald Lines Jacobus, *Descendants of Robert Waterman* (New Haven: E. F. Waterman, 1939).

JMN: *The Journals and Miscellaneous Notebooks of Ralph Waldo Emerson*, ed. William H. Gilman et al., 16 vols. to date (Cambridge: Belknap Press of Harvard University Press, 1960–).

LBD: *Lamb's Biographical Dictionary of the United States*, ed. John Howard Brown, 7 vols. (Boston: James H. Lamb, 1900–1903).

Letters of JFC: *The Letters of James Freeman Clarke to Margaret Fuller*, ed. John Wesley Thomas (Hamburg: Cram, de Gruyter, 1957).

Love-Letters: *Love-Letters of Margaret Fuller, 1845–1846* (New York: D. Appleton, 1903).

Martineau's Autobiography: *Harriet Martineau's Autobiography*, ed. Maria Weston Chapman, 2 vols. (Boston: J. R. Osgood, 1877).

Memoirs: *Memoirs of Margaret Fuller Ossoli*, ed. R. W. Emerson, W. H. Channing, and J. F. Clarke, 2 vols. (Boston: Phillips, Sampson, 1852).

Memorial Biographies: *Memorial Biographies of the New England Historic Genealogical Society*, 9 vols. (Boston, 1880–1908).

Miller: *Margaret Fuller: American Romantic*, ed. Perry Miller (Garden City, N.Y.: Doubleday, 1963).

Mt. Auburn: Burial records, Mount Auburn Cemetery, Cambridge, Massachusetts.

MVR: Massachusetts vital records, Boston.

National Cyclopaedia: *The National Cyclopaedia of American Biography* (New York: James T. White, 1898–).

NAW: *Notable American Women, 1607–1950*, ed. Edmund T. James, 3 vols. (Cambridge: Belknap Press of Harvard University Press, 1971).

NEHGR: *The New England Historical and Genealogical Register*.

NEHGS: The New England Historic Genealogical Society, Boston.

OCGL: Henry and Mary Garland, *The Oxford Companion to German Literature* (Oxford: Clarendon Press, 1976).

Paige, *Cambridge*: Lucius R. Paige, *History of Cambridge, Massachusetts* (Boston: H. O. Houghton, 1877).

Peabody Genealogy: Selim H. Peabody, comp., *Peabody* (*Paybody, Pabody, Pabodie*) *Genealogy* (Boston: Charles H. Pope, 1909).

Peabody Sisters: Louise Hall Tharp, *The Peabody Sisters of Salem* (Boston: Little, Brown, 1950).

Plymouth Church Records: *Plymouth Church Records, 1620–1859*, 2 vols. (New York: New England Society, 1920).

Potter Families: Charles Edward Potter, *Genealogies of the Potter Families* (Boston: A. Mudge & Son, 1888).

Prescott Memorial: William Prescott, *The Prescott Memorial* (Boston: H. W. Dutton & Son, 1870).

Randall, *Poems*: John W. Randall, *Poems of Nature and Life*, ed. F. E. Abbot (Boston: G. H. Ellis, 1899).

Rhode Island Biographical Cyclopedia: *The Biographical Cyclopedia of Representative Men of Rhode Island*, 2 vols. (Providence, R.I.: National Biographical Publishing Co., 1881).

Rusk, *Letters of RWE*: *The Letters of Ralph Waldo Emerson*, ed. Ralph L. Rusk, 6 vols. (New York: Columbia University Press, 1939).

Rusk, *Life of RWE*: Ralph L. Rusk, *The Life of Ralph Waldo Emerson* (New York: Scribner's, 1949).

Shepard, *Pedlar's Progress*: Odell Shepard, *Pedlar's Progress: The Life of Bronson Alcott* (Boston: Little, Brown, 1937).

Snow et al., *Alphabetical Index*: Edwin M. Snow et al., *Alphabetical Index of the Births, Marriages and Deaths Recorded in Providence* (Providence, R.I.: Sidney S. Rider, 1881–).

STC Letters: *Letters, Conversations, and Recollections of S. T. Coleridge*, ed. Thomas Allsop (London: E. Moxon, 1836).

Stern, "Phrenologist-Publishers": Madeleine B. Stern, "Margaret Fuller and the Phrenologist-Publishers," *Studies in the American Renaissance*, 1980, pp. 229–37.

Sturgis of Yarmouth: Roger Faxton Sturgis, ed., *Edward Sturgis of Yarmouth, Massachusetts* (Boston: Privately published by Stanhope Press, 1914).

Tuckerman Family: Bayard Tuckerman, *Notes on the Tuckerman Family of Massachusetts* (Boston: Privately printed, 1914).

Vose Descendants: Ellen F. Vose, *Robert Vose and His Descendants* (Boston: [S. Usher, Fort Hill Press], 1932).

VR: vital records.

Wade: *The Writings of Margaret Fuller*, ed. Mason Wade (New York: Viking Press, 1941).

Whiting, *Memoirs*: William Whiting, *Memoir of Rev. Samuel Whiting* (Boston: Rand, Avery, 1872).

Whittier Family: Daniel B. Whittier, *Genealogy of Two Branches of the Whittier Family, from 1620 to 1873* (Boston: A. Mudge & Son, 1873).

Wilpert, *Schiller-Chronik*: Gero von Wilpert, *Schiller-Chronik* (Stuttgart: A. Kroner, 1958).

WNC: Margaret Fuller Ossoli, *Woman in the Nineteenth Century, and Kindred Papers*, ed. Arthur B. Fuller (Boston: John P. Jewett, 1855).

Works: Manuscript copybooks, Fuller family papers, 3 vols., in Houghton Library, Harvard University.

THE LETTERS OF MARGARET FULLER

1. To Timothy Fuller

April [24 1817?][1]
[Canton, Massachusetts]

dear Father

it is a heavy storm i hope you will not have to come home in it little eugene[2] is aslep whil i am writing.

Ps caroline has been here in the rain[3]

AL (MH: fms Am 1086 [9:1]); MsC (MH: fms Am 1086 [9:1]). *Addressed:* Mr Timothy Fuller. *Endorsed:* Sarah Margaret Fuller's / *First* Letter— / written 24. April 1817—

Timothy Fuller (1778–1835), fourth of the eleven children born to the Reverend Timothy (1739–1805) and Sarah Williams Fuller (d. 1822), graduated from Harvard in 1801, studied law, and served in the Massachusetts Senate from 1813 to 1816. In 1817 he began the first of his four terms as United States representative from Cambridge. After his retirement from Washington in 1825, Fuller was elected to the Massachusetts House, where he became Speaker in 1825 and a member of the Executive Council in 1828. On 28 May 1809 he married Margarett Crane (1789–1859), the second of the four children born to Peter (1752–1821) and Elizabeth Jones Weiser Crane (1755–1845) (Fuller: William Hyslop Fuller, *Genealogy of Some Descendants of Thomas Fuller of Woburn* [n.p., 1919], pp. 142–48, and Arthur B. Fuller, *Historical Notices of Thomas Fuller and His Descendants* [Boston, 1859]; Crane: Endicott, *BMD*; Huntoon, *Town of Canton*; MVR 21:75).

1. Dated from endorsement, but the childish scrawl of the letter suggests an earlier year than 1817.

2. Eugene Fuller (1815–59) was the next oldest surviving child of the Timothy Fuller family. He graduated from Harvard in 1834, studied law with George F. Farley in Groton, and was admitted to the Middlesex bar. Finding no success in his law career, Eugene went to New Orleans, where he married Anna Eliza Rotta, a Philadelphia widow. On 21 June 1859 Eugene was lost overboard from a ship sailing from

Timothy Fuller. Courtesy of Willard P. Fuller, Jr.

New York to Boston (Thomas Cushing, *Memorials of the Class of 1834 of Harvard College* [Boston, 1884], pp. 19–20; *Groton Historical Series*, no. 3, p. 6).

3. Probably Caroline Kuhn (1806–85), daughter of Margarett Crane Fuller's half sister, Nancy Weiser (1780–1860), who had married George Kuhn (1777–1847) (MVR 33:8, 239:119, 365:70; Middlesex Probate, 1st ser., no. 36014). Another possibility is Caroline Williams Belcher (1812–83), daughter of Clifford (1778–1832) and Deborah Fuller Belcher (1782–1865) of Farmington, Maine ("Farmington, Franklin County, Maine: Marriages—Births—Deaths. 1784–1890," NEHGS, p. 15; Francis Gould Butler, *A History of Farmington* [Farmington, Me., 1885], pp. 380–81; Suffolk Probate, no. 54797).

2. To Timothy Fuller

Canton 13 Jany 1818

Dear Father

I received your letter by todays mail dated 4 Jan.[1] I have taken several lessons in Musick to raise and fall the notes I have not learned to sing a tune by note. I have writen every day a little but have made but little improvement as you will see by this letter. I have been reviewing Valpy's Chronology.[2] We have not been able to procure any books [on] either Charles 12th of Sweden or Philip IId of Spain[3] but Mama intends to send to Uncle Henry.[4] I hope to make greater proficuncy in my Studies I have learned all the rules of Musick but one. Eugene speaks of you sometimes. William Henry wakes in the Morning as usual.[5] I should have liked to have been with you to have seen the pictures gallery at NYork.[6]

We were much delighted to hear from you as we were anxious to hear of your safe arrival at Washington. I hope you will write to me frequently. I can read your letter. I do not write well at all. Whenever we speak of you Eugene asks for your knife. Mama wants me to hold the baby while she writes to you, she has written to you once Farewell, dear Papa

SARAH MARGARET FULLER.

ALS (MH: fMS Am 1086 [9:3]). *Addressed:* Hon. Timothy Fuller. Washington. / District of Columbia. *Endorsed:* From my Daughter. / Sarah Margarett Fuller / Recd 19. Jan. 18—

1. In his letter (MH), her father had inquired about her studies and her music.

2. Richard Valpy's *Poetical Chronology of Ancient and English History* (London, [1795?]) had been published in Boston in 1816.

3. Fuller was reading about warrior kings. Charles XII of Sweden (1682–1718), who reigned 1697 to 1718, was the central figure in the Great Northern War, and Philip II of Spain (1527–98), who reigned from 1556 to 1598, was most noted for

his support of the Counterreformation, for the conquest of Portugal in 1580, and for the exploitation of Spain's American colonies.

4. Fuller refers here to her uncle Henry Holton Fuller (1790–1852), who had been in law partnership with her father. Henry graduated from Harvard in 1811, studied law in Litchfield, Connecticut, served in the Massachusetts House of Representatives, and founded the *Atlas,* a Whig newspaper. A witty conversationalist, he had a reputation for old-fashioned dress and for wearing his beaver hat with the fur brushed the wrong way. In 1826 he married Mary Buckminster Stone (1804–52), the daughter of Daniel Stone of Framingham (Henry A. Fuller, "Henry Holton Fuller," *Memorial Biographies,* 1:410–22).

5. Her brother William Henry Fuller (1817–78) became a likable, enthusiastic young man, the most personable of the boys. He never went to college, deciding instead to enter business. He failed several times before he established himself in Cincinnati. In 1840 he married Frances Elizabeth Hastings (1819?–87), the daughter of Daniel and Deborah Hammond Hastings (1793–1886) (*CVR;* Roland Hammond, *A History and Genealogy of the Descendants of William Hammond* [Boston, 1894], p. 236).

6. Timothy Fuller mentioned visiting the Academy of Arts in New York City, where he saw a number of religious paintings.

3.   To Timothy Fuller

24 Feby 1818
[Canton]

Dear Father

Why do you not write to me. I want to read letters if I cannot books. Uncle Henry has not sent us any books. I wish you to buy me the play you saw performed at the Theatre.[1] Caroline and Nancy have written to me once.[2] It is Nancys first letter that she has written to me. I have written to them. I never have so much to say as Mama. I wish you to buy a few books for me of the sort you think most fit. Give my love to Uncle Abraham.[3] How does he do. Your afectionate daughter

SARAH M FULLER

Ps Do you see Uncle Abraham often.

ALS (MH: fMS Am 1086 [9:3]). *Addressed:* Hon. Timothy Fuller. M C. / Washington. / District of Columbia. *Endorsed:* From my Sarah Margarett / Recd 3. March 1818—

1. In his November letter her father described his visit to the theater, observing that it was "much inferior to Boston." The unnamed play, however, was "very entertaining," and he admitted he "was ashamed to have so many tears to spare" (Timothy Fuller to Margaret Fuller, November 1817, MH).

2. Caroline and Nancy are the Kuhn sisters. On Caroline, see Letter 1, note 3; her sister Nancy was born in 1801 and died in 1871 (MVR 239:119).

3. Abraham Williams Fuller (1784–1847), Timothy's next younger brother, made a modest fortune in real estate and the law. He never married (Suffolk Probate, no. 35086).

4. To Timothy Fuller

Canton 5 March 1818

Dear Papa

I was very much disappointed not to receive a letter from you. I cannot think my letters go. It is three mails since I wrote to you. I think I have improved a good deal in writing and I can sing one part whil Aunt Abigail sings another.[1] I geuss you will buy my pianno forte. Has Uncle Abraham set out to come home. I am sorry Aunt Kuhn could not come here this winter. I cannot write any more at present so farewell till night.

Evening of the 5 of March. Ellen being here I delayed writing till evening.[2] Now I shall write a little every week but they will not be long. Grandpapa has got better of the rheumatism.[3] Tomorrow we are going to have a singing meeting. Perhaps you will laugh to see the word guess in my letter but I think Slave holder far more disgraceful. I remember what you said in your letter but though I knew the meaning of the word Uankee yet I did not that of Slave holder.[4] I wish you would send me a sheet of gilt egded paper. The time is almost expired when you will get home. O how glad I shall be to see you. Your affectionate daughter

SARAH M FULLER

ALS (MH: fMS Am 1086 [10:86]). *Addressed:* Hon. Timothy Fuller. MC / Washington. *Endorsed:* From my daughter / Sarah Margarett / Recd 14. March 1818—

1. Third of the four children of Peter and Elizabeth Crane, Abigail (1792–1876) was an unmarried aunt who frequently visited the Fullers during Margaret's childhood (MVR 284:218).

2. Ellen Crane (1810–85) was the daughter of Simeon (1774–1821) and Elizabeth (Betsey) Crane Crane (1785?–1856), eldest of the four children of Peter Crane. In 1837 Ellen married David Hill (1812–82) (MVR 365:253, 338:237; *CC*, 19 April 1837).

3. Her grandfather Peter Crane.

4. In his letter of 4 January 1818, her father had explained how the epithets "Yankee" and "slaveholder" were used when New Englanders met southerners in Washington. He went on to give her a brief lesson in colloquial usage by noting the habit of saying "I guess" in the North and "I reckon" in the South, and warned that "both are improper" (Timothy Fuller to Margaret Fuller, 4 January 1818, MH).

5. To Timothy Fuller

Cambridgeport. 16 Dec. 1818.

Dear Papa.

I was very sorry to hear of your accident.[1] I dreamed the night Mamma recieved your letter that you were sick and your life was despaired of when you suddenly recovered. I hope the latter will be accomplished not the former. Papa I do not suppose you think it a good excuse to say that I could not write. No Papa nor do I either for I could have done it. But I have been like Basil in the "Tomorrow" and have determined to be so no longer. I am resolved to write you every week. I have requested Mamma often to let me learn to make puddings and pies. Now I will tell you what I study Latin twice a week and Arithmetick when Aunt Elizabeth is here.[2] If you have spies they will certainly inform you that we are not very dissipated. We have been three times to Dr. Williams[3] and once to Mr Gannetts[4] Aunt Elizabeth often goes to Boston. Eugene has got well but William Henry is rather fretful today. Eugene was very much pleased to recieve your letter but I found it began to grow dirty and took it into custody. Mamma has given me one of the arches to put my letters in for I hope you will write to me when you are not more usefully employed. I do not see how I have contrived to write without being forced to search my brain for something to say except your letter" furnished a variety of topics for I cannot write a long letter seldom more than a page and a half neither do I see how you and Mamma write so much. Perhaps I shall now though. It will take you fifteen minutes to read this letter and me an hour to write it. You say a relation of your pain would be uninterresting to any but an affectionate wife. Do not forget that I am Your afectionate Daughter

SARAH M FULLER

ALS (MH: fMS Am 1086 [9:4]). *Addressed:* Hon. Timothy Fuller MC / Washington / District of Columbia. *Endorsed:* From my Daughter / Sarah Margarett / Recd 22. Dec. 1818— / 27. Dec. 1818—Answered.

except your letter] except your ↑ letter ↓

1. During the trip from Boston to Washington, Fuller's stage had overturned. He reported to his family on 4 December that he was bruised but otherwise unhurt (MH).

2. Another unmarried aunt, Elizabeth Fuller (1775–1856), was a frequent visitor when her brother was in Washington (Princeton VR).

3. Dr. John Williams (1747?–1846) and his wife, Abigail Jones (b. 1762), were Cambridge neighbors and close friends of the Fullers (Barre VR; D. H. Hurd, *History of Middlesex County* [Philadelphia, 1890], p. 166).

84

4. Thomas Brattle Gannett (1789–1851) was the first minister to serve the Cambridgeport Congregational (later Unitarian) Church. The son of the Reverend Caleb and brother of Ezra Stiles Gannett, Thomas Brattle graduated from Harvard in 1809, was ordained in 1814, and settled on 1 January 1814 at Cambridgeport, where he served until his voluntary resignation in 1833. He was later town clerk for Cambridge and twice representative to the Massachusetts General Court. Gannett was twice married: first to Deborah Foxcroft White (1791–1822) of Plymouth; then, following her death, to her sister Sarah Whitworth White (1801–81) (Paige, *Cambridge*; *Gannett Descendants*, pp. 81–82).

6. To Timothy Fuller

Cambridge Port. 6th Jan. 1819

Dear Papa

I was delighted to receive your letter. I had been expecting it for several weeks and had deferred writing till I received it. I shall write to you as often as you to me. Mary Allen[1] brought me a letter from Miss Kilshaw[2] which if you have not got you soon will. The Triton will sail the 18th of this month. Perhaps you would like to write to her if you have not already. I am going into town this week. It is I believe the first time since you went away. Susan Wiliams is to have a ball tomorrow.[3] Papa who shall we send to bring Miss Ellen over. I have asked my Uncles they tell me to send Uncle Abraham but he is unwilling to go. I do not know any body but you that will go and if you did perhaps She would not come. Your affectionate daughter

SARAH M FULLER

ALS (MH: fMS Am 1086 [9:5]). *Addressed:* Hon T Fuller. / Washington. *Endorsed:* From my Daughter / Sarah Margarett— / Recd 12. Jan. 1819—

1. Probably Mary B. Allen (1808–44), daughter of James Allen of Cambridge (*CVR*).
2. Ellen Kilshaw, whom Fuller called "the first angel of my life," was the daughter of John Kilshaw, a Liverpool merchant. She had spent fourteen months during 1816–17 in the United States, visiting her sister and brother-in-law, John H. Greene, a Boston merchant. After she returned to Liverpool, she corresponded often with the Fullers, with whom she had become good friends. Ellen Kilshaw later married a Mr. Cowan and had three children (MH: fMS Am 1086 [2:24–72]; these letters from Kilshaw to the Fullers give the only details we have of the friendship).
3. Margaret often visited her father's cousin Susan Ann Buckminster Williams (1806–71), the daughter of Thomas (1768?–1827) and Susan Atwood Williams. In 1835 Susan Ann Williams married John C. Hayden, a Boston physician ("Hollis Street Church," pp. 466–67; Mt. Auburn; *CC*, 10 October 1835; MVR 139:114).

7. To Timothy Fuller

Cambridge Port 8th Jan 1819.

Dear Papa

This paper is blotted but it is not my fault. While I was writing Eugene stood by the table. He laid the point of a penknife he had in his hand on it and in taking it up he made a blot. I do not think he did it intentionally and I should not have told you of it but I was afraid you would think me careless. I wrote a short letter to you as a forerunner to this. I think your maxim with regard to letter writing[n] is good, but it is not easy for me to use it. For anybody whose ideas flow fast it is easy but as mine do not it is not to me. Like you Papa I have no faith in dreams. I want to ask you a question. Whether my manners ought to increase with my growth or with my years. Mamma says people will judge of me according to my growth. I do not think this is just for surely our knowledge does not[n] increase because we are tall. Do you go to the Theatre often. Perhaps Mama has told you that Mr Wheeler is going to be married. He is to be married to the widow Balch of Dorchester.[1] She is a very young widow for she is not more than[n] 25 and is not likely to meet the fate of his former wives. Sarah Hartwell a favorite of Uncle Elishas is married to Mr Peirce.[2] Weddings Balls Parties all are nothing[n] to me, for I am not invited to them. I am soon to have lessons in drawing. Because of these Aunt Elizabeth has changed her mind and we shall go into Town Tomorrow morning so that I must finish this letter to night or else let it lie[n] till Monday which I do not like to do. Mamma and my two Aunts are gone out Betsy is ironing in the kitchen William has got the old brush after vain efforts to get the new one and is pushing the fire out while Eugene is trying to prevent him from doing it. So Papa I am Your[n] affectionate Daughter

SARAH M FULLER

ALS (MH: fMS Am 1086 [9:6]). Published in Wade, p. 544. *Addressed:* Hon Timothy Fuller MC. / Washington. D.C. *Endorsed:* 2d. / From my Daughter / Sarah Margarett / Recd 13. Jan. 1819— / 30. Jan. 1819—Answered—

regard to letter writing] regard ↑ to letter writing ↓
knowledge does not] knowledge does ↑ not ↓
not more than] not mo⟨t⟩re than
all are nothing] all are nothin ↑ g ↓
let it lie] let it li⟨g⟩e
I am Your] I am ⟨y⟩ Your

1. Ann Clap (1792–1868) was the daughter of Ebenezer and Mary Glover Clap of Dorchester. In 1811 she married Alexander Balch, who died on 5 July 1812 at twenty-

six. On 10 January 1819 the widow Balch married John Wheeler of Cambridge, a man already twice widowed (*NEHGR* 15:232; MVR 213:50; *CVR*).

2. On 5 December Sarah Hartwell (1788–1871) of Lincoln married Abijah H. Pierce (1782–1860), a Boston rum dealer (Lincoln VR; *CVR*; *CC*, 9 January 1819; MVR 139:106, 239:156). Elisha Fuller (1794–1855), Timothy's youngest brother, graduated from Harvard in 1815, attended the Divinity School, was licensed to preach, and filled several Unitarian pulpits until 1821, when he left preaching for the law. After being admitted to the bar in 1824, Fuller moved first to Concord and then to Lowell. A sociable, engaging man, Elisha married in 1830 Susan Adams (1806–61), the daughter of John Adams of Concord (Nathaniel Paine, "Hon. Elisha Fuller," *Memorial Biographies*, 2:353–57).

8. To Timothy Fuller

Cambridge 8th. May [1819?]

Dear father

I am happy to hear that the day of your return is fixed at last. Every body is enquiring when you are coming home and I can only tell them I do not know. You will be home the 21st and my birth day is the twenty third and a month from that is *Examination*: You do not write to me now which I am very sorry for but I know you have other *business*.—

Aunt Martha has been out here lately two or three days.[1] We have heard from Miss Kilshaw lately and Mr. Greene is out here now[2] He was fifty days on his passage here I shall call on Miss Greene tomorrow with Mrs Stewart.—[3]

What a girl my paper is almost out and I've said very little so, no more from Your affectionate daughter

SARAH M FULLER

ALS (MH: fMS Am 1086 [9:2]). *Addressed:* Hon T Fuller MC / Washington.

1. Timothy Fuller's youngest sister, Martha Williams Fuller (1787–1852), married Simeon Chase Whittier (1780–1859) in 1809. Margaret Fuller often visited the Whittiers in Boston, even though her mother thought the Whittier children undisciplined and too devoted to card playing (Charles C. Whittier, *The Descendants of Thomas Whittier and Ruth Green of Salisbury and Haverhill, Massachusetts* [Rutland, Vt., 1937], p. 13; Margarett Crane Fuller letters, MH).

2. John H. Greene. The Miss Greene mentioned later in the letter is probably his sister, Sarah Greene (*CC*, 28 September 1816).

3. Probably Sarah Thompson Stewart, widow of Thomas Stewart, a shipping merchant and Cambridge resident. She died in December 1821 at age thirty-six (*CC*, 22 December 1821; Middlesex Probate, 1st ser., no. 21444).

9. To Ellen Kilshaw

Cambridge 20th Nov 1819

Dear Miss Ellen

As the slow messenger Mercury will soon bend his[n] course toward England I sit down to the pleasant duty of writing you a letter. It is pleasant because while I am writing to you I think[n] I am with you and it is a duty because it is your wish and all your wishes ought to be a duty to me. I am resolved it shall be the longest letter I have ever written to you I hope I shall receive in return a long letter from you. I do not write often enough to write as easy as some persons who seem to have so much to say that they cannot[n] write fast enough and they have not paper enough to hold all they have to say. When I have some event to talk about I think will be interesting to the person to whom[n] I am writing, then indeed I can talk fast enough.

Friday night the ropewalk in Boston was burnt.[1] It has been burnt once before. Some new machinery had been bought which sparing a good deal of labor several workmen were dismissed and by that means brought out of employment. They were Irishmen of a fierce vindictive[n] spirit. As they departed they declared they would be revenged and told the proprietor of the ropewalk he should not enjoy it long. That night it was set on fire and one entirely burnt It was rebuilt and scarcely finished[n] before it was again set on fire. Part of the new one and the whole of another were destroyed. That it was set on fire by incendiares there can be no doubt, every circumstance confirms it. Its being twice burnt the fires breaking out at two ends besides Mr Lewis the proprietor of the rope walk going into it the night before it was burnt discovered behind the door a heap of shavings matches and all the implements necessary for starting a fire. No attempt was made to injure it that night doubtless the villians saw him go in and knew it would be watched The fire was a most awful spectacle which if I attempted to describe I should not be able to give you an adequate idea of its grandeur.

On the same night the Aurora Borealis or Northern Light shone out in splendor. We had walked out to have a nearer view of the fire. When we were returning, papa observed some streaks of it but it was not till we had entered the house we saw it in full splendour. At last I grew weary even of grandeur and went to bed or to express it more elegantly retired to rest. I shall expect when our faithful Hermes returns (whether he is faithful I know not but I know he is not nearly as swift as his namesake the messenger of the gods) I shall expect a long letter from[n] you. You will certainly fulfil my wishes.

How tall do you think I am dear Ellen? So tall some persons think I am thirteen. How do you think I look? Just as I did two years ago. Ah Ellen I can remember just how you looked. I shall not put any miss to your name unless you bid me to do it. It does not look half so friendly and it conveys an idea[n] of respect with it that I do not like at all. How old is Miss Elisa K Greene now—her betrothed lover[n] is in his 3d year.[2] Do you think it would do any harm to let them be married at 13. I have heard of a French[n] princess who was married at 10 years old and a prince betrothed at 6 months. Does she continue to be industrious and does she still read bottom upwards. I am William Henrys elder sister and as he's so young I take the charge of inquiring into these things myself. I doubt not if Wm Henry were to see her he would be charmed with her. As to nobility of blood our family needs no ennobling I as you well know am a queen William Henry unites a prince and king in his single person and Eugene is prince of Savoy I am beside being a queen the duchess of Marlborough. But I remember I told you over all our titles in a former letter so I shall dwell[n] upon this no longer—

Do you not think Dear Ellen some respect is due to elder sisters I am five[n] years older than my eldest brother yet I receive no respect from him Determine this cause dear Ellen and till it is determined I rest Your affectionate friend

MARGARET FULLER

ALS (MH: fMS Am 1086 [9:258]). *Addressed:* Miss Ellen Kilshaw— / Liverpool *England.* By the Mercury. *Endorsed:* Sarah M. Fuller / to / Miss Ellen Kilshaw— / 20. Nov 1819 / Not Sent.

soon bend his] soon bend ⟨d⟩his
you I think] you I thin⟨g⟩k
they cannot] they cann ↑ ot ↓
person to whom] person ↑ to ↓ whom
fierce vindictive] fierce vin⟨e⟩dictive
and scarcely finished] and scarcely finis⟨?⟩ed
long letter from] long letter ⟨to⟩ ↑ from ↓ you
conveys an idea] conveys an⟨d⟩ idea
her betrothed lover] her betrot⟨?⟩hed lover
of a French] of a ⟨fre⟩ French
I shall dwell] I shall dwe⟨e⟩ll
I am five] I⟨f⟩ am five

1. The Davis and Lewis rope works had a history of fires. It had been destroyed in 1818, rebuilt, and burned again early in October 1819. The principal owner, Isaac P. Davis (1771–1855), established his business on the western side of Charles Street (now part of the Public Garden). He was a prominent businessman who made a fortune dealing with the navy (John Ward Dean, "Mr. Isaac P. Davis," *Memorial Biographies,* 2:327–34; Dexter, "BVR," 1:56).

2. Fuller is referring to her brother William Henry and Ellen Kilshaw's niece, Eliza Greene.

10.   To Timothy Fuller

Cambridge. 19. Dec. 1819.

My Dear father

I have asked mama to leave a space here that I might write a few lines. A few lines it must be now but [   ] day, I shall write you a very long letter for then our[n] examination will be over and I hope to have a great deal to say. I shall send you a copy of my composition and my specimen of writing.— Eugene has been for about a fortnight begging mama to get him a bladder, at last she has got him one and now he wants a sledge and a pair of skaits. Mama told him he must wait till he could use them, he intreated at least to have his when mama got hers.— Uncle Elisha came here the other day and asked what time of day our examination was, he intends to go to it I believe And now papa I must subscribe myself Your affectionate daughter

S M FULLER

ALS (MH: fMS Am 1086 [9:7]). *Addressed:* Hon. Timothy Fuller. MC / Washington / District of Columbia. / *Postmark:* Boston Dec 20 MS. *Endorsed:* 5. / From my dear Wife / & Sarah Margarett— / Recd. 24. Dec. 1819. / Dated 19. Dec. / Inclosing letters from Eugene & Wm. Henry / Written by—

then our] then ⟨y⟩our

11.   To Timothy Fuller

Cambridge. 25th Dec 1819

My Dear Father

I should have written to you immediately after the examination but mamma was out the two next days. But yesterday Uncle Elisha came here. He heard me recite and mended my pen. It is not at all a good one. He is coming to hear me recite Fridays and Teusdays. I have been two afternoons to a writing school of which Mr Gould is the master.[1] He is a most elegant writer. He keeps once in a week and his terms are one dollar a quarter. Mamma doubtless has written[n] to you about the Examination. I enclose you my composition and specimen of writing. I assure you I wrote the former off much better and made *almost* as many corrections as your critical self would were you at home. But Mr Dickinson kept the theme I corrected as he always does the theme[n] which is written at the end of the quarter.[2] I think this is the best theme I ever wrote Write My Deserted Village goes on slowly.[3] I have only translated a page and a half. However I am determined to finish it before New Years day which is about six days from this time—

Last night was very cold. The wind was very cold and keen and the ground was covered with snow.

William Henry the other day took his tier and having filled it[n] with coals went around to ask us to eat some "tesnuts Eugene has broke his bladder with kicking it about and now he has given up the sledge and skaits and wants a watch. This morning he asked mamma to give him a twenty cent piece. She told him he must earn it. He said if she would give it him he would earn it. Now he drinks sugar though mamma has offered to give him two cents a week if he will not drink it.

I have read papa that Zeluco is a very intelligent sensible book therefore as I assure you I have been a very good girl.[4] I beg you will send me "carte blanche" to read Zeluco. Do not forget it dear papa. I have been reading a novel of the name of Hesitation.[5] Do not let the name novel make you think it is either trifling or silly. A great deal of sentiment[n] a great deal of reasoning is contained in it.[n] In other words it is a moral-novel. Miss Argyle the principal heroine has not such superhuman[n] wit beauty and sense as to make her an improbable character. Fitsroy earl of Montague is a sensible well informed man posessing a superior genius and deeply versed in the human character but improbably[n] delicate in his ideas of love. Grosvenor a virtuous well bred youth but inexperienced and possessing ardent. Lady Clervaux a lady whose affections were withered and whose feelings were checked by being taught to believe that fashion is every thing. Sir Thomas has no character. Lord Percival Lorn is a person of very shallow judgement and very malignant feelings[n] two things apparently incompatible. I can sketch no more at present you shall have the rest in another letter. I am your affectionate daughter

SARAH-MARGARET FULLER

ALS (MH: fMS Am 1086 [9:10]). *Addressed:* Hon. Timothy Fuller / Washington / DC. *Endorsed:* From my Daughter / Sarah Margarett / Recd 31. Dec. 1819.

doubtless has written] doubtless ↑ has ↓ written
does the theme] does the ⟨the⟩ theme
having filled it] having filled ⟨so⟩ it
deal of sentiment] deal of sentime ↑ nt ↓
contained in it] contained in ⟨it⟩ it
not such superhuman] not such superhuma ↑ n ↓
but improbably] but impro⟨p⟩bably
malignant feelings] malignant ⟨f⟩ feelings

1. Possibly Lewis Gould (1771–1851), a Harvard graduate of 1797 (Harvard archives).

2. Edwards Dickinson (1796–1831) graduated from Harvard in 1818 and became a doctor in 1823. In 1824 he married Susan Henry (1805–43) and returned to his native Holliston, where he practiced medicine until his death (Harvard archives; Harvard class of 1818 secretary's notes; Holliston VR; *CC*, 28 April 1824).

3. Fuller was translating Oliver Goldsmith's 1770 poem "The Deserted Village" into Latin.

4. John Moore, *Zeluco: Various Views of Human Nature Taken from Life and Manners, Foreign and Domestic* (London, 1789).

5. [Mrs. Ross], *Hesitation: or, To Marry, or Not to Marry?* (London, 1819). An American edition had been published in New York the same year. Her father's response was chilly: he wanted her to "acquire a taste for books of higher order than tales & novels" (Timothy Fuller to Margaret Fuller, 25 January 1820, MH).

12. To Amelia Greenwood

[ca. 1820]
[Boston?]

Dear Amelia,

I do hope and presume you reached your domicil well and safe. I should have written before had I anything to relate. Two evenings I have been out with my *aunts* and *Caroline* and passed eight long long hours, in duress vile, a damsel all forlorn, sad victim to politeness. I have been unfortunate in my visitors and have not seen one interesting person except Mr Robbins and Almira Penniman,[1] with whom I passed a pleasant hour—

I have read naught save Massinger, Miss Baillie and now and then some of Burns—[2]

Elizabeth Randall is coming here tonight.[3] How did Marian enjoy her ride?[4] Almira Penniman was in raptures about her. I shall call on you Saturday "all other things being equal" either before twelve in the morning or rather late in the afternoon. Have you finished Delphine?[5] I wish you would write me a note today and tell to me what events have diversified your journey through life since our roads parted and what reflections, if any, such events have suggested to your youthful mind. Love to my friend Ann.[6] Dites Moi ses nouvelles aussi.[7]

Yrs M.

ALS (PSt). *Addressed:* Miss Amelia Greenwood, / Portland St.

Catharine Amelia Greenwood (1810–67), daughter of William Pitt (1766–1851) and Mary Langdon Greenwood (1773–1855), was Margaret Fuller's closest childhood friend. In 1834 she married George Bartlett (1806–64), who graduated from Harvard in 1827 and became a doctor (Isaac J. Greenwood, "William Pitt Greenwood," *Memorial Biographies,* 1:268–71; *CC,* 15 November 1834; Harvard archives; Roxbury VR).

1. Almira Cornelia Penniman (1807–68) was another close friend from childhood. The daughter of Elisha (1778–1831) and Sybil Allen Penniman (1785–1875) of Brookline, Almira married David Hatch Barlow (1805–64) in 1830. The couple separated in 1840, and Almira went with her children to live at Brook Farm. A woman of striking beauty, she provided part of the model for Zenobia in Hawthorne's *Blithedale Romance.* Mr. Robbins is unidentified; he is probably not Chandler Robbins ("Hollis Street Church"; Brookline VR; *CC,* 19 May 1830; *DivCat;* notes on Barlow family, MH: bMS Am 1910 [175]).

2. Philip Massinger (1583–1640) was best known for his comedy *A New Way to Pay Old Debts* (1633). Joanna Baillie (1762–1851) wrote plays and poems, the best known of which were *De Montfort* and *The Family Legend.*

3. Elizabeth Wells Randall (1811–67) was the oldest of the five children born to John (1774–1843) and Elizabeth Wells Randall (1783–1868). Her father had graduated from Harvard in 1802, received a degree in medicine in 1806, and practiced in Boston. In 1836 Elizabeth married Alfred Cumming of Georgia, who became governor of the Utah Territory from 1857 to 1861 (Harvard archives; Randall, *Poems,* pp. 41–61).

4. Marian Marshall (b. 1812), the daughter of Josiah (d. 1841) and Priscilla Waterman Marshall (1782–1860), was a friend through Margaret Fuller's childhood and into her adult years. Marian married John G. Holbrook in 1844 (Jacobus, *Descendants of Robert Waterman,* p. 365).

5. Madame de Staël's *Delphine* was published in Geneva in 1802.

6. Probably Amelia's sister, Angelina Greenwood (1812–50), who married Richard Warren in 1836 (Isaac J. Greenwood, "William Pitt Greenwood," *Memorial Biographies,* 1:271; *CC,* 15 October 1836).

7. "Tell me her news also."

13. To Timothy Fuller

Cambridge. 16 January 1820[n]

My dear father

I received your letter of the 29th about a week ago[.] I should have written to you much sooner but have been very busy. I begin to be anxious about my letter of the 28th which you do not mention having received in any of your letters. If it has not miscarried it reached you a fortnight ago. Your letter to me was dated the day after mine was written but you do not mention it in any of your letters to Mamma.—

I attend a school which is kept by Aunt Abigail for *Eugene* and *myself* and my *cousins* which with writing and singing schools and my lessons to Uncle Elisha takes up *most* of my time—[1]

I *have* not written to[n] Miss *Kilshaw yet as* there is no opportunity of sending our letters. *Deep rooted* indeed is my affection[n] for her May it flourish an *ever* blooming flower till[n] our kindred spirits absolved from earthly day mount together to those blissful regions where never again we[n] shall be seperated. I am not romantic, I am not[n] making professions when I say I love Ellen better than my life. I love her better and reverence her more for her misfortunes.[2] Why should I not she is[n] as lovely as sweet tempered as before. These were what I loved before and as she possesses all these now why should my love diminish. Ought it not rather to increase as she has more need of it. It is for herself alone I grieve for the loss of fortune She will be exposed to many a trial a temptation she would otherwise have escaped Not but I know she will go through them all No But I shall feel *all* her sorrows—

You will let me read Zeluco? will you not and no conditions. Have you been to the theatre this winter? Have they any oratorios at Washington?— I am writing a new tale called The young satirist. You must expect the remainder of this page to be filled with a series of unconnected intelligence[n] My beautiful pen now makes a large mark I will write no farther. 17th January 1820[n]

Yesterday I threw by my pen for the reason mentioned above. Have you read Hesitation yet. I knew you would (though you are no novel reader) to see if they were rightly delineated for I am possessed of the greatest blessing of life a good and kind father. Oh I can never repay you for all the love you have shown me But I will do all I can

We have had a dreadful snowstorm today. I never look around the room and behold all the comforts with which Heaven has blessed me without thinking of those *wretched* creatures who are wandering in all the snow without food or shelter. I am too young No I am not. In nine years a great part of my life I can remember but two good actions done those more out of sefishness than charity. There is a poor woman of the name of Wentworth in Boston she would willingly procure a subsistence but has not the means. My dear father a dollar would be a great sum to this poor woman. You remember the handsome dollar that I know your generosity would have bestowed on when I had finished my Deserted Village I shall finish it well and desire nothing but the pleasure of giving it to her. My dear father send it to me immediately I am going into town this[n] week I have a thousand things to say but neither time or paper to say them in.

Farewel my dear Father I am Your affectionate daughter

MARGARET FULLER

P S I do not like Sarah, call me Margaret alone, pray do![3]

ALS (MH: fMS Am 1086 [9:11]). Published in part in Chevigny, pp. 52–53. *Addressed:* Hon. Timothy Fuller. M.C. / Washington. / District of Columbia. *Endorsed:* From my daughter / Sarah Margarett / Recd 23. Jan. 1820—.

January 1820] January 18⟨19⟩20
not written to] not w⟨h⟩ritten to
my affection] my affection⟨s⟩
till] till⟨y⟩
again we] again ↑ we ↓
am not] am ↑ not ↓
she is] she ↑ is ↓
unconnected intelligence] unconnected ↑ intelligence ↓
January 1820] January 18⟨19⟩20
town this] town ⟨next⟩ this

1. Margaret was reciting both Latin and Greek for her uncle Elisha. Her father had told her in his letter of 29 December, "I wish too you would read frequently in Grumbach's Greek testament, & commit as much of the grammar to memory as your Uncle E. thinks proper to make" (Timothy Fuller to Margaret Fuller, 29 December 1819, MH).

2. The "misfortunes" suffered by the Kilshaws were the sickness of Ellen's sister and the financial ruin of her father and brother during the Liverpool panic of the time. A few months after this letter, Ellen's engagement ended.

3. When he answered this letter on 25 January, her father pointedly ignored her request in his address and salutation, but he called her "my dear Margaret" in the body of the letter. He closed by giving permission to give the dollar to the poor woman "& to *charge* it to me" (Timothy Fuller to Margaret Fuller, 25 January 1820, MH).

14. To Timothy Fuller

Cambridge 3d February 1820

My dear father

Yesterday[n] I wrote you a short epistle in Latin, now I sit down to address you in my native language. I am half through the fifth book[n] of Virgil[1] In my last lesson I got the whole of the fourth book and Uncle Elisha said I got it extremely well— Who would believe that it was February. The winter has passed very quickly to me. Shall you be here the first of April alias April fool day? I remember when I was only 6 years[n] old that morning you told me to look out of the window and see that little bird perched on a tree I looked[n] and was very much surprised to see none.—

Thank you for your kind permission to read Zeluco but Mamma will not let me have it till I have recited to Uncle Elisha. Next year shall I not be old enough to go to Dr Parks school.[2]

I have spent five days in Boston and returned day before yesterday. My Aunt carried me to Dr Clarkes.[3] He has lately failed in trade and boards out. After much research we at length arrived at Mrs. Mansfields.[4] A ragged, dirty little boy came to the door[n] Does Dr Clark board here. The boy s[c]ratched his head. Do'nt know ma'am. In he went and presently returned with a Wo'nt you walk in. Well we went in and were ushered into the greasy kitchen[n] from that were introduced to a narrow wet passage into a back door to a neat parlor The Doctor is a healthy man about 3 and 40. Mrs Clarke is a pretty, interresting woman apparently on the verge of thirty. She has five children 4 sons and one daughter

I saw a head of her daughters painting which looked very natural Five or six pencils and brushes lay upon a window sill—and a portrait was upon a wooden frame. I saw also a beautiful landscape This young ladys name is Sarah She has a singular taste for painting—

William Henry is sitting on the rug singing "Phosannur in de sidest." The little rogue alias student of roguery[n] does this in imitation of us. These words are in the Chorus Anthem Hosanna in the highest.—[5]

Miss Kimball informs me that Miss Mary Elliot[6] went through Virgil in thirty days and I have studied with renewed vigor ever since [   ] shall surpass me if possible I shall finish this letter with the Lords prayer in Latin Farewell I am your afectionate daughter

SARAH M FULLER

Noster pater qui estis in coelo sis sacrum tuum nomen, tua voluntas esto factus in terra ut in coelo, da nos eum diem nostrum quotidianum cererem et da veniam nobis nostra peccata ut da veniam eis qui peccant nobis duco nos non temptationem et trade a peccato tuum est imperium, potestas et gloria semper. Amen

PS Correct it for me papa will you?[7] I had almost forgot, Thank you for your pen.

ALS (MH: fMS Am 1086 [9:13]). *Addressed:* Hon Timothy Fuller DC / Washington. *Endorsed:* From my daughter / Sarah Margarett / Recd 9. Feb. 1820. / Answered. 22d. Feb. 1820—

Yesterday] Yesterday⟨y⟩
the fifth book] the fi ↑ f ↓ th book
only 6 years] only 6 ⟨in⟩ years

I looked] I loo⟨?⟩ked
to the door] to the door ⟨I⟩
greasy kitchen] greasy ⟨kitchen⟩ kitchen
student of roguery] student of roguery⟨t⟩

1. In the fifth book of the *Aeneid* Aeneas is driven to Sicily, where he institutes the funeral games and builds a city for all who are unfit for war.

2. From 1811 to 1831 Dr. John Park (1775–1852) conducted the Boston Lyceum for Young Ladies. A New Hampshire man, Park graduated from Dartmouth in 1791, studied medicine, then sailed in 1799 as a ship's surgeon to the West Indies, where he investigated the transmission of yellow fever. In 1804 he left medicine to establish a Federalist newspaper in Boston. He sold the paper (later to become the *Daily Advertiser*) to open his school in 1811. Following a bout of ill health, Park retired to Worcester. After the death of his first wife, Louisa Adams, he married an English-woman, Agnes Major (1782?–1857), in 1814 (Journal of Dr. John Park, 5 vols., MB; MVR 113:225; Hall, "Dr. John Park").

3. This is Margaret Fuller's first meeting with the Clarke family, with whom she became close friends. Dr. Samuel Clarke (1779–1830) was a doctor/druggist who had a shop in Boston until 1829, when he moved to Newton to open a chemical factory. It was destroyed by fire the same year. In 1805 Clarke married Rebecca Parker Hull (1790–1865), a descendant of General William Hull. The children Fuller mentions later in the paragraph are Samuel C. Clarke (1806–97); Sarah Ann (1808–96); James Freeman (1810–88); William Hull (1812–78); and Abraham Fuller (1814–86) (William W. Johnson, *Clarke-Clark Genealogy: Records of the Descendants of Thomas Clarke, Plymouth, 1623–1697* [North Greenfield, Wis., 1884]; Newton VR; Clarke, *Richard Hull*, p. 12; Puella F. Mason, *A Record of the Descendants of Richard Hull of New Haven* [Milwaukee, 1894], pp. 57–58; *Boston Evening Transcript*, 26 February 1897).

4. The Boston directory lists Mrs. Nancy Mansfield as the owner of a boarding-house.

5. Charles Wesley's hymn from *Hymns on the Lord's Supper* (1745).

6. Probably either Mary Joanna Eliott (b. 1805) of Cambridge, daughter of Joel and Mary Eliott, or Mary Fleet Eliot (b. 1808) of Boston, daughter of Ephraim and Mary Eliot (*CVR*; *Boston Births*).

7. After criticizing her translation, her father wrote, "I would not discourage you, my girl, by being too critical and yet I am anxious to have you admit to one *fault*, which you will remember I have often mentioned, as the source, the very fountain of others—carelessness" (Timothy Fuller to Margaret Fuller, 22 February 1820, MH).

15. To Timothy Fuller

Cambridge 21st March 1820

My dear Father

As Mr Dickinson will keep school another quarter, mamma has determined on sending me. Besides as the walking is at present I could not go into town. Mr D called here yesterday to see if I was going to school. I have got through Virgil and I shall go into Cicero as soon as I go to school. I do not know what to do for want of a Cicero. Uncle Elisha promised if he could get me one he would either call here with it or send it but he has not sent or brought it and he knows that school begins tomorrow Uncle Henry has got one but I cannot get it before I go to school I must borrow one of Mr Dickinson till I get your answer and then if you have not got one I can either borrow Uncle Henrys or buy one.—

William Henry improves[n] in talking. He formerly said *"Winny"* but now he says *"Willy"*. He says it with a singular accent but on the whole it sounds pretty. From "Samoddy he said "Sannardet. The other day he said "I'm satisfied pend upon't"—

The other day I saw Sotherbys Oberon in the bookcase[1] I never read any thing that delighted me so much as that book My father When I get the card that has *Best* upon it at school may I read it again? Answer me this in your next letter to mamma, will you?—

Papa do you think that anybody could learn French in 16 lessons. If Mr Hamilton can teach it perfectly in so short a time he is[n] a wonderful man indeed. I should not think any one could learn the grammar in that time should you?—

Miss Vose and Miss Susan Messinger came here last night and brought mamma a beautiful bouquet.[2] There was a superb rose just opening and a lovely little bud; periwinkle blossoms of a delicate blue, two kinds of geraniums, the lauristenus bearing a large bunch of little flowers of a cream colour myrtle with leaves no wider than a fine needle. Miss Vose keeps her flowers in bloom in the middle of winter while mine (from want I suppose of proper management) have not a leaf on them—

The other day I bought the children two very pretty watches I thought they[n] were real at first for they had a chain and key. After they had played with them a little while mamma put them away. William Henry was going to cry when mamma told him[n] he must keep it to show to pa when he came home and he very quietly assented.—

I am glad that Ellen is to marry so well though I wish she had married Uncle Henry[3] However may she be happy for she must to ensure me happiness. Do you think she will come here now she is married? I do not think she will but Uncle Elisha thinks[n] she will Do you remember what a fascinating smile she had? I do I can remember just how she looked. Oh she was a magnet that attracted every one especially me. Mamma wishes to write to you therefore I must bid you farewell. I am your affectionate daughter

SARAH M FULLER

ALS (MH: fMS Am 1086 [10:87]). *Addressed:* Hon. T Fuller DC / Washington *Endorsed:* From my daughter / Sarah Margarett / Recd 26. March 1820. / Inclosing Eugene's &c.

William Henry improves] William Henry ⟨?⟩ improves
he is] he ⟨are⟩ is
I thought they] I thoug ↑ ht ↓ they
mamma told him] mamma ⟨?⟩ ↑ told ↓ him
Uncle Elisha thinks] Uncle ↑ Elisha ↓ thinks

    1. William Sotheby, *Oberon: or, Huon de Bourdeaux; A mask. And Orestes: a tragedy* (Bristol, 1802). Sotheby (1757–1833) based his work on Christoph Martin Wieland's poem of the same name.

    2. Miss Vose is undoubtedly one of the children of Robert Vose (1760–1803), a Cambridge rum and real estate dealer, who married Rebecca Knapp Ritchie in 1795. They had three daughters: Harriot, Mary Knapp, and Rebecca Ritchie (*Vose Descendants,* p. 183; *CVR*; *CC*, 6 January 1796). Susan Bowen Messinger (d. 1830) was the daughter of Henry (b. 1773) and Frances Bowen Messinger (1777–1815). The father was a Cambridge hatter. Susan married Thomas Nelson in 1824 (*CVR*; *CC*, 13 November 1830; Bowen,*Woodstock Families*, 2:523).

    3. The news of Kilshaw's engagement had been prematurely announced by her brother-in-law. Her fiancé, a Catholic, was accepted as a suitor, but when his mother demanded Ellen's conversion, the young woman broke the engagement, apparently with little regret.

16. To Margarett C. Fuller

Cambridge 17enth April 1820

My Dear Mother

    As I promised to write to you concerning the behaviour and health of the children I take the opportunity to fulfil my promise. They are both in perfect health and William Henry has been a very good boy I wish I could say the same of Eugene. He was a good boy till he went to meeting There he behaved very ill. To punish him I did not let him go to meeting in the afternoon[n] and ever since he has behaved as bad as he possibly can. He says he will spoil this letter if I write how he has behaved.

    Uncle Kuhn carried a letter from Papa this morning into town I expect to have another today which I shall send with this short letter I have a very bad pen therefore you must excuse this bad writing Believe me mama I am Your affectionate daughter

SARAH M FULLER

ALS (MH: fMS Am 1086 [9:14]). *Addressed:* Mrs M Fuller / Canton. *Endorsed:* Sarah M. Fuller / to / her Mother— / *1820.*

    meeting in the afternoon] meeting ⟨this⟩ ↑ in the ↓ afternoon

Margarett Crane Fuller. Courtesy of Willard P. Fuller, Jr.

17.   To Mary Vose

Cambridge 7. Aug 1820—

My dear friend,

As I am in a fair way to be very idle very dull and very cross this afternoon if I do not write to somebody I will give the preference to employment and to you I do not imagine you will thank me but it is not because I have any thing pretty or new or even remarkable to tell you but to rid myself of the burden of an insupportable idleness.

Ah my poor Mary I fear that the die is cast and that you have lost the generous independant noble highminded and spirited Redmond.[1] What a pity that a man of such elegant manners should throw himself away upon Susan Messinger. You were the only person fit for him. You alone could equal his fine talents uncommon genius and superior understanding. How happy would you have been with him and perhaps if you lived here and the air did you good you might have children equal to their father in beauty and genius. How I should admire to see my sweet cool Mary in the midst of a parcel of children vexed with one scolding another and whipping a third. It wou'd do my heart good.

And now what can I say having once entered on this delightful theme Is it possible for you to quit it and descend to common subjects? Doubtless not but I being heartily tired of it must beg leave to quit the subject.

Do you then you impatiently explain mean to extend the limits of your letter any farther Yes my dear Mary but I am not unreasonable I will not expect you to read more than a line on each page. It will sufficiently inform you of what stuff my letters are composed Indeed you might have guessed from my delightful and edifying conversation what charming lovely letters I write. As I love to oblige my friends I will ask this of you If you do not like to read my letters write a line and tell me so. You shall be no longer troubled with them I do not fear to hear the truth

Abba writes me that T Hawton (Horton) is sick[2] It is lucky poor mr Dickenson does not know it for fear it should place him in the same condition.

If you ever write to me leave out that name Sarah. Out upon it I will not be content to be called by it till I am sixty years old Then I will take it for it is a proper, good, old maidish name. I will be willing to sit down and knit stockings look cross and be called Miss Sarah Fuller for the rest of my life. But for the present time I will be addressed by the name of Margarette or as Ellen calls it Marguerite since I cant change it

Mrs Olney asked me to recommend a name for her little girl[.][3] Helen Angelica I said You will laugh but I selected it as her name that I might amuse myself with the mistakes of the good country folk who I'll warrant would call the poor little thing Hellun Arnchellika or perhaps to improve it might say Arnchela or Anshellicka I have a cousin named Eleanor and they call her Hellin And another whose name was Juliet A good woman wishing to speak to her called I remember the time very well I was walking with poor Juliet She said to me and Miss Sally Woont you tell your cousin Shulet to step this way I ran away feigning not to have heard her and ran away to where I could laugh unrestrained by the fear of her seeing me

Yours affectionately

MARGARETTE F

MsC (MH: fMS Am 1086 [9:15]). *Addressed:* Miss Mary Vose / Walpole— *Endorsed: Copy* / Sarah M. Fuller / to / Miss Mary Vose / 1820 / Copy by T. Fuller.

Mary Knapp Vose (1798–1840), second daughter of Robert and Rebecca Vose, married William Palfrey Rice (1790–1843) in 1839 (*Vose Descendants,* p. 183).

1. Probably "Redmond" is Thomas Redman of Natchez, Mississippi, who in 1821 married Mary Elizabeth Messinger (b. 1780). He died at Natchez in 1837, aged thirty-nine (*CC*, 15 April 1837; *CVR*; Bowen, *Woodstock Families,* 2:523).

2. Temperance Horton (1799–1870) was the daughter of Gideon and Temperance Horton of Brewer, Maine. In 1823 she married Warren Colburn (1793–1833), the author of a famous pair of arithmetic texts and a manufacturer in Lowell (*DAB*; *CC*, 3 September 1823; *MVR* 230:101). Abba may be Margaret's aunt Abigail Crane.

3. Mrs. Olney was another member of the Crane family of Canton, but she was not directly related to Margaret's mother. Martha Crane (b. 1790), daughter of Nathan and Esther Crane of Canton, married Anthony Olney (1790?–1859?) of Plymouth. Apparently they ignored Margaret's advice, for the daughter was named Elizabeth (James H. Olney, *A Genealogy of the Descendants of Thomas Olney* [n.p., 1889], p. 95; Endicott, *BMD*).

18. To Sarah W. Fuller

Cambridge 1st Nov. 1820

Honored Grandmamma

The great entertainment and instruction I have recieved from your letters to my father and mother has induced me also to request that I may be favoured with a correspondence with my grandmother.

As this may seem presumptuous in such a little urchin as you doubtless at present think of me, I must entreat that I may henceforth present myself to your "minds eye" in the form of a tall girl five feet two inches high. I suppose this may at first be pretty difficult but multiply my stature[n] with my years and perhaps you may find me grown enough to merit some degree of consideration.—

Of Which of[n] the family does little Ellen resemble?[1] Does she look like her mother and is she pretty Elisabeth and Martha Anne Whittier are quite handsome and Sarah is quite pretty[2] I wish you would come back here and take a view of your grandchildren who I am sure wish to be with you Perhaps if you would come you would find I can talk faster and perhaps a very little better than I write and it would certainly give you a better idea of my length breadth and thickness of which till you behold you cannot have an adequate opinion of I remember precisely how you looked when you were here tho' I am perhaps assisted by seeing your portrait for it is three years I think since I saw you and I have had but one letter from you during all that time Pray my dear grandmother if you write to any of your grandchildren write to me you cannot be more beloved by any of them.

I am Your affectionate gran[d daughter]

SARAH M FULLER

ALS (MH: fMS Am 1086 [9:12]).

Margaret's paternal grandmother, born Sarah Williams, was the daughter of the Reverend Abraham Williams of Sandwich. She married the Reverend Timothy Fuller (1739–1805) in 1771; she died in 1822 (Princeton VR).

multiply my stature] multiply my ⟨feet⟩ ↑ stature ↓
Of which of] Of ⟨which⟩ ↑ which ↓ of

1. Ellen Kilshaw Fuller (1820–56), Margaret's sister, was born on 7 August of this year. She became a lovely young woman with a strong temper. She was ill with tuberculosis her entire adult life. On 23 September 1841 she married William Ellery Channing, by whom she bore five children.

2. Tryphosa Elizabeth Fuller Whittier (1812–84) later married Dr. Robert Cony (1806–71) of Augusta, Maine. Martha Ann (1815–82) married Alonzo F. Palmer (b. 1810) of Hallowell, Maine. The girls were daughters of Simeon (1780–1859) and Martha Fuller Whittier (1787–1852) ("Hallowell Family Records," NEHGS; Hallowell, Me., VR; *Whittier Family*, p. 13; Holman, *John Coney*, p. 212).

19. To Timothy Fuller

Cambridge 22d Nov. 1820

My dear father;

Though you have not asked me to write, yet I think you would like to have me do it. I have a very bad pen and hope you will not criticise my writing very severely.

I *did* rewrite my letter to Miss Kilshaw, but I do not think it went. I altered the subject considerably too. I went to Mrs Greene's this morning, and Miss H. G. said the Falcon sailed a fortnight ago.

We recieved your sixth letter to day It came yesterday. Mother got it to day when she went into town. Miss E Fuller went to Framingham in the stage to day.—[1] I should like to see Mr Randolph[n] His speeches are very keen, witty (tho' satirical), and eloquent[2] I hope you will send us all his speeches this winter, my dear Sir I should be charmed to read them I never troubled my head much about any of the speeches except yours unless to laugh at the endless repetitions observable in some. I wish sir you would give me your speeches if you have them I should value them extremely. I assure you notwithstanding[n] the very mean opinion you have of my understanding, I should value one of my dear fathers speeches more than a thousand lighter works. I know well you think me, light, frivolous, and foolish. I believe you have had reason to think so but—I am yet capable of affection to one to whom I stand so highly indebted as to you.—

I must leave the last page for mother. She is going to Professor Fararrs[3] Friday night and is preparing her dress Farewell dear sir I am Your most affectionate daughter

S M FULLER

ALS (MH: fMS Am 1086 [9:16]). *Addressed:* Hon. Timo Fuller. Member of Congress / Washington City. *Endorsed:* 1. / From my daughter / Sarah Margarett / Recd. 27 Nov. 1820. / 3 Dec. Answered—

see Mr Randolph] see Mr Randolph('s)
assure you notwithstanding] assure ↑you↓ notwithstanding

1. Her aunt Elizabeth.

2. The brilliant, eccentric John Randolph of Roanoke (1773–1833) was serving in the U.S. House of Representatives, where he was famous for his oratory.

3. John Farrar (1779–1853) was Hollis Professor of Mathematics at Harvard from 1807 to 1836. A native of Lincoln, Farrar graduated from Harvard in 1803. He married Lucy Maria Buckminster (d. 1824) on 31 August 1819 (Harvard archives; *CC*, 31 August 1819, 11 September 1824).

20. To Timothy Fuller

[25 November 1820]

[Cambridge]

My dear Father

I am sorry mamma sent the letter I wrote you as it was very faulty.

I hope you will pardon the writing, as our pens are good for nothing. Pray write to me soon dear sire I should be delighted if you would. I am afraid[n] you cannot read this writing; is it possible you have been gone a for[t]night? I am yours affectionately,

S M F

ALS (MH: fMS Am 1086 [6:92]). *Addressed:* Hon. Timothy Fuller. M.C. / Washington City / D C. *Endorsed:* No 7 25. Nov. / From my dear Wife— / Recd 29. Nov. 1820—

Margaret's letter is a postscript to her mother's.
afraid] a⟨f⟩fraid

21. To Timothy Fuller

Cambridge 4th Dec. 1820

Dear Father,

I have not yet answered your letter, for I did not wish to until I had a decent pen. Miss Moore mended me one to day and we recieved two which you mended, though one was very much split. As you have often told me not to write a couple of pages about writing I stop here.

Miss Greene told me that she wrote to my beloved friend Miss Kilshaw by the way of Charlestown, I have not seen Mr Henry Fuller but once since you left Cambridge, and was in such a hurry then, I forgot to ask him if my letter went. He is very careful to cheat nobody for your name is taken from the office door and Henry H Fuller upstairs in large golden capitals instead.—

Mr Taylor comes every other lesson at least he has the last three weeks for I keep a list of the days in which he is absent. If he came every time he ought his quarter would be out in January but he is determined I shall not suffer for want of practise, and I think it likely he will make his quarter last till you come home.

Mr Stanisbury is as active and mischivous as ever. He walks to meeting in a plaid cloak hooked so closely across his throat that I should think it would strangle him. He very condescendingly makes me a bow and grants me a smile (and so indeed does the doctor.) He has a great idea of his own genius and wishes extremely to preach here thinking he can illumine our minds.

Mr Waldo was here the other evening and protested as vehemently against novels and *such trash* as you do papa and he is not even so moderate as you for he[n] will not even except historical[n] novels.[1] Well I dare say he as silly *I* when arrived at the same age, shall be as wise, at present though you tell me I am foolish, you are angry at me for being so. I wish I could be wiser, but that person *is* illiberal who condemns Scotts[n] and Edgeworths novels—[2]

Mother is sewing and Ellen after a long fit of crying asleep. She does not sleep half or a quarter so much as she did. I conclude she thinks as she grows older she is more entertaining but as she grows larger it is no pleasure to hold a heavy child certainly. I am your affectionate daughter

MARGARETT FULLER

ALS (MH: fMS Am 1086 [9:17]). *Addressed:* Hon Timo' Fuller. Member of Congress / Washington City. *Endorsed:* 2. 4. Dec. / From my daughter / Sarah Margarett. / Recd 10. Dec. 1820—

you for he] you f⟨f⟩or he
even except historical] even except⟨ing⟩ historical
who condemns Scotts] who conde⟨?⟩mns Scotts

1. The Reverend Daniel Waldo (1762–1864) served in the Connecticut militia before entering Yale. After taking his A.B. in 1788, he studied theology and was ordained as a Congregational minister in 1792. In 1795 Waldo married Nancy Hanchett (1777–1855). He served as a visiting minister at Cambridgeport in 1810 and 1811 (Waldo Lincoln, *Genealogy of the Waldo Family* [Worcester, Mass., 1902], pp. 256–58).

2. Though Fuller admired Scott's novels all her life, her enthusiasm for Maria Edgeworth (1767–1849) did not last.

22.   To Timothy Fuller

Cambridge 21 December 1820

Dear Father

Will you accept the inclosed trifle. It has no other recommendation it is true than that it is the work of your daughter but that I know will be one to you. Will you my dear sir write to Mr Elisha Fuller that I may continue my studies with him I am in haste for it is full time that this should be gone and must now declare myself your affectionate[n] daughter

SARAH M FULLER

ALS (MH: fMS Am 1086 [6:104]). *Addressed:* Hon. Timothy Fuller MC / Washington City / DC. *Postmark:* Boston MS 23. *Endorsed:* 19. 22.Dec / from my dear Wife— / Recd 27. Dec. 1820.

Margaret's letter is a postscript to her mother's.
myself your affectionate] myself your ⟨self⟩ affectionate

23. To Timothy Fuller

Cambridge 5th Jan. 1821

Dear Father,

And it is January my dear sir; How the winter has flown. You have been gone two months. It seems as if there were neither nights or days the hours fly so quickly We have no reason to complain of the slow foot of time.[1] We had a ball here the other night and nearly three days were absorbed in preparations and reparations. However it was delightful and I danced as much as I wished. But mamma doubtless has given you a full description of it. I wish you would mend some pens and send them me You would very much oblige me if you would do it.

I expect sir that when you come home you will bring me home a complete case of jewels or something equal to it and if you cant do that I will be satisfied with a gold ring plain or twisted or even with one made of tortoise shell. Aunt Fuller has taught me to play "Bounding billows" and sing it. I am sorry my dear sir you write to me so seldom. Has your affection decreased? I fear it has; I have often pained you but I hope you still love me I should be most happy to be Dr Parks scholar.[2] I will endeavor to gratify all your wishes. Dr Park has increased the number of his scholars if you write to him soon you may with ease get me a place Susan Williams said half in jest half in earnest she would take me to board and in earnest she said she wished I could come and live there that we might study together.[3] I will tell you something highly to Susans honor. She has refused all invitations to go out that she may give all her time to study. This you know is really a considerable exertion of fortitude in a young lady who has such an extensive acquaintance as Susan has I think I should do so too, but I should not have nearly so many temptations to break my resolution as Susan has therefore it would not be so honorable in me as in her.

Did you ever see Mozarts requiem Mary Parker used to sing it There are remarkable circumstances about the writing of it which I will acquaint you with another time.[4] The requiem is exceedingly beautiful and there is great variety in it.

Mrs M'Keig has been five years at Paris and it is the native tongue of her daughter and assistant Mrs Colman who was born in France; French is spoken entirely at her school and if any one speaks English they are fined[n] two cents. Eliza Williams goes to her now[5] Are you not tired of my prating? At any rate I shall cease. Farewell dear father I am Your affectionate daughter

S M Fuller

Aunt Fuller sends best love she would write but her thoughts are taken up with balls and her hands with a great work viz hemming handkerchiefs[6]

ALS (MH: fMS Am 1086 [10:88]). Published in part in Chevigny, pp. 53–54. *Addressed:* Hon. T Fuller. MC / Washington City. *Endorsed:* From my daughter / Sarah Margarett— / Recd 11. Jan. 1821.

are fined] are fi(?)ned

1. Probably she refers to the jests about time between Rosalind and Orlando in *As You Like It*, III.ii.302–36.

2. It was still uncertain whether Dr. Park was to take Margaret as his pupil. She did enroll, however, in late January or early February. The school was well equipped and offered a curriculum that included Latin, French, Italian, ancient and modern history, arithmetic, geometry, trigonometry, natural history, geography, and composition. The texts included Caesar, Horace, Voltaire, Molière, Alfieri, and Tasso (Hall, "Dr. John Park," pp. 83–87).

3. Her cousin.

4. Mozart's *Mass in D Minor for the Burial of the Dead* was commissioned by a stranger who mysteriously refused to disclose his name or his patron. The mortally ill Mozart agreed to the task and set to work. As the work progressed he came to believe that he was writing his own burial mass. He lived to complete the "Requiem" and "Kyrie." He sang part of the work the day of his death and seemed to have it in his thoughts as he died. Not until years later was the patron, Count von Walsegg of Austria, identified. The mass was finished by Franz Xavier Sussmayer, Mozart's close friend, and was first performed on 5 December 1791 in Vienna (William Pole, *The Story of Mozart's Requiem* [London and New York, 1879], pp. 63–68). The Mary Parker that Fuller mentions may be the daughter (1805–35) of Eleazer and Mary Parker of Groton. She later married Dr. Nehemiah Cutter (*GVR*; *CC*, 28 May 1825, 22 August 1835).

5. Elizabeth McKeige (d. 1853) was the second wife of Clotworthy McKeige, a Halifax merchant who moved to Boston. He died aged eighty-three on 29 January 1824. Mrs. Fuller, in a letter to her husband, called him "a very great dunce" who had "stumbled into a fortune" about eight years before (Margarett C. Fuller to Timothy Fuller, 7 February 1821, MH). Mrs. McKeige had a school in Jamaica Plain in 1818–19, when Lydia Jackson (later Waldo Emerson's second wife) and her sister Lucy went to school (Ellen Tucker Emerson, *The Life of Lidian Jackson Emerson*, ed. Delores Bird Carpenter [Boston, 1980], pp. 28–29). Mrs. Colman was Elizabeth McKeige's widowed daughter (*CC*, 31 January 1824; Suffolk Probate, no. 38825). Eliza Williams was the daughter of Dr. John and Abigail Jones Williams of Cambridgeport.

6. Elizabeth Fuller was staying with the Timothy Fullers.

24.   To Timothy Fuller

Cambridge 15th Jan 1821

My dear Father

I fear I have not very punctually kept my resolution of writing to you once in a week. Yet as I have not any thing very witty, very agreeable, or very entertaining to commit to paper I do not think the omission is much to be regretted.

I went to Mrs M'Keig's Thursday evening. Mrs M'Keig is a very polite woman The young ladies play country dances and cotillons on the piano forte for each other to dance. Mrs M'Keig took particular care that I should dance with young ladies with whom I was acquainted." Miss Eliza M'Keig plays with great taste and execution on the piano forte and harp.[1]

I have persuaded mamma to ask Mr Stiles Ganet to come here twice in a week in order to hear me recite in Caesars Commentaries and the Greek Grammar.[2] I knew I should study much better if I had an instructor.

Mr Greene says there are letters from Miss Kilshaw at New York I think it probable we shall not recieve them until he leaves America. I intend to write today; I hope he will call here if he does not we must send our letters to Mr Greene senior I am sorry he is going so soon as a fortnight; I have not had time to ask him any thing about Miss Ellen. Have you heard from Mr Kilshaw lately?

What is the reason of my uncle Elisha's meditating and expedition to the South. Is it merely for pleasure? I should think so. If he had not I should have wished him to have given me lessons as he did the preceding winter, what time in the winter does he intend to go for my dear father the welcome time of your return approaches, and I should think he would wish to be at Washington with you not only for the pleasure of having a brother in an unexplored city but, likewise that you might introduce him to your acquaintance for I conclude there are not many with whom he is acquainted in Washington Aunt Martha alias Aunt Whittier is" paying us a visit as well as Sarah[3] and (as is the case at present) she is exiled into the kitchen while the parlour is made fit for our residence; in my opinion this little kitchen is a much pleasanter place than the parlour.

"Men grow wiser" "every day" but in reality I find a difficulty" in imagining myself an infant. I have endeavored to lately but I believe the warm weather is not favorable to imagination I think more in winter about keeping myself warm for if I imagine myself in sunny gardens fanned by the zephers along comes the cold north wind and the snow, and I believe there has not been such a cold winter this great while Farewell my dear father. I am your affectionate daughter,

S M FULLER.

ALS (MH: fMS Am 1086 [9:18]). *Addressed:* Hon. Timothy Fuller MC. / Washington City / DC. *Postmark:* Boston MS Jan 20. *Endorsed:* From my daughter / Sarah Margarett— / Recd 24. Jan. 1821.

whom I was acquainted] whom I w⟨ere⟩as acquainted
Aunt Whittier is] Aunt Whittier ⟨has⟩ is
I find a difficulty] I find ⟨it⟩ a difficulty

1. Eliza McKeige, another daughter of Elizabeth and Clotworthy McKeige, married Dr. Hiram Hoyt (1800–1866) in 1826 (*CC*, 29 August 1826; Galusha B. Balch, *Genealogy of the Balch Families in America* [Salem, 1897], p. 99).

2. Ezra Stiles Gannett (1801–71) was in his first year of study at the Divinity School after having graduated at the head of the Harvard class of 1820. He was ordained in 1824 and became first Dr. Channing's assistant at the Federal Street Church, then his successor in 1842. Gannett was a founder and president of the American Unitarian Association. In 1835 he married Anna Linzee Tilden (1811–46) (*Gannett Descendants*, pp. 82–83; *Heralds*, 3:138–47).

3. Sarah Williams Fuller Whittier (1810–93) married Hiram Fuller (b. 1809) of Hallowell, Maine, in 1836. This Hiram Fuller should not be confused with the Hiram Fuller for whom Margaret worked in Providence (*Whittier Family*, p. 13; Emma H. Nason, *Old Hallowell on the Kennebec* [Augusta, Me., 1909], p. 179).

25. To Timothy Fuller

Cambridge 25 Jan 1821

My dear father

I am very sorry that you do not write to me more frequently. Your letters are very pleasant to me The ship with letters from Miss Kilshaw has not arrived and it must be either wrecked or blown on to the southward She has been[n] has been out eighty days a long voyage even in winter I fear it is wrecked. It is excessively cold, there was a man froze to death last night in Boston and a man froze his face and ears in this place.

I thank you my dear sir for writing to doctor Park: It will be rather fatiguing walking in and out again every day to be sure, but then I shall have a pleasant walk to pay for it The doctor begins at nine, and ends at two, so as to keep five hours a day and I shall have to study all the time out of school. He teaches Latin French and Italian.

Ellen is tolerably good natured generally, but at present the cold weather makes her feel uncomfortable and consequently does [*illegible*] she may not be perfectly well however. I think she is well; she wants to get up in the morning very much and always cries if not permitted to get up. I wish I could think of something entertaining to say to you but I cannot I believe we are all dull here." now perhaps the cold weather has that effect. I must now close my tedious scrawl and declare myself your affectionate daughter

S M Fuller

ALS (MH: fMS Am 1086 [6:119]). *Addressed:* Hon. Timothy Fuller MC / Washington City / DC. *Postmark:* Jan 26 Boston MS. *Endorsed:* 34. 25. Jan. / From my dear Wife— / Recd 30. Jan 1821—

    Margaret's letter is a postscript to her mother's.
    she has been] ⟨it⟩ She has been
    are all dull here] are all ⟨?⟩ dull here

26. To Timothy Fuller

Cambridge 29th Jan 1821

My dear Father

I now begin to count how many days will elapse before the welcome day of your return. It is not six weeks before that time arrives. I must still continue to regret that I have received but one letter from you. I know that you are very much occupied if you were not I am sure you would write to me.

Miss Sarah Greene called here this afternoon. She fears that the ship with our letters has been lost I think it must have been shipwrecked. She was a new vessel; and I think it was very wrong to make her first voyage such a long one. I shall be very sorry if our letters are lost. It was very providential that Mr Greene did not as he at first intended come in that vessel which he would have done had all his things been ready.

This place is quite barren of incident lately except it be of deaths Several have died lately. Mr Wellman and Mrs Rainy[1] among others." The former died of old age merely I believe.

I have not painted my box yet but I expect I shall soon. Have you put my watch paper into your watch?" I have given each of my uncles one.

When Mr Randolph makes a speech pray send it to me. I wish you would send us some letter paper. We received the quills today and they were very good; it is with one of them I am now writing. I am glad you send some, sometimes. There was a fire in Boston the other night, it burnt up a stable in which there were two horses. There has been but two fires in Boston since you have been gone. Mamma wants to write the rest. I am your affectionate daughter

S MARGARETT FULLER.

ALS (MH: fMS Am 1086 [6:121]). *Addressed:* Hon. Timothy Fuller. MC. / Washington City / DC. *Postmark:* Boston MS Jan 30. *Endorsed:* 36. 29. Jan. / From my dear Wife / Recd 5. Feb. 1821.

Margaret's letter is a postscript to her mother's.
among others] among ↑ others ↓
your watch] your wa⟨th?⟩tch

1. Stephen Wellman (1746–1821) died on 23 January. A veteran of the Revolutionary War, Wellman was twice married, twice widowed. His first wife was Dorothy Jenkins (1742–75); his second was Hannah Chapin of Waltham, who died in 1807, aged fifty-three (Joshua Wyman Wellman, *Descendants of Thomas Wellman* [Boston, 1918], p. 197; manuscript list of baptisms and deaths, Cambridgeport Church, 1814–20 [1833], MHi). Abigail Torrey Englesby (1769–1821) married William Reaney in 1800. Of Mrs. Reaney's death, Mrs. Fuller says mysteriously in her letter, "many dark surmises are whispered about the cause." The Reverend Thomas B. Gannett simply wrote "sudden" in his church record book (*CC*, 27 January 1821; Frederic C. Torrey, *The Torrey Families and Their Children in America* [Lakehurst, N.J., 1924]; Cambridgeport Church, 1814–20 [1833], MHi).

27. To Timothy Fuller

Cambridge 14th Feb 1821

My dear father

We recieved to day our dear Miss Kilshaws letters by the vessel that I supposed was lost. Ever affectionate ever kind she has sent us charming letters. But you will be better able" to judge of them from sight, than from my praises. Have you heard from Mr Kilshaw lately; when you write to him present my respects. You sent a brief letter to day you must have a multiplicity of business on your" hands. Little William has the earach he is now asleep in mamma's lap He has cried several times to night. He told Miss Moore to day, he did not read beautiful to Miss Osgood.[1] The former is very fond of him, and the children always bring him an apple nut or almond requiring as a recompense that he should only say 'thank you dear' with his own peculiar accent. I have not yet I believe acknowledged your kind letter. Mamma intended going to Mrs Wheelers to night but was prevented by a violent snow storm accompanied by hail.[2] I must leave room for her to write and declare myself Your affectionate daughter

S M F

ALS (MH: fMS Am 1086 [6:128]). *Addressed:* Hon Timothy Fuller MC / Washington City / DC. *Endorsed:* 43. 14. & 15. Feby— / From my dear Wife— / Recd 21. Feb. 1821— / Inclosing Miss Kilshaw's / letter.

Margaret's letter is a postscript to her mother's.
be better able] be ↑ better ↓ able
business on your] business ⟨i⟩on your

1. Probably Mary Osgood (1803–49), daughter of Peter (1770–1835) and Mary Pritchard Osgood of Cambridge (Ira Osgood, *A Genealogy of the Descendants of John, Christopher, and William Osgood* [Salem, 1894], p. 105).
2. Undoubtedly Mrs. Ann Balch Wheeler, the Fullers' neighbor (see letter 7).

28. To Margarett C. Fuller

Boston. 2d Dec. 1821

Dear Mother

I received today your affectionate letter dated 28th Nov. I should be very much pleased to hear some particulars of the conversation which pleased you so much between Mr Frey and Mr Cushman.[1] I am very sorry for your disappointment at the theatre. It was hardly worth the trouble of dressing oneself. Miss Abba Crane has not as yet done me the favor of writing to me I dare say she will not this winter. Pray if you hear from her tell me how the children do. Tell my dear father that I have not cried once since he went away. I am as happy here as I can be separated from you. I walked out to C P yesterday afternoon. Sophia Williams is better She sent her love to you and intreats you to write to her.[2] She can speak much more distinctly. Poor Mrs Stuart is much better.[3] The Physicians say that she may probably linger on a month. I called on Mrs Mycall and repented of it for she kept me almost an hour to hear good advice.[4] Uncle Thomas is worse.[5] He has a very good nurse.

5th Dec I have for different reasons defered finishing my letter until now. Poor Susan Williams is threatened with a fever. I hope she will not lose all her places, she is a very sweet tempered, amiable girl. I love her very much and I hope that she will not have to go to the foot in all the classes. If she can get well by next Tuesday for the rest of the week is vacation because it is Thanksgiving. Professor Everett will preach for us Thanksgiving day and thus I shall have the opportunity I have long desired of hearing this celebrated preacher.[6] Grandmamma intends to write to papa very soon Tell him I am writing a long composition but it will be three weeks before it is given up. He will not have it till I know what the Dr. says to it. I am next to the head in the second class in E parsing. Perhaps I may get up to the head and so get a medal I have had three medals, but Susan Channing[7] who went into the class three months before I did[n] has been up to the head a long time it has brought[n] her seventeen medals and she has had three medals for composition and one accurate and now she has got the eye of Intelligence because she has made up her twenty one medals but she would not have had it this year if it had not been for that class, if I can get up to the head I shall keep there for I have not made one mistake in that class; indeed I have taken great pain not to, perhaps I may have the eye, before you return[n] which is the highest medal in school. But dear mother I forget, this is probably not as interesting to you as it is to me. Farewell I am your affectionate daughter

SARAH M FULLER

ALS (MH: fMS Am 1086 [9:19]). *Addressed:* Hon. Timothy Fuller. / Washington City. / District of Columbia. *Postmark:* Boston MS Dec 7. *Endorsed:* Our daughter / Sarah M. Fuller— / Recd 11. Dec. 1821.

before I did] before I ⟨did has been up to⟩ did
it has brought] it has ⟨brought h⟩ brought
the eye, before you return] the eye, ↑ before you return ↓

1. In her letter of 28 November, Mrs. Fuller described to Margaret two of the passengers who had accompanied the Fullers to Washington. She spoke of "the learned & animated debate on sacred literature, & points of faith between Mr. Frey a converted Jew & our fellow traveller the Rev. Hon Cushman from Maine" (Margarett C. Fuller to Margaret Fuller, 28 November 1821, MH). Joshua Cushman (1761–1834) served in the Revolution, then graduated from Harvard in 1787. After studying theology, he was licensed to preach, and settled in Winslow, Maine (then part of Massachusetts). He was a Congregational minister for twenty years before entering politics. He served in the Massachusetts Legislature and the U.S. Congress for two terms, 1821–25. Of Frey nothing more is known (*Biographical Directory*).

2. Sophia Williams (b. 1786) was the daughter of Dr. John and Abigail Jones Williams.

3. Sarah Thompson Stewart died on 20 December (*CC*, 22 December 1821).

4. In 1804 Elizabeth Parsons Chandler, widow of Samuel Chandler of Newburyport, married John Mycall, a widower. A former schoolteacher, businessman, and printer, "Squire Mycall" acquired a landed estate. He died aged eighty-three in 1833;

his wife died at eighty-six in 1845 (Newburyport VR; *CC*, 21 November 1804; Harvard VR; Henry S. Nourse, *History of the Town of Harvard, Massachusetts, 1732–1893* [Harvard, Mass., 1894], pp. 438–41).

5. Thomas Williams.

6. A brilliant speaker, Edward Everett (1794–1865) was then professor of Greek at Harvard. The first American to receive a Ph.D. from Göttingen, Everett was successively a member of the U.S. Congress, governor of Massachusetts, ambassador to England, president of Harvard, and U.S. senator from Massachusetts. In 1822 he married Charlotte Gray Brooks (1800–1859), daughter of Peter Chardon Brooks (1767–1849) (*DAB*; *NEHGR* 14:85).

7. Susan Cleveland Channing (1807–77), daughter of Francis Dana (1775–1810) and Susan Higginson Channing (1783–1865), married Dr. Francis J. Higginson in 1831 (Higginson, *Reverend Francis Higginson*, p. 31).

29. To Margarett C. Fuller

Boston. December 9th. 1821

Dearest mother,

I received or rather grandmother did my fathers[n] letter on the 7th. I do not think his plan of making you his secretary a very feasible plan. I fancy you will be too much engaged besides you do not write half so fast as he can, and are not sufficiently fond of letter writing; do tell my father that I expect some letters from him. You know mother that I am not a very good dancer. I wish to go to Mr Park's dancing school.[1] I do not think it would interfere with my studies as it will keep only Thursday an[d] Saturday and I should have all the evenings to myself. I wish you would let me know your determination as quickly as possible as this quarter will finish a week from next Tuesday. Uncle Williams is better, but he says it is very hard for him to lie in bed so, and so hungry too. Poor Susan is confined to her bed. Last Teusday night she had shivering fits, she went to bed but was attacked again in the morning, and is now quite ill. I went to Mr Frothingham's on Thanksgiving day and heard Mr Everet.[2] I liked his sermon or rather lecture much except two or three expressions which I could not understand such as "the active centres of fermentation and in my opinion his pronunciation was not very good. The meeting house was very much crowded and there was some excellent singing. They say that the choir at Mr. F's is the best in Boston. I believe I did not tell you in my former letter that uncle Abraham had carried me and aunt Sarah and the two girls to the ampitheatre. The performance was Blue Beard,[n] in which we had the pleasure of seeing fire, smoke, battles, death, blood, skeletons and all the ghostly preparations.[3] But there were many beautiful horses and some of the performances really wonderful. One of the little ponies being ordered to jump through a balloon went and stuck his nose through the paper and then not liking the sport ran back. An Arabian horse kept excellent time to the tune of Nancy Dawson. By the way uncle Abraham says that he had as lieve see Mr Whittiers children take a cane and ride around the room as hear me play on the piano and that it came as near to these performances as my music did to that of Mrs Holman and Mrs French.[4] Uncle Elisha asked me if I talked to him about it on purpose to quarrel with him I shall not ever play before him I fancy tho' he says I may when he is asleep. My best love to papa I am your affectionate daughter

SARAH M FULLER.

ALS (MH: fMS Am 1086 [9:20]). *Addressed:* Hon. Timothy Fuller. MC. / Washington City. *Postmark:* Boston MS Dec 9. *Endorsed: 2.* / From our Daughter—Sarah Margarett— / Recd 13. Dec. 1821— / 23. Dec. Answered—

did my fathers] did ⟨y⟩my fathers
was Blue Beard] was ⟨blue⟩ Beard

1. Dana Parks (1780–1861) (not to be confused with Dr. John Park) had a dancing school in Boston. In 1826 he married Sarah Lefevere (1806–92) of Topsfield (MVR 149:72, 429:178; *CC*, 27 September 1826).

2. Nathaniel Langdon Frothingham (1793–1870) graduated from Harvard in 1811, taught at the Boston Public Latin School, and in 1815 became minister at the First Church, where he remained until 1850. The conservative Frothingham was known as an author and composer of hymns. He was Edward Everett's brother-in-law, having married in 1818 Ann Gorham Brooks (d. 1863), daughter of Peter Chardon Brooks (*DAB*; *Heralds*, 1:32).

3. *Bluebeard*, the popular melodramatic opera written by George Colman the younger (1762–1836), was first performed at Drury Lane on 23 January 1798 and then in New York on 8 March 1802 (*DNB*). The "two girls" were probably Fuller's cousins Elizabeth and Martha Anne Whittier.

4. Shortly before his death the actor Joseph George Holman (1764–1817) married a Miss Lattimer (d. 1859), a beautiful English singer. Though she married twice more, she kept Holman as her professional name. Mrs. Holman made her debut in Charleston before moving to New York and then to Boston in 1818. Mrs. French was born Anna Maria Mestayer (d. 1881), a member of a famous Philadelphia stage and circus family. In 1831 she married Charles Thorne, an actor (Brown, *American Stage*; MH, Theatre Collection).

30. To Margarett C. Fuller

Boston. Dec. 23d. 1821.

Dear Mother

On Thursday last I received your most welcome letter of the 13th.

I think it is singular you should receive both my letters at nearly[n] the same time, as one of them was dated three days later than the other. In the afternoon on Thursday poor Mrs Stuart departed this life, and was buried on Saturday. It was her request that she should be opened for the benefit of others afflicted with the same disease. Her case was an uncommon one. Uncle Elisha can tell you what it was. I would have gone to the funeral, but the walking was much too bad to go any where. Uncle E says that Mr. Hayward will set off for Washington in a few days and will call on me before he goes; do you remember that you invited him to take tea with you at W; he means I believe to accept the invitation, at any rate he will visit you.[1] I can tell you nothing concerning Abbi, she has not written to me, but Aunt Kuhn called here though I unfortunately had gone out and said the dear children were well. I have bought the doll for Willy. Uncle Williams has had a paralytic shock and is now obliged to sit up all day in consequence of it. Susan is almost recovered but is so delicate that she cannot go to school all winter and she regrets it very much.

Aunt Kuhn was at the funeral

Yesterday, Miss Heard, Miss Cunningham, Miss Hart, and Miss Greenleaf, Dr Parks oldest sholars left school after having made and received very elegant presents to and from the scholars. The Dr addressed them in a very pathetic manner no one could restrain her tears and he was so much affected, that he could hardly speak as he bid them farewell. The four ladies shed abundance of tears and could not prevail on themselves to go, untill the last minute. Then kissing us all round they went, but still it seemed to give them great pain.

I think that we are all sisters, it is hard for me to stand unconnected; and all girls who have no intimate friends are not so much beloved.[n] Tell papa that I do not believe I shall be happy if I leave school soon. Ask him mamma whether I shall not stay more than a year. Ah I hope I shall for I love the Dr so much, and my companions seem so amiable that I long to stay. I talk about this too much perhaps but it is the uppermost in my thoughts. And now I will tell you about our ball[n] [at] Mr Parkss. Sarah Whittier danced uncommonly well. She danced the garland of three, which her master thinks his handsomest dance, and many others not quite so handsome. Among other dances which received the most applause were a short dance by Caroline Coffin a gavotte by Annie Coffin and the garland of twelve in which Tissy [illegible] was one. Martha Anne and Miss Fairbanks who are of a size danced the garland of two and no dance was more applauded; indeed they danced sweetly. Martha Anne demanded of her mother what they meant by "slapping their hand so" and said they were foolish people. Mary Bean went with us it rained and we were in a hack.[2] Mary and I[n] were I believe as much entertained as any body. There was a great ball[n] after the children had done and I danced thirteen times. Twelve of my partners were grown up gentlemen and of course very bad dancers but I had one good partner who knew what he was about and he was one of the scholars. Mr M'Lay and his two daughters were there Mr and Mrs Pierpoint and divers other gentry[3] for my part I had rather they should have staid at home as they did not dance[n] for the room was very much crowded eight cotillons standing up at the same time and four country dances. I really think some of the ladies were indecently dressed, for most of them could not be content without shewing their bosoms and shoulders completely, there was one lady with her sash brought up so as to come over a part of her bosom and nothing more. Mr Whittier said he hoped she would dance her gown completely off and that he expected nothing more than that she would jump out of her clothes. I am sure I was ashamed for her, for she was not a young girl neither but rather in the decline of life and her neck none of the whitest. My love to my dear father. Farewell

SARAH M FULLER

Dr and Mrs Randall were at the ball poor little Abra is not at all well but the Dr says it is his teeth he has got one already.[4] I have a medal for accurate recitation Uncle E says he is glad of that

ALS (MH: fMS Am 1086 [9:21]). *Addressed:* Hon. Timothy Fuller. / Washington City / DC. *Endorsed:* Sarah Margt Fuller / to her Mother— / Recd 31. Dec. 1821— / At Washington.

at nearly] at ⟨?⟩ nearly
friends are not so much beloved] friends ↑ are not so much beloved ↓
about our ball] about ⟨your⟩ our ball
Mary and I] Mary and ⟨?⟩ I
a great ball] a ⟨?⟩ great ball
at home as they did not dance] at home ↑ as they did not dance ↓

1. James Hayward (1798–1866), Harvard 1819, was at this time a tutor at the college. He became College Professor of Mathematics and Natural History in 1826. In 1828 he married Catharine S. Frisbie. Later in life Hayward was a civil engineer and railroad president (*CVR;* Harvard archives).

2. Probably Mary E. Bean, daughter of Dr. Horace Bean. Married in 1828 to James Hooton, she died in 1897, aged ninety (*CC,* 22 October 1828; *Boston Evening Transcript,* 26 May 1897).

3. The Reverend John Pierpont (1785–1866), minister at the Hollis Street Church since 1819, and his wife, Mary Sheldon Lord (1787–1855) (*Heralds,* 2:192; MVR 94:93).

4. Abraham Williams Fuller Whittier (1821–61), third and surviving Whittier son to be so named (*Whittier Family,* p. 13).

31. To Timothy Fuller

Boston March 13th 1822.

My dear father,

On the day after tomorrow Dr Park will have an examination, which will I think go off with great splendour. Although I am immersed in the studies which are necessary to prepare me to support my part, I leave them for a moment to write to you. I received a letter from you a few days ago. Grandmamma had one to day, I did write to you in French, but Ma said the letter was too short. You shall soon have a longer one.— The reason" that you have not had a letter from me, is that I promised to write to you in French. I shall have a vacation of a fortnight, which I shall spent at Canton, and I shall then have ample leisure to write to you. Indeed you must excuse my errors in every thing in this letter, I am surrounded by tasks and even now my maps which lie before me, seem to call for my attention and divide it with my letter." I am glad that you cannot witness my first Examination. I know what your feelings would be, mine are sufficient. My uncle Abraham will be there, he will acquaint you with my success, perhaps it may be a failure, but I hope not, be assured that I will do my utmost to acquit myself well. I hardly dare trust that I shall be right in Geography, the numberless questions on the map quite disconcert me. History unless I am frightened quite out of my wits I am sure of and 'tis very improbable that I shall miss in parsing or Latin (by the bye I have learned to scan and parse) or French and I think my Italian will be right. I wonder if this is as interesting to any body else as it is to me, I think of nothing else. Goodbye my dear father, you will soon hear from me again Your affectionate daughter

S M FULLER.

P S Grandma has written to you she was much pleased with your letter to day she bids me tell you she gets better slowly.

ALS (MH: fMS Am 1086 [9:22]). *Addressed:* Hon. Timothy Fuller. / MC. / Washington City. / DC. *Postmark:* Boston MS Mar 14[?]. *Endorsed:* 3. March / From my daughter / Sarah Margarett— / Recd 18. March 1822—

The reason] ⟨My⟩ The reason

Attention and divide it with my letter] attention and ⟨divided my attention⟩ ↑ divide it with my letter ↓

32. To Timothy Fuller

Canton 22d March, 1822

My dear father,

I have passed through all the dangers and perils of Examination without any failure. I made out much better than I had expected I should, but I was so unfortunate as to have a bad cold, and I was in consequence extremely hoarse. I left Boston last Teusday. Little Ellen knew me^n again. The love of contradiction so natural to her; has taught her to say "shant, didnt, no, and 'tis." She says ayme instead of yes. W H says "how bid you are." The other day he said "aunt Abba want two days londer than two months," she said no, and he answered "yes they are I know better than you, for I am a man." All the family are in good health: but E K has been unwell. Farewell my dear Father I am Your affectionate daughter

S M FULLER.

ALS (MH: fMS Am 1086 [7:26]). *Addressed:* Hon. Timothy Fuller MC / Washington / DC. *Endorsed:* 25. 22 Mar / From my dear Wife— / Recd 27. March 1822.

Margaret's letter is a postscript to her mother's.
Ellen knew me] Ellen kn⟨?⟩ew me

33. To Timothy Fuller

Canton. March 29th. 1822

My dear father,

I shall tomorrow leave Canton and return to school. I received yesterday your kind letter of the 22d inst. You say you wish that I had written to you more frequently, ah! my dear father, I write so ill that I am quite ashamed to look at my letters when written, even when I take considerable pains with them. You say in one of your letters to mamma, that you wish she would write to Miss Ellen and inclose it to you, and you would send it to her. I intend to write when I go to Boston and send it to you I hoped we should have heard from her this spring, but the Falcon has arrived and has brought no letters, at least I have not heard of any. Little William Henry has just brought his little sister's chair to the fire for her. He has put his plate of cheese, or chee as Ellen calls it, in my lap and says "tum Ellen dont you want some more." He has a great notion of courting and Miss

Clara Crane is selected by him as the object of his admiration.[1] Ellen has learned since I have been here to say, did, do, see, come, back, and sick, with the last word she is very much pleased. She is a lovely little creature. She is not very well now she has caught a bad cold. There is an examination this afternoon at William Henry's and Eugenes school, that is the Canton people go there to hear the children read and spell. W H is not at the head of his class he studied a great deal this morning and yesterday afternoon. I am glad I have not little children to teach, tis in my opinion a disagreeable occupation to repeat twenty times to a stupid child A B C and at last not to have him remember it in all probability. Poor W H is all the time teasing Ma, aunt Abba, Grandma, and me, to send him on errands. I remember he used to say been errand. Eugene sends[n] his love to you and an hundred kisses. Dinner is ready and Grandma says; I must come as no time is to be lost. Farewell dear Pa I am Your affectionate daughter

S M FULLER

ALS (MH: fMS Am 1086 [7:29]). *Addressed:* Hon. Timothy Fuller MC / Washington / DC. *Endorsed:* 28. 29 March / From my dear Wife— / Recd 2 Apl 1822— / From Sarah Margarett.

Margaret's letter is a postscript to her mother's.

Eugene sends] Eugene ⟨h⟩ sends

1. Clara Crane (1802–72), daughter of Friend and Rebekah Crane of Canton, was a distant relative of Mrs. Fuller's. In 1824 Clara married Mrs. Fuller's cousin Jepthah Crane (Endicott, *BMD*, p. 184; Norfolk Probate, no. 4616).

34. To Timothy Fuller

Cambridge. 22d Dec. 1822

Dear Sir,

I received your letter of the 15th on Friday. It gave me great pleasure as I have been long expecting it.[n]

I have left the good Dr's with much regret. The[n] Dr. made an address to us (Jane Welles and myself) in which[n] he particularised each of us.[1] He began with saying that he never *flattered,* then paid some fine *compliments,* and concluded with some advice about religion and our conduct through life. Previous to my departure she requested me to put my two[n] last pieces into the book of selections, and as I had no time, he copied them for me. I really do love him, for he has a very kind and sweet disposition. He requested me to come and see him often, and I think that I shall. As to the presents Dr Park has forbidden[n] us to make any while we remain at school but my uncles think it would be well for me to make a few to those with whom I was intimate, "comme les petits presens entretiennent de l'amitié,"[2] likewise to invite about forty to dance at our house, as they think it would be the best time just after I leave school, as I am to visit many of the girls, and the expense of it would not be great, since suppers are not fashionable[n] now. Will you be so good as to answer me as soon as possible on both these subjects as I[n] shall wait for your opinion. I saw a Mr Tazewell the other evening, and some one told me that he was son to one of the first senators of Virginia. Do you know his father?[3]

I have read Bracebridge Hall lately.[4] I was much disappointed in it, it seems to me to possess very little incident or originality of idea; I think that although it has considerable wit, yet that is often far-fetched. The style is good, but I think this work is much inferior to any of Irving's preceding works, which I have seen. In one respect it is certainly superior to any book which[n] I ever read, and that is the size of the print, it might be read by the weakest eyes without either pain or danger.

Have you seen Mrs Eustis yet, and did she inquire after me.[5] I hope that she did for I was so much pleased with her that I was anxious to interest her in my favor. I am much obliged to you for the pens which you mended for me. I have given Eugene a little book as a reward for getting his lessons well. He can recite his lessons easily, and is much more diligent and attentive than he has been. Your little Arthur is much prettier than he was before you left us.[6] Ellen K[ilshaw] has been pretending great sorrow to induce us to pity her. We are all of us very anxious for the return of William, indeed, we do not know how to live any longer without him. Here's a long letter all about self, I have read your speeches on the subject of the Piracy bill, and rejoice in your success.[7] I have much more to say to you, but it grows late, and Mother says that I must write no longer lest I should hurt my eyes, which are weak at present. Goodnight my dear father I am Your affectionate daughter

S M FULLER.

ALS (MH: fMS Am 1086 [10:89]). *Addressed:* Hon. Timothy Fuller. / MC. / Washington. DC. *Postmark:* Boston MS Dec 23. *Endorsed:* From my daughter / Sarah Margarett— / Recd 27. Dec. 1822—

long expecting it] long expect(?)ing it

much regret. The] much regret. ⟨and many⟩ The
myself) in which] myself) ⟨and⟩ in which
put my two] put ⟨two⟩ my two
Dr Park has forbidden] Dr Park ↑ has forbidden ↓
are not fashionable] are ⟨of⟩ not fashionable
subjects as I] subjects ⟨as soon as possible⟩ as I
to any book which] to any ⟨which⟩ book which

1. Jane Welles (1805?–80) was the daughter of John Welles, a wealthy and respected Boston merchant. She never married ("Hollis Street Church"; Suffolk Probate, no. 64518).

2. "As little gifts keep up friendship."

3. The Tazewells were distinguished Virginia aristocrats. Fuller met either Henry (1805–28) or John Nivison Tazewell (1807–69), sons of Littleton Waller Tazewell (1774–1860) and his wife, Anne Nivison (d. 1858). The elder Tazewell had served in the Virginia General Assembly; later in his career he was a U.S. senator and governor of Virginia. Both the Tazewell sons had enrolled in the Harvard class of 1826 but neither graduated. Henry died a suicide after being rejected by a young woman; John Nivison studied law with his father and became a lawyer (Littleton Waller Tazewell Book, ms. genealogy, Southern Historical Collection, NcU [copy at ViU], pp. 118, 165, 190–92; Harvard archives; *DAB*; William H. Stewart, *History of Norfolk County, Virginia* [Chicago, 1902], p. 586).

4. Two editions, an English and an American, of Washington Irving's *Bracebridge Hall: or, the Humourists* had been published in May 1822.

5. Caroline Langdon (1781?–1865) had married William Eustis (1753–1825) in 1810. He was a former surgeon in the Revolutionary War, a secretary of war under Madison, and ambassador to the Netherlands; he was soon (1823) to be governor of Massachusetts. Timothy Fuller was a political ally of Eustis's (*DAB*; Paige, *Cambridge*, p. 244).

6. Arthur Buckminster Fuller (1822–62), sixth of the Timothy Fuller children, had been born on August 10 of that year. After graduating from Harvard in 1843, Arthur went to Illinois, where he established a school. Finding education on the frontier to be unsatisfactory, he returned to Cambridge. He graduated from the Divinity School in 1847 and was ordained in 1848. He served as a chaplain in the Civil War but resigned his position to enlist in the army. He was killed the next day in the battle at Fredericksburg. Arthur Fuller was married twice: first, in 1850, to Elizabeth Davenport (1831–56), daughter of Joseph and Mary Daniels Davenport; then, in 1859, to Emma Reeves (1833–1904), daughter of Walter and Elmira Reeves (Richard F. Fuller, *Chaplain Fuller* [Boston, 1863]; ms. Davenport genealogy, MH: fMS Am 1086 1:136; MVR 1904, 30:139).

7. Her father had spoken on the floor of the House on 13 December 1822 in support of a bill that would provide enough ships to suppress piracy in the Gulf of Mexico. The measure passed.

35. To Timothy Fuller

Cambridge 30 Dec 1822

My dear father,

Yesterday I did not write to you as I went to church all day. Even if we had not had company, I could not have written to you in the evening, as my eyes are so extremely weak. I hoped to have been able to have studied this week eight hours each day, but I have determined not only not to study, but not to look into a book for seven days. I am very sorry to be obliged to do this for I had begun "Smiths Wealth of Nations and I wished to finish it. I wished for two books "Bacon's Essays" and "Paleys Internal Evidences" but mother can not find them in either of the bookcases.[1] I thought that, when I asked you whether we had them, you said yes. Did I misunderstand you? The Dr. told me that he thought me sufficiently advanced in my studies to begin some works upon ethics, and that I had better begin as soon as possible. I shall expect on Wednesday," the first of January, an answer to my letter of the 22d. A letter from you will be as good as a New year's present. This letter must be sent directly, or it will not be in time for the mail, therefore I must break of[f] abruptly, with the sincerest wishes for your health and happiness for the ensuing year and many others.

Your affectionate daughter

S M FULLER

P S I hope you will send us Mr K's letter, as we sent you his sister's.[2]

ALS (MH: fMS Am 1086 [7:55]). *Addressed:* Hon. Timothy Fuller. / MC. / Washington. / D.C. *Endorsed:* No. 14. 30, Dec. / From my dear Wife— / Recd 3. Jan. 1823. / & From Sarah Margarett—

   Margaret's letter is a postscript to her mother's.
   shall expect on Wednesday] shall expect ⟨the day after⟩ on Wednesday

   1. Adam Smith's *An Inquiry into the Nature and Causes of the Wealth of Nations* (Dublin, 1776) had been published in Philadelphia in 1789 and Hartford in 1818. Bacon's *Essayes* (London, 1597) had been published in Boston in 1807 as *Essays. Moral, Economical, and Political.* William Paley's *Natural Theology: or, Evidences of the Existence and Attributes of the Deity, Collected from the Appearances of Nature* (London, 1802) had gone through many editions; the first American edition was published in Philadelphia in 1802.

   2. Probably the Kilshaws.

36.   To Timothy Fuller

Cambridge 5 Jan 1823

Dear Father,

My eyes are much better and in a few days I intend to write you a long letter." [Th]ank you for your kindness in consenting to m[y part]y and for answering me soon on that sub[ject.] It is fixed for a week from next Wednesday. Uncle Elisha is to be my manager. Pray take care of your own health and do not continue your [   ] too long. Your brother Elisha can lift a hundred and twenty pounds on his little finger. I have seen Mathews, never was so pleased in my life.[1] Mr H. G. Otis and Mr Webster were at the theatre.[2] Mr Otis came into the next box to us, to see Mary Boardman, his son's wife's sister.[3] Write to me soon.

Yours affectionnately

S M Fuller.

ALS (MH: fMS Am 1086 [7:58]). *Addressed:* Hon. Timothy Fuller MC. / Washington / DC. *Postmark:* Boston Jan 7 MS. *Endorsed:* No 17. 5 & 6. Jan. / From my dear Wife— / Recd 11. Jan. 1823.

Margaret's letter is a postscript to her mother's.
a long letter] a long letter (in a few days)

1. Charles Mathews the elder (1776–1835), an English comedian, had made a successful American tour that included Boston (Brown, *American Stage*, p. 238).

2. Harrison Gray Otis (1765–1848) served in both houses of the state and federal legislatures. A leader of the Hartford Convention in 1814, the Federalist Otis had just lost a mayoral election in Boston and was to lose his first race for governor before being elected mayor for the first of three terms in 1829. In 1790 he married Sally Foster. Daniel Webster (1782–1852) was at this time a congressman from Boston (*DAB*).

3. Harrison Gray Otis, Jr. (1792–1827), married Eliza H. Boardman, daughter of William H. Boardman of Boston (*CVR*; *CC*, 10 May 1817). Her sister Mary Gilman Boardman (1800–1870), whom Fuller mentions here, married John Douglas Bates in 1834 (*CC*, 18 January 1834; MVR 231:40).

37.   To Timothy Fuller

Cambridge. 12th Jan. 1823

My dear father,

I cannot but regret tho'[n] I do not feel surprised that I do not receive an answer to my letter and postscript. As to this party I have issued about ninety invitations, and received nine answers. It is the twelfth and my party is fixed for the fifteenth. I think it is very rude and very inconvenient to the host not to send answers until the day of the party. Richard Fuller is coming he is a Southerner, do you know what his family is?[1] He has but one rival in his class, the Sophomore. I made the wedding call on Sarah Dix alias Williams. Your brother Elisha says that Edward has not any right to put an Esq. to his name and has laughed a great deal, because the marriage was put into the newspaper that on Wednesday at St. Paul's by the rev. Dr. Jarvis Edward Williams *Esq.* to Miss Sarah Anne Elisabeth Dix, daughter of the late Alexander Dix Esq. Now I say that I am much pleased that my relations should be thus ennobled, and beside Mr Dix certainly has a right to the title here allotted him, for he, died in a duel, which proves him beyond doubt a gentleman.[2] Your sisters Martha and Sarah, who, you must know, pique themselves on being modish and fashionable, derided me extremely for wearing a coat to make this wedding call on the coldest morning I have known this winter. They thought I would have understood the propriety of things better, and indeed seemed marvellously afraid that they should be forever disgraced by taking me with them dressed in so improper a habit, as a merino mantle, dark blue cloth coat, and chinchilli cap. However my aunt Sarah pinned four shawls on her shoulders[n] my aunt Martha tossed a veil upon her head, and put a white shawl on over a thin black silk gown, and away we went; when we got to the drawing room door, Jane ushered my aunts into an antichamber, and said to me, "Miss Fuller will you go in now" I said "No I would wait" tho I could not help smiling to see that even the waiting maid perceived that I was the only one that was properly drest. And when we entered, it was as I expected, there was not one without her bonnet and coat I teased them well for it, and what do you think the answer was, "In truth there was nobody there fit to be seen. I am much obliged to Miss Adeline Brown for her kindness, I cannot copy music, but I will take off some patterns and send her.[3] Miss Brinley shewed me the other day a newly invented instrument to copy music.[4] Mr Hayward wishes me to request you to buy for him "The Lost song of David". He says that you will find it at Thomson's, and that it will be expensive.[5] Your son Eugene is much changed since he went to Mr Frosts' school, he is become a wit, and when you come home he will amuse you much, I think he has a very good understanding.[6] William, I think, is the most boisterous boy I have known. If it were not for his sweet temper, nobody could bear him. I do not believe that four other boys would make the noise that he does, and at this time when we are all busy he exerts this faculty to the utmost. I have heard that Mr Motte is dead, is it true?[7] I wish to have some further particulars of Miss Holmes.[8] Goodbye my dear father, believe me Your affectionate daughter,

S M FULLER.

ALS (MH: fMS Am 1086 [9:23]). *Addressed:* Hon. Timothy Fuller. / MC. / Washington. DC. *Postmark:* Boston MS Jan 14. *Endorsed:* 12. Jan. / From my daughter S. Margtt / Recd 18. Jan. 1823.

but regret tho'] but regret th⟨oug⟩o'
on her shoulders] on her shoulders ⟨Mar⟩

1. Richard Fuller (1805–76) (who was not related to Margaret's family) was a Harvard student (class of 1824) from South Carolina. He became first a lawyer and then a Baptist clergyman (Harvard archives).

2. Her father's cousin Edward A. Williams (1793–1871), son of Thomas and Susan Williams, married Sarah Anne Elizabeth Dix (1805–74), daughter of Alexander (1782–1809) and Temperance P. Smith Dix (1781–1807). The young couple had been married by the Reverend Dr. Samuel F. Jarvis (1786–1851), rector of St. Paul's Episcopal Church in Boston. The elder Dix had indeed died in a duel. He was killed by Martin Blake in Canada on the evening of 23 March 1809 (Dix: *CC*, 15 June 1805, 29 March 1809; Dexter, "BVR," 1:55, 63; *Worcester Births, Marriages, and Deaths* [Worcester, 1894]; Williams: Mt. Auburn; *CC*, 4 January 1823).

3. Adeline Brown was the daughter of Uriah Brown, a miniaturist painter who was living in Washington.

4. Possibly Catharine Hutchison Brinley (d. 1832), daughter of George Brinley, a Boston businessman (*CC*, 28 July 1832).

5. Pishey Thompson was a "bookseller and stationer, and importer of foreign books, optical, mathematical, and surveying instruments" in Washington (Judah Delano, *The Washington Directory* [Washington, 1822], p. 147). "The Lost Song of David" may be *The Last Words of David (2 Sam. xiii) Divided According to Metre, with Notes Critical and Explanatory, by Richard Grey* (London, 1749).

6. John Frost (1800–1859) of Kennebunk, Maine, graduated from Harvard in 1822. He taught in Boston, then in Cambridgeport (where both Margaret and Eugene went to his school), and finally in Philadelphia (Harvard archives; Havard Class of 1822 Secretary's Record Book).

7. Mellish I. Motte (b. 1801) was not to die till 1881. A South Carolinian, he had graduated from Harvard in 1821; among his classmates were Emerson and Josiah Quincy. He became a Unitarian minister (he had the South End Church in Boston from 1828 to 1842) and a foe of slavery. In 1829 he married Marianne Alger (b. 1812), daughter of Cyrus Alger, a wealthy foundry owner (*CVR*; Harvard archives; Arthur M. Alger, *A Genealogical History of That Branch of the Alger Family Which Springs from Thomas Alger of Taunton* [Boston, 1876], p. 26).

8. Probably Ann Susan Holmes (1804–77), daughter of the Reverend Abiel Holmes of Cambridge ("A Record of Some of the Descendants of John Holmes," NEHGS, p. 5).

38. To Timothy Fuller

Cambridge 30 Jan 1823

My dear father

My party was exceedingly agreeable, and I was very happy in it. I went to a cotillon party in Cambridge last night. Your Lady would not consent to go and it was lucky she would not. I staid till after two and if she had staid as long, I do not know what would have become of the poor child. I had a delightful evening. Professor Hedge told me "that you had obliged him exceedingly by sending him a packet of *Congressional Dockments*.[1] Elliot, Hilliard and Stearns were the Managers.[2] Your three brothers attended. The gentlemen were almost all Southerners. I saw Henry McKean, they say that he bears a strong resemblance to his father; he has a fine face, and I thi[nk] that he is the tallest man I ever saw.[3] Mr Tasewell is gone to Virginia, he would have come to my party, but he was engaged to go to Captain Hull's.[4] I was delighted to receive your letter of the 19th, which I shall answer soon. I have begun my letter to Ellen.[5] I intend to finish it today.[n] Goodbye dear father, Your affectionate daughter

SARAH MARGARET FULLER

ALS (MH: fMS Am 1086 [7:67]). *Addressed:* Hon. T. Fuller. MC. / Washington. DC. *Postmark:* Boston Jan 30 MS. *Endorsed:* No 26. 30 Jan. / From my dear Wife / & Sarah Margarett / Recd. 3. Feb. 1823.

Margaret's letter is a postscript to her mother's.

finish it today] finish it tod⟨y⟩ay

1. Levi Hedge (1767–1844) graduated from Harvard in 1792. He was first a tutor, then College Professor of Logic and Metaphysics from 1810 to 1827, and then Alford Professor of Natural Religion, Moral Philosophy, and Civil Polity from 1827 to 1832. His son, Frederic Henry (1805–90), became Margaret Fuller's good friend (*DAB*).

2. Fuller names Stephen Elliott (1804–66), Francis Hilliard (1806–78), and William G. Stearns (1804–72). Elliott first became a lawyer in his native Beaufort, South Carolina, then was ordained in the Episcopal church in 1835. He became the first bishop of Georgia in 1841 (Harvard archives; *LBD*). Hilliard, the son of William Hilliard, married Catherine Dexter Haven (*CVR*; Dexter, "BVR," 2:99). Stearns became a Boston lawyer, the partner of Theophilus Parsons, and was a steward of Harvard College for twenty-six years (Harvard archives; Davis, *Suffolk County*, 1:142).

3. Henry Swasey McKean (1810–57) was the son of Joseph McKean (1776–1818), a minister at Milton and the founder of Harvard's Porcellian Club (*CVR*; Sarah M. Folsom Enebuske, "Charles Folsom and the McKeans," *Cambridge Historical Society Proceedings* 25 [1938–39]:97–112; Harvard archives).

4. Possibly Captain Isaac Hull (1773–1843), formerly the commander of the *Constitution* (*LBD*).

5. Ellen Kilshaw.

39. To Timothy Fuller

Cambridge 2d Feb 1823.

My dear father,

Have I not been good this winter. Confess that I have kept my promise of writing every fortnight. Mamma says that you expect an account of the party, and that I must give it you. I need not tell you why she has elected me to this office, as to you my peculiar talent at narrative is well known. To state things fairly, I began to write you a full account three days afterwards,[n] but after I had proceeded half a page, mother would not allow me to proceed, because, *she said,* I wrote so ill; you well know, sir, what the anger of a disappointed author is; I threw away my pen and indignantly exclaimed, I'll write no more. Nothing but gratitude could have induced me to break my resolution. As to the party, Miss Locke of Billerica, whom Mary Stearns brought with her, was a belle.[1] Mary Stearns herself was another. There were but few from Boston. Every thing went on well. Miss Sales was here and your brother Elisha made an eulogium on her to the man who played on the clarionet.[2] I feel myself much obliged to Uncle Elisha, who took a great deal of trouble on my account. The two Misses Frost were here they are very handsome, and much admired in Cambridge.[3] Mrs Fay could not come without her husband, who was detained until ten oclock at court, and as he returned was sent for by somebody who kept him till eleven.[4] She might have come then. Mrs William Sullivan does not go out till nine in the evening she thinks it vulgar to go to a party before that time.[5] Dr Parks son came to my party accompanied by John Howard. Catherine Howard was prevented from coming by a severe cold.[6] Julia Davis's departure for Washington prevented Helen and Margaret from coming.[7] It seems to me now that I never shall wish to see Helen again, she has been so unfeeling towards Julia and so unkind to Mrs Park. Julia tenderly loved her, and deserved better treatment from her, but I should think that even for her own sake, even if Helen did not love her sister, she would have paid her proper attention. I send you inclosed my letter to Ellen. Will you be so good as to seal after you have read it. Your affectionate daughter

S M FULLER.

ALS (MH: fMS Am 1086 [10:90]). *Addressed:* Hon Timothy Fuller. MC. / Washington DC. *Endorsed:* From my daughter / Sarah Margarett / Recd. 8. Feb. 1823.
three days afterwards,] three days afte(?)rwards,
1. One of the daughters of Joseph (1772–1853) and Lydia Goodwin Locke: Harriet (1807–83), Mary Ann (1809–73), or Frances Caldwell (1811–80) (Billerica VR; Henry A. Hazen, *History of Billerica, Massachusetts* [Boston, 1883], p. 92; MVR 257:387, 320:303, 347:333, 438:126). Mary Stearns (1802–36) was the daughter of Asahel (1774–1839) and Frances Wentworth Shepard Stearns and the sister of William G. Stearns (see letter 38, note 2) (*Groton Historical Series*, 4:314–15; Chelmsford VR; *CVR*).
2. Mary C. Sales (d. 1884) was the only child of Francis (d. 1854) and Mary Hilliard Sales (d. 1847). Her father was an instructor of Spanish at Harvard from 1816 to 1854. Mary Sales never married (*CVR*; MVR 356:67; Harvard archives).
3. Possibly Fuller refers here to Eliza and Lavinia Frost, daughters of John Frost, Jr., of Cambridge, a blacksmith who died in 1818 (Middlesex Probate, 1st ser., no. 8600).
4. The Fays were good friends of the Fullers. Samuel Prescott Phillips Fay (1778–1856), judge of Probate Court of Middlesex County and a former member of the Governor's Council, graduated from Harvard in 1798 (with William Ellery Channing), married Harriet Howard (1782–1847), and raised a large family in Cambridge (*CVR*;

Mt. Auburn; Christina Baker, *The Story of Fay House* [Cambridge, Mass., 1929], p. 88; *Fay Genealogy*, p. 68).

5. In 1802 Sarah Webb Swan (1782–1851), daughter of James and Hepzibah Clarke Swan, married William Sullivan (1774–1839), the second son of Governor James Sullivan (*Groton Historical Series*, 3:286; *DAB*; Thomas C. Amory, *Materials for a History of the Family of John Sullivan* [Cambridge, Mass., 1893], p. 152).

6. John Cochran Park (1804–89) graduated from Harvard in 1824 and was admitted to the bar in 1827. He served in the legislature, became district attorney for Suffolk County, and was prominent in the militia. In 1829 Park married Mary F. Moore, daughter of Colonel Abraham Moore (Harvard archives; *CC*, 28 November 1829; Davis, *Suffolk County*, 1:219). John Howard (1805–44), son of Dr. John Clark (1772?–1810) and Hepzibah Swan Howard (1778?–1833) of Boston, graduated from Harvard in 1825, became a doctor, and married Elizabeth Chase in 1829. His sister Catharine (1807–88) married James Cunningham, a Boston merchant, in 1830. The Clark children were cousins of William Sullivan (Herman Howard, *The Howard Genealogy* [Brockton, Mass., 1903], pp. 84–85, 164; MVR 393:213).

7. The Davis sisters were daughters of Daniel (1762–1835) and Louisa Freeman Davis, sister of the Reverend James Freeman. Julia, then twenty-two, died of consumption the same week that this letter was written. Her sisters, Helen (1798–1887) and Margaret (1803–79), never married (Frederick Freeman, *Freeman Genealogy* [*Samuel of Watertown*] [Boston, 1875], p. 407; Davis, *Suffolk County*, 1:186; *Records of the Church in Brattle Square, Boston* [Boston, 1902], p. 288; MVR 311:59, 382:284).

40. To Timothy Fuller

Cambridge. 18th Dec 1823

My dear Father,

You desired me when you left me[n] to write to you very often, and of myself. But as I hoped to find something besides my own affairs to relate to you, I have deferred a little while, the pleasure of writing to you. I am compelled however to begin on the old theme. You ask if I study Greek. I do study it, but I could go on much faster and with far greater ease if I had the aid of an instructor.[n] It is very unpleasant to me to meet with so many words, which I cannot penetrate, and am therefore obliged to pass over. Perhaps you think that as my attention has been so much devoted to the languages, I ought to be able to study the language without any assistance. But a teacher or even a companion in my studies, would greatly facilitate my progress in them. You promised to let me know whether you had determined that I should go to Mr Emerson's school.[1] If you intend that I should go; I hope that you will desire one of my uncles to see when I can be admitted, for if it is deferred until your return, I could not probably enter till next winter. I learn a portion of Tacitus every day, and am writing a translation of Cicero against Cataline. If I send it to you, may I hope that you will give yourself the trouble to correct it. My English style is exceedingly defective and I never have had but very little attention in that particular.

My dear father, I hope you do not miss me the thousandth part as much as I do you. This, you must own, is very disinterested. I feel your absence more I think every day. I hope you in [te]nd to write to me sometimes. Miss Bainbridge is very ill, dangerously I believe.[2] I intend to go and see her if possible next week. She was going to Miss Pratts ball, but was taken very suddenly ill the day before. Aunt Fuller received a note from Uncle Elisha to day; he is well, happy, full of spirits and of business. Uncle Henry has much more of the latter than the former I think. He complains of not having a minute to himself he could not spare time to go either to Miss Otis's wedding or party, he was invited to both.[3] He seems in good health however. Ellen and the boys send a budget of love and kisses.

Dear father, Yr ever afft daughter

SARAH M. FULLER.—

P S. Eugene studies pretty well.

ALS (MH: fMS Am 1086 [10:91]). *Addressed:* Hon. T. Fuller. M.C. / Washington. DC. *Postmark:* Boston MS Dec 19. *Endorsed:* From my daughter / Sarah Margarett— / Recd 23. Dec. 1823.

you left me] you left ⟨you⟩ me
of an instructor] of ↑an↓ instructor

1. When her father answered this letter, he told her to make a list of difficult passages and then "enquire of your Uncle or Mr Gannett or Mr Gage; who can probably solve your difficulties." Timothy went on to tell her she was going to the Prescott school in Groton, not the Emersons' in Boston: "I am certain that you are in need of some of the instruction & feminine discipline which Miss P. is said to excel in" (Timothy Fuller to Margaret Fuller, 24 December 1823, MH). William Emerson (1801–68) had established a young ladies' school in Boston and had the aid of his brother Ralph Waldo (1803–82), who began teaching in the school in 1821 (Rusk, *Life of RWE*, pp. 76–101). Margaret Fuller did not meet Waldo Emerson until 1836.

2. Either Susan, Lucy Ann, or Louisa Alexina Bainbridge, daughters of Commodore William Bainbridge (1774–1833), the heroic commander of the *Constitution*. The Bainbridges, who were then living in Cambridge, were good friends of the Fullers. Susan married Captain Thomas Hayes of the navy in 1825; Lucy Ann (1814–84) married Ashbel Green Jaudon (1800–1864) of Philadelphia in 1833; Louisa (d. 1882) married Henry Kuhn Hoff (1809–78), who became a rear admiral in 1867 and commander of the North Atlantic Fleet in 1868 (*DAB*; Edwin J. Sellers, *An Account of the Jaudon Family* [Philadelphia, 1890], p. 20, and *The Jaudon Family of Pennsylvania* [Philadelphia, 1924], p. 29; *National Cyclopedia*, 4:486; *Boston Daily Advertiser*, 13 October 1882; *CC*, 30 March 1825).

3. Sophia Harrison Otis (1799–1874), daughter of Harrison Gray Otis, became the second wife of the widower Andrew Ritchie (1786–1862) of Boston on 9 December 1823 (*CC*, 13 December 1823; William A. Otis, *A Genealogical and Historical Memoir of the Otis Family in America* [Chicago, 1924], p. 202).

41. To Timothy Fuller

Cambridge 23 Dec 1823

Dear Sir,

I had not intended to have written to you again, till I had received an answer to my last letter, as I consider regularity as proper in all things, but in consideration of the pleasure my very interesting letters must give you, I h[ave] altered my resolution. If you should see Miss Adams pray give my respects to her, I am much obliged to her for remembering me though to tell the truth I had nearly forgotten her, and did not think her by any means as interesting as her mother.[1] I believe this is the only occasion on which you have mentioned your very dutiful and affe daughter

SARAH M. FULLER

ALS (MH: fMS Am 1086 [7:86]). *Addressed:* Hon. Timothy Fuller MC / Washington DC. *Postmark:* Boston 24 MAS. *Endorsed:* 10. 23 Dec / From my dear Wife— / Recd 28. Dec. 1823.

Margaret's letter is a postscript to her mother's.

1. Which Adams family Fuller mentions is unclear, but comments in letters from her mother to her father suggest a Boston family that was visiting Washington.

42. To Timothy Fuller

Cambridge. 25th. Jan. 1824.

My dearest father,

I was delighted a short time ago by receiving a letter from you. I should very much prefer going to Mr Emerson's on every account, and if I go to Miss Prescott's I must be compelled to give up seeing you at all.[1] But if you wish it, I am willing to go, only, I hope you will not keep me there very long. I would give you the particulars of Miss Pratts party, as you desire, but it is so long ago I have really forgotten them. I was very happy, I am passionately fond of dancing and there is none at all[n] in Cambridge except at the Cotillon parties. I thank you most sincerely, my beloved father, for the interest you take in my pleasures. Be assured, I will do all that is in my power to manifest my gratitude for the indulgence and kindness you have ever shown in endeavoring to gratify even my slightest wishes. I think there never was so kind and affectionate a father[n] as you and I am most profoundly and ardently sensible of it. At Miss Wells's there was dancing to the piano, singing, music, and chess. I played "Mary list awake," Bruce's address to his army,"—and "Oh this is the spot." Miss[e]s Gray and Wells accompanied me on the flute and flageolet. Miss Channing Miss Cochran and Miss Brewster, who have all delightful voices sang and played.[2] I was particularly pleased with Miss Cochran's singing, for though her voice is neither very powerful, nor of great compass; I think it is the most soft and melodious I ever heard. Miss Howard did not sing well at all.[3] There was great difficulty in prevailing on her to sing and when she did, she played without any apparent diffidence to the middle of the tune, when she suddenly b[r]oke off and buried her face in her hands. Every one thought that she was very silly and affected, and some gentlemen told me she always did just the same thing, and they supposed she thought it graceful and practised it at home for effect. Misses Spooner and Pratt played for us to dance, and my partner for the two first dances was Mr Ripley, who had the first part last Commencement, and as you thought spoke so finely.[4] Afterwards I danced with Messrs Lunt, Newell, Emerson and Denny, Adeline Denny's brother.[5] There is to be a Cotillon party this week.[n] If you were at home, I am sure Mother would be willing that I should go, when she knew you I wished[n] it. Elisabeth Ware, Charlotte M'Kean, Abba D'Wolfe, the Misses Hilliard indeed all the young ladies of my age in Cambridge except Harriette Alston H Fay and poor Sarah M. Fuller are going, and Sarah M. is going to Groton next summer and in all human probability will not go to a dance this two years.[6] If there was time for Mother to receive a letter from you, signifying your desire, that I should go, I am sure she would let me, but that cannot be, as the party is on Thursday.

You have I suppose received a letter from Uncle Elisha, giving you the particulars of his being exposed to the infection of the small pox. But I do not believe he can have caught it. Uncle Abraham has written to him advising him not to avoid it by any means. Uncle A has been inoculated for the kine pock again, and mother thinks she shall be so too. Mother was very unwell yesterday, she seemed very feverish and I feared that she would be sick, but she appears much better to day.[7] Have you any objection to my having my music bound. I can get it done in two volumes, half binding for two dollars. I am extremely obliged to you for your permission to buy a Graeca Minora.[8] Dearest father, yr most affectionate daughter

SARAH MARGARET FULLER.

ALS (MH: fMS Am 1086 [9:24]). *Addressed:* For / Hon. T. Fuller. M.C.— / Washington.— / DC.— *Endorsed:* From my daughter / Sarah Margarett— / Recd 31. Jan. 1824.

none at all] none ⟨?⟩ at all
affectionate a father] affectionate ⟨?⟩ a father
party this week] party ⟨next⟩ this week
she knew you I wished] she knew ↑ you ↓ I wished

1. Susan Prescott (1796–1869), daughter of Judge James Prescott, conducted a girls' school in Groton for a decade before marrying John Wright (1797–1869) of Lowell in 1829 (*Prescott Memorial*, pt. 1, p. 106; MVR 221:152; "Miss Prescott's School," *Groton Historical Series* 1, no. 5:8–11).

2. Robert Burns's "Robert Bruce's March to Bannockburn," also known as "Scots, wha hae wi' Wallace bled," first appeared in the newspaper *The Morning Chronicle* (London) on 8 May 1794, then in a series of pamphlets, Poetry: Original and Selected (Glasgow, 1798?), and finally in George Thomson's *Original Scotish Airs* (London, 1799), where Fuller probably read the song (J. W. Egerer, *A Bibliography of Robert Burns* [Carbondale, Ill., 1964], p. 46). Fuller's friends are nearly impossible to identify with certainty, though Miss Wells is probably the Jane Welles mentioned in letter 34; Miss Channing is probably Susan Cleveland Channing, whom Fuller knew at Dr. Park's school. Miss Brewster may be Catherine Brewster (b. 1805) of Cambridge, and Miss Cochran is probably Agnes Gordon Cochran (1810–88), whom Fuller knew and who maried Stephen Higginson in 1831 (Brewster: *CVR*; Cochran: *Cleveland and Cleaveland*, p. 1064).

3. Possibly the Catharine Howard mentioned in letter 39.

4. Since the Fullers knew the family of Dr. William Spooner (1760–1836) of Boston, the reference here is probably to one of his daughters: Charlotte (d. 1841), Elizabeth (1806?–56), Martha Waldoe (d. 1837), or Hannah. Elizabeth married Samuel W. Spooner in 1835 (Davis, *Suffolk County*, 3:278; *CC*, 21 March 1835, 2 September 1835, 11 October 1837). George Ripley (1802–80) had graduated from Harvard in 1823 and was at this time studying at the Divinity School, from which he graduated in 1826. He became pastor at Purchase Street Church in Boston from 1826 until he left the ministry in 1841 to found Brook Farm. In 1827 he married Sophia Dana (1803–61), daughter of Francis and Sophia Dana of Cambridge. Sophia studied with Dr. Park in Boston before helping her mother with a school in Cambridge (*DAB*; *NAW*).

5. Her partners could have been several recent Harvard graduates and members of the class of 1824: William Parsons Lunt (1805–57) or his brother George (1803–85), both of whom became Unitarian ministers; George Newell (1797?–1831), an 1823 graduate, or his brother William (1804–81), who became minister of the new Unitarian parish that split off from the Congregational church in Cambridge in 1830; Edward Bliss Emerson; and Thomas Denny (1797–1874), a graduate in 1823. Adeline Denny (1799–1831) married the Reverend Elisha Goodrich Smith in 1830 (Lunts: Newburyport VR, Harvard archives; Newells: Harvard archives; Paige, *Cambridge*, pp. 301–4; Emerson: *Ipswich Emersons*, p. 264; Denny: Leicester VR, Harvard archives).

6. Elizabeth Ware (1808–66), daughter of the elder Henry Ware, married the Reverend George Putnam in 1831 (*CVR*; MVR 193:267). Charlotte Agnes McKean (1807–75) was the daughter of Joseph McKean (*CVR*; MVR 275:85). Abby Bradford DeWolfe (1810–88) was the daughter of Charles and Mary Goodwin DeWolfe (Mary LeBaron Stockwell, *Descendants of Francis LeBaron of Plymouth, Massachusetts* [Boston, 1904], pp. 129, 275). Elizabeth Hilliard was born in 1810; her sister Sarah Ann Hilliard (1808–48) married Charles C. Little, the publisher (*CVR*; MVR 40:142). Harriet M. Allston (d. 1886) was a niece of the painter Washington Allston (Joseph A. Groves, *The Alstons and Allstons of North and South Carolina* [Atlanta, 1901]; Suffolk Probate, no. 75766). Harriet Howard Fay (1810–85), Judge Fay's daughter, married William Greenough in 1831 (*CVR*; Mt. Auburn).

7. On 21 January, Elisha Fuller had written Mrs. Fuller (MH) saying that he had

been exposed to smallpox at Dr. Bartlett's home, where Fuller was staying in Concord. Though Bartlett had thought himself immunized, he contracted the disease after examining the body of one of its victims.

8. Andrew Dalzel's edition of *Collectanea Graeca Minora* (Edinburgh, 1787) had gone through five American editions by this time.

43. To Timothy Fuller

Cambridge. 22d Feb 1824.

My dearest father,

It was with the greatest pleasure that I received your letter of the 12th. I am extremely happy to hear that you think my[n] hand improved and hope to profit by your observations on it. I am sure I shall remember them as it is the first and dearest wish of my heart to conform *to your* wishes in every thing.[1] I very often study lessons in Latin and French. As to Greek I will own that I do not think I shall ever take any pleasure in it till I have either a companion or instructor in the study. I learn lessons in Alfieri occasionally.[2] But I do not study a great deal and I am very sensible that I should improve much more at school I hope dear sir that wherever you send me this spring you will arrange it so that I may go as soon at least as soon as you return I could wish it to be sooner if possible. My wishes feelings and judgement are decidedly on Mr Emersons' but if one is not applied to quickly I shall not be able to gain admittance to either and shall remain at home as I did last summer. If I go to Miss Prescotts of course I shall not see you the whole year round. Yesterday was a most lovely day. In the afternoon I went up to see Elizabeth Ware whom I have not seen for some time as she has just lost her sister in law of whom she was very fond[3] I met her coming down to see me. I turned back with her and passed the rest of the afternoon at her house. She walked part of the way back with me and I went and took tea with Mrs Fay She had invited Mr. Brenan and Germanicus and Edward Hedge to meet Mr Constant.[4]

AL (MH: fMS Am 1086 [10:92]).

you think my] you t(?)hink my

1. After recalling how his father had corrected him, Timothy told his daughter, "These things can only be corrected by *degrees*, & your letter shows *so much* improvement, that I am encouraged to expect more" (Timothy Fuller to Margaret Fuller, 12 February 1824, MH).

2. Vittorio Alfieri (1749–1803), an Italian dramatist, was the author of nineteen classical tragedies, as well as sonnets, odes, comedies, and an autobiography.

3. Elizabeth Watson Waterhouse (1793–1824), daughter of Dr. Benjamin Waterhouse, had married Henry Ware, Jr., on 15 October 1817. She died on 5 February 1824 (*CVR*; *CC*, 11 February 1824).

4. Brenan is probably Richard Brenan, who graduated from Harvard in 1825 and became a lawyer in Charleston, South Carolina (Harvard archives). Germanicus is most likely Frederic Henry Hedge, Brenan's classmate. His brother, Edward Hedge (1807–37), was in the Harvard class of 1828 (*CVR*; Harvard archives). According to a letter from Mrs. Fuller to her husband dated 19 February 1824 (MH), Mr. Constant was a Frenchman who lived with the family of Dr. John Williams and tutored Sophia in French.

44.   To Timothy Fuller

Cambridge 19th April 1824

My dear father,

I received, with delight, your very kind letter of the third. I thank you most sincerely for the assurances of your continued affection which have set my heart at ease. I shall willingly go to Groton for the summer, at your pleasure, though nothing else could in the least reconcile me to it. I shall entirely depend on an immediate visit from you according to your promise.[1] You told me sometime ago that you would consent to my making some little presents to Elisabeth Ware and two or three other of my friends "comme les petites presens entretiennent de l'amitie" and I intend to take up a small sum from my uncle for that purpose. I hope you will write to me as soon as you hear from Mr Lawrence.[2]

Miss Bainbridge has pressed me so much to pass some days with her, that I intended to have accepted of her invitation, but I find myself so much engaged that I fear it will not be in my power. She attends Exhibitions with me. It will be a week from next Tuesday.

I went to the theatre the other evening with uncle Elisha and Mrs Whittier to see Tom and Jerry, with which I was exceedingly entertained.[3] It is exceedingly witty I think and the character of Logic inimitably hit off. Miss Clarke danced to the tamborine in the afterpiece.[4] The night was rainy, and the house rather thin, although Tom and Jerry has had a run of thirty five nights, and always drawn crowded houses before. It is a very great favorite among the students, one hundred and forty went to it in one night.

Eugene desires me to inform you that he is at the head in two classes, and got two certificates last Saturday. He is so much elated that he wants a watch directly, as Charles Fay and Wendell Holmes have one.[5] Commodore Billy has one with its pink ribbon and seal, which he wears with an air of great majesty, and contributes to the public service with true philanthropy, by telling the hour to every old woman and dirty little boy that he comes across.

I believe the little politicks of Cambridge do not much interest you "engaged in loftier thoughts the nation's rise or fall. Neither is there much to relate. As music is allowed in the evening the Anti-Harmonics go out with fifes and tin kettles to the great annoyance of the government and the peaceful inhabitants of C— How much I regret to leave this charming place, where I am beloved and go to one where I am an entire stranger and where[n] I must behave entirely by rule. I hope you have no intention of keeping me there four years. My very affectionate Aunt Fuller and my excellent uncles wish me to stay four years. But I hope *you* are not quite so anxious to get rid of your *little* daughter. I thank them for their good will, but do not feel myself particularly obliged to them for such testimonials of it. I always hold, that, those who love me, will wish to have me with them. I hope you will write to me directly. I am to board with Miss Prescott I suppose. I intend to call on Miss Chaplin before I go and learn the regulations which I presume are not very strict.[6] Your ever afft daughter.

SARAH M. FULLER.

ALS (MH: fMS Am 1086 [10:93]). *Addressed:* Hon. Timothy Fuller MC / Washington / DC. *Postmark:* Boston Apr 19. *Endorsed:* From my dear Wife / & Sarah Margarett— / Recd. 23. Apl 1824.

stranger and where] stranger and ⟨go to one⟩ where

1. Her father, who told her in his letter that he saw a need for her to have "a few months with a judicious country lady, who will be *free & faithful* in watching & correcting your faults," closed by saying, "I shall soon write again, & shall visit you immediately upon my return. Depend upon my undiminished affection, as long as you continue dutiful" (Timothy Fuller to Margaret Fuller, 3 April 1824, MH).

2. Amos Lawrence (1786–1852), who with his brother Abbott helped establish the textile industry in Massachusetts, had returned from Boston to his native Groton (*DAB*).

3. *Tom and Jerry or Life in London: a Burletta of Fun, Frolic and Flash in Two Acts* had opened in Boston on 19 December 1823. This comedy, which was second only to *The Beggar's Opera* in popularity, was written originally by Pierce Egan (1772–1849), a British sports reporter, and adapted for the stage by William Thomas Moncrieff (1794–1857) (William W. Clapp, Jr., *A Record of the Boston Stage* [Boston, 1853], p. 216; George C. D. Odell, *Annals of the New York Stage* [New York, 1928], 3:59; L. W. Conolly and O. P. Wearing, *English Drama and Theatre, 1800–1900* [Detroit, 1978]; *DNB*).

4. The *Boston Daily Advertiser* lists "Miss W. Clarke" in a variety of roles in the 1820s.

5. The son of Judge Samuel P. P. Fay, Charles (1808–88) graduated from Harvard

in 1829 and became an Episcopal minister (*CVR*; *Fay Genealogy*, pp. 154, 289; *Vermont Historical Gazetteer*, 2:154; *Boston Evening Transcript*, 8 November 1888). Oliver Wendell Holmes (1809–94), son of the Reverend Abiel Holmes and a friend of Fuller's in Cambridge, was a doctor before he turned to literature with *The Autocrat of the Breakfast-Table* (*DAB*).

6. Miss Chaplin is probably Eliza O. Chaplin (1808?–62), daughter of Dr. James P. and Hannah Gardner Chaplin. Eliza married William G. Hubbard of Boston in 1828 (Paige, *Cambridge*; *CC*, 19 January 1828, 30 October 1832).

45.   To Timothy Fuller

Groton, May 21st. 1824

Dear Sir,

I received your letter, on Teusday, with delight. I am much obliged to you for writing so soon, much sooner indeed than I had supposed you would; as I know how much you are engaged. I am happy to hear, that I have a fourth brother, though I hardly think he will rival my pet, Arthur in my affections. As to a name for him, I like Frank best, Frederick next, and I wish he might have three names.[1]

By a letter from my uncle Elisha, I find that my uncle Henry is elected a Representative.[2] If he wished for the dignity, I am happy that he has gained it, and beg that you will congratulate him in my name, as I think that I shall not very speedily find time to write to him, and should be sorry not to offer my felicitations on *such an accession* of *dignity*. I am contented here, which I think is as much as could be expected. Miss Prescott has about twenty boarders, and from twenty to thirty day scholars. There are among the boarders six young ladies from Cambridge, Miss Chaplin, whom you know, Miss Warland, who is, I suppose, a sister of Mrs Manning, Miss Holmes, whose father is carpenter to the University, two Miss Frains, whose father has some office about the State Prison, and a Miss White from Lechmere Point.[3] The others are Virginia Shaw, daughter to the late Commodore Shaw, who boards here with her stepmother, Miss Soley of Charlestown, Miss Nash, daughter to a sea captain in Boston, a Miss Prescott, and Miss Patten from—I know not where, and two Miss Fiskes, with Miss Hale, a ward of Mr *Amos* Lawrence's.[4] Miss Caroline James is my chum, and I have likewise in the room with me a Miss Wood,[n] Miss Clarke of Princeton comes to the school and rooms at Mr Butler's.[5] Among the Groton young ladies who attend the school I like Miss Butler and Miss Brasier best, Miss Lawrence and Miss Dana very well.[6] I will describe them all sometime.

I study Hedge's Logick, Blair's Rhetorick and Colburn's Arithmetick.[7] I feel myself rather degraded from Cicero's Oratory to One and two are how many It *is* rather a change is it not? I do not believe the two former will do any good except as an exercise of the memory, but Miss Prescott knows best, of course. I wish you would write to Miss Prescott, for I do not know myself exactly what were your wishes with regard to the course of my studies.

The school hours are from half past eight to twelve in the morning, and from two to half past four in the afternoon. We have prayers at half past six in the morning and at eight in the evening. I walk every evening immediately after tea with some young ladies; I take a great deal of pleasure in these walks, for this part of the country is exceedingly beautiful.

I will give you a full length portrait of Miss Prescott, when I have more room. I dislike miniatures, they are seldom correct. Suffice it at present that I really love and admire her, though I did not intend to like her at all. She has two sisters, I like them both but prefer Miss Mary.[8] I wish you would have the goodness to send me my Milton's Paradise lost, my Hedge's" Logick and Bible. I wish too that when it is convenient you would send me a newspaper. I shall depend on your writing directly to let me know how my dear mother is. I shall expect your June visit most impatiently, and hope my mother will then be well enough to accompany you. I hope by this time Aunt Fuller is safely returned from her journey, and that it was pleasant. Love to my brothers, sister if she is at home. I am, dearest father, your ever affectionate daughter

Sarah M. Fuller.

ALS (MH: fMS Am 1086 [9:25]). *Addressed:* Hon T. Fuller. / Boston. / Massachusetts. *Endorsed:* My daughter / Sarah Margarett Fuller— / Recd 23. May 1824— / her birthday—she is / fourteen years old— / 25. May—Answered—

Miss Wood] Miss Wood ⟨a very disagreeable girl, whom I would not tolerate except to please Miss Prescott⟩

lost, my Hedge's] lost, ⟨H⟩ my Hedge's

1. Richard Frederick (1824–69), seventh of the Fuller children, born 15 May 1824, became Margaret's favorite brother. Richard graduated from Harvard in 1844, studied law with George Davis in Greenfield, and returned to Cambridge to graduate from the Harvard Law School. He was for a time a partner with his uncle Henry Holton Fuller but found that his melancholic temper was unsuited to the partnership. Richard was married twice: first, in 1849, to Sarah Batchelder (1829–56), daughter of Francis and Sarah Kolloch Batchelder; then, in 1857, to Adeline Reeves, daughter of Jacob and Mary Griffin Reeves (Richard F. Fuller, *Recollections of Richard F. Fuller* [Boston, 1936]; MVR 103:127; *CVR*; Endicott, *BMD*, p. 261; MVR 1917 12:240).

2. Her uncle Henry Holton Fuller had just been elected to the first of his four nonconsecutive terms in the Massachusetts lower house (Henry A. Fuller, "Henry Holton Fuller," *Memorial Biographies*, 1:417).

3. Elizabeth Bell Warland, daughter of Thomas and Elizabeth Warland of Cambridge, had married the Reverend John Abbott, who died in 1814. Her second husband was Dr. Samuel Manning, Jr. Her sister, Lucy Warland (1789–1830), at thirty-five was certainly too old to be in school. Fuller probably confused the Warland families and was in fact describing Mary Madelia Warland (1809–72), daughter of John and Sarah Bates Warland of Cambridge. Mary Madelia married Royal Richardson in 1831 (Paige, *Cambridge*, pp. 677–78; *CVR*). Miss Holmes is probably Mary Ann Holmes (b. 1808), daughter of Richard Holmes, a "housewright" (John Holmes, *The Descendants of George Holmes of Roxbury* [Boston, 1908], p. 140). The Frains and Miss White are unidentified.

4. Virginia Shaw was the daughter of Commodore John Shaw (1773–1823) and his first wife, Elizabeth Palmer. Following Elizabeth's death, the commodore married Mary Breed (d. 1868), daughter of Ebenezer Breed (d. 1817) of Charlestown. In 1828 Virginia Shaw married Lieutenant William Lynch of the U.S. Navy, who in the 1840s was in charge of the Dead Sea exploration and who later became an officer in the Confederate Navy (*LBD*; *DAB*; Middlesex Probate, no. 41402; Thomas Bellows Wyman, *Genealogies and Estates of Charlestown* [Boston, 1879], 1:122). Mary Russell Soley (1807–81), daughter of John and Rebecca Henley Soley of Charlestown, remained a friend of Fuller's for many years. In 1835 Mary married William Bradford DeWolfe (1810–62), son of Senator James DeWolfe, the prominent slave trader of Bristol, Rhode Island (Calbraith B. Perry, *Charles D'Wolf of Guadaloupe* [New York, 1902], pp. 126–27; Hunnewell, *Town Life*; "De Wolfe Cemetery, Bristol, Rhode Island," NEHGS). The Boston papers of the time mention three seagoing Nashes with daughters: Captain Joshua Nash and Mary Ann; Captain Luther Nash and Mary; Captain Timothy Nash and Susan (*CC*, 9 December 1826, 23 February 1828, 27 June 1835). Prescott genealogies record two girls of the right age to be at the Groton school: Mary Brigham (b. 1809), daughter of Levi and Mary Townsend Prescott of Bolton, and Mary (b. 1811), daughter of James and Mary Owen Prescott (*Prescott Memorial*, p. 115). Miss Patten (Patton?) is unidentified, as are the Fiskes. The Middlesex Probate Court records William (not Amos) Lawrence was the guardian of Elizabeth Hale, daughter of the deceased Samuel and Betsey Brown Hale (Middlesex Probate, 1st ser., no. 10085; *GVR*).

5. Letters of Margaret's mother identify Caroline James (1806–67) as the daughter of Eleazer James of Barre. She married the Reverend Alexander Young, an anti-Transcendentalist Unitarian minister, in 1826 (Barre VR; William Buell Sprague, *Annals of the American Pulpit* [New York, 1857], 8:524; MVR 204:81). Miss Wood is unidentified. Miss Clarke is probably Mary Abbott Clarke (1812–35), daughter of Aaron and Eliza Clarke of Princeton. Mary Clarke married William Putnam in 1833 (Princeton VR; *CC*, 19 June 1833; Rutland, Vt., VR). The girls were rooming in Groton at the home of Caleb (1776–1854) and Clarissa Varnum Butler (1782–1862) (*GVR*; Green, *Historical Sketch*; Frances Brooks, "Caleb Butler," *Memorial Biographies*, 2:266–79).

6. Fuller refers here to either Susan (1809–26) or Rebekah Butler (1811–44), daughters of Caleb and Clarissa Butler (*GVR*); Mary Saltonstall Brazer (1808–29), daughter of William Farwell (1782?–1835) and Phebe Varnum Brazer (*GVR*; *Groton Historical Series*, 4:256); Anna Maria Lawrence (1806–95), daughter of Luther and Lucy Bigelow Lawrence (*GVR*; Robert M. Lawrence, *The Descendants of Major Samuel L. Lawrence of Groton, Massachusetts* [Cambridge, Mass., 1904], p. 76); and either Rebecca (1805–1903) or Martha Barrett Dana (1809–83). Rebecca and Martha were daughters of Samuel (1767–1835) and Rebecca Barrett Dana (d. 1834), who became close friends of the Fullers and from whom Timothy bought his Groton farm (*GVR*; Butler, *Town of Groton*; *Dana Family*, p. 309).

7. Levi Hedge's *Elements of Logick: A Summary of the General Principles and Different Modes of Reasoning* (Cambridge, 1816) was a widely used text that went through numerous editions, as did Hugh Blair's *Lectures on Rhetoric and Belles Lettres* (London, 1783). Blair (1718–1800) was a Scottish minister and professor of rhetoric. His book was required reading at Harvard in the 1820s. Warren Colburn's work transformed the teaching of arithmetic by focusing the student's attention on a reasoned solution of

problems. Fuller probably used either *Colburn's First Lessons. Intellectual Arithmetic, upon the Inductive Method of Instruction* (Boston, 1821) or *Arithmetic: Being a Sequel to First Lessons in Arithmetic* (Boston, 1822).

8. The Prescott women were children of James (1766–1829) and Hannah Trowbridge Champney Prescott (1768–1836). James graduated from Harvard in 1788, became a lawyer, and then held two judgeships simultaneously—he was chief justice of the Court of Common Pleas and judge of probate. In 1821 he was impeached and convicted of judicial misconduct. The daughters not previously identified are Lucretia (b. 1798), Lucy (b. 1800), and Mary Oliver (1806–30) (*Prescott Memorial*, pt. 1, p. 106; Samuel Abbott Green, *An Account of the Lawyers of Groton* [Groton, 1892], p. 27).

46.   To Abraham W. Fuller

Groton. 14th July 1824.—

Dear Sir,

My answer to your letter has been delayed so long merely on account of a deficiency in interesting material, for its composition. But I do not find that there is any probability of my being able to collect any that is so, and must write as I can.

I was happy to hear that you found your journey so pleasant, and very sorry that you did not find it convenient to take Groton on your way home. I hope, if possible, that you will visit me again this term, and that Mr. H. H. Fuller will accompany you.[n] I have not heard any tidings of of the last named gentleman, since I came into these regions but, conclude he is still in the land of the living, (having received no information to the contrary through the medium of the newspapers) and, if I am right in my conjecture, shall be very happy to see him[n] if it should be only for the sake of novelty.

Mrs. Littlefield is perfectly recovered, very pretty and interesting.[1] Her illness has not taken from her bloom, which is as fine[n] as ever. She has not the sort of face which I admire, but I like her very well. Miss Anna Maria Lawrence is going to Sunderland this week, to stay sometime, with an uncle, I think.[2] I see her so little, that I shall not miss the light of her countenance. Mr. and Mrs. Bigelow of Medford visited Mrs Lawrence last week, a circumstance which we had reason to regret, as it prevented Mrs L. and Miss Anna Maria from honoring our play with their presence.[3] Votre chere amie, Miss Mary Braser attends school in the afternoon to *practise the art of painting*. She had a party a week or two since. Miss Mary Prescott, Miss James and *I* were there, so were all the gentlemen in town, Miss Clarke and Miss Butler. Miss Clarke sends her respects to your Honor. Caroline increases daily in grace and goodliness. She would have gone to a party at Judge Dana's last night, if she had not missed it.[4] Eight of us that were going were prevented by the rain which had the impertinence to interpose its veto. They expected thirty, and but four individuals were present three[n] ladies and one gentleman. So much for the uncertainty of human affairs in this sublunary state. I am sure of two things that my father has not written to me for a week, and that I adore Miss Prescott, which is nothing new to say, and will not surprise you, who have seen her and know how charming she is. I have told you all the novelties with which I am acquainted, and hope that you will do the same for me. I shall hope to receive[n] a very interesting letter from you next week, superior to all that I have received, and very long[n] as well as very good, in which hope I steadfastly remain Your very afft niece,

SARAH M. FULLER.

ALS (MH: fMS Am 1086 [9:27]). *Addressed:* For / A. W. Fuller. Esq.— / Boston,— / Mass. *Postmark:* Groton MS July 14. *Endorsed:* July 15th. 1824 / Thursday 9 Oclk a.m / Pr mail / Miss Sarah M. Fuller / July 15th 1824 / Pr Mail / Answered Pr Mail / July 30th 1824.

will accompany you] will acompany ↑ you ↓
to see him] to see ⟨?⟩ him
which is as fine] which ↑ is ↓ as fine
were present three] were present ⟨four⟩ three
hope to receive] hope to rec⟨ie⟩eive
and very long] and ⟨l⟩ very long

1. Henrietta Butler (1805–64), daughter of Caleb and Clarissa Varnum Butler, had married Nathaniel Littlefield on 1 September 1823 (*GVR*; Frances Brooks, "Caleb Butler," *Memorial Biographies*, 2:266–79).

2. The previous January, Joshua Green (1797–1875), a doctor in Sunderland, had married Eliza Lawrence (1796–1874), sister of Luther Lawrence, Anna Maria's father (John Montague Smith, *History of the Town of Sunderland, Massachusetts* [Greenfield, Mass., 1899], p. 380).

3. The Reverend Andrew Bigelow (1795–1877) of Medford was Anna Maria Lawrence's cousin. The son of the Honorable Timothy Bigelow, Andrew married Amelia Sargent Stanwood (1806–93) in January 1824 (*GVR*; Medford VR; Gloucester VR; *DivCat*; MVR 438:403).

4. Samuel Dana had been a lawyer in Groton since 1789, a member of the Massachusetts legislature (where he served three terms as president of the Senate), and chief justice of the Circuit Court of Common Pleas from 1811 to 1820 (Butler, *Town of Groton*, p. 266).

47. To Abraham W. Fuller

Groton 29th September. 1824.

Dear Sir,

I understood[n] with extreme regret only a few days since that you had been very ill on your journey, but that you were now in Boston and happily recovering. I am extremely sorry that you should be thus disappointed of the pleasure which you had anticipated from your journey, and that you should be ill when away from home, which is disagreeable to any one, but is I know particularly so to you. I hope however that you had the advantage of being either with my Aunt Martha or aunt Ann, who would of course pay you every attention in their power. I have my own selfish regrets on the subject, for I had firmly expected a visit from you of which I shall now, I suppose, be deprived; and I know you will here sympathise with me, as you will regret not[n] seeing Miss Prescott if you do not, losing the pleasure of an interview with my very honorable self.

There is a young lady here who says she is acquainted with you, hight Miss Marianne Davis;[1] I believe her father deals in brass, but she has none of it about her, for if she be not absolutely of the pure ore of fine gold, she is at least quite free from dross, indeed, a very pretty girl and ladylike in her manners. Miss Prescott is I think proved to be gold without alloy, if trial will prove it, for I have seen her tried seventy times seven times, which is I think the number of times which you said would satisfy you; and her original splendor far from being tarnished gains each time additional brightness; and she is fairly seventy times seven times, brighter, fairer, lovelier, in my eyes than when I first described her to you, which I then thought so impossible; how people change their ideas. I doubt whether if I were to commit to paper my present set of ideas, I should let the end of the year find one, that had not turned over thirty times.

Mrs. Littlefield wishes to know how you do, and when she may expect the pleasure of seeing you at Groton. I tell you this because it is of importance; and will just observe, en passant, that Mrs Braser and Miss Mary, made the same remark, though the idea was originally Mrs Littlefields. Yr affectionate niece,

SARAH M. FULLER.

ALS (MH: fMS Am 1086 [9:28]). *Addressed:* / For / Abraham W. Fuller. Esq. / Boston, / Mass. *Endorsed:* ⟨Sept⟩ / Oct 2nd, 1824 / Sat. 12 Oclk / N. / Miss Sarah M. Fuller / Oct 2d. 1824 / Pr mail / Answered Pr mail / Novr 9 A 1824.

I understood] I un⟨t⟩derstood
regret not] regret ↑ not ↓

1. Mary Ann Davis (d. 1881) was the daughter of James (1777–1862) and Hannah Ingols Davis. James Davis owned the Boston brass foundry that became the Revere Copper Company. In 1832 Mary Ann Davis married Henry Winsor (1803?–89) (S. T. Snow, *Fifty Years with the Revere Copper Co.* [n.p., 1890], pp. 9–28; *CC*, 2 June 1802, 2 June 1832; Suffolk Probate, no. 66690; *Boston Evening Transcript*, 28 October 1889).

48. To Timothy Fuller

Groton 20th December. 1824.

Dear father,

I was too busy to write to any being while I was at home, or you would have heard from me ere this; and, if I had staid at home, (as I purposed to do), another week, I would have written you a very *very* interesting epistle, as it is, I fear I shall prove very dull, for whatever I heard in Cambridge, new, original, interesting[n] and eccentric, has become old and lost all its valuable qualities by this time.

I left home on Wednesday 15th at half past one p. m. and passed the night at Concord; reached Groton next morning; I should not have come so soon if it had not so chanced that uncle came to Cambridge on Monday and persuaded me to go back with him on the grounds of expediency, and I, like a little simpleton, consented. I shall not return for fourteen weeks and you will be at home three weeks before me I hope you will write to me as often (if possible) as once in the fortnight; and tell me what is interesting to you, not what you think will please me. Whenever you can send me a newspaper I wish you would; it gives me more pleasure to read them, than you, who live where they make the news, can easily imagine.

You will have the pleasure of seeing your good friend Judge Samuel Dana at Washington this winter, and, I believe, Miss Ann intends to accompany him.[1] You will undoubtedly be very happy to see him. I am very sorry Miss Ann will not be here this winter, for I like her much.

I saw but very little of my uncles while I was at home, my uncle Abraham was so much occupied with the cares of the church that he had not a word to say on other subjects. He had at last fixed on Mr Barrett, who has lately preached in Philadelphia for his favorite congregation.[2] Mr Upham has been ordained and Miss A. S. Holmes is to be married next spring, but, I suppose there will be no rejoicings for that event in Cambridge, as she probably will go immediately to Salem.[3] The good people of C. were wonderfully pleased when pretty Sarah McKean married that stupid, awkward man; I was told that no event had enlivened them so much for a year.[4] Mr T Curtis is married (you know it I dare say) to Maria Sargeant, that living resemblance of the sweet Julia Davis; she is not quite so handsome I think as Julia was, but the likeness is extremely striking.[5] Uncle Williams is so much better I think he must recover entirely.

Susan gives a ball Tuesday and when I went there she and aunt were very busy and happy as queens. I think that aunt is quite in her element in the bustle and preparation requisite for a great rout. She desired to be particularly and affectionately remembered to you; Susan the same or something like it. Goodbye Yr most afft daughter

SARAH M FULLER.

ALS (MH: fMS Am 1086 [9:26]). *Addressed:* Hon. Timothy Fuller M.C. / Washington. D.C. *Postmark:* Groton MS Dec 22. *Endorsed:* My daughter S. Margtt / Recd 27. Dec. 1824.

original, interesting] original, interest⟨t⟩ing

1. Ann Dana (1800–1864), daughter of Samuel and Rebecca Dana of Groton, married John Sever of Kingston on 10 October 1825 (*GVR*; *Dana Family*, p. 41).

2. The Reverend Samuel Barrett (1795–1866) had received calls from churches in Philadelphia, Baltimore, and Keene, New Hampshire, but took instead the Twelfth Congregational Society of Boston, where he was ordained on 9 February 1825. A graduate of Harvard (1818), Barrett was active in the organization of the American Unitarian Association. In 1832 he married Margaret Fuller's friend Mary Susan Greenwood (1805–74) (*Heralds*, 2:239–41; Harvard archives; Isaac J. Greenwood, "William Pitt Greenwood," *Memorial Biographies*, 1:271).

3. Son of a judge, Charles Wentworth Upham (1802–75) graduated from Harvard in 1821 and was ordained in 1824 at Salem. He retired from the ministry in 1844 and began a successful career in politics. On 24 March 1826 he married Ann Susan Holmes, daughter of the Reverend Abiel Holmes of Cambridge (*Heralds*, 3:144–47).

4. Susanna Sarah McKean (1805–87), daughter of Joseph and Amy Swasey McKean, married Charles Folsom (1794–1872), then a teacher at Harvard and later the librarian of the Boston Athenaeum (*CVR*; *MVR* 383:78; *DAB*).

5. Thomas Buckminster Curtis (1795–1871), son of Thomas Curtis of Boston, was a distant relative of Timothy Fuller's. First a naval officer, then a merchant, Curtis married Maria Osborne Sargent (1803–35), daughter of the Honorable Daniel and Mary Frazier Sargent, on 1 December 1824 (*CVR*; *CC*, 8 December 1824; Samuel C. Clarke, *Records of Some of the Descendants of William Curtis, Roxbury 1632* [Boston, 1869], p. 192; Richard D. Pierce, *The Records of the First Church in Boston*, Publications of the Colonial Society of Massachusetts, vols. 39–41).

49. To Timothy Fuller

Groton January 5th. 1825

My dear father,

I have had the pleasure of receiving two letters from you this term, one on the thirtieth of December and one yesterday, accompanied by the Albion.[1] You mention in yesterdays letter, that you had sent me two or three numbers of the Albion; I received but one before yesterday, but I have a number of the "Baltimore patriot."[2]

This house at present bears no slight resemblance to a hospital; Miss Prescott has been very ill for the last two days; she is better today. I have been very unhappy that I could not go and help take

145

care of her how delightful it would be to me, now, to be her sister and then I should have an undeniable right to attend on her. But are not the privileges of a daughter superior to those of a sister? Miss Prescott has honored me by allowing me to call myself her adopted daughter, but it seems no one, (when it comes to the proof) will allow my claims to relationship any validity. I have been very sick myself but I am now well I am very grateful not only to my beloved friend, but to her amiable sisters Mary and Lucretia for their kindness and attention to me. I will not say that they supplied the place of my own mother, whom I have never seen equalled in the tenderness and assiduity with which she devotes herself to her sick friends, but they have done all I could wish; far more than I could expect. Miss Davis, Virginia and Miss Whitney are, the two first recovered, and the latter convalescent.[3] Miss Stedman and Miss Tarbell are now sick and Mary Prescott quite unwell.[4]

I am very glad you have given your two hundred thousand to La Fayette. Had the bill not passed the house an indelible stain would have been left on American glory.[5] I wish the sum had been doubled; then it would have been a noble reward as it is it seems a more honest[n] compensation for his past services. But it is sufficient as it will enable our brave friend if he pleases to end his glorious life in the country of his adoption.

I received a letter from mother (the first since I left home) on Monday with one from my uncle, I think it did me more good than any medicine I swallowed. I fear she is not very well though she does not mention her own health I study this term Geo Enfields Philosophy, Chemistry and Lord Kames's Criticisms.[6] I shall be glad, on the whole, when I have finished this[n] course of study and go back to my beloved study, the languages. Not that this is[n] disagreeable to me but I love them best. Your affectionate daughter

S. M. FULLER

I folded the letter in such a hurry that I did not observe that the third page was not dry I spoil every thing by my impetuosity but if you will excuse the blots this once the next letter shall be very fair

ALS (MH: fMS Am 1086 [9:29]). *Addressed:* For / Hon. Timothy Fuller, M.C. / Washington D.C. *Postmark:* Groton M. Jany 5. *Endorsed: Jan.* / From Sarah Margarett— / Recd 10. 5. Jan. 1825—

more honest] more ⟨?⟩ honest
I have finished this] I have ↑ finished ↓ this
that this is] that this ⟨was⟩ is

1. The *Albion* was an eclectic weekly magazine founded in 1822 by Dr. John S.

Bartlett (1790–1863), a British physician and journalist who had settled in Boston. It was known for its high literary quality (*DAB*).

2. The *Baltimore Patriot & Mercantile Advertiser*, established in 1812, was being published by Isaac Munroe.

3. Virginia must be Virginia Shaw, but which Miss Whitney she means is unclear. A catalogue for the Prescott school in 1826 lists Mary Wyman Whitney of Boston and Sophia Whitney of Cambridge as students, but we do not know whether either of them was enrolled in 1824–25 (*Catalogue of the Teachers and Pupils of the Young Ladies' Seminary, in Groton, Mass., for the Year Ending November, 1826* [Concord, 1826]).

4. Miss Stedman is unidentified; Miss Tarbell is probably Mary Elizabeth Tarbell (1809–98), daughter of John and Amelia Tarbell of Cambridge, whom the Fullers knew quite well. She was later married twice: first to George Blake, Jr., then, following his death, to Charles O. Whitmore (1807–95) (*CVR; CC*, 7 October 1835; Francis Whitmore, *The Whitmore Genealogy* [n.p., 1907], p. 101). The Mary Prescott mentioned here is a student, not the teacher.

5. In recognition of the service of the Marquis de Lafayette to the nation, bills were introduced in both houses of Congress on 21 December 1824 to grant him $200,000 and one township of land on any of the unappropriated lands in the United States. The House bill passed on 22 December with the support of Timothy Fuller (*Register of Debates in Congress*, 18th Congress, 2d sess.).

6. William Enfield's *Institutes of Natural Philosophy, Theoretical and Experimental* (London, 1785) had gone through four American editions, the most recent published in Boston in 1824. Beginning with the second English and first American editions, the *Institutes* had "an introduction to the first principles of chemistry." Henry Home, Lord Kames, wrote *Elements of Criticism* (Edinburgh, 1762), a standard text at this time.

50. To Timothy Fuller

Groton 31st Jany 1825.

My dear father

I received on Thursday the Albion with a few lines from you which gave me pleasure as they afforded me the assurance that you were well. I heard the same day through the medium of Miss Ann Dana, that you were in fine health and spirits. As the great the eventful day approaches, I am sensible that you must be more and more deeply engaged, and, I do not indulge the hope of hearing from you till the great political contest is terminated; I hope, by a happy and honorable event. I suspect by the Stoical tone of indifference and calmness which you would assume that the hopes of Mr Adams's friends are not so high as formerly. Indeed, (when I was at home) I perceived that you were by no means as sanguine as you had almost uniformly been from the commencement of the canvass. Your letters last winter so often closed with the decisive sentence of "Mr Adams *will* be president," and now you appear to waver in your expectations between Mr A and General Jackson.[1] Pray, does the General ever

147

remind you of your Seminole speech?[2] I reperused it the other day. I begun intending certainly to write a long letter but I cannot fill my paper, our messenger goes to the post office immediately Adieu you shall hear from me again this week Yr aff daughter

AL (MH: fMS Am 1086 [9:30]). *Addressed:* Hon Timothy Fuller. M.C. / Washington. D.C. *Postmark:* Groton MS Jany 31. *Endorsed:* Sarah Margarett F.— / Recd 6. Feb. 1825— / Answd Same day—

1. In the contest for the presidency in 1824, Timothy Fuller had worked for John Quincy Adams.

2. On 2 and 3 February 1819, Fuller spoke during the debate on a resolution to disapprove the proceedings in the trial and execution of Alexander Arbuthnot and Robert Ambrister, two British subjects whom Andrew Jackson had captured in the first Seminole war. While he praised Jackson's service in New Orleans, Fuller denounced the general for his conduct of the war against the Seminoles (*The Debates and Proceedings of the Congress of the United States*, 15th Cong., 2d sess.).

51. To Timothy Fuller

Groton 14th Feb. 1825.

My dear father,

Your letter of the 6th inst reached me yesterday accompanied by the Albion. That, dated the 15th, was not received until Thursday, mine, I think, was mailed on Wednesday, consequently I could not acknowledge the receipt of yours. I believe, papa, if you will take the trouble to overlook my letters, that you will find (though, I confess, my general want of that exactitude necessary to please *men* of *business* may have given you just reason to suspect me) that I *have endeavored* to comply with your wishes in this respect, as far as I know them; the receipt is always mentioned, I fancy though perhaps the dates may not be. I will try to remember in future. I have received six of the following dates the 22d and 27th Dec, 3d 13th and 27th Jan, and one this month already mentioned. You desired me, sometime since to send you the notes of the [*illegible*] it is so seldom that I have it in my power to do any thing to compensate you in the least degree for your multiplied kindnesses, that it is a subject of extreme regret to me when you express the slightest wish which I cannot fulfil (the superlative is not inapplicable here) but it is not in my power to comply with your desire on this head, for I cannot copy music and although I have the notes, they are bound in one of my music books. I should always, as you have desired send you word how I do, but when I reperuse the letter, these formal notices of my health and well being look *so* egotistical, they remind me so forcibly of the invariable beginning of the little girl's letters with whom I used to go to school "I take this opportunity to inform you that we are all well and hoping that you enjoy the same blessing." Besides, mon cher pere, you do not conform to your own rule; not once this winter have you told me whether you are well, ill, or indifferent. However, if you wish it 't is enough, here it comes without any more prosing. "J' ai un rhume avec une tous qui me génent beaucoup, d' ailleurs, je me trouve asser bien.[1]

By the emphasis laid on the word slovenliness I see what you think of my letters. I confess that I do not bestow on you that attention that I do on other correspondents, who will I think be more critical and less kind.[2] I have abused your indulgence I own. I must request that you will burn my letters, all that you now have, let this affair of confessions, extenuations and palliations share the common lot; and I will in future assume a *fairer outer* guise at least in my epistles though this matter may not recommend them more highly to your eye, mind's eye I mean. Indeed, I cannot make myself interesting to you; to your strictures on my conduct manners &c however valuable to me I can return nothing but thanks; my delineations of such scenes and characters as I meet with in my retired situation, however much matter of reflection they may afford to me, would not probably interest you, who can contemplate human nature on so much more extensive a scale and under so many diversified forms, neither if I thought my ideas and conclusions would interest you, should I be willing to impart them to the paper which might prove not a sure, though a senseless confidant. I have numberless things to say to you, that I hope will interest you who I know my dear, kind father makes all the views and affairs of his *little daughter* his own, and when we all meet again (and I trust that time is not far distant we shall have a delightful time by our own fireside then, we will all sing.

"Through pleasures and palaces though we may roam
Be it ever so humble theres no place like home."[3]

We have been in great trouble about poor Mr Clay the *peoples* were quite disappointed after all their long faces and "What a dreadful thing it *is's*" they heard he was alive and well, and even now they are at a loss whether to assume blue and black, or not.[4] The good Dr Eustis is gone, it seems;[5] you will have lamented his death, I know, goodbye Your ever affectionate daughter

SARAH M. FULLER.

149

ALS (MH: fMS Am 1086 [9:31]). *Addressed:* Hon. Timothy Fuller. M.C. / Washington D.C.— *Endorsed: 14. Feb.* / Sarah Margarett F.—Recd 19. Feb. 1825—

1. "I have a cold with a cough that inconveniences me a great deal, but other than that I am well enough."

2. In his letter of 6 February (MH) her father admonished her to acknowledge all his letters by date, to record her health in each, and to remember his lessons in "chirography" and "particularly to join all the letters & syllables of each word." He went on to say, "In looking at some of my letters written when in college & since, I was lately very much mortified to find them studied & quaint, not however in general liable to the charge of slovenliness." Margaret read the sentence as an implied criticism of her letters—which it may have been.

3. From John Howard Payne's *Clari, the Maid of Milan* (1823).

4. The *Boston Daily Advertiser* for 8 February 1825 said: "A report was current at Baltimore on Wednesday [the second], and at New York on Friday, that Mr. [Henry] Clay had fallen in a duel with a member of the Pennsylvania delegation. The mail of the following day afforded proof that the report was without foundation."

5. William Eustis had died on 6 February (*DAB*).

52. To the Marquis de Lafayette

[Boston?]

[16? June? 1825?]

Sir,

I expect the pleasure of seeing you tonight.[1] If I should not be disappointed, the timidity appropriate to youth and the presence of many strangers will probably prevent me from expressing the ardent sentiment of affection and enthusiastic admiration[n] which pervades my soul whenever I think of you; I cannot resist the desire of placing my idea before your mind if it be but for a moment; I cannot resist the desire of saying, "La Fayette I love I admire you;" I am sure that this expression of feeling, though from one of the most insignificant of that vast population whose hearts echo your name, will not be utterly inconsequent to you; I am sure that not one of that people in whose cause you consumed, amid the toils and hardships of a camp, the loveliest years of human existence and from whom you are now receiving a tribute of gratitude unparalleled in the annals of history as your extraordinary life, is inconsequent to you. Sir the contemplation of a character such as yours fills the soul with a noble ambition. Should we both live, and it is possible to a female, to whom the avenues of glory are seldom accessible, I will recal my name to your recollection

Accept the sincere homage of a youthful heart and dear friend of my country, farewell.

SARAH MARGARETT FULLER.

ALS (NIC).

enthusiastic admiration] enthusiastic ⟨?⟩ admiration

1. The Marquis de Lafayette (1757–1834) was on a triumphal tour of America in 1824–25. Twice he was in Boston: from 21 August to 2 September 1824 and from 15 to 21 June 1825. He was feted almost every night, but only two of the gatherings seem likely choices for the one Fuller mentions here: on 27 August 1824 Governor William Eustis, Timothy Fuller's friend, gave a state banquet, and on 16 June 1825 Mayor Josiah Quincy gave a reception at his home. It was probably the latter party to which Fuller went, though she may have seen Lafayette at any time during his two visits to Boston (J. Bennett Nolan, *Lafayette in America Day by Day* [Baltimore, 1934], pp. 244–47, 292–93).

53. To Susan Prescott

Cambridge, 11 July 1825

Having excused myself from accompanying my honored father to church, which I always do in the afternoon, when possible, I devote to you the hours which Ariosto and Helvetius ask of my eyes,—as, lying on my writing-desk, they put me in mind that they must return this week to their owner.[1]

You keep me to my promise of giving you some sketch of my pursuits. I rise a little before five, walk an hour, and then practise on the piano, till seven, when we breakfast. Next I read French,—Sismondi's Literature of the South of Europe,—till eight, then two or three lectures in Brown's Philosophy.[2] About half-past nine I go to Mr. Perkins's school and study Greek till twelve, when, the school being dismissed, I recite, go home, and practise again till dinner, at two.[3] Sometimes, if the conversation is very agreeable, I lounge for half an hour over the dessert, though rarely so lavish of time. Then, when I can, I read two hours in Italian, but I am often interrupted. At six, I walk, or take a drive. Before going to bed, I play or sing, for half an hour or so, to make all sleepy, and, about eleven, retire to write a little while in my journal, exercises on what I have read, or a series of characteristics which I am filling up according to advice. Thus, you see, I am learning Greek, and making acquaintance with metaphysics, and French and Italian literature.

"How," you will say, "can I believe that my indolent, fanciful, pleasure-loving pupil, perseveres in such a course?" I feel the power of industry growing every day, and, besides the all-powerful motive of ambition, and a new stimulus lately given through a friend.[4] I have learned to believe that nothing, no! not perfection, is unattainable.

I am determined on distinction, which formerly I thought to win at an easy rate; but now I see that long years of labor must be given to secure even the *"succes de societe,"*—which, however, shall never content me. I see multitudes of examples of persons of genius, utterly deficient in grace and the power of pleasurable excitement. I wish to combine both. I know the obstacles in my way. I am wanting in that intuitive tact and polish, which nature has bestowed upon some, but which I must acquire. And, on the other hand, my powers of intellect, though sufficient, I suppose, are not well disciplined. Yet all such hindrances may be overcome by an ardent spirit. If I fail, my consolation shall be found in active employment.

ELfr, from *Memoirs*, 1:52–54; also in Chevigny, pp. 55–56.

1. The poet Lodovico Ariosto (1474–1533) published his *Orlando Furioso* in 1516 (revised in 1532). The author of comedies, satires, and sonnets, Ariosto served members of the Este family for a number of years. The freethinking Claude Adrien Helvétius (1715–71) was one of "Les Philosophes," a group of eighteenth-century authors whose members included Diderot and Condorcet. Helvétius' *Oeuvres complètes* (1774) was published at Liège.

2. Leonard Simonde de Sismondi (1773–1842) was a friend of Madame de Staël. A Geneva-born historian and political economist, Sismondi published *De la littérature du midi de l'Europe* (1813) in four volumes. Thomas Brown (1778–1820), professor of moral philosophy at Edinburgh, had published his *Lectures on the Philosophy of the Human Mind* in Edinburgh in 1820. American editions had been published at Andover in 1822 and at Philadelphia in 1824. This and other references in her letters show Fuller to have been acquainted with the Scottish common-sense philosophers.

3. George William Perkins (1804–56), son of the Honorable Enoch Perkins of Hartford, graduated from Yale in 1824 and taught for a year at Cambridgeport before attending the Yale Divinity School, from which he graduated in 1828. He later served pulpits in Connecticut, Chicago, and Montreal. His first wife was a Miss Dickenson (d. 1832) of Montreal and his second was a Mrs. Munger of Rochester, New York. Among Fuller's classmates in Perkins' school was Richard Henry Dana, Jr. (*Record of the Class of 1824 in Yale College* [New Haven, 1875], p. 30).

4. Probably Lydia Francis, whom Fuller describes in letter 56.

54. To Susan Prescott

Cambridge, 5 March 1826

Duke Nicholas is to succeed the Emperor Alexander, thus relieving Europe from the sad apprehension of evil to be inflicted by the brutal Constantine, and yet depriving the Holy Alliance of its very soul. We may now hope more strongly for the liberties of unchained Europe; we look in anxious suspense for the issue of the struggle of Greece, the result of which seems to depend on the new autocrat.[1] I have lately been reading Anastasius, the Greek Gil Blas, which has excited and delighted me; but I do not think you like works of this cast.[2] You did not like my sombre and powerful Ormond,—though this is superior to Ormond[3] in every respect; it translates you to another scene, hurls you into the midst of the burning passions of the East, whose vicissitudes are, however, interspersed by deep pauses of shadowy reflective scenes, which open upon you like the green watered little vales occasionally to be met with in the burning desert. There is enough of history to fix profoundly the attention, and prevent you from revolting from scenes profligate and terrific, and such characters as are never to be met with in our paler climes. How delighted am I to read a book which can absorb me to tears and shuddering,—not by individual traits of beauty, but by the spirit of adventure,—happiness which one seldom enjoys after childhood in this blest age, so philosophic, free, and enlightened to a miracle, but far removed from the ardent dreams and soft credulity of the world's youth. Sometimes I think I would give all our gains for those times when young and old gathered in the feudal hall, listening with soul-absorbing transport to the romance of the minstrel, unrestrained and regardless of criticism, and when they worshipped nature, not as high-dressed and pampered, but as just risen from the bath.

ELfr, from *Memoirs*, 1:54–55.

1. Alexander I, emperor of Russia since 1801, died on 1 December 1825. After a three-week interregnum, his youngest brother, Nicholas, became tsar of Russia instead of his older brother, Constantine (A. W. Ward, G. W. Prothero, and Stanley Leathes, eds., *Cambridge Modern History* [New York, 1907], 10:190–204; G. M. D. Howat, *Dictionary of World History* [London, 1973]). The Greeks had begun a rebellion against Turkey on 2 April 1821. The two countries fought alone until 1824, when the Turks were aided by Mehemet Ali of Egypt. A month after Fuller's letter, the English and Russians signed the Protocol of St. Petersburg, the first formal step toward Greek independence. Greece did not achieve independence until January 1833, when Otto I, a Bavarian, assumed the Greek throne (*Cambridge Modern History*, 10:179–204).

2. *Anastasius: or, Memoirs of a Greek* (London, 1819) was a picaresque tale published anonymously by Thomas Hope (ca. 1770–1831), a wealthy London art connoisseur. *The Adventures of Gil Blas of Santillane* (Paris?, 1715–35), which Fuller compares to Hope's novel, was written by Alain-René Le Sage (1668–1747). The French novel, too, was a picaresque romance, known for its positive view of humanity.

3. In her notebook for 9 February 1825, Fuller copied extracts from Charles Brockden Brown's *Ormond; or, the Secret Witness* (New York, 1799) (MH: fMS Am 1086 [Box C]).

55. To Susan Prescott

Cambridge, 14 May 1826

I am studying Madame de Stael, Epictetus, Milton, Racine, and Castilian ballads, with great delight.[1] There's an assemblage for you. Now tell me, had you rather be the brilliant De Stael or the useful Edgeworth?[2]—though De Stael is useful too, but it is on the grand scale, on liberalizing, regenerating principles, and has not the immediate practical success that Edgeworth has. I met with a parallel the other day between Byron and Rousseau, and had a mind to send it to you, it was so excellent.[3]

ELfr, from *Memoirs*, 1:55.

1. Fuller early knew the work of Anne Louise Germaine, baronne de Staël-Holstein (1766–1817), including *Corinne* (Paris, 1807), *Delphine* (Geneva, 1802), and *De l'Allemagne* (Paris, 1813). The "Castilian ballads" were probably John Gibson Lockhart's *Ancient Spanish Ballads, Historical and Romantic* (Edinburgh, 1823).

2. Maria Edgeworth was known for her moral didacticism.

3. Fuller was enthusiastic about both George Gordon, Lord Byron (1788–1824), whose poetry she often quoted, and Jean-Jacques Rousseau (1712–88), whose novels were quite familiar to her (though the reference here may well be to his *Confessions*).

56. To Susan Prescott

Cambridge, 10 January 1827

As to my studies, I am engrossed in reading the elder Italian poets, beginning with Berni, from whom I shall proceed to Pulci and Politian.[1] I read very critically. Miss Francis and I think of reading Locke, as introductory to a course of English metaphysics, and then De Stael on Locke's system.[2] Allow me to introduce this lady to you as a most interesting woman, in my opinion. She is a natural person,—a most rare thing in this age of cant and pretension. Her conversation is charming,—she brings all her powers to bear upon it; her style is varied, and she has a very pleasant and spirited way of thinking. I should judge, too, that she possesses peculiar purity of mind. I am going to spend this evening with her, and wish you were to be with us.

ELfr, from *Memoirs*, 1:55–56.

1. Francesco Berni (1497–1536) was a satirist and burlesque poet. Luigi Pulci (1432–84) wrote an epic, *Il Morgante Maggiore*, in 1483. "Politian" was Angelo Poliziano (pseudonym of Angelo Ambrogini) (1454–94), an Italian humanist and poet.

2. Lydia Maria Francis (1802–80), a longtime friend of Margaret Fuller's, married David Child (1794–1874) in 1828. She was an editor, author, and abolitionist (*NAW*). The two young women were probably reading Madame de Staël's *De l'Allemagne*, bk. 2, pt. 3, chap. 2, "De la philosophie angloise," which discusses Locke.

57. To Susan Prescott

Cambridge, 3 January 1828

I am reading Sir William Temple's works, with great pleasure.[1] Such enlarged views are rarely to be found combined with such acuteness and discrimination. His style, though diffuse, is never verbose or overloaded, but beautifully expressive; 't is English, too, though he was an accomplished linguist, and wrote much and well in French, Spanish, and Latin. The latter he used, as he says of the Bishop of Munster, (with whom he corresponded in that tongue,) "more like a man of the court and of business than a scholar."[2] He affected not Augustan niceties, but his expressions are free and appropriate. I have also read a most entertaining book, which I advise you to read, (if you have not done so already,) Russell's Tour in Germany.[3] There you will find more intelligent and detailed accounts than I have seen anywhere of the state of the German universities, Viennese court, secret associations, Plica Polonica, and other very interesting matters. There is a minute account of the representative government given to his subjects by the Duke of Weimar.[4] I have passed a luxurious afternoon, having been in bed from dinner till tea, reading Rammohun Roy's book, and framing dialogues aloud on every argument beneath the sun.[5] Really, I have not had my mind so exercised for months; and I have felt a gladiatorial disposition lately, and don't enjoy mere light conversation. The love of knowledge is prodigiously kindled within my soul of late; I study much and reflect more, and feel an aching wish for some person with whom I might talk fully and openly.

Did you ever read the letters and reflections of Prince de Ligne, the most agreeable man of his day?[6] I have just had it, and if it is new to you, I recommend it as an agreeable book to read at night just before you go to bed. There is much curious matter concerning Catharine II.'s famous expedition into Taurida, which puts down some of the romantic stories prevalent on that score, but relates more surprising realities. Also it gives much interesting information about that noble philosopher, Joseph II., and about the Turkish tactics and national character.[7]

ELfr, from *Memoirs*, 1:56–57.

1. Sir William Temple (1628–99) was an English author, diplomat, and statesman (*DNB*).

2. Temple wrote of Christopher Bernard von Ghalen, prince-bishop of Münster, "He speaks the only good *Latin* that I have yet met with in *Germany,* and more like a Man of Court and Business than a Scholar" (*The Works of Sir William Temple, Bart* [London, 1740], 2:4). In June 1665 Temple was sent on a mission to Münster to induce the bishop to attack Holland during the Anglo-Dutch war. The scheme fell through, however, when the bishop outwitted the English in spite of Temple's efforts.

3. John Russell, *A Tour in Germany and Some of the Southern Provinces of the Austrian Empire, in the Years 1820, 1821, 1822* (Edinburgh, 1824).

4. Russell devotes the whole of chap. 3 of his book to the German universities, especially Jena. He later spends four pages describing "plica polonica," a disease of the scalp that was prevalent in the ghetto in Cracow. In chap. 2 Russell praises the administration of Karl August, Herzog von Sachsen-Weimar (1757–1828), "the most popular prince in Europe." The Grand Duke is best known as Goethe's patron in Weimar (*OCGL*).

5. Rammohun Roy (1772?–1833) was a Brahmin from Bengal who had converted to Christianity. In 1820 he published *The Precepts of Jesus, the Guide to Peace and Happiness* (Calcutta) in an effort to convert his countrymen. In November 1821 Roy became an object of controversy between the Unitarians and Congregationalists in Boston when the *Christian Register* published an article about his supposed sympathy with Unitarian principles. Fuller probably read the edition of Roy's book published in New York in 1825.

6. Charles-Joseph, prince de Ligne (1735–1814), became a general in the Austrian service. A friend of Voltaire and Madame de Staël, Ligne wrote *Mélanges militaires, littéraires, sentimentaires* (Dresden, 1795–1811).

7. Ligne devotes several chapters of his *Mélanges* to Catherine II of Russia (1729–96). He wanted, he said, to correct the popular view of the ruler. The ambitious Catherine had extended Russian dominion to the Black Sea by moving into the Crimea (or Taurica, as it was then known). Joseph II (1741–91) of Austria was Holy Roman emperor from 1765 to 1790. Not only did he strengthen the power of the Habsburg dynasty, but he also reformed criminal law, abolished serfdom in 1781, and wrote a Patent of Toleration for Protestants in the same year. Ligne observes that the Turks did indeed have a military method, despite their general reputation to the contrary. He describes their practice of crying "Allah!" and of displaying chopped-off heads to intimidate their enemies.

58. To [?]

17 December 1829

The following instance of beautiful credulity, in Rousseau, has taken my mind greatly. This remote seeking for the decrees of fate, this feeling of a destiny, casting its shadows from the very morning of thought, is the most beautiful species of idealism in our day. 'T is finely manifested in Wallenstein, where the two common men sum up their superficial observations on the life and doings of Wallenstein, and show that, not until this agitating crisis, have they caught any idea of the deep thoughts which shaped that hero, who has, without their feeling it moulded *their* existence.[1]

"Tasso," says Rousseau, "had predicted my misfortunes. Have you remarked that Tasso has this peculiarity, that you cannot take from his work a single strophe, nor from any strophe a single line, nor from any line a single word, without disarranging the whole poem? Very well! take away the strophe I speak of, the stanza has no connection with those that precede or follow it; it is absolutely useless. *Tasso probably wrote it involuntarily, and without comprehending it himself.*"[2]

As to the impossibility of taking from Tasso without disarranging the poem, &c., I dare say 't is not one whit more justly said of his, than of any other narrative poem. *Mais, n' importe,* 't is sufficient if Rousseau believed this. I found the stanza in question; admire its meaning beauty.

I hope you have Italian enough to appreciate the singular perfection in expression. If not, look to Fairfax's Jerusalem Delivered, Canto 12, Stanza 77; but Rousseau says these lines have no connection with what goes before, or after; *they are preceded,* stanza 76, by these three lines, which he does not think fit to mention.

> "Misero mostro d'infelice amore;
> Misero mostro a cui sol pena e degna
> Dell' immensa impietà, la vita indegna.
>
> Vivrò fra i miei tormenti e fra le cure,
> Mie giuste furie, forsennato errante.
> Paventerò l'ombre solinghe e scure,
> Che l'primo error mi recheranno avante:
>
> E del sol che scoprì le mie sventure,
> A schivo ed in orrore avrò il sembiante.
> Temerò me medesmo; e da me stesso
> Sempre fuggendo, avrò me sempre appresso."[3]
>
> La Gerusalemme Liberata, C.XII.76,77.

ELfr, from *Memoirs,* 1:222–24.

1. Fuller refers here to Schiller's *Wallenstein* trilogy, *Wallensteins Lager, Die Piccolomini,* and *Wallensteins Tod* (Tübingen, 1800), based on the life of Albrecht Wallenstein (1583–1634), a general in the Thirty Years' War.

2. The reference is to bk. 7 of Rousseau's *Confessions.*

3. Torquato Tasso (1544–95) published his heroic epic poem *Gerusalemme Liberata* in 1575. Edward Fairfax (d. 1635) translated the poem as *Godfrey of Bulloigne, or the Recoverie of Jerusalem* (London, 1600). His translation of the lines quoted by Fuller is as follows:

A sad example must I still remain;
A woeful monster of unhappy love,
Who still must live, lest death is comfort prove:

Still must I live in anguish, grief, and care;
Furies my guilty conscience that torment,
The ugly shades, dark night, and troubled air,
In grisly forms her slaughter still present;
Madness and death about my bed repair,
Hell gapeth wide to swallow up his tent;
Swift from myself I run, myself I fear,
Yet still my hell within myself I bear.

59. To [?]

19 December 1829

I shall always be glad to have you come to me when saddened. The melancholic does not misbecome you. The lights of your character are *wintry*. They are generally inspiriting, life-giving, but, if perpetual, would glare too much on the tired sense; one likes sometimes a cloudy day, with its damp and warmer breath,—its gentle, down-looking shades. Sadness in some is intolerably ungraceful and oppressive; it affects one like a cold rainy day in June or September, when all pleasure departs with the sun; everything seems out of place and irrelative to the time; the clouds are fog, the atmosphere leaden,—but 't is not so with you.

ELfr, from *Memoirs*, 1:80.

60. To [?]

[ca. winter] 1829–1830

I have hesitated much whether to tell you what you ask about my religion. You are mistaken! I have not formed an opinion. I have determined not to form settled opinions at present. Loving or feeble natures need a positive religion, a visible refuge, a protection, as much in the passionate season of youth as in those stages nearer to the grave. But mine is not such. My pride is superior to any feelings I have yet experienced: my affection is strong admiration, not the necessity of giving or receiving assistance or sympathy. When disappointed, I do not ask or wish consolation,—I wish to know and feel my pain, to investigate its nature and its source; I will not have my thoughts diverted, or my feelings soothed; 't is therefore that my young life is so singularly barren of illusions. I know, I feel the time must come when this proud and impatient heart shall be stilled, and turn from the ardors of Search and Action, to lean on something above. But—shall I say it?—the thought of that calmer era is to me a thought of deepest sadness; so remote from my present being is that future existence, which still the mind may conceive. I believe in Eternal Progression. I believe in a God, a Beauty and Perfection to which I am to strive all my life for assimilation. From these two articles of belief, I draw the rules by which I strive to regulate my life. But, though I reverence all religions as necessary to the happiness of man, I am yet ignorant of the religion of Revelation. Tangible promises! well defined hopes! are things of which I do not *now* feel the need. At present, my soul is intent on this life, and I think of religion as its rule; and, in my opinion, this is the natural and proper course from youth to age. What I have written is not hastily concocted, it has a meaning. I have given you, in this little space, the substance of many thoughts, the clues to many cherished opinions. 'T is a subject on which I rarely speak. I never said so much but once before. I have here given you all I know, or think, on the most important of subjects—could you but read understandingly!

ELfr, from *Memoirs*, 1:135–36; also in Chevigny, pp. 166–67.

61. To [?]

[ca. winter] 1829–1830

I have had,—while staying a day or two in Boston,—some of Shirley's, Ford's, and Heywood's plays from the Athenaeum.[1] There are some noble strains of proud rage, and intellectual, but most poetical, all-absorbing, passion. One of the finest fictions I recollect in those specimens of the Italian novelists,—which you, I think, read when I did,—noble, where it illustrated the Italian national spirit, is ruined by the English novelist, who has transplanted it to an uncongenial soil; yet he has given it beauties which an Italian eye could not see, by investing the actors with deep, continuing, truly English affections.

ELfr, from *Memoirs*, 1:115.

1. Fuller had been reading the English dramatists James Shirley (1596–1666), John Ford (b. 1586), and John Heywood (1497?–1580?). Several of Shirley's plays had been reprinted in the mid-1820s; John Ford's *Dramatic Works* appeared in London in 1827 (*DNB*).

62. To Susan Prescott

Cambridge, January 1830

You need not fear to revive painful recollections. I often think of those sad experiences. True, they agitate me deeply. But it was best so. They have had a most powerful effect on my character. I tremble at whatever looks like dissimulation. The remembrance of that evening subdues every proud, passionate impulse. My beloved supporter in those sorrowful hours, your image shines as fair to my mind's eye as it did in 1825, when I left you with my heart overflowing with gratitude for your singular and judicious tenderness.[1] Can I ever forget that to your treatment in that crisis of youth I owe the true life,—the love of Truth and Honor?

ELfr, from *Memoirs*, 1:57.

1. Fuller describes this crisis in *Memoirs*, 1:50–52.

63. To James F. Clarke

16 March 1830
[Cambridge?]

Half-past six, morning.—I have encountered that most common-place of glories, sunrise, (to say naught of being praised and wondered at by every member of the family in succession,) that I might have leisure to answer your note even as you requested. I thank you a thousand times for "The Rivals."[1] Alas!! I must leave my heart in the book, and spend the livelong morning in reading to a sick lady from some amusing story-book. I tell you of this act of (in my professedly unamiable self) most unwonted charity, for three several reasons. Firstly, and foremostly, because I think that you, being a socialist by vocation, a sentimentalist by nature, and a Channingite from force of

circumstances and fashion, will peculiarly admire this little self-sacrifice exploit. Secondly, because 't is neither conformable to the spirit
of the nineteenth century, nor the march of mind, that those churlish
reserves should be kept up between *the right and left hands,* which
belonged to ages of barbarism and prejudice, and could only have
been inculcated for their use. Thirdly, and lastly, the true lady-like
reason,—because I would fain have my corespondent enter into and
sympathize with my feelings of the moment.

As to the relationship; 't is, I find, on inquiry, by no means to
be compared with that between myself and ———,[2] of course, the
intimacy cannot be so great. But no matter; it will enable me to answer
your notes, and you will interest my imagination much more than if
I knew you better. But I am exceeding legitimate note-writing limits.
With a hope that this epistle may be legible to your undiscerning eyes,
I conclude,

your cousin only thirty-seven degrees removed,

M.

EL, from *Memoirs,* 1:62–63.

James Freeman Clarke, one of Fuller's closest friends, graduated from Harvard in
1829 and from the Divinity School in 1833. He went to Louisville, where he served
the Unitarian church until 1840, then returned to Boston in 1841 to organize a new
Unitarian congregation, the Church of the Disciples. In 1839 he married Anna (1814–
97), daughter of Harm Jan Huidekoper of Meadville, Pennsylvania. An early follower
of Goethe and Emerson, Clarke represented the development of radical thought among
the Unitarian clergy. He and Fuller worked closely together in the early 1830s, when
they both began to read German literature (Newton VR; Clarke, *Richard Hull,* p. 12;
MVR 474:141). This letter answers one from Clarke published in *Letters of JFC,* p.
9, in which he jokingly asked Fuller to investigate the degree of family relationship
between them and to see if it were not as close as that between her and another
distant cousin, George T. Davis. Clarke's maternal grandmother was Sarah Fuller,
daughter of Abraham Fuller of Newton (not to be confused with Margaret's uncle
Abraham W. Fuller); she married Colonel William Hull. This Fuller family descended
from Captain Matthew Fuller, who settled in Cambridge in 1644. Margaret's family
descended from Thomas Fuller of Woburn, a branch not connected to Captain Matthew (Samuel C. Clarke, *Records of Some of the Descendants of John Fuller Newton, 1644–
98* [Boston, 1898], pp. 8–11; William Hyslop Fuller, *Genealogy of Some Descendants of
Captain Matthew Fuller* [n.p., 1914], pp. 97, 128).

1. [Gerald Griffin], *The Rivals; Tracy's Ambition* (London, 1829).

2. George Davis (1810–77). Another member of the Harvard class of 1829, Davis
became a lawyer in 1832 and began a practice in his native Greenfield. Although he
was later a member of both houses of the Massachusetts Legislature and the U.S.
House of Representatives, he first devoted himself to journalism and founded the
Franklin Mercury. Though Thackeray once called him the "best conversationalist he met
in America," Fuller thought Davis' humor cruel. The details of his friendship with her
are meager, but it is clear from the Fuller family correspondence as well as from
fragmentary letters from Margaret to Davis (see letter 73) that she loved him during the
late 1820s and early 1830s. In 1834, however, he married Harriet T. Russell (1811–

62), a Boston woman whom Fuller and Clarke knew well (Greenfield VR; Francis M. Thompson, *History of Greenfield Shiretown of Franklin County, Massachusetts* [Greenfield, Mass., 1904], p. 1172).

64. To James F. Clarke

[ca. 24? March 1830]
[Cambridge?]

I cannot bring myself to write you what you wished.[1] You would be disappointed, at any rate, after all the solemn note of preparation; the consciousness of this would chill me now. Besides, I cannot be willing to leave with you such absolute *vagaries* in a tangible, examinable shape. I think of your after-smiles, of your colder moods. But I will tell you, when a fitting opportunity presents, all that can interest you, and perhaps more. And excuse my caution. I do not profess, I may not dare, to be generous in these matters.

ELfr, from *Memoirs*, 1:66.

Dated from Letters of JFC, *p. 11. This fragment is clearly from the letter Clarke mentions on 27 March 1830 and probably answers his of 19 March.*

1. Clarke had asked Fuller to comment on "my Louisa affair" (*Letters of JFC,* p. 10). During his undergraduate days at Harvard he had been in love with his cousin Sarah Louisa Hickman (1811–32), daughter of his aunt Ann Binney Hull Hickman (1787–1846). On 10 December 1828 Louisa married Samuel J. Smith. Years later, on a bizarre impulse, Clarke went to Louisa's tomb, opened her coffin, and meditated on her death (Clarke, *Richard Hull,* pp. 11, 14–15; *CC,* 12 November 1828, 13 February 1830; Arthur S. Bolster, Jr., *James Freeman Clarke: Disciple to Advancing Truth* [Boston, 1954], p. 65).

65. To James F. Clarke

[28? March 1830]
[Cambridge?]

I thank you for your note.[1] Ten minutes before I received it, I scarcely thought that anything again would make my stifled heart throb so warm a pulse of pleasure. Excuse my cold doubts, my selfish arrogance,—you will, when I tell you that this experiment has before had such uniform results; those who professed to seek my friendship, and whom, indeed, I have often truly loved, have always learned to content themselves with that inequality in the connection which I have never striven to veil. Indeed, I have thought myself more valued and better beloved, because the sympathy, the interest, were all on my side. True! such regard could never flatter my pride, nor gratify my affections, since it was paid not to myself, but to the need they had of me; still, it was dear and pleasing, as it has given me an opportunity of knowing and serving many lovely characters; and I cannot see that there is anything else for me to do on earth. And I should rejoice to cultivate generosity, since (see that *since*) affections gentler and more sympathetic are denied me.

I would have been a true friend to you; ever ready to solace your pains and partake your joy as far as possible. Yet I cannot but rejoice that I have met a person who could discriminate and reject a proffer of this sort. Two years ago I should have ventured to proffer you friendship, indeed, on seeing such an instance of pride in you; but I have gone through a sad process of feeling since, and those emotions, so necessarily repressed, have lost their simplicity, their ardent beauty. *Then*, there was nothing I might not have disclosed to a person capable of comprehending, had I ever seen such an one! Now there are many voices of the soul which I imperiously silence. This results not from any particular circumstance or event, but from a gradual ascertaining of realities.

I cannot promise you any limitless confidence, but I *can* promise that no timid caution, no haughty dread shall prevent my telling you the truth of my thoughts on any subject we may have in common. Will this satisfy you? Oh let it! suffer me to know you. [   ]

No other cousin or friend of any style is to see this note.

ELfr, from *Memoirs*, 1:66–68; also in Chevigny, pp. 102–3.

Her letter apparently answers his of 27 March 1830 (Letters of JFC, *pp. 11–12*).

1. Clarke had told Fuller, "I should have been happy in going further with you than with all before, but there must be an answering store" of emotional honesty (*Letters of JFC*, p. 12).

66.   To Amelia Greenwood

Tuesday Eveg.
Cambridge 30th March [1830]

My dear Amelia,

I have escaped from the parlour where Ive been sitting the livelong eveg playing auditor to Judge Weston, his jokes and anecdotes are pleasant enough but I fairly ache sitting three hours in boarding-school attitude hemming a ruffle and saying never a word.[1] Pa—always thinks my presence gives a finish to the scene;—but I absconded at last to read in solitude over an excellent little supper of dry bread and *lime-water*.

—How do you live or *do* you live? I hope so! Oh days of spring balm and still summery gloss my spirit is inebriate with your delights!— You know, Amelia, I've long wished that the customs of society would permit to be intoxicate *only once* as Ive read them to be in the [*illegible word*] et cetera— Well! I was so yesterday; Im sure of it— In the morng I went into the fields and passed the morng reading Moores Byron and inspiring delight in every breath. *Then* I was *happy*— But after I came home I sat down where the *west* wind could blow on my cheek and read Moore beginning with that song which made Byron's friend's wife so melancholy for three hours or so;[2] and I was in a kind of delireum I read senselessly and dreamed consciously at the same time; I have not been able to read so for ages. My heart was not gay and light as with hope nor proudly throbbing as with—oh words!!—it floated in luxury of realized bliss No! not *bliss felicity*.— But what skills it talking?— I only meant to tell your La' ship my wish was fulfilled

My whole being is Byronized at this moment c'est a dire my whole mind is possessed with one desire—to comprehend Byron once for all.

—I passed yesterday eveg at Mr Higginson's. Miss Storrow was so unkind to herself and me as to have the sick headach.—[3] What a splendid quantity of tragick talk is going on in society; every body hoping to have life diversified and self complacency flattened by somebody taking the trouble to knock down or shoot. I was at Helen's Friday, she walked back with me and on the way who should we meet but J. T come back from the asylum he had so sighed for near a week before 'twas necessary.[4] Ah quel rencontre! I was sadly *de trop* I assure you However this is neither the first time nor the last of my being so I grieve to say— Have you seen James?[5] he asked after you in the most *fraterial* way as T. Hook might phrase it. He brought me Retsch's Illust. of Hamlet spoiled in copying I presume for they were the weakest burlesque—and one could not trace any talent in the designs either.—[6]

Now I've written to you because I wished to do so and can only hope this farrago wont find you very triste or very *sâge*. I have not *yet* a bed to offer; mais le bon tem viendra Helen would have hurried your visit but I could not. You cant think how droll, dreary, and domestick she and M. looked sewing; writing;—drinking—molasses and water—[7] Adieu child of

M.

ALS (ICHi).

1. Nathan Weston (1782–1872), a Dartmouth graduate of 1803, was at this time associate justice of the Supreme Court of Maine. He became chief justice in 1834. In 1809 Judge Weston married Paulina Bass Cony (1787–1857), daughter of Judge Daniel C. Coney (*National Cyclopedia*, 7:503; Holman, *John Coney*, p. 169; MVR 302:255).

2. Thomas Moore edited *Letters and Journals of Lord Byron: With Notices of his Life* (London, 1830), which includes the anecdote about Byron's habit of sadly singing Moore's "Tyrolese Song of Liberty." Since Mary Shelley describes the scenes in her journal, she is undoubtedly the "friend's wife" Fuller mentions. Moore's poem appears in *The Works of Thomas Moore* (New York, 1825), 3:65–66, and in the Philadelphia edition of 1829, 2:385–86, the two editions most likely to have been available to Fuller.

3. Stephen Higginson (1770–1834), the steward at Harvard from 1818 to 1827, had first married Martha Salisbury (1771–1803), then Louisa Storrow (1786–1864). Undoubtedly Miss Storrow is either Louisa Higginson's sister, Ann Gillam Storrow, who lived with them, or their niece, Ann Louisa Storrow (1810–37). The tone of Fuller's comment suggests the younger woman. The Higginsons were the parents of Thomas Wentworth Higginson (1823–1911), Margaret Fuller's biographer (Higginson, *Reverend Francis Higginson*, p. 28; *CC*, 23 June 1837; John Clark, *Records of the Descendants of Hugh Clark of Watertown* [Boston, 1866], p. 83; John Wentworth, *The Wentworth Genealogy* [Boston, 1878], 1:514).

4. Presumably this is Helen Davis, a friend of both Fuller and Amelia Greenwood; J. T. is unidentified.

5. James Freeman Clarke.

6. Moritz Retzsch (1779–1857), a German painter and designer, had published *Gallerie zu Shakspeare's dramatischen Werken* (London and Leipzig, 1828).

7. If Helen is Helen Davis, then M. is probably her sister, Margaret.

67. To James F. Clarke

Saturday evening, 1 May 1830
[Cambridge?]

The holy moon and merry-toned wind of this night woo to a vigil at the open window; a half-satisfied interest urges me to live, love and perish! in the noble, wronged heart of Basil;[1] my Journal, which lies before me, tempts to follow out and interpret the as yet only half-understood musings of the past week. Letter-writing, compared with any of these things, takes the ungracious semblance of a duty. I have, nathless, after a two hours' reverie, to which this resolve and its preliminaries have formed excellent warp, determined to sacrifice this hallowed time to you.

It did not in the least surprise me that you found it impossible at the time to avail yourself of the confidential privileges I had invested you with. On the contrary, I only wonder that we should ever, after such gage given and received, (not by a look or tone, but by letter,) hold any frank communication. Preparations are good in life, prologues ruinous. I felt this even before I sent my note, but could not persuade myself to consign an impulse so embodied, to oblivion, from any consideration of expediency.

ELfr, from *Memoirs*, 1:68–69.

1. The main character in the anonymous *Basil Barrington and His Friends* (London, 1830).

68. To James F. Clarke

4 May 1830
[Cambridge?]

I have greatly wished to see among us such a person of genius as the nineteenth century can afford—*i.e.*, one who has tasted in the morning of existence the extremes of good and ill, both imaginative and real. I had imagined a person endowed by nature with that acute sense of Beauty, (*i.e.*, Harmony or Truth,) and that vast capacity of desire, which give soul to love and ambition. I had wished this person might grow up to manhood alone (but not alone in crowds); I would have placed him in a situation so retired, so obscure, that he would quietly, but without bitter sense of isolation, stand apart from all surrounding him. I would have had him go on steadily, feeding his mind with congenial love, hopefully confident that if he only nourished his existence into perfect life, Fate would, at fitting season, furnish an atmosphere and orbit meet for his breathing and exercise. I wished he might adore, not fever for, the bright phantoms of his mind's creation, and believe them but the shadows of external things to be met with hereafter. After this steady intellectual growth had brought his powers to manhood, so far as the ideal can do it, I wished this being might be launched into the world of realities, his heart glowing with the ardor of an immortal toward perfection, his eyes searching everywhere to behold it; I wished he might collect into one burning point those withering, palsying convictions, which, in the ordinary routine of things, so gradually pervade the soul; that he might suffer, in brief space, agonies of disappointment commensurate with his unpreparedness and confidence. And I thought, thus thrown back on the representing pictorial resources I supposed him originally to possess, with such material, and the need he must feel of using it, such a man would suddenly dilate into a form of Pride, Power, and Glory,—a centre, round which asking, aimless hearts might rally,—a man fitted to act as interpreter to the one tale of many-languaged eyes!

What words are these! Perhaps you will feel as if I sought but for the longest and strongest. Yet to my ear they do but faintly describe the imagined powers of such a being.

ELfr, from *Memoirs*, 1:69–70; also in Miller, pp. 28–29.

69. To Timothy and Margarett C. Fuller

Cambridge 21st August 1830.

Dear father and mother,

I congratulate you on your good-fortune with respect to the weather —more enchanting I have never known it; I think you must have had a short passage to Bangor; the wind on Tuesday was so favorable and I trust all has gone well with you— Here at home we are innocently industrious and tranquilly happy. The children are very well and gay; they were at home nearly all yesterday[n] because "Miss Kuhn wished to buy some worsted" and I believe that 'tis to be vacation all next week as aunt K. goes to Canton. She came here a day or two since; I was not at home but she left word that she would call again and I shall write to grandmother by her.

I have not bought a dinner *yet* but we shall fare sumptuously tomorrow as I expect Eugene. He has written to "*papa*"; but the letter is nowise worth sending. Polly's whole soul is wrapt up in the counterpanes; she has cut out, for *my* doing, enough patchwork to drapery the pyramids. Silver has painted the floors and chamber stairs; if the weather be fair they will be dry by Monday. I have postponed the bannisters till your return for sundry admirable reasons. I have been out twice—on Wednesday to Charlestown— The girls were much disappointed that I could not come for the week— Catharine goes in a few days. I thought them more lovely than ever. They liked my pink dress very much and did not think it would be too *decided,* for Phi Beta so I shall wear it for they have excellent taste. Mary S. insisted that *I* should wear her gold net as *she* is in mourning —it is very beautiful and marquée so I felt extremely unwilling but whether I do or no I am pleased by the care for me she has shown. They had no company except Mr Prescott his sister and Dr Hunter of the Navy.[1]

Dr Randall and Elizabeth have been here; I saw the former only for a moment; he left E. on his way to Mr Quincy's.[2] She is much better and is now gone to Stow to pass the next week. Marian Marshall rode out to see me; she brought Amelia and Mrs Woods's little boy in the carriage; never did I see any one so changed in so short a time!, she must have been dreadfully sick and seems now too weak to stand two minutes—[3] Anna S. H. has not been to see me yet; her ague has not left her; but she wrote a droll billet and is coming Monday "if she recovers her beauty" I shd have preferred another day as Miss Gray is to be here but she will not come early. Sarah Coffin called. Miss E. Williams has been very kind she and Caroline [*illegible*] have brought a "wild profusion" of books to entertain what I believe they think a dreary solitude; though fully occupied I am glad of the books.[4] I have (by the way) finished nearly all my own sewing which weighed so heavily on my mind. Arthur reads "Sandford and Merton" to me evegs while I work; he seems to like it very much and I think we form quite a nice little domestick groupe.[5] Lloyd says often that I am "a nice good girl as ever was." Arthur seems anxious to hear of your safety and asks why we dont have a letter. I have not known the other two to notice your absence which surprizes me— Mr Willard has called and an elderly gentleman and lady who did not leave their names.—[6] Mr Folsom wrote to father concerning the Phi Beta meeting at Mr Gray's; I supposed an answer unnecessary.[7] The very night of your departure some evil-minded persons came as soon as the doors were fastened, loudly rang the door-bell and ran away. I was somewhat vexed but nothing of the kind has since occurred; and indeed I think such tricky persons may well be terrified for Silver declares publickly "he should not value shooting any one so coming—in the legs."—

My dear father and mother— Though not particularly well arranged I suppose this will do for a *domestick* letter. I have jotted down these little items of intelligence as they rose to my mind. I am anxious to hear from you and shall expect a letter from Hallowell[8] My love to William and Ellen I hope they are as happy as the birds. Remember me affectionately to my aunts and other Maine friends and amid the pleasures of novelty do sometimes think with tender complacence on your deserted but dutiful daughter

MARGARET.

ALS (MH: fMS Am 1086 [10:94]). *Addressed:* Hon. Timothy Fuller. / Hallowell, / Maine. *Postmark:* Boston MS Aug 21. *Endorsed:* Miss Sarah Margtt Fuller / Recd 23. Aug. 1830—

at home nearly all yesterday] at home ↑ nearly ↓ all ⟨day⟩ yesterday

1. Fuller was visiting the Soley family in Charlestown. Among the six children of John and Rebecca Tyng Henley Soley were Catharine Henley (b. 1806), who later married Alvin Edson, and Mary, who married William Bradford DeWolfe (Hunnewell, *Town Life,* pp. 222, 224). Their visitors may have been Benjamin James Prescott, son of James Prescott of Groton, and one of his sisters. Lewis Boudinot Hunter (1804–87), son of Andrew and Mary Stockton Hunter of Princeton, graduated from the University of Pennsylvania medical school in 1828 and then joined the navy. He became the fleet surgeon under Admiral David Dixon Porter in the Civil War (J. Montgomery Seaver, "Hunter Family Records," NEHGS, p. 73; Edward W. Callahan, *List of Officers of the Navy of the United States and of the Marine Corps from 1775 to 1900* [New York, 1901], p. 285).

2. Josiah Quincy (1772–1864) was president of Harvard from 1829 to 1845. A prominent member of a prominent family, he had served in the Massachusetts Legislature and had been mayor of Boston from 1823 to 1827 (*DAB*).

3. Fuller's visitors were Marian Marshall, Amelia Greenwood, and Marian Marshall's older sister, Almira (1804–63), who had married Alva Woods in 1823. The son may have been Marshall Woods (1824–99) (Jacobus, *Descendants of Robert Waterman,* 1:365–66).

4. E. Williams is probably Eliza Williams, the Fullers' Cambridge neighbor. The other women are not identified.

5. Thomas Day's *History of Sandford and Merton: A Work Intended for the Use of Children* (London, 1783–89), a well-known "improving work" for children.

6. Sidney Willard (1780–1856) graduated from Harvard in 1798 (with William Ellery Channing and Joseph Story), was librarian at the college from 1800 to 1805, and became professor of Hebrew and Oriental languages from 1807 to 1831. After his retirement from teaching he was several times a member of the Massachusetts General Court. Willard was married twice: first to Elizabeth Andrews (1789–1817) of Ipswich and after her death to Hannah Heard (1789–1824) (*CVR;* Harvard archives; *CC,* 20 September 1817, 28 June 1824; Ipswich VR; Paige, *Cambridge,* pp. 692, 815).

7. Charles Folsom, director of the University Press, a commercial printing firm in Cambridge, and (probably) Francis Calley Gray (1790–1856), a lawyer and member of the legislature (*DAB*).

8. Several members of the Fuller family were then living in Maine. Fuller's aunt Deborah Allen Fuller had married Clifford Belcher of Farrington; Ann Buckminster Fuller had married Henry Titcomb of Farmington; her uncle, Simeon Whittier, was a native of Hallowell.

70.   To Amelia Greenwood

Lynn Oct 17 1830

My dear, amiable, arrogant friend,

I just met the gentle Jamis[1] who says there's a letter in the P.O. from

thee to me, whereupon je vous ecris (rhyme you may par parenthèse)[n]—
I went thereunto yesterday and not finding said epistle according to
thy promise did in a rage vow to leave thee, promise breaker, in
ignorance of all the interesting tidings to me appurtaining but I find
you as heretofore better than my thought. I am *"perfectly happy"* Deep
in a vale the cottage stands of David and Almira"[2] I spend all the
sunny hours[n] in rambling over richly wooded hills which overlook
your pet ocean! The house is, to my taste, charming and a lovely
brook fusses and babbles before it— Almira is enchantingly droll and
piquante— Elisabeth is more sweet and lovely than ever and I in
highest glee—[3] We have seen some very decent world's people; I have
no books but in lieu have amused the odd minutes in exploring Mr
and Mrs B's private correspondence. I was right glad to see James
Stuart's bright handsome face. He was not gay though. Tomorrow we
are going to Nahant, Mr Dodge's &c I believe. James Clarke looks
wondrous well; like former times today; I have no ideas in my head
and cannot give you what I dont possess. If you'd ride down some
afternoon I know Almira would be glad to see you; why cant you
come with Marian if she's well enough?
Love to Ann—[4]

M.

ALS (MH, Autograph File). *Addressed:* Miss Amelia Greenwood. / Boston— *Endorsed:*
From Margaret Fuller.

ecris— (rhyme you may par parenthèse)] ecris— ↑ (rhyme you may par parenthèse) ↓
all the sunny hours] all the sun⟨y⟩ny hours

1. Probably James Clarke.
2. David and Almia Barlow, whom Fuller was visiting. Barlow was pastor of the
Unitarian church in Lynn from 1829 to 1833 (*DivCat*).
3. Elizabeth Randall.
4. Amelia Greenwood's sister Angelina.

71. To Almira P. Barlow

Cambridge, Nov 19. 1830
Having some reason to flatter myself with present possession of a
vacant evening, a vacant heart, head, &c, &c, I think this a suitable
occasion to address the apprehensive ear of my amiable Almira. I
wish the evening to be free from interruption, expecting the letter to
occupy half an hour in the inditing; and the "tenderly playful" remi-

niscences which cluster round your once-invoked image, four or five additional. A vacant heart and head because,— but oh! it is too tedious to why and wherefore in this style.

My dear Simplicetta, why don't you get well? Really this additional pain in your fascinating ankles is *too* heart-breaking. The Trevetts, Coffins, Breeds &c, are too exciting for you I know.[1] Never before have your *ankles* been excited, even by my overwhelming power. Close your door, I entreat you, against the Lynn population. Rude health would be in much better keeping with the elegant simplicity of your abode, than these complicated ills. Come and see me; I will *reason* you out of them.

Many things have happened since I echoed your farewell laugh. Elizabeth and I have been fully occupied.[2] She has cried a great deal, fainted a good deal and played the harp most of all. I have neither fertilized the earth with my tears, edified its inhabitants by my delicacy of constitution, nor wakened its echoes to my harmony,—yet some things have I achieved in my own soft feminine style. I hate glare, thou knowest, and have hitherto successfully screened my virtues therefrom. I have made several garments fitted for the wear of American youth; I have written six letters, and received a correspondent number; I have read one book,—a piece of poetry entitled "Two Agonies", by M. A. Browne, (pretty caption, is it not?) and J. J. Knapp's trial;[3] I have given advice twenty times,—I have taken it once; I have gained two friends, and recovered two; I have felt admiration four times,—horror once, and disgust twice; I have been a journey, and shewed my penetration in discovering the beauties of Nature through a thick and never-lifted shroud of rain; I have turned two new leaves in the book of human nature; I have got a new pink bag, (beautiful!) I have imposed on the world time and again, by describing your Lynn life as the perfection of human felicity, and adorning my visit there with all sorts of impossible adventures,—thus at once exhibiting my own rich invention and the credulous ignorance of my auditors (light and dark you know, dear, give life to a picture). I have had tears for others' woes, and patience for my own,—in short, to climax this journal of many-colored deeds and chances, so well have I played my part, that in the self-same night I was styled by two several persons "a sprightly young lady", and "a Syren!!" Oh rapturous sound! I have reached the goal of my ambition; Earth has nothing fairer or brighter to offer. "Intelligency" was nothing to it. A "Supercilious", "satirical", "affected", "pedantic" "Syren"!!!! Can the olla-podrida[4] of human nature present a compound of more varied ingredients, or higher gusto?

Loveliest of created minister's wives! I have egotized as became a friend so interesting as myself, to one so sympathizing as thyself. For the present I pause. When, oh when shalt thou gather strength to come and hear the remainder? Let the hour hasten forward. I sigh to laugh with thee. And we *will* laugh, my beloved! as Leila said to Mignoun,[5] in those beautiful Persic poems we have so often conned together in more studious hours. "Let fate do her worst &c!" I send thee the candy: six cents and a quarter I did remit to Boston for it, I do assure thee, small as the package may seem. May it visit thy palate with the sweetness of manna! Adieu; say unutterable things from me to Frederic and Josephene, and forget not my regards to Mr Barlow.

P. S. Write soon and let the letter be sentimental. Sentiment now bears unbounded sway in the palace of my heart. But write soon, or the tide may ebb. Have any new philosophical works supplanted Combe and Coleridge?[6] Have you heard from Miss Peabody?[7] Did Mr Barlow tell you about the bandbox-lid? Be prolix in your answers. Faithfully yours,

M<small>ARGARET</small> F.

MsC (MH: fMS Am 1086 [Works, 1:1–5]). Published in part in Higginson, *MFO*, pp. 39–40, and Chevigny, pp. 101–2.

1. Fuller probably refers to Robert W. Trevett (1788?–1842), a Lynn lawyer who was interested in history and literature; Dr. Edward Lummus Coffin (1794–1845); and Henry A. Breed (1798–1887), a prominent factory owner. Coffin and Breed were among the founders of the Unitarian parish when the liberals separated from the Congregationalists in 1823. Breed was married three times: to Mary W. Adams (1798–1823), Catherine Hathorne (1798–1844), and Mary Hathorne (1804–74). Coffin married Mary Rhodes (1801–25) and, following her death, Frances Cutler (b. 1802) (Parsons Cooke, *A Century of Puritanism and a Century of Its Opposites* [Boston, 1855], p. 375; Trevett: *History of Lynn*, p. 409; Lynn VR; Breed: Lynn VR; *CC*, 4 September 1822, 3 December 1825; Salem VR; *Boston Evening Transcript*, 18 April 1887; MVR 265:231; Coffin: Harvard archives; *History of Lynn*, pp. 533–34; *CVR*).

2. Elizabeth Randall.

3. Fuller may have read a poem by Mary Ann Browne (1812–44), who had published three books of verse by this date (though none of them has a poem by this name). The day before this letter was written, Joseph Jenkins Knapp of Salem had been condemned to die for hiring his brother, John Francis, to kill Joseph White of Salem on 6 April 1830. The trial had begun on 9 November. White was related by marriage to Joseph Knapp, who had confessed his part in the plot, thinking to escape death. He was, however, executed on 31 December, at the age of twenty-five. John, who was twenty, had been executed on 28 September (Salem VR; *Boston Daily Advertiser*, 7–8 April, 11–18 November 1830).

4. A sort of Spanish stew; a miscellaneous mixture.

5. Characters in Goethe's *Wilhelm Meister*.

6. The Combe brothers, George (1788–1858) and Andrew (1797–1847), were phrenologists, disciples of Johann Spurzheim. Fuller had a lifelong interest in phre-

nology and mesmerism (Stern, "Phrenologist-Publishers"). Fuller knew the prose of Samuel Taylor Coleridge (1772–1834) better than his poetry.

7. Elizabeth Peabody (1804–94), daughter of Dr. Nathaniel (1774–1855) and Elizabeth Palmer Peabody (1778–1853), had been an unpaid assistant to Dr. William Ellery Channing but was teaching school in New Bedford during the winter of 1830–31 (*Peabody Genealogy*, p. 85; *DAB*; *NAW*).

72. To [?]

[ca. winter] 1830–1831

I was very happy, although greatly restrained by the apprehension of going a little too far with these persons of singular refinement and settled opinions. However, I believe I did pretty well, though I did make one or two little mistakes, when most interested; but I was not so foolish as to try to retrieve them. One occasion more particularly, when Mr. G[reenwood],[n] after going more fully into his poetical opinions than I could have expected, stated his sentiments: first, that Wordsworth had, in truth, guided, or, rather, completely vivified the poetry of this age; secondly, that 't was his influence which had, in reality, given all his better individuality to Byron. He recurred again and again to this opinion, *con amore*, and seemed to wish much for an answer; but I would not venture, though 't was hard for me to forbear, I knew so well what I thought. Mr. G[reenwood]'s Wordsworthianism, however, is excellent; his beautiful simplicity of taste, and love of truth, have preserved him from any touch of that vague and imbecile enthusiasm, which has enervated almost all the exclusive and determined admirers of the great poet whom I have known in these parts. His reverence, his feeling, are thoroughly intelligent. Everything in his mind is well defined; and his horror of the vague, and false, nay, even (suppose another horror here, for grammar's sake) of the startling and paradoxical, have their beauty. I think I could know Mr. G[reenwood] long, and see him perpetually, without any touch of satiety; such variety is made by the very absence of pretension, and the love of truth. I found much amusement in leading him to sketch the scenes and persons which Lockhart portrays in such glowing colors, and which he, too, has seen with the *eye of taste*, but how different![1]

ELfr, from *Memoirs*, 1:105–6.

Mr. G] *George Davis's copy of the* Memoirs, *now owned by Joseph Deiss, has an annotation identifying the Reverend F. W. P. Greenwood as the speaker Fuller mentions.*

1. John Gibson Lockhart (1794–1854), Scott's son-in-law, had written four novels (which probably are the source of Fuller's comment here): *Valerius, Adam Blair, Reginald Dalton,* and *Matthew Wald.* He is best known for his seven-volume *Memoirs of the Life of Sir Walter Scott* (Edinburgh, 1837–38).

73. To George T. Davis

2 February 1831

My cousin and (at this moment) dearest friend. I expressed to you last night either nothing of wh. I felt or something directly opposite to it. I did not know what I said; I was so troubled and surprized that you cd. still excite a new sensation.

I feel that but for you I should[?] be free at least in the common [*illegible*] sense of the world. You are the only person who can appreciate my true self. This thought has been most grevious to me.

You alone can now see me as I truly am.

O would to heaven my cousin that I could act out my present feelings and show gratitude to the person who has embellished my life with one sweet[?] emotion. Alas! I dare not hope it

Do you ever pray my cousin if so pray for me (you alone can do it understandingly) pray that I may act religiously[?] until[?] the time comes for my feeling so. O if I could look forward to an era: I would wait. In my thoughts I have fixed it six years hence. Long ere that my cousin may you be happy and untroubled by me. My heart does not wish this but my reason does.

MsCfr, in the hand of Thomas Wentworth Higginson (MB: Ms. Am. 1450 [18]). *Higginson identifies the recipient in his notes.*

74. To [?]

1832
[Cambridge?]

I am thinking how I omitted to talk a volume to you about the "Elective Affinities."[1] Now I shall never say half of it, for which I, on my own account, am sorry. But two or three things I would ask:—

What do you think of Charlotte's proposition, that the accomplished pedagogue must be tiresome in society?

Of Ottilia's, that the afflicted, and ill-educated, are oftentimes singled out by fate to instruct others, and her beautiful reasons why?

And what have you thought of the discussion touching graves and monuments?

I am now going to dream of your sermon, and of Ottilia's china-asters. Both shall be driven from my head to-morrow, for I go to town, allured by despatches from thence, promising much entertainment. Woe unto them if they disappoint me!

Consider it, I pray you, as the "nearest duty" to answer my questions, and not act as you did about the sphinx-song.[2]

ELfr, from *Memoirs*, 1:118.

Probably written to Clarke.

1. Johann Wolfgang von Goethe, *Die Wahlverwandschaften, ein Roman* (Tübingen, 1809). Fuller was an early champion of this novel, a scandalous one to many readers because of its unconventional attitude toward infidelity.

2. From Goethe, by way of Carlyle. In *Wilhelm Meisters Lehrjahre* a wandering pedestrian tells Wilhelm, "Das Sicherste bleibt immer, nur das Nächste zu tun was vor uns liegt." Carlyle translated the passage, "The safe plan is, always simply to do the task that lies nearest us." He undoubtedly recalled Goethe when he said in *Sartor Resartus*, "Do the duty which lies nearest thee" (Goethe, *Gedenkausgabe*, 7:454; *Centenary Edition of the Works of Thomas Carlyle*, ed. H. D. Traill [London, (1907)], 24:2, 1:156). The sphinx-song is unidentified.

75. To [?]

January 1832

All that relates to ——[1] must be interesting to me, though I never voluntarily think of him now. The apparent caprice of his conduct has shaken my faith, but not destroyed my hope. That hope, if I, who have so mistaken others may dare to think I know myself, was never selfish. It is painful to lose a friend whose knowledge and converse mingled so intimately with the growth of my mind,—an early friend to whom I was all truth and frankness, seeking nothing but equal truth and frankness in return. But this evil may be borne; the hard, the lasting evil was to learn to distrust my own heart and lose all faith in my power of knowing others. In this letter I see again that peculiar pride, that contempt of the forms and shows of goodness, that fixed resolve to be anything but "like unto the Pharisees," which were to my eye such happy omens. Yet how strangely distorted are all his views! The daily influence of his intercourse with me was like the breath he drew; it has become a part of him. Can he escape from himself? Would he be unlike all other mortals? His feelings are as false as those of Alcibiades.[2] He influenced me, and helped form me to what I am. Others shall succeed him. Shall I be ashamed to owe anything to friendship? But why do I talk?—a child might confute him by defining the term *human being*. He will gradually work his way into light; if too late for our friendship, not, I trust, too late for his own peace and honorable well-being. I never insisted on being the instrument of good to him. I practised no little arts, no! not to effect the good of the friend I loved. I have prayed to Heaven, (surely we are sincere when doing that,) to guide him in the best path for him, however far from me that path might lead. The lesson I have learned may make me a more useful friend, a more efficient aid to others than I could be to him; yet I hope I shall not be denied the consolation of knowing surely, one day, that all which appeared evil in the companion of happy years was but error.

ELfr, from *Memoirs*, 1:83–84.

1. Probably George T. Davis, for the discussion closely parallels that in letter 73.

2. Alcibiades (c.450–404 B.C.), an Athenian general and politician, was a nephew of Pericles and a friend of Socrates. He switched his allegiance from Athens to Sparta, then back to Athens.

76. To [?]

6 July 1832

I believe I behaved very badly the other evening. I did not think so yesterday. I had been too surprised and vexed to recover very easily, but to-day my sophistries have all taken wing, and I feel that nothing good could have made me act with such childish petulance and bluntness towards one who spoke from friendly emotions. Be at peace; I will astonish you by my repose, mildness, and self-possession. No, that is silly; but I believe it cannot be right to be on such terms with any one, that, on the least vexation, I indulge my feelings at his or her expense. We will talk less, but we shall be very good friends still, I hope. Shall not we?

ELfr, from *Memoirs*, 1:79; also in Chevigny, p. 103.

77. To James F. Clarke

[ca. 1 August 1832]
[Cambridge?]

I have not anybody to speak to, that does not talk common-place, and I wish to talk about such an uncommon person,—about Novalis! a wondrous youth, and who has only written one volume.[1] That is pleasant! I feel as though I could pursue my natural mode with him, get acquainted, then make my mind easy in the belief that I know all that is to be known. And he died at twenty-nine, and, as with Körner,[2] your feelings may be single; you will never be called upon to share his experience, and compare his future feelings with his present. And his life was so full and so still. Then it is a relief, after feeling the immense superiority of Goethe. It seems to me as if the mind of Goethe had embraced the universe. I have felt this lately, in reading his lyric poems.[3] I am enchanted while I read. He comprehends every feeling I have ever had so perfectly, expresses it so beautifully; but when I shut the book, it seems as if I had lost my personal identity; all my feelings linked with such an immense variety that belong to beings I had thought so different. What can I bring? There is no answer in my mind, except "It is so," or "It will be so," or "No doubt such and such feel so." Yet, while my judgment becomes daily more tolerant towards others, the same attracting and repelling work is going on in my feelings. But I persevere in reading the great sage, some part of every day, hoping the time will come, when I shall not feel so overwhelmed, and leave off this habit of wishing to grasp the whole, and be contented to learn a little every day, as becomes a pupil.

But now the one-sidedness, imperfection, and glow, of a mind like that of Novalis, seem refreshingly human to me. I have wished fifty times to write some letters giving an account, first, of his very pretty life, and then of his one volume, as I re-read it, chapter by chapter. If you will pretend to be very much interested, perhaps I will get a better pen, and write them to you.

ELfr, from *Memoirs*, 1:118–19.

1. Friedrich, Freiherr von Hardenberg (1772–1801), known as Novalis, fell in love with twelve-year-old Sophie von Kühn. His grief at her death led him to a religious experience that culminated in *Hymnen an die Nacht*, written in 1799, published in 1800. After Novalis died, Friedrich Schlegel and Ludwig Tieck gathered his writings into a two-volume edition, *Novalis Schriften* (Berlin, 1802). These volumes were issued in 1826 in one volume, probably the one Fuller had read. In addition to the *Hymnen*

and some aphorisms, the posthumous edition contained two fragmentary novels, *Die Lehringe zu Sais* and *Heinrich von Ofterdingen* (*OCGL*).

2. Karl Theodor Körner (1791–1813) was the son of Christian Gottfried Körner, a friend of Schiller's. The younger Körner, who wrote five tragedies and five comedies, was killed in battle in the Wars of Liberation (*OCGL*).

3. Fuller's manuscript notes (MH) show that she had access to the authoritative *Goethes Werke: Vollständige Ausgabe letzter Hand*. The original edition of forty volumes (Stuttgart, 1827–30) was expanded to sixty volumes with the addition of *Goethes nachgelassene Werke*, ed. J. P. Eckermann and F. W. Riemer (Stuttgart, 1832–42). The first three volumes of the complete edition are devoted to poetry; volume 3 contains the "Lyrisches" (Waltraud Hagen, *Die Drucke von Goethes Werken* [Berlin, 1971]).

78. To James F. Clarke

7 August 1832
[Cambridge?]

I feel quite lost; it is so long since I have talked myself. To see so many acquaintances, to talk so many words, and never tell my mind completely on any subject—to say so many things which do not seem called out, makes me feel strangely vague and movable.

'T is true, the time is probably near when I must live alone, to all intents and purposes,—separate entirely my acting from my thinking world, take care of my ideas without aid,—except from the illustrious dead,—answer my own questions, correct my own feelings, and do all that hard work for myself. How tiresome 't is to find out all one's self-delusion! I thought myself so very independent, because I could conceal some feelings at will, and did not need the same excitement as other young characters did. And I am not independent, nor never shall be, while I can get anybody to minister to me. But I shall go where there is never a spirit to come, if I call ever so loudly.

Perhaps I shall talk to you about Körner, but need not write. He charms me, and has become a fixed star in the heaven of my thought; but I understand all that he excites perfectly. I felt very *new* about Novalis,—"the good Novalis," as you call him after Mr. Carlyle.[1] He is, indeed, *good*, most enlightened, yet most pure; every link of his experience framed—no, *beaten*—from the tried gold.

I have read, thoroughly, only two of his pieces, "Die Lehrlinge zu Sais," and "Heinrich von Ofterdingen." From the former I have only brought away piecemeal impressions, but the plan and treatment of the latter, I believe, I understand. It describes the development of poetry in a mind; and with this several other developments are connected. I think I shall tell you all I know about it, some quiet time after your return, but, if not, will certainly keep a Novalis-journal for you some favorable season, when I live regularly for a fortnight.

ELfr, from *Memoirs*, 1:119–21.

1. The most influential British writer of his day, Thomas Carlyle (1795–1881) deeply affected not only Fuller but Emerson, Thoreau, and Melville, among many others. He gave Fuller a topic, suggested a critical method, and remained a model for her criticism (*DNB*). He had published "Novalis" in *The Foreign Review and Continental Miscellany* 4 (July 1829):97–141.

79. To [?]

September 1832

"Not see the use of metaphysics?" A moderate portion, taken at stated intervals, I hold to be of much use as discipline of the faculties. I only object to them as having an absorbing and anti-productive tendency. But 't is not always so; may not be so with you. Wait till you are two years older, before you decide that 't is your vocation. Time enough at six-and-twenty to form yourself into a metaphysical philosopher. The brain does not easily get too dry for *that*. Happy you, in these ideas which give you a tendency to optimism. May you become a proselyte to that consoling faith. I shall never be able to follow you, but shall look after you with longing eyes.

ELfr, from *Memoirs*, 1:123–24.

Although Clarke is the most likely recipient of this letter, the "six-and-twenty" does not match his age. The letter may be misdated in the Memoirs.

80. To [?]

14 Dec 1832

I have had no reason to complain of Arthur this past week.[1] He has learned all his lessons very well.— M. F.

ALfrS (NN-M).

1. Probably her brother Arthur.

81. To [?]

1833
[Groton]

Heaven's discipline has been invariable to me.[1] The seemingly most pure and noble hopes have been blighted; the seemingly most promising connections broken. The lesson has been endlessly repeated: "Be humble, patient, self-sustaining; hope only for occasional aids; love others, but not engrossingly, for by being much alone your appointed task can best be done!" What a weary work is before me, ere that lesson shall be fully learned! Who shall wonder at the stiff-necked, and rebellious folly of young Israel, bowing down to a brute image, though the prophet was bringing messages from the holy mountain, while one's own youth is so obstinately idolatrous! Yet will I try to keep the heart with diligence, nor ever fear that the sun is gone out because I shiver in the cold and dark!

ELfr, from *Memoirs*, 1:145.

1. Fuller is probably expressing her despair at having to move from Cambridge to Groton.

82. To Eliza R. Farrar

Groton April 25, 1833

[   ] day in which[n] I came hither, summoned home by the intelligence that our poor brother[n] had received a violent blow on the eye from a large piece of wood thrown by our careless man servant and must probably lose the use of it.[1] I found the poor child, (who had kept[n] me so full of joy and eagerness that I thought almost with a sigh (not of envy) how happy he at least would be here,) in a dark room burning with fever and both his eyes closed to the light. He had expected me very impatiently and was very faint lest it should not be Margaret who had driven up— I confess I greeted my new home with a flood of bitter tears.— He is [   ] perhaps will condemn. [   ] much more highly his talents than any of my young brothers' —and feeling as I have, that I must devolve my hopes and ambition on others I had thought that in him I might see[n] the fruits of what I had thought felt and suffered— The vision seemed to have basis, for my influence over him is great!— And now he may be possibly

quite blind, certainly greatly injured for all this world's glory— An object of pity too rather than affection, ah! dear Mrs. Farrar if the value I set upon talent and beauty has been over-great I am indeed punished.— You wished me to give you an [   ]

ALfr (MH: fMS Am 1086 [Box A]); MsCfr (MH: fMS Am 1086 [Works, 3:351–53]). Published in part in *Memoirs*, 1:146.

Elizabeth (Eliza) Rotch (1791–1870), oldest daughter of Benjamin (1764–1839) and Elizabeth Barker Rotch (1764–1857), married the widowed professor John Farrar in 1828. She had taken an interest in Margaret Fuller several years before this letter was written and occupied a special place among Fuller's circle of friends. In 1836 Mrs. Farrar published *The Young Lady's Friend*, a popular book of manners (Bullard, *Rotches*, pp. 126–30).

day in which] day ⟨when⟩ in which
that our poor brother] that ⟨y⟩our poor brother
who had kept] who had ⟨?⟩ kept
I might see] I ⟨had⟩ might see

1. Arthur Fuller apparently recovered completely from the accident.

83.   To James F. Clarke

Groton, May, 1833

I think you are wrong in applying your artistical ideas to occasional poetry. An epic, a drama, must have a fixed form in the mind of the poet from the first; and copious draughts of ambrosia quaffed in the heaven of thought, soft fanning gales and bright light from the outward world, give muscle and bloom,—that is, give life,—to this skeleton. But all occasional poems must be moods, and can a mood have a form fixed and perfect, more than a wave of the sea?

ELfr, from *Memoirs*, 1:121.

84.   To James F. Clarke

[ca. 20 May 1833]
[Groton?]

I have read nothing,—to signify,—except Goethe's "Campagne in Frankreich."[1] Have you looked through it, and do you remember his intercourse with the Wertherian Plessing?[2] That tale pained me exceedingly. We cry, "help, help," and there is no help—in man at least. How often I have thought, if I could see Goethe, and tell him my state of mind, he would support and guide me! He would be able to understand; he would show me how to rule circumstances, instead of being ruled by them; and, above all, he would not have been so sure that all would be for the best, without our making an effort to act out the oracles; he would have wished to see me what Nature intended. But his conduct to Plessing and Ohlenschlager shows that to him, also, an appeal would have been vain.[3]

Do you really believe there is anything "all-comprehending" but religion?[4] Are not these distinctions imaginary? Must not the philosophy of every mind, or set of minds, be a system suited to guide them, and give a home where they can bring materials among which to accept, reject, and shape at pleasure? Novalis calls those, who harbor these ideas, "unbelievers;" but hard names make no difference. He says with disdain, "To *such*, philosophy is only a system which will spare them the trouble of reflecting." Now this is just my case. I *do* want a system which shall suffice to my character, and in whose applications I shall have faith. I do not wish to *reflect* always, if reflecting must be always about one's identity, whether "*ich*" am the true "*ich*" &c.[5] I wish to arrive at that point where I can trust myself, and leave off saying, "It seems to me," and boldly feel, It *is* so to me. My character has got its natural regulator, my heart beats, my lips speak truth, I can walk alone, or offer my arm to a friend, or if I lean on another, it is not the debility of sickness, but only wayside weariness. This is the philosophy *I* want; this much would satisfy *me*.

Then Novalis says, "Philosophy is the art of discovering the place of truth in every encountered event and circumstance, to attune all relations to truth."

Philosophy is peculiarly home-sickness; an overmastering desire to be at home.[6]

I think so; but what is there *all-comprehending*, eternally-conscious, about that?

ELfr, from *Memoirs*, 1:122–23.

This letter answers Clarke, who had sent Fuller a letter-journal (Habich, "JFC's 1833 Letter-Journal).

1. Drawing on his experience in the German invasion of France in 1792, Goethe wrote *Campagne in Frankreich 1792* in 1820–21 and published it in 1822 as part 6 of *Aus meinem Leben.*

2. Friedrich Viktor Plessing (1749–1806) had written Goethe complaining of a

Wertherian melancholy. Goethe met Plessing in 1777 on a trip to the Harz Mountains and urged the young man to cure himself. Apparently the advice was salutary, for Plessing later became a professor of philosophy (Richard Dobel, *Lexikon der Goethe-Zitate* [Zurich and Stuttgart, 1968], col. 1132).

3. Adam Gottlob Oehlenschlager (1779–1850), a Danish writer of German descent, met Goethe a number of times between 1805 and 1809 (Dobel, *Lexikon der Goethe-Zitate*, col. 1131; *OCGL*).

4. Fuller is replying directly to Clarke, who had written in his letter-journal to her, "There was no all-comprehending idea. Every man leant on his favourite one—carried before him his own flag. One said, My Profession—another, My Country—another Mankind. One shouts, Self-sacrifice—another, Truth. All are excellent ideas—very well to lean on them & gather strength from faith & action. But why make your watchword, the scale of all excellence?"

5. Johann Gottlieb Fichte (1762–1814) developed a philosophy based on the distinction between the *Ich* and the *nicht-Ich* (ego and non-ego) (*OCGL*).

6. From Novalis, *Fragmente und Studien*, 9:566: "Die Philosophie ist eigentlich Heimweh—Trieb überall zu Hause zu sein" (*Novalis Schriften*, ed. Paul Kluckhohn [Leipzig, n.d.], 3:162).

85. To James F. Clarke

June 1833
[Groton?]

I return Lessing.[1] I could hardly get through Miss Sampson. E. Galeotti is good in the same way as Minna. Well-conceived and sustained characters, interesting situations, but never that profound knowledge of human nature, those minute beauties, and delicate vivifying traits, which lead on so in the writings of some authors, who may be nameless. I think him easily followed; strong, but not deep.

ELfr, from *Memoirs*, 1:121.

1. Gotthold Ephraim Lessing (1729–81) influenced modern German drama with such plays as *Miss Sara Sampson, ein bürgerliches Trauerspiel* (1755), *Minna von Barnhelm, oder das Soldatenglück* (written 1763, produced 1767), and *Emilia Galotti* (1772) (*OCGL*). Fuller appears to have known both Lessing's drama and his criticism. Clarke, who had been reading *Miss Sara Sampson*, may have taken the book to Fuller when he visited her in Groton.

86. To James F. Clarke

3 June 1833
[Groton]

I part with Plato with regret. I could have wished to "enchant myself," as Socrates would say, with him some days longer. Eutyphron is excellent. 'T is the best specimen I have ever seen of that mode of convincing. There is one passage in which Socrates, as if it were *aside*,—since the remark is quite away from the consciousness of Eutyphron,—declares, "qu'il aimerait incomparablement mieux des principes fixes et inébranlables à l'habilité de Dédale avec les tresors de Tantale."[1] I delight to hear such things from those whose lives have given the right to say them. For 't is not always true what Lessing says, and I, myself, once thought,—

F.—Von was fur Tugenden spricht er denn?

Minna.—Er spricht von keiner; denn ihn fehlt keine.[2] For the mouth sometimes talketh virtue from the overflowing of the heart, as well as love, anger, &c.

"Crito" I have read only once, but like it. I have not got it in my heart though, so clearly as the others.

The "Apology" I deem only remarkable for the noble tone of sentiment, and beautiful calmness. I was much affected by Phaedo, but think the argument weak in many respects.[3] The nature of abstract ideas is clearly set forth; but there is no justice in reasoning, from their existence, that our souls have lived previous to our present state, since it was as easy for the Deity to create at once the idea of beauty within us, as the sense which brings to the soul intelligence that it exists in some outward shape. He does not clearly show his opinion of what the soul is; whether eternal *as* the Deity, created *by* the Deity, or how. In his answer to Simmias, he takes advantage of the general meaning of the words harmony, discord, &c. The soul might be a result, without being a harmony. But I think too many things to write, and some I have not had time to examine. Meanwhile I can think over parts, and say to myself, "beautiful," "noble," and use this as one of my enchantments.

ELfr, from *Memoirs*, 1:116–17.

Recipient identified by Clarke's letter-journal, where he reports on his reading of Plato, especially of "Phaedo" (Habich, "JFC's 1833 Letter-Journal").

1. One of Plato's Early Dialogues, "Euthyphro" is among the best examples of the Socratic method. The passage Fuller quotes in French may be translated as "that he would love fixed and immovable principles incomparably more than the competence of Daedalus together with the treasures of Tantalus." Benjamin Jowett translates this passage, with its context, as follows:

Euthyphro: "Nay, Socrates, I shall still say that you are the Daedalus who sets arguments in motion; not I, certainly, make them move or go round, for they would never have stirred, as far as I am concerned."
Socrates: "Then I must be a greater than Daedalus; for whereas he only

made his own inventions to move, I move those of other people as well. And the beauty of it is, that I would rather not. For I would give the wisdom of Daedalus, and the wealth of Tantalus to be able to detain them and keep them fixed" ["Euthyphro," in *The Works of Plato* (New York, n.d.), 3:79–80].

2. Fuller quotes from *Minna von Barnhelm,* act 2, scene 1, in which Minna responds to a question by Franziska, her maid. "Of what virtues does he talk, then?" asks Franziska about Major von Tellheim. "He talks of none," answers Minna, "for he is wanting in none" (Brander Matthews, ed., *Great Plays* [New York, 1901], p. 208).

3. "Crito" defines the nature of honorable living; "Apology" is a defense of the Socratic method; "Phaedo" is Plato's argument for the immortality of the soul.

87. To James F. Clarke

[30? June 1833]
Sunday eveg 3d hour
of the most superb
moonlight.

My dear Friend

I am spiritually impelled to say a few words— I have strangely wished you were here this evening— I have thought of a thousand things to say to you—but I shall not write them or ever say them perhaps. And yet I felt vexed that I should think of you, should think of any earth-born people when I was feeling so pure, so free! Why should not I have a vision?— O I have been so happy—have done and felt every-thing with such enjoyment— It was really Sabbath— I felt so very right when I was going to and from church and so prayerfull in it. The day has been divine as if nature wished to make up for her late coldness by crowding all june into one day. Such gorgeous light, such rich deep shadows—such sweet, *sweet* west wind! And this evening I have been sitting in the piazza hearing it rustle the vines against the Moon's benignant face and thinking through Alroy which I have been reading—[1] I lived it all through and set it to musick in my soul. This is an era— I never have been happy on a moonlight evening (I mean in a constant happy mood— I always have high flights and keen flashes) except in two instances and those were rapture—but this is such a sweet and strange composure. I never felt any-thing like it except on Thanksgiving day which you may remember I told you about.[2] But that was far better— I shall never know a day like that again—it was like the mansions of the blest. Today I am wide awake and notice every-thing— I am quite well today and can let Heaven's free wind blow upon me without being shudderingly reminded that I am framed of "suffering clay."

I send you this leaf of geranium which I have been wearing in a nosegay Whose roses all their fragrance and worse almost all their petals have shed or you should have one of those in preference. all this fine time. You may put it in a locket and wear it as a memento that the most striving souls have their halcyon hours—

And now adieu— Perhaps I shall write tomorrow but not as today I know— This mood is distinct so should be its expression.—

M.

ALS (MH: bMS Am 1569.7 [462]). Published in *New England Quarterly* 30 (September 1957):378–79.

Dated from Clarke's letter to Fuller, June 1833, in Letters of JFC, *p. 42.*

1. Benjamin Disraeli, *The Wondrous Tale of Alroy: The Rise of Iskander* (London, 1833).

2. Her account of this 1831 religious experience is in *Memoirs*, 1:139–42. She describes it further in letter 189.

88. To James F. Clarke

[1? July 1833]
Tuesday aft

I send inclosed a somewhat and tautological[n] epistle dating Sunday. I have been still more moonstruck since, for last eveg surpassed Sunday's in beauty as much as that does a hideous, glaring January noon— Eclipse of the Moon on one side Heavens dome Opposite incessant glows of the very finest lightning above those deep blue, (but then black) hills which you remember and the air one continued sigh of delight. Verily the beauties of nature may be sympathized withal, nor can such hours of communion leave behind dregs and bitterness they *are* "marvellously good." I think I should prefer a desert for my dwelling place to a convent.

And to-day is so luxurious,[n] so warm so fragrant. O! it would be Elysium to have just performed some great and glorious deed, or to have just finished some beautiful work the Apollo Belvidere[1] for instance or Shakespeare's Tempest and to pause this day and feel creation and one's self a worthy part thereof. But it is sad to stand by Nature's side and feel one's self a bungling pupil, not gifted[n] to bring into life and shape one of her beautiful thoughts or pay back aught for her bounteous instruction. But why do I write this now— I am not feeling, only remembering it. For I have been working in nature's garden, digging round and watering two or three plants not fragrant indeed, no nor stately, but she placed them there and probably intended them to grow by some means. "The nearest duty" is comfortable doctrine whether true or no? Mais assez de cela?—

You are right[n] to send the "*scratches*"!—the kind of Faith is right.[2] Also I am glad that you have this new interest. An elegant female writer hath observed "that every new torch kindled in the mind's cavern makes those already lit burn more brightly"[3] This figure of speech is not, I presume, philosophically correct but the idea is so. The head of Prometheus is *fine* but of these anon—when I see you c' est à dire. Alas— Helas!— I shall not be able any more to say "when I see you"—I could be sentimental quite à la Morgan about it—[4] *Is* not that sketching number in Blackwood *very* good? "I ask for information. I like the review of Mr Motherwell (odious rustick name) better than his poetry though some of *that* pleased me too— But the article on Cornwall and Devon made me laugh to die and think tis as good as the old Noches—so degagée and overflowring![5] Voici Titan![n] I have not been able to get into Richter's stream—[6] I read here and there before E, whom I may call my external sensibility arrived—[7] But she and Jean Paul to-gether were de trop. Too rambling and melting— I found necessary to balance and harden myself with some good onward books all plan and method else I should have been dissolved by this time, and such a catastrophe would not suit the style of the 19th century, however natural it seemed in ancient days.— I do not even know why the book is called Titan so if you do pray tell me for I fancied a reason.

I have had a letter from H. Hedge in which he says you are better qualified to translate transcendentalism than he had supposed.[8] You are a good-for nothing young man not to write about Eugene.[9] What do you suppose I care for aught else in comparison?— If it is bad why *dont* you tell it—?

M.

ALS (MH: bMS Am 1569.7 [463]).

Somewhat and tautological] somewhat ⟨silly⟩ and tautological *After canceling* silly *Fuller inserted the following note above the line:* inexpressive rather. Though I said silly when I read it over, I do suppose perhaps I should not dispatch it if I really thought so.

so luxurious] so ⟨r⟩luxurious
not gifted] not gi⟨v⟩ted
You are right] ⟨?⟩ You are right
Voici Titan! I] Voici Titan! ⟨?⟩ I

1. The Apollo Belvedere is an early Roman marble, discovered in 1485 and preserved in the Vatican.

2. Clarke had sent Fuller a portfolio of drawings, saying: "Do not laugh at my designs—or rather laugh at them, but not at me for sending you thus every rude scratching . . ." (*Letters of JFC*, p. 42).

3. Perhaps Fuller's own words.

4. Sydney Owenson (1783?–1859), an Irish writer of sentimental verse and prose, had married Sir Thomas Charles Morgan (1783–1843) and, as Lady Morgan, had published *Dramatic Scenes from Real Life* (London, 1833). Fuller had probably read this work (perhaps in its New York edition), or possibly Morgan's earlier, more famous novel, *The Wild Irish Girl: A National Tale* (London, 1806) (*DNB*).

5. Clarke had sent a copy of *Blackwood's Edinburgh Magazine* to Fuller with a comment to note the article on sketching and the one on Motherwell. In the issue for April 1833 (vol. 33), "The Sketcher, No. 1" (pp. 682–88) gave advice to amateurs on sketching landscapes, with a reference specifically to Gaspard-Poussin (Gaspard Dughet) (1613–75), the French landscape painter. William Motherwell (1797–1835) was a Scottish poet and journalist whose *Poems, Narrative & Lyrical* was reviewed in that issue of the magazine (*DNB*). The reviewer called Motherwell "a stronger-minded man by far and away than Alfred Tennyson, and of equal genius." A travel article, "Devonshire and Cornwall Illustrated. No. 1," appeared on pp. 689–704.

6. Clarke had asked Fuller to return his copy of Johann Paul Friedrich Richter's *Titan*. Richter (1763–1825) was known as Jean Paul. *Titan*, his best-known book, was noted for its stylistic density, verbal play, and comic extravagance (*OCGL*).

7. Probably Elizabeth Randall.

8. Clarke was translating Schiller's *Jungfrau von Orleans*. Hedge, in his letter to Fuller of 24 June (MH-AH), praised Clarke in the words she uses here but went on to say that Schiller's book "is not worth translating."

9. Her brother Eugene was a member of Harvard's class of 1834.

89. To Frederic H. Hedge

Groton 4th July. 1833.—

I think I cannot commemorate the anniversary of our independence better than by writing to you, since all of freedom that has fallen to my lot, is that of thought and unrestrained intercourse with my friends. The citizens of this place, I grieve to state, are quite ungrateful for the blessings of their estate— No speech, no procession, no glorification of any kind, not so much as a cannon to please the boys with its bobbing report— I am only reminded of the occasion by loud shouts from the juvenile citizens of this family who cannot sufficiently express their joy at being released for one day from all obligation to "intellectual progress."

Your letter was very grateful to me and I confess I had not expected such a token of remembrance.[1] Since I came here I have had much reason to believe that there exists more^n warmth of feeling in the little world wherein I have been living than I had supposed. I expected that my place would be immediately filled by some person "about my age and height." I have not found it so. My former intimates *sigh* at least, if they do not pine, for my society[n] I rejoice to see that it is[n] so for their sakes more than my own. They must be living since they can feel peculiar wants. I could not expect that you should miss me—but since you do, why not come here? The journey is short, the weather is delightful, the country in perfect beauty, and either Lucy or Mary will, I am sure, be inclined to acompany you.[2] Both will be welcome.

I do, indeed, wish you might succeed your Father.[3] The place would suit you exactly and I know of none other that would. Could you once be brought into unison with your day and country without sacrificing your individuality all would be well. Let me once more intreat you to *write*, to bring your opinions into collision with those generally received.[4] Nobody can be more sensible than myself that the pen is a much less agreeable instrument for communication than the voice, but all our wishes will not bring back the dear talking times of Greece and Rome. And believe me, you cannot live, you cannot be content without acting on other minds "it's no possible." I should be very willing to join in such a society as you speak of and will *compose a piece*, if you will give me a subject—[5] Why will you not continue Novalis's novel, I should think your experiences might suffice. As to my German studies, I have not done much. My time has been much broken up, although not frittered away (to use a favorite expression of my mothers.). I have with me those works of Goethe which I have not read and am now perusing Kunst and Alterthum and Campagne in Frankreich.[6] I still prefer reading Goethe to anybody and as I proceed find more and more to learn.— feel too that my general idea of his mind was less perfect than I supposed and needs testing and sifting. I brought your beloved Jean Paul with me, but have been obliged to send him back before I was half through Titan.

I found considerable difficulty in reading it, my knowledge of German is so imperfect and there are so many compound and coined words in his works that 'twas almost like learning a language: thus perhaps I cannot judge so well, but I think he and I shall not be intimate. I prefer wit to humour, and daring imagination to the richest fancy, his infinitely variegated and I confess most exquisitely coloured web fatigues my attention. I like widely extended plan, but the details more distinc[t.] Besides his philosophy and religion seem to be of the sighing sort, and having some tendency that way myself I want opposing force in a favorite author. Perhaps I have spoken unadvisedly—

if so I shall recant on further knowledge.— You kindly offer me books— I have some of yours which should by rights have been returned, but I wish to make some further translations from them. I shall not keep them always— and should like Serapions Bruder, which you mention. I have never seen it.—

I highly enjoy being surrounded by *new* and beautiful natural objects. My eyes and my soul were so weary of Cambridge scenery— my heart would not give access to a summer feeling there. The evenings lately have been those of Paradise and I have been very happy in them: The people here are much more agreeable than in most country-towns—there is no vulgarity of manner, but little of feeling and I hear no gossip— They are very kind to us and if they do not give great pleasure will not, I believe annoy or pain me. I have met with few characters strongly marked enough to be amusing, but I am not yet *intimate* with any of the lower class. I have not the advantages of a clergy man. The length of this letter gives it right to be called a lady's if not a ladylike letter. Farewell. Commend me to Lucy and your family. Sincerely your friend

MARGARET F.

ALS (MH: fMS Am 1086 [10:96]); MsCfr (MH: fMS Am 1086 [Works, 3:353–55]); MsCfr (MB: Ms. Am. 1450 [177]). Published in part in *Memoirs*, 1:146–47, and Higginson, *MFO*, pp. 43–45, 141. *Addressed:* Rev. F. H. Hedge. / West Cambridge. / Mass. *Endorsed:* Margaret Fuller.

there exists more] there ⟨?⟩ exists more
for my society] for my ⟨absence⟩ ↑ society ↓
that it is] that ↑ it ↓ is

1. On 24 June Hedge had written, "I have often yearned for an hour's communion with you & have felt the want of your society more keenly than I myself could have anticipated or than I have ever given you reason to suppose that I should" (Hedge to Fuller, 24 June 1833, MH-AH).

2. Hedge's wife, Lucy Pierce (1808–91), and his sister Mary (1803–65). Hedge was pastor at West Cambridge from 1829 to 1835 (*CVR*; *CC*, 15 September 1830; *Boston Evening Transcript*, 13 April 1891; *MVR* 184:56; Mt. Auburn; *DivCat*).

3. In his letter, Hedge told Fuller that he had been "talked of" as his father's replacement at the Divinity School, and that long before Levi Hedge retired it had been "a favourite dream" that he might succeed him. Hedge became professor of ecclesiastical history, but not until 1857.

4. Only a few months earlier, Hedge had done exactly what Fuller was urging. He published "Coleridge's Literary Character" in the *Christian Examiner* 14 (March 1833):108–29, where he reviewed *Biographia Literaria, Poetical Works, Aids to Reflection*, and *The Friend*.

5. Hedge, in his letter of the 24th, had proposed a society of friends based on those portrayed by E. T. A. Hoffmann in *Serapionsbrüder* (Berlin, 1819–21) and by Ludwig Tieck in *Phantasus*:

> A few friends meet together, converse on various topics relating to Literature, Art & Life, read essays, or tales which they have composed at some leisure

Frederic Henry Hedge. Courtesy of the Unitarian-Universalist Association.

hours & when in this way matter enough has been collected the book is finished. Books composed in this manner have always seemed to me the most
agreeable & useful; they unite variety of form with oneness of spirit, they
give you the benefit of a fair discussion without wearying you with all the
formalities of argument. . . . Now it has seemed to me that we, that is you &
I & some of our friends, might do something in this way, if not for the public,
at least for our own instruction, & amusement.

Tieck (1773–1853), a prolific writer of fiction and drama, published a compendium
of short prose works, *Phantasus*, in Berlin from 1812 to 1816. Hoffmann's tales are
based on the stories told by a mad hermit who thinks he is St. Serapion (*OCGL*).

6. Goethe's *Über Kunst und Altertum* was first published in six volumes from 1816
to 1832. It was later included as volume 43 of *Goethes Werke: Vollständige Ausgabe
letzter Hand*.

90. To James F. Clarke

[September? 1833]
[Groton?]

Do you remember a conversation we had in the garden, one starlight
evening, last summer, about the incalculable power which outward
circumstances have over the character? You would not sympathize
with the regrets I expressed, that mine had not been formed amid
scenes and persons of nobleness and beauty, eager passions and dignified events; instead of those secret trials and petty conflicts which
make my transition state so hateful to my memory and my tastes.
You then professed the faith which I resigned with such anguish,—
the faith which a Schiller could never attain,—a faith in the power
of the human will. Yet now, in every letter, you talk to me of the
power of circumstances. You tell me how changed you are. Every one
of your letters is different from the one preceding, and all so altered
from your former self. For are you not leaving all our old ground,
and do you not apologize to me for all your letters? Why do you
apologize? I think I know you very, very well; considering that we
are both human, and have the gift of concealing our thoughts with
words. Nay, further—I do not believe you will be able to become
anything which I cannot understand. I know I can sympathize with
all who feel and think, from a Dryfesdale up to a Max Piccolomini.[1]
You say, you have become a machine.[2] If so, I shall expect to find
you a grand, high-pressure, wave-compelling one—requiring plenty
of fuel. You must be a steam-engine, and move some majestic fabric
at the rate of thirty miles an hour along the broad waters of the nine-

teenth century. None of your pendulum machines for me! I should, to be sure, turn away my head if I should hear you tick, and mark the quarters of hours; but the buzz and whiz of a good large life-endangerer would be music to mine ears. Oh, no! sure there is no danger of your requiring to be set down quite on a level, kept in a still place, and wound up every eight days. Oh no, no! you are not one of that numerous company, who

> ——live and die,
> Eat, drink, wake, sleep between,
> Walk, talk like clock-work too,
> So pass in order due,
>   Over the scene,
> To where the past— *is* past,
> The future—nothing yet, &c &c

But we must all be machines: you shall be a steam-engine;—shall be a mill, with extensive water-privileges,—and I will be a spinning jenny. No! upon second thoughts, I will not be a machine. I will be an instrument, not to be confided to vulgar hands,—for instance, a chisel to polish marble, or a whetstone to sharpen steel!

ELfr, from *Memoirs*, 1:85–86.

Dated by reference in a letter from Clarke to Fuller, 9 September 1833, in Letters of JFC, *pp. 59–61.*

1. Jasper Dryfesdale is the revengeful old steward in Walter Scott's *Abbot,* and Max Piccolomini is a major character in Schiller's *Piccolomini* and *Wallensteins Tod.*

2. Clarke had written, "Indeed, without the blessing of your confidence and intimacy I should have a very machine-like feeling, in going about my works" (*Letters of JFC,* p. 61).

91. To Richard F. Fuller

Boston 17th Octr 1833

My dear Richard,

As Ellen and Arthur both have letters I think it right to address you and Lloyd, although you are *juniors*.[1] I hear from Father that you are a very good boy— I hope you will not forget your resolves about study but that when I return you will have a grand account to give me of what you have learned— I think a great deal of my brothers and always paint them to myself as neatly dressed, speaking in a polite gentlemanly way to one another or learning some good thing. Dont let me feel disappointed and sad when I come home. Frank Rotch, only eleven years old, has made such progress in Mathematicks that his Master sent him back to his parents saying that he had no boys who could keep up with little Frank.[2] When shall we have any thing so pleasant said of Richard?— Two years hence?"

I have looked at some building-blocks—but find that the really good" ones, those which have little books with them showing how to build the foreign churches &c are 1-25 a set—" I fear we cannot afford this— What do you think about it? The cheaper-sets are mere baby's toys and would give no knowledge of Architecture.

Give love to all I do love. I should be glad to get a neatly written letter from you— Do you write a copy every day?— Your afft sister

M

ALS (MH: fMS Am 1086 [9:33]); MsC (MH: fMS Am 1086 [Works, 2:613–15]). *Addressed:* Richard F. Fuller. / Groton.

Two years hence?] Two years ⟨?⟩ hence?
the really good] the ⟨?⟩ really good
are 1-25 a set—] are 1-25 ↑a set↓ —

1. Margaret Fuller's youngest brother, James Lloyd Fuller (1826–91), was a troubled soul. He was either emotionally disturbed or mentally retarded; the family correspondence often talks of "poor Lloyd" without describing his handicap.

2. Eliza Farrar's nephew, Francis Morgan Rotch (1822–63), was the son of Francis (1788–1874) and Ann Waln Morgan Rotch (1800–1884) (Bullard, *Rotches*, p. 443).

92. To James F. Clarke

Boston 25th Octr 1833.

I must write to you, dear James, I feel such a want of enthusiasm this eveg—and you are the only person I can think of whose recollection makes me feel pleasantly.— I have been passing several days in what is called a very gay manner, and the jarred and saddened state in which this always leaves me brings your remembrance very forcibly upon me— 'Tis unaccountable that I should always feel so inclined to tell you my mental wants and troubles when I know you cannot minister any remedy which I cannot procure for my self— I can only suppose it is because I feel that you are upon the right path and that therefore your words and thoughts soothe me indirectly for they breathe the perfumes of a healthful atmosphere and fertilized soil.— How very silly? This does not bear rereading immediately.—" I am not going to tell you what vexes me but you must write and direct to me at Boston, care of Henry H. Fuller—that I may receive the letter as soon as I return— As soon as I return for I am going to N. York in a day or two with your" Mother and Elizabeth—[1] I shall stay a week.

I think I shall be much refreshed by new thoughts and new objects on which to muse this winter in the *icy* seclusion of Groton! But do not anticipate much *pleasure*. E. too feels very cold about the change she has wished so long.— I have been much engrossed of late by her plans and preparations— I am allowed to tell you in greatest confidence that William P. has offered himself—that is to say he has expressed ardent attachment, regret for the past, and a hope that if he can place himself in a proper situation to claim her hand she may favor his suit.[2] This she is willing you should [k]now as you have been made acquainted with those particulars of their connexion so unfavorable to William P.

I do not know whether to be glad or sorry— On the one hand this cancels the bitter part of his experience in some measure. She has no longer the misery of remembering the person she has loved heartless or ungrateful— She does not now feel that her young affections have watered but the desert though they have produced but "weeds of rank luxuriance, tares of haste" She need not feel herself utterly powerless and gets rid in short" of the victim—the Mrs Hemans part of her troubles—[3] On the other hand he is not worthy of her and could never keep her good and happy and if he were so and could so, her father will never consent to her marrying" him— And I fear she will now be infinitely less likely to forget him— He talked of going to Louisville to see *you* (I cant imagine for what purpose) if he should you will be discreet.

I passed last eveg at Mr Everett's.— All the dramatis personae changed from last autumn except Mr and Mrs E[,] M. Soley and myself—and!! Mr Osgood in Mr Angier's place—at least so it seemed on a slight survey.[4] Pray has this youth dignity or independence of feeling? I only ask for information—

Mr Robbins has had a call to Mr *Emerson's*[5] I went all Sunday with Sarah to Brattle St to hear Mr Channing preach. I was deeply interested in the morning sermon which was upon the text— Work out your salvation with fear and trembling—[6] That of the afternoon on the omnipresence of the Deity was very beautifully written but did not come so home to my previously unfinished trains of thought— He does not read the hymns well. His emphasis is faulty, cadences governed by no rule and manner much too rapid, indeed very conversational. I hope you read the hymns well— I think you do for I always thought your manner of reciting poetry showed that sensibility which commands attention and sympathy even where exception is taken to the taste and emphasis in detail.

What fault do you find with Goethe's lyricks—[7] Each one gives a mood of the mind with marked expression and intense and beautiful language— Does not the perusal of them rouse your imagination and make you think or in some cases rouse you to unexpected passion— What would you have? If you want sympathy read Schiller. I have been quaffing more Martineau sherbet of late with much satisfaction.[8] I believe I told you in my last of her letter to Mr Ware.

Do you study now or are you so happy as to be obliged to write and act all the time. Let me know the texts of some of your sermons I wish to write some in the style of Saturday evening.[9] By the way you have never answered what I said about that book. Always answer my questions if possible— I cannot forget a question till I get it answered.

I wish to study ten-thousand, thousand things this winter— Every day I become more sensible to the defects in my education— I feel so ignorant and superficial. Every day hundreds of questions occur to me to which I can get no answer and do not know what books to consult. Today at the Navy yard!— I did so wish I had had some person of sense with me to explain sundry things— I must study Architecture at all events. That is part of my plan this winter I *will* know the minutiae of *that*— I am tired of these general ideas. They did well enough for conversation but cannot satisfy me when I am alone. I hope I shall greet you with some new ideas when you return. Whatever I learned at Groton makes a very defined impression upon me because I cannot talk it out and draw my inferences.—

Here is a man talking to Bill about Frankenstein—[10] After getting the *story* from her he says "a very good outline but where is the moral?— Tieck would have been delighted— Moral of Frankenstein forsooth?—

I would fain say some thing very fine before I close, but I cannot— I cannot— Adieu worse written than ever I grieve to say.—

P S. I am now on very pleasant terms with Sarah She talks to me plentifully.[11]

AL (MH: bMS Am 1569.7 [464]). Published in part in *New England Quarterly* 30 (September 1957):379. *Addressed:* Rev. James F Clarke. / Louisville— / Kentucky— *Postmark:* Boston MS Oct 26. *Endorsed:* S. M. F. Oct 26.

How very silly? This does not bear rereading immediately.—] ↑ How very silly? This does not bear rereading immediately.— ↓

two with your] two with ⟨Mrs⟩ your

gets rid in short] gets rid ↑ in short ↓

consent to her marrying] consent to ↑ her ↓ marry ↑ ing ↓

1. Probably Elizabeth Randall.

2. John Wesley Thomas identifies this man as William Pickering. Clarke, in his reply dated 12 November, discusses Pickering's unsuccessful attempt to woo Elizabeth Randall (*Letters of JFC*, pp. 64–65).

3. Felicia Dorothea Hemans (1793–1835), a writer of popular verse, is best known for her "Casabianca," which contains the line "The boy stood on the burning deck" (*DNB*).

4. Edward Everett was at this time a member of the U.S. House of Representatives (*DAB*). M. Soley is Mary Soley of Charlestown. Samuel Osgood (1812–80) was a Harvard theological student (class of 1835). Mr. Angier is Joseph Angier (1808–71), a close friend of Clarke's and a graduate of the Divinity School in 1832 (*DivCat*).

5. Emerson had sent a letter of resignation to the Proprietors of the Second Church, Boston, on 11 September 1832; they accepted it on 28 October (Rusk, *Letters of RWE*, 1:355–56). The pulpit was vacant for over a year, until Chandler Robbins (1810–82) was ordained and assumed the ministry of the church on 4 December 1833. Robbins, the son of Dr. Peter G. and Abba Dowse Robbins, occupied the pulpit until he retired in 1874 (*Heralds*, 3:335–39).

6. Phil. 2:12. William Henry Channing (1810–84), Dr. Channing's nephew, was at this time preaching at Brattle Street Church, where he was being considered for a call. The church did not invite him to become its minister, however, and Channing soon went to Europe. Son of Francis Dana (1775–1810) and Susan Higginson Channing (1783–1865), William Henry had graduated from the Divinity School in 1833. In 1836 he married Julia Allen (1813–89). A socialist and associationist, Channing later served several pulpits and became a contributor to and editor of radical papers and magazines. After helping to found the Religious Union of Associationists, which he served as president, he moved to England. Except for a period during the American Civil War, he lived there until his death. Three days before Fuller wrote this letter, Clarke had written Channing, "I wonder why you and M. Fuller have never come nearer to each other. Is it that you feel her defects to be similar to your own, & she not being on the right way would exercise a bad influence on the growth of your mind? I admire her character as I do the torso of Hercules—it is imperfect but it denotes a higher style than the Apollo's Gladiators" (Octavius B. Frothingham, *A Memoir of William Henry Channing* [Boston, 1886], pp. 90–91; *DAB; Cleveland and Cleaveland*, p. 1072; Higginson, *Reverend Francis Higginson*, pp. 31–32; Clarke to Channing, 22 October 1833, MH: bMS Am 1569 [284]).

7. In his letter of 9 September, Clarke had admitted to Fuller that he no longer had an enthusiasm for Goethe's poetry. "I cannot understand his poetry as I fancied I did his prose. Those little *Lieder*, proverbs, etc., are darkness visible to me" (*Letters of JFC*, p. 60).

8. Fuller had probably been reading some of Martineau's Illustrations of Political Economy, a series of pamphlets begun in 1832 and published in an American edition by L. C. Bowles in Boston.

9. [Isaac Taylor], *Saturday Evening* (London, 1832). Taylor (1787–1865) was an artist, author, and lay theologian (*DNB*).

10. Mary Wollstonecraft Shelley, *Frankenstein: or, the Modern Prometheus* (London?, 1818).

11. Sarah Clarke, James's sister.

93. To [?]

[ca. 1834?]

Mr.—— says the Wanderjahre is "*wise.*" It must be presumed so; and yet one is not satisfied. I was perfectly so with my manner of interpreting the Lehrjahre; but this sequel keeps jerking my clue, and threatens to break it. I do not know our Goethe yet. I have changed my opinion about his religious views many times. Sometimes I am tempted to think that it is only his wonderful knowledge of human nature which has excited in me such reverence for his philosophy, and that no worthy fabric has been elevated on this broad foundation. Yet often, when suspecting that I have found a huge gap, the next turning it appears that it was but an air-hole, and there is a brick all ready to stop it. On the whole, though my enthusiasm for the Goetherian philosophy is checked, my admiration for the genius of Goethe is in nowise lessened, and I stand in a sceptical attitude, ready to try his philosophy, and, if needs must, play the Eclectic.

Did I write that a kind-hearted neighbor, fearing I might be *dull*, sent to offer me the use of a *book-caseful* of Souvenirs, Gems, and such-like glittering ware? I took a two or three year old "Token," and chanced on a story, called the "Gentle Boy," which I remembered to have heard was written by somebody in Salem. It is marked by so much grace and delicacy of feeling, that I am very desirous to know the author, whom I take to be a lady.[1]

ELfr, from *Memoirs*, 1:167–68.

Perhaps two letter fragments.

1. The author was, however, the young Nathaniel Hawthorne (1804–64), whose "Gentle Boy" had appeared in *The Token* (Boston, 1832), pp. 193–240. Exactly when Fuller met Hawthorne is not clear, but they had a cordial, if not a warm, friendship in the 1840s. Hawthorne later came to dislike her aggressiveness and bitterly denounced both her and Ossoli in his journal (Julian Hawthorne, *Nathaniel Hawthorne and His Wife* [Boston, 1884], 1:259–60).

94. To Almira P. Barlow

Groton, March 9. 1834.

Are you not ashamed, oh most friendship-less clergywoman! not to have enlivened my long seclusion by one line? You can write to Mistress Mary Hedge, forsooth! to her you confide the history of your

intellectual efforts, of your child's mental progress and various mala-
dies, and of your successes in Brooklyn society.[1] Who is she, that you
should prefer her to me as the depositary of all these interesting particulars? Can the Brooklyn Society have exercised so depraving an influence on your heart and tastes? Or does the Author of the "Lecture
delivered with much applause before the Brooklyn Lyceum", despise
and wish to cast off the Author of "Essays contumeliously rejected by
that respected publication, the Christian Examiner?"[2] That a little success should have such power to steel the female heart to base ingrati-
tude! Oh Ally! Ally! wilt thou forget that it was I, (in happier hours
thou has full oft averred it) who first fanned the spark of thy Ambition into a flame? Think'st thou that thou owest nought to those long
sweeps over the insignificant, inexpressive realities of literature, when
thou wert obliged to trust to my support, thy own opinions, as yet
scarce budding from thy heels or shoulders? Dost thou forget,— but
my emotions will not permit me to pursue the subject; surely I must
have jogged your conscience sufficiently. I shall follow the instructions of the great Goethe, and having, in some degree vented my feelings, address you as if you were what you ought to be. Still remains
enveloped in mystery the reason why neither you nor my reverend
friend came to bid me good-bye before I left your city, according to
promise. I suspected the waiter, at the time, of having intercepted
your card; but your long, *venomous* silence has obliged me to acquit
him. I had treasured up sundry little anecdotes touching my journey
homeward, which, if related with dramatic skill, might excite a smile
on your face, oh laughter-loving blue-stocking! I returned home under
the protection of a Mr Fullerton, fresh from London and Paris, who
gave me an entirely new view of continental affairs. He assured me
that the German Prince was an ignorant pretender, in the face of
my assurances that I had read and greatly admired his writings;[3] and
gave me a contemptuous description of Waldo Emerson *dining in boots*
at Timothy Wiggin's, absolument a faire mourir![4] All his sayings were
exquisite. And then a sui generis *Mother* whom I met with on board
the steamboat. All my pretty pictures are blotted out by the rude hand
of Time; verily, this checking of speech is dangerous. If all the matter
I have been preserving for various persons, is in my head, packed
away, distributed among the various organs, how immensely will my
head be developed when I return to the world,—not admissible in
good society, I fear. This is the first time in my life that I have known
what it is to have nobody to speak to, c'est à dire, of my own peculiar
little fancies. I bear it with strange philosophy, but I do wish to be
written to. I will tell you how I pass my time, without society or exer-

cise. Even till two o'clock, sometimes later, I pour ideas into the heads of the little Fullers; much runs out;—indeed I am often reminded of the chapter on home-education, in the New-Monthly.[5] But the few drops which remain mightily gladden the sight of my Father. Then I go down stairs and ask for my letters from the Post; this is my only pleasure; according to the ideas most people entertain of pleasure. Do you write me an excellent epistle by return of mail, or I will make your head ache by a minute account of the way in which the remaining hours are spent. I have only lately read the "Female Sovereigns" of your beloved Mrs Jameson, and like them better than any of her works.[6] Her opinions are clearly expressed, sufficiently discriminating, and her manner unusually simple. I was not dazzled by excess of artificial light, nor cloyed by spiced and sweetened sentiments. My love to your reverend husband, and four kisses to Edward,[7] two on your account, one for his beauty, and one abstract kiss, symbol of my love for all little children in general. Write of him, of Mr B's sermons, of your likes and dislikes, of any new characters, sublime or droll you may have unearthed, and of all other things I should like.

Affectionately your country friend, poor and humble,

MARGARET.

MsC (MH: fMS Am 1086 [Works, 1:7–11]). Published in Wade, pp. 545–46.

1. The Barlows had moved to Brooklyn, where David Barlow had become the minister of the Unitarian church on 17 September 1834 (*DivCat*).

2. *The Christian Examiner and General Review* had begun publishing in 1824 as a continuation of *The Christian Disciple*. More than an organ of Unitarianism, the *Examiner* was a major religious review, with a broad scope and high literary standards. No trace of rejected Fuller essays survives (Frank Luther Mott, *A History of American Magazines, 1741–1850* [New York, 1930], pp. 284–92).

3. Hermann, Fürst von Pückler-Muskau (1785–1871), was a Prussian officer in the Russian army during the Wars of Liberation. He then traveled extensively in Africa and Asia Minor and became popular as a writer. His *Briefe eines Verstorbenen* had been published in four volumes from 1830 to 1832. Mrs. Sarah Austin translated it into English, but Fuller may have read the original (*OCGL*).

4. Timothy Wiggin (1773–1856), originally from New Hampshire, became an auctioneer, dry goods dealer, and importer in Boston. He went to England, where he and his brother Benjamin grew quite wealthy (J. H. Wiggin, *Wiggin Family* [Boston, 1888], p. 77; Franklin C. Thompson, "Wiggin Genealogy," NEHGS, p. 59). Emerson was touring Europe and England from late 1832 to October 1833 (Rusk, *Life of RWE*, pp. 168–97); "It is absolutely to die."

5. Founded in 1814, the magazine had several well-known editors, including Thomas Campbell, Bulwer-Lytton, and Thomas Hood (*Oxford Companion to English Literature*, ed. Paul Harvey, 3d ed. [Oxford, 1946]).

6. Anna Brownell Jameson, *Memoirs of Celebrated Female Sovereigns* (London, 1831). A prolific writer, Jameson (1794–1860) was a friend of Elizabeth Barrett, Lady Byron, and Ottilie Goethe. Her *Visits and Sketches at Home and Abroad* (London, 1834) helped to popularize German culture (*DNB*).

7. Edward Barlow, Almira's oldest son.

95. To Amelia Greenwood

Groton 20th March 1834.

My always dear Amelia,

I was neither hurt nor offended—I wrote the exact truth in my note. My life was so monotonous, on so different a level from yours that I really seemed to have nothing to communicate— I should have at any-time have been very glad to hear from you but did not feel distressed about you as I was sure you were well and happy—

You were not the least egotistical— I took much pleasure in hearing of your happiness—but somehow your engagement seems to have changed our relation to one another and we have not been sufficiently together yet for me to feel easy under this change—[1] Then I sincerely dislike to talk or write about myself— Only when *drawn out* can I do it with comfort— Pride not modesty is the occasion for this— The past I will not mourn over but cannot love to contemplate— The present— I can use or endure, but not enjoy— I cannot de[   ] of either at least not to old friends [   ] I am perfectly free forgetting the [   ] onward to those "before" but you, [   ] the conflicts of my soul and I am invo[   ] tempted to recur to them?

To recur for they are over? My soul is [   ] by passion and inflated by vainglorious [   ] I look upon my situation and contem [   ] perform and suffer.

I do not cast gloom over my family and the few who see me probably esteem me cheerful or gay.

I have now been at home nearly five months— You know I had adopted the idea that the edn of my little brothers[n] and sister was my nearest duty— Circumstances not necessary to detail induced me to promise my father if he would allow William to come home this winter I would take charge of him also.

Four pupils[n] are a serious and fatiguing charge for one of my some what ardent and impatient disposition. Five days in the week I have given daily lessons in three languages, in geography and history besides many other exercises on alternate days— This has consumed often eight, always five hours of my day— There has been a great deal of needle-work to-do, and is now nearly all finished and I shall not be obliged to pass my time about it when every-thing looks beautiful as I did las[t] summer— We have had[n] very poor servants and for [some time past,] only one— My mother has been often [ill. My grand]mother (who passed the winter with [us) has been ill. Thus] you may imagine as I am the *only* [grown-up daughter, that] my time has been considerably [taxed.]

[But as, sad or merry, I must always be learning, I laid down a course of study at the beginning of winter, comprising certain] things about which I had always [felt deficient. These] were— The history and [Geography of] modern Europe, beginning the former in the fourteenth century The elements of Architecture—the works of Alfieri with his opinions on them—the hist and critical works of Goethe and Schiller and an outline of hist of our own country.

All this you see Dear, is might dry and would not interest you like the things I used to be learning. Thus I chose this time when I should have nothing to distract or dissipate my mind— I have nearly completed this course in the style I proposed (not minute or thorough, I confess) though I have had only three evenings in the week and chance hours in the day for it. I am very glad I have done it and feel the good effects already. I occasionally try my hand at composition but have not completed any thing to my satisfaction— I have sketched a number of plans but if ever accomplished they must be so in a season of more joyful energy, when my mind has been renovated and refreshed by change of scene or circumstance.— I have other plans but they are too undecided to be worth mentioning. My trans of Tasso cannot be published a present if ever—[2] I regret this principally because I expected to have had a certain sum of money at my own disposal.

I have now, my dear Amelia, written to you of myself more freely and fully than to any one for some-time— Do not impart [   ] other person this long recital of my doings: it [   ] very Pharisaical—but I esteemed it the propo[   ] your letter you will see that very little in my [   ] pro[   ] me to communication by writing [   ]— Yet I [   ] shall talk to you a great deal when we meet—

That may chance in May— At that time—I shall lay on the shelf books needles and children—and if Elizabeth R. returns from Georgia I shall visit Boston for a short time— I will then pass a couple of days with you if you wish it— Meanwhile write to me if you feel like it and if you do not receive immediate answer—do not suppose me either alienated or sad— I have done some good— I have trust that Providence will enable me to do more— My parents are *both* perfectly satisfied with me— I am *some what less diss*atisfied with myself than heretofore— I am not absolutely without society— Goethe!! says live a [   ] retired as we will we must soon become either d[   ] creditors. It has been so with me— There are sev[   ] here to whom I am debtor for much kindness as [   ] of considerable cultivation and enlargement. I do not however esteem their characters worth drawing for *you.*

I have letters pretty frequently from Mrs Farrar, A Higginson, A Barker, E Randall and James.—[3] The latter seems to anticipate seeing us again with much pleasure— He has had many things to try him but has endured them as you and I would expect— I had an extremely witty letter from Mrs Barlow yesterday which I should like to show you if you were here— Mr B has had a call and they will remain— Present my regards to Dr Bartlett love to your mother, Angy and Emma[4] and believe me silent or communicative your Friend as ever

M F.

If there is news of M. Peabody I should like to hear of it I never he[ar]d she went but concluded she did.[5]

ALS (MH: fMS Am 1086 [Box A]); MSCfr (MH:fMS Am 1086 [Works, 3:363–67]). Published in part in *Memoirs*, 1:149–51. *Addressed:* Miss Amelia Greenwood, / Care of Revd Mr Barrett / Boston / Mass. *Postmark:* Groton MS March 22.

The manuscript is badly torn. Matter in square brackets has been supplied from the Memoirs *version.*

my little brothers] my ↑ little ↓ brothers
Four pupils] Four pupi(s)ls
We have had] We ↑ have ↓ had

1. Amelia Greenwood apparently had just announced her engagement to Dr. George Bartlett.

2. The translation was never published in Fuller's lifetime. Her brother Arthur included it in his edition of *Art, Literature, and the Drama* in 1860. On 25 October 1833 Sarah Clarke wrote her brother James that Eliza Farrar had shown Fuller's preface to the translation to Charles Folsom of the college press with the idea of publishing it anonymously and pretending it came from England (Sarah Clarke, "Letters of a Sister," corrected proof sheets, MH: bMS Am 1569.3 [12]; these letters were edited by Lillian F. Clarke and published in *The Cheerful Letter*, a magazine, between November 1903 and January 1910).

3. Anna Hazard Barker (1813–1900) married Samuel Gray Ward in 1840 (*Barker Genealogy*, p. 180; Mt. Auburn). James is James Clarke.

4. Amelia was staying with her sister Mary Susan (1805–74), the wife of the Reverend Samuel Barrett; Angy is her sister Angelina. Emma was their youngest sister, Emmeline (1816–96), who married Charles L. Hayward (1812–90) in 1840 (Isaac J. Greenwood, "William Pitt Greenwood," *Memorial Biographies*, 1:271; *CC*, 12 September 1832, 15 November 1834; Isaac John Greenwood, *The Greenwood Family* [n.p., 1934], p. 145).

5. Mary Tyler Peabody (1806–94), daughter of Dr. Nathaniel and Elizabeth Palmer Peabody, had been in Cuba since December 1833. She had been looking after her sister Sophia, who had gone there for her health. The Peabodys stayed in Cuba until April 1835. In 1843 Mary married the widower Horace Mann (1796–1859), with whom she collaborated in reforming public education in America (*Peabody Genealogy*, p. 85; *Peabody Sisters*, pp. 71–73; *NAW*; *DAB*).

96. To Arthur B. Fuller

Boston 4th June 1834.

I could not but regret, my dear Arthur that your letter, which would otherwise have given me so much pleasure to receive should require to be prefaced and concluded with so many apologies for bad writing, brevity &c— you are old enough to write a neat and a long letter and I hope your next will be both.

I have seen Wentworth often but can tell you little about him as he has preserved a modest silence in my presence except that he looks very bright and happy.[1] He gave me a letter for you which I *very carelessly* left at Cambridge— I have sent for it and hope it will arrive in time to go by Father, if not I will send it by the first opportunity. I have not seen the Nortons but hear they are making great progress in their studies.[2] They learn Latin, French, Italian and history besides dancing lessons, sewing &c— They have few disengaged hours and feel that, at their age, to be quite right. They went Election day with Mrs Farrar, Frank Rotch and Mr Cleveland and passed the afternoon at Horn Pond.—[3] Ellen will describe to you her visit to the Websters, her rides upon the Donkey and the wild times they have had at College—[4] When I return I will, if you remind me, give you an account of the Tableaux vivans, or living pictures I saw at Miss Davis's—[5] The State's prison &c At present I have no time adieu, my dear, I hope you are doing *nothing* for which I shall be sorry and *something* for which I shall be glad Say the same to Richard with my love. Do not let weeds grow in my garden. I trust to have radishes from it when I return. Remember me to Rebecca I hope she is enjoying life. Affectionately your sister

M.

ALS (MH: fMS Am 1086 [9:36]); MsC (MH: fMS Am 1086 [Works, 1:611–13]). *Addressed:* Arthur B. Fuller / Groton. *Endorsed:* S. M. Fuller / June 9th 1834.

The endorsement was added at a later time.

1. Probably Thomas Wentworth Higginson.

2. The younger Fuller children were longtime friends of the children of Andrews (1786–1853) and Catharine Eliot Norton. The elder Norton is now best known for his attacks on Transcendentalism. The children were Louisa (1823–1915), Jane (1824–77), Charles Eliot (1827–1908), and Grace (b. 1834) (*Heralds*, 2:193–98; MVR 1915, 53:312, 473:540, 293:60; *DAB*; Sarah Norton and M. A. DeWolfe Howe, *Letters of Charles Eliot Norton* [Boston, 1913], 1:11, 80; 2:77).

3. Mr. Cleveland may have been Stephen Higginson Cleveland (1811–56) or George William Cleveland (d. 1848), who graduated from Harvard in 1832 (*Cleveland and Cleaveland*, p. 509; Harvard archives). Election Day sermons were given in Massachusetts from 1634 until 1884. Beginning in 1641, Election Day was the last Wednesday in May, but in 1832 it was changed to the first Wednesday in January to coincide with the meeting of the legislature. For many years, however, people still celebrated "Election Day" in May. By 1834 the holiday was expanded to a full week's activities, which included meetings of religious and charitable organizations. In 1834, for instance, they included the Prison Discipline Society, the Bible Society of Massachusetts, the New

Arthur Buckminster Fuller during the Civil War. Courtesy of Willard P. Fuller, Jr.

England Anti-Slavery Society, the American Unitarian Association, and the Massachusetts Temperance Society (A. W. Plumstead, *The Wall and the Garden* [Minneapolis, 1968], pp. 6–12; Lindsay Swift, "The Massachusetts Election Sermons," *Publications of the Colonial Society of Massachusetts* 1 [1895]:388–451; *Christian Register*, 24 May 1834).

4. On 19 May, Harvard had erupted in one of its occasional battles between students and faculty. A quarrel between the freshman class and an instructor in Greek who was unable to keep discipline led to a general rebellion. On 29 May President Quincy suspended the entire sophomore class (1836) for its part in the fracas, but that action caused even more disorder in the Harvard Yard (Harvard archives HUD 234.04.B). The Websters were the family of John White (1793–1850) and Harriet F. Hickling Webster (1793–1853). Webster, the Erving Professor of Chemistry at Harvard, later was the center of Boston's most famous murder trial; he was convicted and hanged for the 1850 murder of Dr. George Parkman (*CVR*; Arthur W. Hodgman, "Elias Parkman of Dorchester and His Descendants," NEHGS, p. 140; "The Dabneys and the Hicklings of the Azores Islands," NEHGS; Robert Sullivan, *The Disappearance of Dr. Parkman* [Boston, 1971]).

5. Fuller probably had visited Helen Davis in Boston.

97. To James F. Clarke

Boston 28th Septr 1834.

You requested me not to answer you rashly— I have therefore taken a week to reflect upon your letter before I replied to it.[1]

I passed a month at Newport and in my few solitary moments the remembrance of our last interview would almost always obtrude itself upon me. My mind refreshed and calmed by new thoughts, tender attentions, and a change of scene stood firm to the decision it had formed in a suffering and excited state. I felt, as I had expected to feel, deep regret: I *knew* that your loss could not be made up to me, but still I thought that my impressions had been correct and the words I had spoken words of sooth— I believed you had recognized them to be such and neither expected nor wished to hear from you again— I looked upon this deprivation with a saddened but a resolved soul.—

But I cannot resist the frank and kind spirit in which your letter is written— I do not "cast you from me"— I will not "insist" that all is over. In yielding to your wishes and your judgement I have good hope that we may begin a new era and that we may alter the *nature* of our friendship without annihilating its soul. I cannot, indeed, see any reason why we cannot all our days have such an one, for instance, as exists between Mrs Farrar and Mr Dewey.[2] There is, I believe, *no* reason except that I am not a reasonable woman and must needs be putting more of feeling into my intercourse with others than is any wise necessary or appropriate. I cannot, however, *promise* that I will shew myself a reasonable woman on this occasion but I will attempt it— I am willing to resume correspondence with you and time will decide whether we can resist the changes in one another. Time only can do it— I shall therefore say nothing further on the subject but begin here—

My dear Friend—

I need not speak to you of the high tone of spirits and bright springing thoughts which are sure to accompany a residence on the sea-shore. The scene is fled, the mood is o'er yet dear to memory that month upon the lovely Island though the return to my old haunts caused pain enough, most would think, to counterbalance any pleasure I might have received.— We were six miles from Newport, in a farm house just between the beautiful glen and Dr Channings—[3] We rode almost every^n day sometimes to Newport but more frequently to beautiful spots on the Island or across the beaches— Two long rides on horseback I remember with peculiar pleasure. The family was generally large; sometimes they were all on R. I.; sometimes only Anna with one of her sisters two^n of her brothers and myself.[4] Newport was a place of very fashionable resort and every aftn and eveg large parties generally Newyorkers and Philadelphians with a few from further South were out at Mr Barker's. All these people amused me though generally speaking they were not of a description with whom I could form any permanent acquaintance having all the outwardness and heartlessness which should only belong to the society of an old country without its graces and accomplishments. I liked only one lady of all whom I saw. She was young, considered very fashionable with the most crude, inconsistent opinions on all subjects but with a lively, eager mind and warm generous heart. I saw a great deal of her. Among the gentlemen who visited most constantly at the house I liked two very much and several well enough to talk with— All the moonlit evegs we walked in the beautiful glen or sat on the rocks by that arm of the sea which embraces that part of the Island— The waves there made wash and murmur enough to be delightful symphonies to conversation though only on Newport beach could we enjoy their full majesty.

Dr Channing was absent the first three weeks of my stay— I saw him however several times and had considerable opportunity for conversing with him one eveg that I passed there. I was charmed by the cle[ar]ness of his expressions and the kind simplicity of his manner— He had much more flow than I expected and I think if I be so fornunate as to see him hereafter I shall find it very easy to communicate with him— Do you know that the Gn Prince is just coming to this country— I read his Tutti Frutti while at N.; *that* and some particulars told me by an English gentleman who lent it me have rather lowered my opinion of him— Still I would give much to see him and should like you to read Tutti— The journey among the Riesengebirge and account of his ascent in the Balloon struck me particularly.[5]

Anna B. came on with me and we have been passing a fortnight with Mrs Farrar. Mr Dewey was there four or five days but I have not space to tell you about him. I have been made acquainted with Mrs Robinson but made no progress with her. I have seen Mr Angier and think him quite *un*regenerate.[6] I have seen H. Hedge who asked me many questions about you. I saw Mr Channing who spoke of you with much affection.[7] He asked whether I saw you much and enjoyed seeing you— I told him No, that our minds were on different levels— He said I ought to be glad to see you higher on the hill of Truth than myself— Said how much pleasure your letters had given him— This is Elizabeth's birthday—[8] She is twenty three and seems in a tolerably happy frame of mind. There are several pictures in town of which I shd like to give an account but have no room for that or a myriad more new-old things— I go next Thursday to Worcester to pass a week or more there before returning to Groton for the winter— Farewell, very sincerely yours

S. M. F.

ALS (MH: bMS Am 1569.7 [467]). Published in part in *New England Quarterly* 30 (September 1957):382. *Addressed:* Revd James F. Clarke. / Louisville, / Kentucky. *Postmark:* Boston MS Oct 1.

rode almost every] rode ↑ almost ↓ every
sisters two] sisters ⟨and,⟩ two

1. Sometime during the summer of 1834 a serious break threatened the friendship of Fuller and Clarke. Apparently she wrote that she had "lost" him and then berated him for the situation. He replied on 8 September, defending himself and concluding: "I beg you not to determine rashly, from a pride of Understanding, that our friendship is over—and so make it over. . . . I can never find such another as you, and I think you will not meet with exactly such another friend as [I]" (*Letters of JFC*, pp. 78–80). Fuller is responding to that letter.

2. From 1823 to 1833 Orville Dewey (1794–1882) had been the minister at the Unitarian church in New Bedford, where Eliza Farrar's family was prominent. After a breakdown, Dewey left the ministry, but he later assumed the pastorate of the Church of the Messiah in New York City. He was a prolific writer on religious topics and an accomplished preacher (*Heralds*, 3:84–89; Harvard archives).

3. Fuller had visited the Jacob Barkers in Newport. The Glen was the summer home of Mary Rotch (1777–1848), daughter of William Rotch, Sr., the Quaker shipper and patriarch of the Rotch family in New Bedford. Mary is the "Aunt Mary" of many later letters (Bullard, *Rotches*, p. 94).

4. Jacob Barker (1779–1871) had become extremely wealthy in New York as a shipper. In the early 1830s he lost his fortune and moved to New Orleans, where he

soon made an even larger fortune. He married Eliza H. Hazard (1782–1866) in 1801 and raised a large family. Which of Anna's brothers was in Newport that summer cannot be determined, but the sister had to be either Elizabeth (1817–78) or Sarah (b. 1819) (*Barker Genealogy*, p. 180; *LBD*). Fuller often vacationed in Newport, staying either with the Barkers, the Channings, or the Rotches.

5. Hermann Pückler-Muskau, *Tutti-frutti: Aus den Papieren des Verstorbenen* (Stuttgart, 1834). Fuller mentions two sections: "Extracts from my Note-book," which describes the balloon, and "Scenes and Sketches of a Tour in the Riesengebirge."

6. Therese Albertine Louise von Jakob Robinson (1797–1870), a philologist and translator, knew and impressed Goethe. The daughter of a Halle professor, Ludwig Heinrich von Jakob, she married Edward Robinson (1794–1863) in 1828. After moving to America, she studied the American Indians, wrote on the Slavic languages, and had a lively salon in New York City in the 1840s (*DAB*). Mr. Angier is Joseph Angier.

7. William Henry Channing.

8. Elizabeth Randall.

98. To Almira P. Barlow

Worcester, Oct 6, 1834.

My dear Almira,

Why have I not answered your kind and pleasant letter of last Spring? Not because I loved you not, but because my mind has been engrossed or dissipated a thousand ways.

I know not precisely why, but during the last three or four days that I have been here, my mind has been turning incessantly towards you; I have wished again and again that I could drink a cup of the strongest coffee, and then sit down to pass an afternoon and evening with you and your spouse.

Surely the intercourse I used to have with you and other friends of my youth, was penetrating, was satisfying, compared with that I have with people now. I am more and more dissatisfied with this world, and *cannot* find a home in it. Outward things how vain! when we lean on them merely, and Heaven knows I have striven enough to make my mind its own place. I have resolution for the contest, and will not shrink or faint, but I know not, just at this moment, where to turn.

I have been wandering about somewhat since I saw you last; one month in Rhode-Island, where I was so happy! Had you seen me then I could have flashed and sparkled, and afforded you some amusement. I had many little stories to tell, ludicrous and pathetic, and many ideas, not very deep, 'tis true, but tasteful and brilliant, which I had been throwing to right and left, to people who would hardly trouble themselves, and would give me nothing in return, except experience.

Experience! why cannot I value thee, and make thee my peculiar household deity, as did our Master, Goethe? I suppose I could, if I had the same reproducing power; but, as it is, Experience only gives me "Byron headache."[1] My mind still leadeth me to new things; I wish to try and try,—and am ashamed too, to be still in this region of experimental philosophy, still afloat. I have thought several times I had grasped "First Principles", but those elegant beings elude me.

Well, I have scolded enough. By dint of scribbling, I have evaporated some of the dissatisfaction which had been weighing on my heart for some three weeks past. How art thou? Is thy tongue fluent? thy mind busy? thy heart warm? Is thy health good, and thy visage in right order? Dost thou find any new friends, whether among literati deceased or foreign, or living, chatty practicals? And thy lovely boy,— is he growing to be a good or an evil angel?

For me, I have been wandering about, as I told thee; I have studied little nor none in books. The German Prince's new work, "Tutti Frutti" I would mention among the noteworthy. I have seen many new human beings, many vapid and aimless, some interesting, some few wise and good. I have not seized any of them by the hand. Have had some hours of most pleasant communing with Nature, but do not find these a panacea. I am passing a week here with a friend enjoying the agricultural festivities of the season, and shall return next Saturday to immure myself at home for the Winter. I saw H. Hedge while in Cambridge; he gave some amusing sketches of his journey. Staid at Mrs Farrar's three or four days, while Mr Dewey was there; you are likely to have him for a neighbor in N. Y. He spoke with due admiration of the Rev W. Emerson, that only clergyman of all possible clergymen who eludes my acquaintance.[2] Mais n' importe! I keep his image bright in my mind. Let me hear from you soon, for my heart is warm toward you.

M. F.—

MsC (MH: fMS Am 1086 [Works, 1:13–17]). Published in part in Higginson, *MFO*, p. 62.

1. Perhaps an allusion to *Childe Harold's Pilgrimage*, canto 1, stanza 8:

> Strange pangs would flash along Childe Harold's brow,
> As if the memory of some deadly feud
> Or disappointed passion lurked below.

2. Apparently Emerson eluded her for another two years, for the scanty record shows no meetings before 1836. Ralph Waldo Emerson (1803–82) was a central figure

in Fuller's life, for she found in him an imaginative union of spirituality and literary excellence. When, in 1839, they joined efforts on the *Dial*, they formed an axis that symbolically united the solitude of Concord with the sophistication of Boston.

99. To Frederic H. Hedge

Groton 9th Novr 1834.

My dear Friend,

I was disappointed by not finding you at home when I lately called on your sister Mary. I wished to consult you on one or two subjects.

I have done with dissipation for the present and hope (though I am to resume Miss Gabbins-izing) to have some time to myself this winter. I want to read the Bible with some good commentary and of the Divines[n] whom I at present have the honor to number among my acquaintance I know of no one so likely to understand[n] what will suit me as yourself— Will you give me your advice in writing on this subject?[1]

Do you still hold in mind your intent of visiting the Planets?[2] I can truly say that from the hour we talked of it[n] until this past week I have not had an hour when my mind was free enough for writing. I do not now retain with sufficient accuracy the plan you marked out for me— Will you give it me again if you still wish my aid and I will see what I can do.—

Please give me any news you have of Mr Barlow and Almira— I feel as if I had wandered a thousand miles from them but love them not the less—[3]

I was not in a sufficiently intellectual mood to enjoy your society when I staid last in Cambridge or I should much lament only having seen you one half-hour— I remember with pure pleasure the conversations we had together last June and have often mused in the still watches of the night on some of the ideas and plans we then discussed— They were of my better world— Perhaps I may live to show myself worthy to be its denizen yet. I meant to have mentioned, in speaking of Mr Barlow, his lines on the death of Edward Emerson.[4] I know not whether it was their beauty or the feelings I have always entertained towards Edward E (though I did not know him) but they drew many tears from my eyes— He was to me, when very young, a living type of noble ambition and refinement. Perhaps this opinion of him was a mistaken one— Fate forbad its being tested— Where such *have* been so I have too often found myself mistaken— But the change which came over his destiny[n] was of a sort which cast a mournful and tender interest round him— We cannot grieve that he was not doomed to linger amid uncongenial scenes and employments far from the scene of his youthful hopes and attachments but I was much affected on seeing his death.

Mary seemed to apprehend your going to Bangor, if so I shall see you no more—[5] But write and let me know what you propose. I am lengthening my intended[n] *note* into a letter— Remember me to Lucy, Mary and your Parents and believe me sincerely yours

M. F.

Please send my trans of Tasso if you have it.[6] Father returns the latter part of this week. Excuse the careless appearance of this— I have been writing six hours and am *too* tired. Another time I will be more *lady like*

ALS (MH: fMS Am 1086 [10:101]).
and of the Divines] and ⟨among⟩ ↑ of ↓ the Divines
so likely to understand] so likely to ⟨know⟩ ↑ understand ↓
say that from the hour we talked of it] say that ↑ from the hour we talked of it ↓
over his destiny] over hi⟨m⟩s ↑ destiny ↓
my intended] my ⟨proposed⟩ ↑ intended ↓

1. In his reply of 17 November (MH-AH), Hedge suggested she read Eichhorn's *Einleitung ins alte Testament*, 3 vols. (Leipzig, 1780–83). Johann Gottfried Eichhorn (1752–1827) had been professor of theology at Göttingen (*Die Religion in Geschichte und Gegenwart* [Tübingen, 1958], cols. 345–46).

2. Fuller refers to Hedge's suggestion that they form a literary club modeled on Tieck. In reply, Hedge said, "I have thought but little about it lately & am not sufficiently master of myself at present to attempt anything of the kind."

3. Of the Barlows, Hedge said, "[David] writes in good spirits though like one who has been much affected by the discipline of life & brought down from his high imaginings."

4. Barlow and Edward Bliss Emerson were classmates in the Harvard class of 1824. Barlow, the class poet, published "Lines to the Memory of Edward Bliss Emerson, who Died at Porto Rico, October, 1834, Aged 29" in the *Christian Register* of 8 November and a different poem on the same subject in the issue for 20 December. Hedge tartly responded to Fuller, "His lines on Edward Emerson possess much beauty & would be excellent were they not somewhat marred by the usual unfinishedness want of taste & unwarrantable licenses of his poetry."

5. Hedge was moving to Bangor, but he did not assume the pastorate there until 3 May 1835 (*DivCat*).

6. Hedge had lent her translation of Goethe's *Tasso* to Emerson, who had not yet returned it.

100. To Frederic H. Hedge

Groton 30th Novr 1834.

My dear Friend,

A severe indisposition has prevented my thanking you sooner for your prompt and kind reply to my note. For the same reason I have not been to ask Mr Robinson whether he can supply me with such of the[n] books as I think I shall want.[1] In a day or two I hope to be able to go out and shall then see him— I will write to you again in a few days by Eugene who will pass a day or two in Boston on his way to Virginia and ask you for such as I cannot have from him;[2] Eichhorn I do not believe he has— I will send also the Tieck which I shall not use as I intended. I have your Uhland and three vols. of Richter which shall be faithfully returned as any other books you have the kindness to lend me.[3] These have been in my possession some months[n] but I have had no quiet time for reading or study— Now I hope to be more free.

My object is to examine thoroughly as far as my time and abilities permit the evidences of the Christian religion— I have endeavored to get rid of this task as much and as long as possible to[n] content myself with superficial notions and knowledge— and, if I may so express it, to adopt the religion as a matter of taste— But I meet with Infidels very often, two or three of my particular friends are Deists—their arguments and several distressing skeptical notions of my own are haunting me for ever— I *must* satisfy myself and having once begun I shall go as far as I can.

With regard to Mr Emerson, I had two *reasons* (if they may deserve to be so called) for wishing him to see my Tasso. It gratified me that a mind which had affected mine so powerfully should be dwelling on something of mine even though 'twere only new dress for the thoughts of another— And I thought he might express something which would be useful to me. I should like very much his corrections as well as yours if it be not too much trouble. I think I may revise it as an exercise. I did wish very much to have it published when I first wrote it, because I expected for it some money which I would much have liked to have at my command. But there was so much difficulty made that I am now tired of the thought.

Mr Robinson brought me your article on Phrenology as "capital— logical, pungent, beautiful style and what not! He said you "were becoming one of the first writers of the day" and borrowed your Election Sermon.[4] In Mrs Farrar's last letter she says "I admire Mr Hedge's[n] article on Phrenoy very much; it is spirited yet perfectly good natured" and other remarks in the same strain— I am much pleased with it myself and have read it twice— It confirms my first opinion that the pen is your true engine of power. I know little of the world which you inhabit while I am here and can ill report its suffrage—[n] *This* has nothing in common with it and letters are poor things at best, though far, far better than nothing.

I rejoice that you and my friend James have taken to writing to one another.[5] Few have appreciated you more fully than he even while you were personally unknown to him. I hope you will be friends. You will always find him *genuine* as far as he goes.— I got a volume of Frazer's Mag and read all the Sartors I could find— Also Memoirs" of Count Cagliostro in two Flights which pleased me mightily— I cannot but wonder however he is willing to write in that odious vulgar magazine.[6] Poor Bulwer is shamefully abused there and without the slightest knowledge of his true faults either. I happened today on B's little critique on Scott which I like very much—though his objections to Scott's want of mannerism, *want of style* as he calls it amused me and I think he would find it difficult to support his assertion that all great prose writers have had style, if by style is meant what might be travestied in the "rejected addresses" as Scott's poetical manner was— Have you read his Pompeii or dont you read his works now?—[7]

No! I have *not* seen Coleridge's Epitaph and I wish you would copy it for me if not too long.[8] I see Mr Hillard's speech about the pirates considerably lauded in newspaper style—[9] Perhaps he may be a distinguished man yet, but I have not much faith in it—he has not health enough, nor what is worse independence enough. Some things about Mr Dewey remind me of H.

I hope you will accept Mr Emerson's invitation and come here at the same time— It would be pleasanter for you in summer and you could see me with more satisfaction but when" the "green and bowery summer" comes—I may not be here and you may be in Bangor— But do not go without reason good I beg— With your habits of mind I think you will regret leaving the vicinity of Boston much and more— Remember me to your friends and believe me most truly yours

M. F.

ALS (MH: fMS Am 1086 [10:98]). Published in part in *Memoirs*, 1:151, and Higginson, *MFO*, p. 63. *Addressed:* Revd F.H. Hedge, / Cambridge, / Mass. *Postmark:* Groton MS Decr 1.

such of the] such ↑ of the ↓
some months] some ⟨time⟩ ↑ months ↓
as much and as long as possible to] as much ↑ and as long ↓ as possible ⟨and⟩ to
admire Mr Hedge's] admire ⟨Mrs Farrar's⟩ ↑ Mr Hedge's ↓
here and can ill report its suffrage] here ↑ and can ill report its suffrage ↓
Also Memoirs] A⟨s⟩lso Memoirs
but when] but ⟨in⟩ ↑ when ↓

1. The Reverend Charles Robinson (1793–1862) became minister of the Unitarian church in Groton in 1826, a position he held until he moved to Medfield in 1838 (*Heralds*, 2:215–17).

2. Her brother Eugene was shortly to begin teaching school in Culpeper County, Virginia.

3. Hedge had asked Fuller for "the 3d 9th & 10th vols of Tieck" (Hedge to Fuller, 17 November 1834, MH-AH). Which of the works of Ludwig Uhland (1787–1862) Fuller read is not clear. A writer of verse tragedies, poems, and ballads, Uhland was also a teacher at Tübingen and a scholar. His *Gedichte* was published at Tübingen in 1815 (*OCGL*).

4. Hedge had published "Pretensions of Phrenology Examined," *Christian Examiner* 17 (November 1834):249–69, a review of Spurzheim's *Phrenology, or the Doctrine of the Mental Phenomena*. His sermon of 2 June 1834 had been published as *A Sermon Preached before the Ancient and Honourable Artillery Company, on their CXCVIth Anniversary, June 2, 1834*. The same issue of the *Examiner* that contained the phrenology essay favorably reviewed the sermon.

5. Despite his reservations about Clarke's career plans (thinking him best suited for a refined and learned congregation), Hedge had enjoyed their correspondence (Hedge to Fuller, 17 November 1834, MH-AH).

6. Thomas Carlyle's writing had been a prominent part of volume 8 of *Fraser's Magazine*. The July and August issues had his "Count Cagliostro: In Two Flights" (19–28, 132–55). *Sartor Resartus* began with the November issue.

7. Bulwer-Lytton's *Last Days of Pompeii* had been published in 1834. Bulwer had been "abused" anonymously by William Maginn in "Mr. Edward Lytton Bulwer's Novels; and Remarks on Novel Writing," *Fraser's Magazine* 1 (June 1830):509–32. The "little critique on Scott" was Bulwer's "Death of Sir Walter Scott," *New Monthly Magazine and Literary Journal* 35 (October 1832):300–304, where Bulwer says: "Scott may be said, in prose, to have *no style*. There are those, we know, who call this very absence of style a merit—we will not dispute it. . . . For our own part, we think him great, in spite of the want of style, and not because of it" (p. 301).

8. Not long before his death on 25 July, Coleridge wrote his epitaph:

> Stop, Christian passer-by!—Stop, child of God,
> And read with gentle breast. Beneath this sod
> A poet lies, or that which once seem'd he.
> O, lift one thought in prayer for S.T.C.
> That he who many a year with toil of breath
> Found death in life, may here find life in death!
> Mercy for praise—to be forgiven for fame
> He ask'd and hoped, through Christ. Do thou the same!

(Walter Jackson Bate, *Coleridge* [New York, 1968], p. 235).

9. The brig *Mexican*, out of Salem bound for Rio, was captured by the *Panda* on 20 September 1832. The disabled ship escaped and returned to Salem to report the piracy. In 1834 a British ship captured and returned the pirates to New England for trial, which began on 11 November 1834. The twelve defendants were represented in court by David Child (Lydia Francis' husband) and George S. Hillard. Despite Hillard's eloquence, seven of the pirates were convicted on 26 November, and six were executed the following year (Edward C. Battis, "The Brig Mexican of Salem," *Essex Institute Historical Collections* 34 (1898):41–63; *Christian Register*, 29 November, 6 December 1834).

101. To Frederic H. Hedge

Groton 26th Decr 1834.

Dear Henry,

I received your package the day before yesterday. I will not now answer to the remarks on the subject of Christianity because I hope to be able to do so more intelligently by and by.

I have been reading Jahn's History of the Hebrew commonwealth together with the old Testament—[1] What is your reason for sending me the 1st and 3d vols Eichorn instead of the 1st and 2d?

Mr Gannett has been turning the heads of my town's people by a Christmas sermon on love to Christ—[2] At an assembly in the eveg twas the grand topick and I was forced to repeat my exoterick opinion of it (to use one of your ancient phrases) some twenty or thirty times— Dr Bancroft,[3] chief beau! of this place in chatting upon this solemn topick and comparing various preachers said there was none under whose ministry he had rather sit than Mr Hedge's of W. Cambridge and was proceeding to give his and other people's opinion of you at full length when a purblind old lady who had but just descried me rushed up and ravenously made prey of all my attention.— I hinted to the parson that Mr Emerson was not far off and might perhaps be induced to act upon our minds from the pulpit— So I shall hope the pleasure of hearing him once this winter. I have been reading your favorite Uhland in some still midnight hours of late and begin to understand the meaning of certain critiques in your article on Schiller—[4] He doth indeed transport the mind into another realm and varnishes nature with none of those false tints which are compounded in the crucible of the human soul.

Have you read Victor Hugo's Hunchback of Notre Dame?[5] I am much fascinated by it— The Lava and the vineyards of a fiery soul!— I dream of the French Faustus and Esmeralda with her foolish, misguided, beautiful love. The Louis XI loses too much when we recollect Scott's fine engraving—[6] Few of the characters can boast originality but they are superb copies.

I should write more if I had better pens— My penmender is gone out and the Fairy (if there be Yankee fairies) who presided at my birth, spitefully denied me the talent which I so much need of fashioning the goose-quill into any perfection as an instrument I thought I would write as Arthur wishes to *call*. Adieu—commend me to those of your household and mention Mary when you write again— very faithfully yours

M. F.

ALS (MH: fMS Am 1086 [10:97]. *Addressed:* Revd Mr Hedge, / Cambridge.
article on] article ⟨of⟩ ↑ on ↓

1. *Jahn's History of the Hebrew Commonwealth* (Andover, 1828) had been translated by Calvin Stowe. Johann Jahn (1750–1816) was an orientalist and a biblical critic.

2. Probably Ezra Stiles Gannett (but the reference may be to Fuller's former minister, Thomas Brattle Gannett).

3. Dr. Amos Bancroft (1767–1848) had a large practice in Groton, where he had settled in 1811 (Green, *Historical Sketch*, p. 101).

4. Hedge had written a favorable review of Carlyle's *Life of Friedrich Schiller* in the *Christian Examiner* 16 (July 1834):365–92.

5. Victor Hugo's *Notre-Dame de Paris* was published in 1831. Her title would indicate that Fuller read a translation.

6. Louis XI is the main character in Scott's *Quentin Durward* (Edinburgh, 1823).

102. To Almira P. Barlow

Groton, January 5, 1835.

Yours was extremely grateful unto me, and I have seized by the front hair the very first leisure hour to answer you. What you say of myself is generally as just as kind,—but I would correct one mistake. You say I have *leisure*; not so,—we can get no servants, and my hours are crammed with the most prosaic tasks. "I have never before told you I loved you?" The tender and weakly souls have need to be fed on *words*, and to such I use them.

I was much pleased with Mr Furness' preachment; his doctrine came to me with a fresher flavor, that I had just closed a Materialist work, whose Author, too, corrected it for the press, on his death-bed.[1]

You say Mrs Butler has become a Unitarian. Do you know her? I am puzzled by the two sides of her character. I could hardly believe that she who could write the lines on a Sleeping Child (not that I like them, but they bespeak a spirit deeply-stirred,) could have given rise to all the foolish talk I heard at Newport.[2] She was staying there while I was so, and it seemed she must find either amusement or pleasure in giving simpletons and coxcombs cause to prattle. What was odd, all the gentlemen I saw, disliked, while the ladies affected to adore her. I say affected, because there was no tinge of discrimination or just appreciation in what I heard said of her by these dressed dolls.

MsCfr (MH: fMS Am 1086 [Works, 1:17–19]).

1. A close friend of both Emerson and Hedge, William Henry Furness (1802–96) was ordained in Philadelphia and served there for fifty years. He was a good German scholar and took a strong stand against slavery. Fuller probably had read Furness' *Spirit of Jesus: A Sermon Preached at the Installation of Rev. D. H. Barlow, in Brooklyn, New York, September 17, 1834* (Brooklyn, 1834) (*Heralds*, 3:133–38).

2. Frances Anne (Fanny) Kemble (1809–93), the English actress, had married Pierce Butler and retired from the stage the year before this letter was written. Apparently she

never joined the Unitarians, but she attended Furness' church and became a good friend of the pastor. Butler's family was aghast at her unconventional parties, for she invited actors to dinner. She later divorced Butler and returned to the English stage (*NAW*). Fuller mentions Mrs. Butler's "Oh child! who to this evil world art come," which appeared in *Francis the First. A tragedy in five acts. With other poetical pieces* (New York, 1833).

103. To [?]

[ca. February 1835]
[Groton]

George Thompson has a voice of uncommon compass and beauty; never sharp in its highest, or rough and husky in its lowest, tones.[1] A perfect enunciation, every syllable round and energetic; though his manner was the one I love best, very rapid, and full of eager climaxes. Earnestness in every part,—sometimes impassioned earnestness,—a sort of "Dear friends, believe, *pray* believe, I love you, and you must believe as I do" expression, even in the argumentative parts. I felt, as I have so often done before, if I were a man, the gift I would choose should be that of eloquence. That power of forcing the vital currents of thousands of human hearts into one current, by the constraining power of that most delicate instrument, the voice, is so intense,—yes, I would prefer it to a more extensive fame, a more permanent influence.

Did I describe to you my feelings on hearing Mr. Everett's eulogy on Lafayette?[2] No; I did not. That was exquisite. The old, hackneyed story; not a new anecdote, not a single reflection of any value; but the manner, the *manner*, the delicate inflections of voice, the elegant and appropriate gesture, the sense of beauty produced by the whole, which thrilled us all to tears, flowing from a deeper and purer source than that which answers to pathos. This was fine; but I prefer the Thompson manner. Then there is Mr. Webster's, unlike either; simple grandeur, nobler, more impressive, less captivating. I have heard few fine speakers; I wish I could hear a thousand.

Are you vexed by my keeping the six volumes of your Goethe? I read him very little either; I have so little time,—many things to do at home,—my three children, and three pupils besides, whom I instruct.

By the way, I have always thought all that was said about the anti-religious tendency of a classical education to be old wives' tales. But their puzzles about Vergil's notions of heaven and virtue, and his gracefully-described gods and goddesses, have led me to alter my opinions; and I suspect, from reminiscences of my own mental history, that if all governors do not think the same 't is from want of that intimate knowledge of their pupils' minds which I naturally possess. I really find it difficult to keep their *morale* steady, and am inclined to think many of my own sceptical sufferings are traceable to this source. I well remember what reflections arose in my childish mind from a comparison of the Hebrew history, where every moral obliquity is shown out with such naïveté, and the Greek history, full of sparkling deeds and brilliant sayings, and their gods and goddesses, the types of beauty and power, with the dazzling veil of flowery language and poetical imagery cast over their vices and failings.

ELfr, from *Memoirs*, 1:124–26.

Probably to Clarke.

1. George Thompson (1804–78), the English abolitionist, came to America in September 1834. He caused a sensation among the conservatives, who detested his appeals. Fuller heard him speak at Groton on 15 January (*DNB*).

2. Everett had delivered his eulogy at Faneuil Hall on 6 September 1834 (Edward Everett, *Orations and Speeches on Various Occasions* [Boston, 1865], 1:459–524).

104.   To James F. Clarke

Groton 1st Feb 1835.

Dear James,

My mind has been so strongly turned towards you these several days that though I owe you no letter I must write. Often in reading or meditating, thoughts strike which I think I wish so much I could communicate to my friend James— If he could only come in this evening as he used to do at Cambridge I would pour forth such a flood. And he—he would gravely listen and then—rise abruptly and go out as if he were disgusted with all I had said but—a month or more after he would come out with an answer which showed that he had thought about it" and if he did not agree at least had not been disgusted— Ah well a day this delightful cornerwise contact of character" is over for ever. The thought makes me melancholy the best" thing I can do since I cannot assail your mind is to assail your pocket and take thence a half-a-dollar for the service of the nation—

So—where was I?— Oh about Reinhard's memoirs—did you, dear "Minister" ever read them for I am going to quote from them for some time—[1] So if you have not read them do so and particy Letter IX and noting what is said therein of the method we should take in examining revelation give[n] me your opinion thereon— *Do it in form*—I want it— Observe the valuable results of his six years patient industry, admire that truly German spirit which produces fruits of such perfect ripeness, those habits of patient investigation, that freedom of spirit joined with candour and humility— See how beautifully his life passed, spirit constantly victorious over the rebellion of matter, every hour employed in pursuits as useful as elegant,[n] that genuine charity, that consistent sweetness and humility— He gave away the fruits of his own soul to the poor; How delightful his domestick life— Oh my friend how lovely is the picture of a good man!— I *hope* it is not flattered— Read it and see if it does not affect you as it does me— I think you will find passages which may be useful to you partiy on the way in which he made general literature and great love of philosophy aid to form the practical part of his religious character. Similar thoughts have occupied your own mind. He seems to have performed what you could conceive and wish therefore are capable of performing. You will not agree with his *doctrine* but that is nothing— And tell me how goes your Unitarianism— Before you went to the west I remember you were grafting sundry notions of your own on that most rational system. Have you decided yet how regeneration is to be accomplished—

Have I ever asked you whether you had read Manzoni's Lucia and which of his two priests you prefer. Surely never did writer invest the clerical character with such grace and dignity— Borromeo is my favourite I dont think any thing can be finer than the scene in which Borromeo rebukes the curate— I have become rather intimate with Manzoni and am marvellously taken with his elevated[n] morality, his tender piety, his various and accurate knowledge and his pictorial power. If you were here I should persecute you with extracts from his writings.[2]

My life has lately been embellished by the establishment of an Atheneum in G. which enables me to read the Foreign and Quarterly reviews—[3] Ever since we have lived here I have had to study when at home because I could get nothing to read and then to suffocate myself with light reading when in Boston that I might keep up with the gallop of the age— *Now* I shall fare better And there is a fine[n] article on Coleridge which I daresay you have read, if you have not—*do* for my sake and if you have sympathize with me. There is some ignorance and much partial judgement but also[n] many brilliant, feeling remarks and interesting particulars— Note the parallel between Coleridges conversational powers and those of Sir J. Mackintosh Also Coleridge's one sided critique on Faust[4] and *above* all a piece new to me entitled "The Pang more sharp than all"—by which I was reminded of some lines of yours which I saw lately *not* where I *should* have seen them first! to wit in print[n] "thus goes the old / Or if it stays, its flower and freshness gone Fetters the limb weighs down the heart like *stone*—[5]

By the way these lines have quite obliterated the impression your yawning account of Niagara made upon me last summer.

And speaking of Niagara I see your friend Dr Lieber's book much abused in the last N. E. Mag—[6] Literary coxcomb is the best name they can afford him.—

Now let me ask you some questions for I feel impertinent to night—[n] How many hours a day do you study and *what*; any thing except sermon writing. Do you feel more or less alone than when with us— Is the promised freedom *joyous* or joyless? Which do you learn most from the book of Nature, Goethe or St Paul—and are you going to stay in the West always?— How are your friends, the Poles?—[n7] My desire to go to the West is revived by the doings at Lane Seminary— That sounds from afar so like the conflict of keen life—[8] There is the greatest fuss about slavery in *this* little nook An idle gentleman weary of his ease has taken to philanthropy as a profession and here are incessant lectures. I rarely go but I attended to hear the English emissary Thomson whom you must have read about in the papers I wish you or any of my friends who need forming as speakers [   ]

ALfr (MH: bMS Am 1569.7 [466]). Published in part in Chevigny, pp. 104–5.

thought about it] thought about ↑ it ↓
of character] of charac⟨h⟩ter
the best] the ⟨f⟩ best
revelation give] revelation ⟨and⟩ give
useful as elegant] useful as ⟨beautiful⟩ elegant
his elevated] his el⟨v⟩evated
is a fine] is a ⟨?⟩ fine
but also] but ↑ also ↓
first! to wit in print] first! ↑ to wit in print ↓
impertinent to night] impertinent to ⟨?⟩ night
How are your friends, the Poles?—] ↑ How are your friends, the Poles?— ↓

1. Franz Volkmar Reinhard's *Geständnisse seine Predigten und seine Bildung zum Prediger betreffend* (Sulzbach, 1810) had been translated by Oliver Taylor as *Memoirs and Confessions of Francis Volkmar Reinhard* (Boston, 1832). Reinhard (1753–1812) was a Lutheran theologian who championed a "supernaturalist" view of justification by grace (Samuel M. Jackson, *The New Schaff-Herzog Encyclopedia of Religious Knowledge* [New York, 1908]). Clarke replied on 16 March, saying that he had read the book but that the "general impression was not so pleasant with me as it appears to have been with you. . . . However, I will read Reinhard again" (*Letters of JFC*, p. 89).

2. In Alessandro Manzoni's *I promessi sposi* (Milan, 1827), Lucia Mondella is be-

trothed to Renzo Tramaglino. Federigo Cardinal Borrommeo is a frugal, learned priest given to the mortification of the flesh. His opposite, Don Abbodino, is self-indulgent and cowardly.

3. According to one contemporary, the Groton Athenaeum was born "during the *antimasonic delusion*, that plague seized it in infancy; it struggled a few months, gasped and died" (Butler, *Town of Groton*, p. 227). Fuller probably read William Fraser's *Foreign Review*, begun in 1829, and the *Quarterly Review*, begun in 1809 as an alternative to the Whiggish *Edinburgh Review*. In 1835 the *Quarterly Review* was edited by John Gibson Lockhart.

4. "The Poetical Works of S. T. Coleridge," *Quarterly Review* 52 (August 1834):1–38. The reviewer (probably John Murray) says, "Those who remember [Coleridge] in his more vigorous days can bear witness to the peculiarity and transcendant power of his conversational eloquence" (p. 2). He praised Mackintosh's brilliance as a conversationalist but said: "To listen to Mackintosh was to inhale perfume; it pleased, but did not satisfy. The effect of an hour with Coleridge is to set you thinking; his words haunt you for a week afterwards; they are spells, brightenings, revelations. In short, it is, if we may venture to draw so bold a line, the whole difference between talent and genius" (p. 4). Sir James Mackintosh (1765–1832) had written an answer to Edmund Burke's *Reflections on the French Revolution*. He and Coleridge disliked each other; the poet went so far as to satirize Mackintosh in verse in 1800 (*DNB*); Robert James Mackintosh, *Memoirs of the Life of the Right Honourable Sir James Mackintosh* [London, 1835]). Murray goes on to recall Coleridge's opinion that *Faust* is a failure because of its "insufficiently and inartificially executed" idea (pp. 20–21). Toward the end of the article, he quotes Coleridge's "The Pang more sharp than all."

5. From Clarke's poem "Niagara. The Bridge by Moonlight. To Ellen Sturgis, August 1834." Never published, the poem now exists in three manuscript copies: "J. F. Clarkes Poems," MHi; "Poems by J.F.C.," MH: bMS Am 1569.3(8); "Commonplace Book," MH: bMS Am 1569.3(6), pp. 9–10.

6. An unsigned review of *Letters to a Gentleman in Germany* (Philadelphia, 1834) called the book "often incomprehensible to the English reader." Clarke, however, favorably reviewed the book in the *Western Messenger* 1 (August 1835):138–43. Francis Lieber (1800–1872), a German-born political philosopher, emigrated to the United States in 1827. He founded the *Encyclopedia Americana*, taught at South Carolina College, and published the influential *On Civil Liberty and Self-Government* in 1853. He was a Kantian who influenced not only Clarke but Hedge, Theodore Parker, and George Ripley as well (*DAB*).

7. Clarke had befriended a group of Lithuanians who had emigrated to Louisville in 1834. In his letter of 22 October 1834 he described his efforts on behalf of "Casimin Mackiewiez" (Casmir Mickiewicz) (*Letters of JFC*, p. 80).

8. Lane Seminary in Cincinnati was founded in 1829 by Ebenezer and William A. Lane, who called Lyman Beecher to be president of their Presbyterian school. In 1834 several students had formed an antislavery society. It was denounced by a trustee resolution, which the faculty supported, on 17 October 1834. In the ensuing controversy, half of the students resigned and withdrew to Oberlin (*Christian Register*, 24 January 1835; *Liberator*, 10 January 1835; *The Autobiography of Lyman Beecher*, ed. Barbara M. Cross [Cambridge, Mass., 1961]; John V. Stephens, *The Founding of Lane Seminary* [Cincinnati, 1941]).

105. To Frederic H. Hedge

Groton 1st Feby 1835;

My dear Friend,

I confess I am disappointed that you should come as far as Concord and not accept my invitation to visit us also for a few days. But I think you must have had some particularly good reason for I would not lightly believe you indifferent to seeing me.

Indeed I do not like the idea of your going to that not wild but *meagre* domain of Maine at all and I do think the Christian Examiner would be just the thing for you— But ah! this money this money it has fettered me always and is like to more and more, what then must it one who does not stand alone but has three other living beings dependant on his care. In sooth it is not "hesitating" between the profitable and the excellent" so much as between the necessary and the excellent. Can you live near Boston on eight hundred a year?— And yet this going into mental solitude is desperately trying. I can appreciate it now-a days— I often try to solace my self by repeating when alone Carlyle's beautiful rhapsodies on the almost miraculous benefits of silence—[1]or by saying Goethe remarked aye even he "We all talk constantly a great deal too much[;] talking is the very worst way of expressing thought, best mature it into action by a silent process as the tree puts forth its fruit"— But to me the expression of thought and feeling is to the mind what respiration is to the lungs and much suffering and probable injury will ensue from living in a thick or harsh atmosphere.— But I *have* nothing "wise" to say no conclusion, the result of nicely balanced[n] arguments, therefore after requesting that you will let me know your decision when it is made, I shall be silent on the subject and "the workman within your own mind will quietly clear away all rubbish as soon as is necessary."

You were quite right about Eichhorn— I have passed over that part of the first volume which discusses the state of the text, different manuscripts &c. It is nonsense for one without[n] learning to read it. I could only follow the wise author blindfold.— I do not get on fast. I dont know how I should like to hear any one else say it but I have long thought my mind must be as shallow as it is rapid and am now convinced of it by the difficulty I find in pursuing this study connectedly. I want to take a general survey of the subject to comprehend the relation which the parts bear to one another, *then* to meditate but the habits of my undisciplined[n] immaterial flutterer are constantly tormenting me— I wish to think before I have proper materials to think upon and at all the picturesque places I have a restless desire to write stories or rather fragments of stories which have nothing to do with my present purpose— I wish, if possible, to be a Christian and to become so not in sickness and adversity but in health and[n] in the full possession of my reasoning powers— I have felt myself a Christian but it was at times of excitement, skepticism returns besides, a religion should not be adopted from taste but conviction. I remember you talked to me once of your friend Mrs Ripley's doubts.[2] I wish you would tell me about this again. I was not interested in the subject then as I should be now but if I mistake not you said she had not perfect faith in the immortality of the soul— I have never been troubled on that score but it so often seems to me that we are ruled by an iron destiny— I have no confidence in God as a Father, if I could believe in Revelation and consequently in an over-ruling Providence many things which seem[n] dark and hateful to me now would be made clear or I could wait— My mind often burns with thoughts on these subjects and I long to pour out my soul to some person of superior calmness and strength and fortunate in more accurate knowledge. I should feel such a quieting reaction. But generally I think it is best I should go through these conflicts alone. The process will be slower, more irksome, more distressing, but the result will be all my own and I shall feel greater confidence in it— Will you write me a short account as to what school of philosophy Eichhorn belonged.—[3] I cannot get at a Conversations Lexicon as I so often wish. And give me an exact definition of the phrase[n] "die hohere Kritik"—[4] I am flattered that Mr Emerson should wish to know me. I fear it will never be but 'tis pleasant to know that he wished it— I cannot think I should be disappointed in him as I have been in others to whom I had hoped to look up, the sensation one experiences in the atmosphere of his thoughts is too decided and peculiar. I forget to tell you that Dr Channing, maugre all my prejudice against Channing women, made me feel as if I might love and reverence him much— Fortunately perhaps, I did not see enough of him to get much P-ized Please write to me as soon and often as is consistent with your engagements— I never felt so much genuine confidence towards you as I do now—in faith yours

M. F.

Is there a 4th vol of Eichhorn?

ALS (MH: fMS Am 1086 [10:99]). Published in part in *Memoirs*, 1:151. *Addressed:* Revd F. H. Hedge, / Cambridge, / Mass. *Postmark:* Groton MS Feb 2.

nicely balanced] nicely balanc⟨ing⟩ed
nonsense for one without] nonsense ⟨with⟩ ↑ for ↓ one ⟨pos⟩without
my undisciplined] my undis ↑ ci ↓ plined
but in health and] but ↑ in health and ↓
things which seem] things which ⟨m⟩seem
of the phrase] of ↑ the phrase ↓

1. "Well might the Ancients make Silence a god; for it is the element of all godhood, infinitude, or transcendental greatness . . ." (Thomas Carlyle, "Characteristics," *Edinburgh Review* 54 [December 1831]:363).

2. Probably Sophia Dana Ripley. When he replied on 20 February (MH-AH), Hedge declined to give details, saying, "With regard to Mrs Ripley's skepticism & all other skepticism & all religious faith I cannot well express myself in a letter on account of the questions which arise at the moment."

3. Hedge said that Eichhorn was "decidedly attached to the modern philosophy of Germany. He was probably a Kantian by which I mean, not a thorough spiritualist, but a critical i.e. an *antidogmatical* philosopher."

4. Hedge replied, "*Höhere Kritik* is a criticism of the inward spirit rather than the letter[,] of the matter rather than the form, a judgment of the opinions of the author & their truth on genuineness & authenticity[,] on the age, country & authorship of a doubtful production;—in poetry—of the degree in which the higher qualifications & true essence of the art have been attained—of the inward & deeper meaning of a work."

106. To Frederic H. Hedge

Groton 6th March 1835—

Dear Henry

Your letter was doubly kind, being written under such circumstances: I fear this unpleasant suspense is wearing you out but must hope this blessed spring season will bring some favorable omen to turn the scale on the right side. Do you love Spring?— I have for years dreaded it but now that my farewell to the Ideal is in one sense completed my feelings are becoming natural and I can welcome the time when "old" enchantments stir the blood,

Like vernal airs that curl the flood.—

I have heard much of Miss Jackson and should think her every-way calculated to make Mr Emerson happy even on his own principle that it is not the *quantity* but the *quality* of happiness that is to be taken into consideration.[1] How is it that men who marry a second time usually select a wife of character and manners entirely[n] unlike their first. This seems the case with Mr E—and I have just heard a similar instance a gentleman in N York married a young girl of my acquaintance, a gentle, fanciful golden-haired blue-eyed maid— Two years she was "crown to his cap and garnish to his dish."[2] She died at the age of 19—two more years pass and here he is engaged to a woman of six and twenty, as ugly, as ungraceful and as simply devoted to duty as possible with[n] a mind, very substantial, indeed, but from which the elegant imaginings de sa premiere could never have elicited a single spark.— This must be on the principle of reaction, or natural desire for balance of character.

Your periodical plan charms me: I think you will do good and what

225

is next best gain fame.[3] Though I have been somewhat jostled in this working-day world I have still a great partiality for the goddess who

vires acquirit eundo

parva metu primō; mox sese attollit in auras,

et caput inter nubilia condit.[4]

I shall feel myself honoured if I am deemed worthy of lending a hand albeit I fear I am merely "Germanico" and not "transcendental"— I go by fits and starts: there is no knowing what I should wish to write upon next January: at present the subject I should select would be the character of King David aesthetically considered (is this English).

I take the satisfaction I expected in the study of the Old Testament. I am gradually creating a new world out of the chaos of old, confused and inaccurate impressions— Soon I shall have finished these vols of Eichhorn and trouble you for more.

You advised me to read[n] Swedenborgian writings by way of counterpoise to Eichhorn,—[5] Which—? perhaps I could procure them— I lately happened on five sermons by one of that sect which pleased me much though the writer as such was no great things— Did I mention to you an avatar of that great man Dr Grigg on these barbarous demesnes. Verily much did he pour into mine ears on the subject of Skullology and very sentimental was he on the subject of certain expressions in your Article which he took à pied de lettre. "What" says he "does Mr H. really think *I* think when holding in my hands the brain of the lamented Spurzheim that I am laying them on the image of the Deity?— Ah *could* I, *did* I"?!!&c—

Your ci-devant tutor Mr Bancroft has been delivering a *curious* address at Deerfield.[6] If I thought you would care for it I would send you the account in Cousin George's paper— My father requested me to write a little piece in answer to Mr B's attack on Brutus in the N.A. Review which he published in the Daily Advertiser some time since—[7] It was responded to (I flatter myself by some big-wig as *we* say in Groton)[n] from Salem. He detected some ignorance in me nevertheless[n] as he remarked that I wrote with "ability" and seemed to *consider me* as an elderly gentleman *I considered* the affair as highly flattering and beg you will keep it in mind and furnish it for my memoirs as such after I am dead.)

I want to know the facts about Goethe and Lili, can you give them me?[8] This somewhat passée affair troubles me; I want to know did he give her up from merely interested (ie selfish) motives.

Tell Mary I recd her note with pleasure and shall write to her when I send you your books. As ever your friend

M. F.

ALS (MH: fMS Am 1086 [10:100]). Published in part in Higginson, *MFO*, pp. 48, 141–42. *Addressed:* Revd F. H. Hedge, / Cambridge, / Mass. *Postmark:* Groton MS March 6.

manners entirely] manners ent⟨?⟩irely
possible with] possible ⟨un⟩with
me to read] me to ⟨?⟩ read
some big-wig as *we* say in Groton] some ⟨elderly⟩ big-wig ↑ as *we* say in Groton ↓
in me nevertheless] in me ⟨rather⟩ nevertheless

1. Lydia Jackson (1802–92), daughter of Charles and Lucy Cotton Jackson of Plymouth, probably met Emerson in January 1835, when he lectured in Plymouth. The couple became engaged by the end of the month and married on 14 September. Emerson thereafter called her Lidian, a name adopted by all their friends (Rusk, *Life of RWE*, pp. 210–26).

2. Samuel Taylor Coleridge, "The Improvisatore: or, John Anderson, My jo, John":

> Yes, yes! that boon, life's richest treat
> He had, or fancied that he had;
> Say, 'twas but in his own conceit—
> The fancy made him glad!
> Crown of his cup, and garnish of his dish!
> The boon, prefigured in his earliest wish,
> The fair fulfillment of his poesy,
> When his young heart first yearn'd for sympathy!

3. Hedge had told Fuller that he and George Ripley were planning "a periodical of an entirely different character of any now existing, a journal of spiritual philosophy in which we are to enlist all the Germano-philisophico-literary talent in the country." Among the contributors Hedge proposed were Emerson, Charles Follen, Caleb Sprague Henry, Richard Henry Dana, James Marsh, William Henry Furness, James Clarke, and Carlyle (Hedge to Fuller, 20 February 1835, MH-AH). Five days after this Fuller letter, Emerson wrote Carlyle, mentioning among other things a "journal, to be called *The Transcendentalist.*" In his next letter to Carlyle (30 April), Emerson included *The Spiritual Inquirer* as an alternate title. No journal emerged from these plans—partly, one assumes, because the *Western Messenger* began publishing in June at Cincinnati (*Emerson–Carlyle Correspondence*, pp. 119, 124–25).

4. Vergil, *Aeneid*, 4:175–77, referring to the goddess Fama. C. Day Lewis translates the lines (*The Aeneid of Virgil* [New York, 1952], p. 77):

> gathering strength as it goes; at the start
> A small and cowardly thing, it soon puffs itself up,
> And walking upon the ground, buries its head in the cloud-base.

5. The work of Emanuel Swedenborg (1688–1772), the Swedish philosopher and theologian, had been popularized in New England by Sampson Reed in the 1820s. In *Nature*, Emerson developed Swedenborg's idea of "correspondence," and in *Representative Men* he gave a chapter to Swedenborg. Fuller, however, never shared his enthusiasm for the Swede.

6. George Bancroft (1800–1891), with whom Hedge had studied in Germany, had given the Washington's Birthday speech at Deerfield on 23 February. The speech was reported in two issues of the *Franklin Mercury*, the weekly paper founded and edited by George T. Davis. Davis had objected editorially to Bancroft's liberal view that "the Tories love authority. The Whig loves money. The Democrat loves equal rights" (*DAB*; *Franklin Mercury*, 3 March 1835).

7. In Northampton Bancroft had given a speech that was published as "The Influence of Slavery on the Political Revolutions in Rome," *North American Review* 39 (October 1834):413–37. "History," said Bancroft, "never manufactured him [Brutus]

into a hero, till he made himself an assassin. Of a headstrong, unbridled disposition, he never displayed coolness of judgment in any part of his career" (p. 432). Fuller responded in her first published work, "In Defense of Brutus," *Boston Daily Advertiser*, 27 November 1834, in which she emphasized Plutarch's account of Brutus. She was answered on 4 December in the same paper by a correspondent from Salem who signed himself "H." H. took issue with her by pointing to Gibbon's and Cicero's accounts of Brutus' moral defects. There is no support for later speculation by some critics that H. was Nathaniel Hawthorne.

8. In 1775 Goethe had fallen in love with Anne Elisabeth (Lili) Schönemann (1758–1817), daughter of a Frankfurt patrician family (*OCGL*).

107. To Frederic H. Hedge

Saturday March
28th 1835.
[Groton]

Dear Henry,

I return your Uhland which has been to me the source of much delight. I have kept him too long but you know I was absent from home a long time. I have three vols of Richter belonging to you which I have never yet opened. As I do not think you at present want them I am reserving them for some still, lonely afternoon. You have never mentioned whether you recd your Tieck I wish you would to set my mind at rest. Will it be too much trouble to send the remainder of Eichhorn to my uncle Henry's?— My father would bring it me the latter part of next week.

I have a letter from James Clarke enclosing a prospectus of the Western Examiner which he is to assist in editing. If he has not sent you one you may find it in last weeks Christian Register.[1] He wishes I should beg you to write something for them, if it be no more than a letter; I hope you will, if well and free enough.

I am impatient to hear the result of your deliberations &c— in great haste yours

M. F.

ALS (MH: fMS Am 1086 [10:101]). *Addressed:* Revd. F.H. Hedge. / Cambridge.

1. The *Christian Register* for 21 March had announced the creation of the *Western Examiner*. The first issue, to be superintended by Ephraim Peabody, was scheduled to appear in April. The founding clergymen announced their principles: "To promote a manly, intelligent, and liberal piety; and faith working by love; to explain and defend the misunderstood and denounced principles of Unitarianism. . . . Also to diffuse sound views on literature, education, schools, and benevolent enterprises." A *Western Examiner*, however, was already being published in St. Louis. Thus the editors renamed the new magazine the *Western Messenger*, the title it carried from its first issue in June 1835

until its end in April 1841. The *Messenger* was a lively, thoughtful journal of religion, social reform, and literature, edited by Ephraim Peabody, James Clarke, James H. Perkins, and William Henry Channing. Both Fuller and Hedge contributed to the journal (Robert D. Habich, "The History and Achievement of the *Western Messenger*, 1835–1841" [Ph.D. dissertation, Pennsylvania State University, 1982]).

108. To James F. Clarke

[29 March 1835]
[Groton?]

My own favorite project, since I began seriously to entertain any of that sort, is six historical tragedies; of which I have the plans of three quite perfect.[1] However, the attempts I have made on them have served to show me the vast difference between conception and execution. Yet I am, though abashed, not altogether discouraged. My next favorite plan is a series of tales illustrative of Hebrew history. The proper junctures have occurred to me during my late studies on the historical books of the Old Testament. This task, however, requires a thorough and imbuing knowledge of the Hebrew manners and spirit, with a chastened energy of imagination, which I am as yet far from possessing. But if I should be permitted peace and time to follow out my ideas, I have hopes. Perhaps it is a weakness to confide to you embryo designs, which never may glow into life, or mock me by their failure.

ELfr, from *Memoirs*, 1:126–27.

1. In her "Reading Journal" for 13 March 1835 (MH), Fuller responded to her reading of Jacques Pierre Brissot and Schiller by planning "two tragedies on the history of G[ustavus] A[dolphus]," one on his early life and one on his life between the battles of Leipzig and Lützen. She noted that she needed "minute information" and "dramatick power" and yearned for a "season of joyous confidence" to "execute one of the many plans which present themselves to my mind whenever I leave it [in] repose." Later, in a notebook for 1840 (MH), Fuller wrote, "My four tragedies are slumbering peacefully in my trunk." The forces of Gustavus II Adolphus (1594–1632) of Sweden met and defeated Wallenstein's forces at Lützen in 1632, but the king was killed in the battle.

109. To Timothy and Margarett C. Fuller

Boston June 2d 1835.

Dearest Father,
    I was very glad to receive your letter although 'twas but brief. You

have of late omitted to write to me when I was absent and I have felt as if you thought of me less than I wished you should.

I have been passing ten days at Cambridge with Mrs Farrar and indeed they were most happy— Every-body so kind—the country beautiful, and my own spirits so light— We made little excursions almost every day— Last Saturday I rode twenty two miles on horseback without any fatigue— Mrs F. had a most agreeable party the day before I came away. But of all these things Ellen will give you the particulars if you are interested to hear them. The Higginsons say Eugene's pupils love him extremely and that Col Storrow too seems much pleased with him—[1] I think we ought to feel satisfied that he should secure so much love and esteem after five or six months close scrutiny. W. H. is still very good and as well disposed as ever— They seem much pleased with him at Avon-place.[2] He passed yesterday with us: he was excused from the store as it was Marsylvia's wedding day— I believe it is the first amusement time he has allowed himself since he left us—

I saw a good deal of your former ward Thornton Davis while in Cambridge but propose giving you the account viva voce.

And now I have something to tell you which I hope—Oh I *hope*— will give you as much pleasure as it does me.— Mr and Mrs Farrar propose taking me with several other delightful persons to Trenton Falls this summer. The plan is to set out about the 20th July—go on to N York, then up the North River to West point, pass a day there— then to Catskill, pass a day there then on to Trenton and devote a week to that beautiful scenery— I said I had scarcely a doubt of your consent as you had said several times this winter you should like to have me take a pleasant journey this summer. Oh I cannot describe the positive extacy with which I think of this journey— To see the North River at last and in such society! Oh do sympathize with me— do feel about it as I do— The positive expences of the journey we have computed at forty seven^n dollars— I shall want ten more for spending money—but you will not think of the money—*will* you? I had rather you would take *two hundred* dollars from my portion than feel even the least unwilling. *Will* you not write to me immediately and say you love me and are very glad I am to be so happy???

It was very unkind in Mr Robinson to have Mr Emerson during my absence. I think I shall join Richard and Arthur in attending Mr Kittredge's—[3] I must write a few words to mother so adieu from your most affectionate daughter

M.

Beloved Mother,

I passed a day while in Cambridge with Aunt Kuhn who is much better and full of love for you— Mrs Story, I understood, was not at all well; I did not see her—[4] Louisa Selfridge tells me she has sent you those seeds:[5] I am very glad— I should not have liked her if she had not— But of our visits to her, Marsylvia's wedding &c Ellen must give you the particulars. I am so full of the North River I can write of nothing else O dear, *dear* Mother—will you not be as glad as I am? Oh I am so delighted, so filled with it that I cannot but dread disappointment. My spirits have been in such an exalted state for some time past, I fear something dreadful must be to happen and nothing seems to me so likely as your making yourself sick— Oh do not I entreat you, think how unhappy you would make me in a moment— Sarah Clarke is to return with me a week from Thursday and then you can set off for Canton at once if you please. I shall not mind having every thing to do—if I can but go to Trenton. Much sewing will be needful but Ellen says she will do every thing she can to help me—do not be vexed with Ellen for staying—she has been a very good girl and would have gone with a good grace at any moment if I had said the word. She is resolved to try not to be selfish but help you all she can. She will tell you about the Danas.[6] I enclose a letter from Eugene which you can read aloud except a passage which I have put in brackets as it relates to another person's affairs. Then please put it away in my drawer. With love to my boys and Rebecca please burn this letter from your *transported* daughter.

M.

ALS (MH: fMS Am 1086 [9:35]); MsC (MH: fMS Am 1086 [Works, 1:153–59]). Published in part in Higginson, *MFO*, pp. 51–53. *Endorsed:* S. Margtt Fuller— / Recd 3. June 1835— / By Ellen—

computed at forty seven] computed at ⟨47⟩ forty seven

1. Samuel Appleton Storrow (1787–1837) served in the Department of Foreign Affairs in 1815, then became judge advocate with the rank of colonel in the U.S. Army from 1816 to 1820. At this time he had a school in Culpeper County, Virginia (George S. Wallace, *The Carters of Blenheim* [Richmond, Va., 1955], p. 64).

2. Her brother William Henry was working in Boston for their uncle Henry Holton Fuller.

3. Emerson had preached twice from Charles Robinson's pulpit in Groton on 31 May (Kenneth W. Cameron, *Index-Concordance to Emerson's Sermons* [Hartford, 1963], 2:701). In 1826, when the Congregational church in Groton called the liberal Robinson, the orthodox minority seceded from the parish and formed the Union Congregational Church. Their first minister, the fiery John Todd, served from 1827 to 1833. On 15 October 1833, Charles B. Kittredge (1806–84), who had studied at Andover, was ordained at Union Church. He was dismissed on 31 August 1835 (Butler, *Town of Groton*, p. 205; Mabel T. Kittredge, *The Kittredge Family in America* [Rutland, Vt., n.d.], p. 99).

4. Sarah Waldo Wetmore Story (1784–1855), daughter of Judge William Wetmore, married Judge Joseph Story (1779–1845) in 1808. A former associate justice of the U.S. Supreme Court, Story was Dane Professor of Law at Harvard (*DAB*; Perley Derby, *Elisha Story of Boston and Some of His Descendants* [Salem, 1915], pp. 24–25; James C. Wetmore, *The Wetmore Family of America* [Albany, N.Y., 1861], p. 455; *NEHGR* 9:375).

5. Louisa Carey Soley (1810?–1896) married Thomas Oliver Selfridge (1804–1902) on 5 March 1833 (Hunnewell, *Town Life*, p. 224; *CC*, 9 March 1833; *Boston Evening Transcript*, 22 September 1896; Benson J. Lossing, *Harper's Encyclopedia of United States History from 458 A.D. to 1905*, 10 vols. [New York, 1905]).

6. The Samuel Danas of Groton.

110. To Timothy and Margarett C. Fuller

Cambridge 13th August. 1835.

Dear Father and Mother,

I arrived here yesterday afternoon, having completed three weeks of such unalloyed pleasure as are seldom allotted to mortals.

You received I trust two letters written by me during our stay at Trenton Falls, one to you and a second to Ellen dated[n] the morning of our last day there. *That* was Sunday. That morning we all rode over to see Miss Mappa, a delightful elderly lady, a Dutch Unitarian whom I shall describe to you more particularly when we meet.[1] From her house we went to church and then had a charming ride home through the woods. That afternoon we passed at the Falls and the evening we all kept together because it was the last at that dear place, and a very happy one too, though touched with sadness by that thought. Next day we went across the country to Little Falls—a very hot ride, too hot to enjoy the scenery but song, and jest, and pleasant chat made the way seem short. We reached Little Falls in time to make a short excursion in a boat and see its romantic rocks more at leisure than before. Next morning we set forth on our homeward journey through the enchanting valley of the Mohawk, and reached Albany about eight oclock. The moon was then casting a charm over that dim and dusky city, so we took a long walk through its streets. We took steam-boat next morning for Kaatskill; it was the Erie, the same one in which we came up. In the town of Kaatskill we stopped half an hour and there, tell our boys, I saw an elephant with a real howdah on his back and a man dressed like a Hindoo upon him parading the streets. Then begun our tedious scramble up the mountain—oh you have no idea what a drag it is—the horses must suffer much. At three o'clock we arrived, having spent four hours in coming these twelve miles. That immense hotel on the top of that mountain seems as if it must have dropped there by magic. We had not more than half an hour to enjoy the gorgeous prospect which spread beneath before it began to rain and as we were obliged to descend the mountain early the next morning we could not see the celebrated fall of water. This is the only contre-temps of our journey. At the house were Mr and Mrs Silsbee and their daughter;[2] as they were acquainted with Mrs Thorndike they joined our party and we passed the evening together;[3] they were very polite to me and sent very kind messages to you which I shall deliver and give you a full account of the acquaintance when I come. Next morning we drove down the mountain at a Jehu pace which contrasted strongly with our snail-like progress of the day before and took boat in the North-America for N York at 10 oclock. Oh that day—it was all beauty and *delight!* We reached N York at sunset, and found Mr Sigourney Barker waiting on the wharf to conduct Mr and Mrs F. Miss Smith and myself to his Father's while the rest of the party went to a hotel.[4] We were recd most hospitably and fared sumptuously but alas! Anna was at Newport and my disappointment great—but Mr Ward, (who has been all kindness throughout) offered to stay with me at Newport as long as I pleased.[5] Here the thread of my narration becomes too entangled to be unwound on paper and how I went to and fro, and how Mrs Thorndike finally took me to Newport and staid over Sunday with me at Mrs Nat. Amory's[6] and how kind *they* were and how I missed Anna and did *not* miss her and how I went to Providence with Mr Jones ([*illegible*] you know;) and how I happened to meet Mrs Farrar again and come on with her and how I heard Dr Channing on the Island and saw him and Mrs Channing &c &c I can only tell you in person. Dear Mrs Thorndike whom I shall ever love has given me and her niece Miss Dana two beautiful rings just alike—they are my friends—[7] may they ever continue so—and I have several others beside— But I must conclude—

Miss Martineau is coming here next Monday to stay the whole week—she brought Mrs Farrar a letter from the celebrated Mrs Summerville and every body that is pleasant is to be here too[8] I have a great many engagements in prospect for the next fortnight and *then* I think I shall come home— I *hope* you are well and long to hear from you— you do sympathize I am *sure* in all my pleasure. I had to give up Bristol. I felt it was so out of Mr Ward's way to go there with me I was somewhat sorry but I have had as much as I deserve— with love to Ellen, the dear children and Rebecca most affly yours

M. F.

Trenton Falls, New York. From *American Scenery*, ed. N. P. Willis (London, 1840). By permission of the Pennsylvania State University Libraries.

234

ALS (MH: fMS Am 1086 [9:37]). *Addressed:* Timothy Fuller Esq. / Groton / Mass. *Postmark:* Cambridge Mass Aug 13. *Endorsed:* Sarah Margarett— / Recd Aug. 1835—

Ellen dated] Ellen ⟨written⟩ ↑ dated ↓

1. Sophia Apollonia Mappa (d. 1860), daughter of Adam Gerard (1754–1828) and Anna Paspoort Mappa (d. 1814), lived near Trenton in a house known locally as Stone Cottage (*DAB*; *Francis Adrian Van Der Kemp: An Autobiography*, ed. Helen L. Fairchild [New York, 1903], pp. 193, 202).

2. She met her father's former colleague Nathaniel Silsbee (1773–1850); his wife, Mary Crowninshield (1778–1835); and their daughter, Mary (1809–87), who married Jared Sparks in 1839. Nathaniel Silsbee served in the U.S. House, the Massachusetts House and Senate, and finally the U.S. Senate. His wife died seven weeks after this letter was written (*Biographical Directory*; Salem VR; MVR 383:79).

3. Sarah Dana (1780–1845), daughter of the Reverend Joseph Dana of Ipswich, married Israel Thorndike (1755–1832), a wealthy Boston merchant, in 1818 (*CC*, 11 July 1818, 9 May 1832; *Dana Family*, p. 32; *DAB*).

4. Andrew Sigourney Barker (1811–46) was the fifth child of Jacob and Eliza Hazard Barker; Miss Smith is unidentified (*Barker Genealogy*, p. 180).

5. Samuel Gray Ward (1817–1907), son of Thomas Wren (1786–1858) and Lydia Gray Ward (1788–1874), roomed with the Farrars during his years at Harvard. He was introduced to Fuller by the Farrars, who invited the young couple to accompany them to Europe in 1836. Ward went; Fuller, whose father died in 1835, stayed home. Upon his return, Ward renewed his friendship with Fuller, who found herself increasingly in love with him. But he rejected her in 1839 for Anna Barker, abandoned his plans for an artist's career, and joined his father in the American office of Baring Brothers (*DAB*; Mt. Auburn; Samuel Gray Ward, *Ward Family Papers* [Boston, 1900], pp. 100–103).

6. Mary Preble (1786–1865), daughter of Eben Preble (1757–1817), had married Nathaniel Amory (1777–1842) in 1808. Amory had been in business in New Orleans but spent several years living on the estate of his father-in-law before he retired to Newport ("Amory: Descendants of Jonathan," NEHGS; George H. Preble, *Genealogical Sketches of the First Three Generations of Prebles in America* [Boston, 1868], p. 153).

7. Fuller probably met Susan Coombs Dana (1817–1900), daughter of Sarah Dana Thorndike's brother Samuel. In 1838 Susan Dana married William R. Lawrence (1812–85) (*Dana Family*, p. 305).

8. Harriet Martineau (1802–76), English reformer and woman of letters, had been touring America since August 1834. Fuller met her and was deeply impressed by her. Mary Fairfax (1780–1872), daughter of Sir William George Fairfax, had been widowed and then had married her cousin, Dr. William Somerville. An accomplished scientist, she wrote a paper on violet rays in 1826 and followed that success with *Mechanism of the Heavens* (London, 1831) and *On the Connexion of the Physical Sciences* (London, 1834) (*DNB*).

111. To Frederic H. Hedge

Tuesday evening,
[18? August? 1835]

My dear friend,

On consulting Miss Jeffrey's note I find that Miss Martineau spends *this* evening at Mr Francis's and tomorrow eveg[n] at Mrs Ripley's—[1] Would I were intimate with that "splendid woman" that she might invite *me*. You are more fortunate and I hope you will go. Mrs Lee and Miss Lucy Searle were here at tea: they had been at Mrs Follen's and met Mr and Mrs Barlow returning.[2] I fear I shall not see Almira. Why could she not come here to see me? when one so seldom has opportunities to meet a friend, no slight punctilio should prevent—

M. F.

ALS (MH-AH). *Addressed:* Revd F. H. Hedge.

tomorrow eveg] tomorrow ↑eveg↓

1. Harriet Martineau was in Cambridge from 17 to 22 August and again late in November (*Martineau's Autobiography*, 1:345). The conjectural dating here is based on the supposition that Fuller would not write so chatty a letter in November, a month following her father's death. Mr. Francis is Convers Francis; Mrs. Ripley is probably Sophia Dana Ripley.

2. Mrs. Lee is probably Eliza Buckminster Lee (1788?–1864), daughter of the Reverend Joseph Buckminster, a distant relative of Timothy Fuller's. She married Thomas Lee of Brookline in 1827. In 1838 she published *Sketches of a New-England Village*. Her *Life of Jean Paul Frederic Richter* (Boston, 1842) was well received and widely read (*DAB*). Fuller's visitor may, however, have been Hannah Farnham Sawyer Lee (1780–1865), wife of George Gardner Lee and also a writer, whose *Three Experiments of Living* (Boston, 1837) became quite popular (*DAB*). Fuller's other guests were Lucy Searle (1794–1863), daughter of George and Mary Atkins Searle of Newburyport; Eliza Lee Cabot Follen (1787–1860), daughter of Samuel and Sally Barrett Cabot and wife of Charles Follen; and David and Almira Barlow (Francis H. Atkins, *Joseph Atkins: The Story of a Family* [Las Vegas, N.M., 1891], p. 73; *NAW*).

112. To[?]

1835, October 25
[Groton]

It appears there will not be more than 21 000 and that we children shall not have above 2000 each.[1]

MsCfr (MH: bMS Am 1280 [111, p. 200]). Published in *JMN*, 11:491.

1. Timothy Fuller died on 1 October 1835. When his estate was settled in the Middlesex Probate Court on 21 January 1836, the inventory showed a total worth of $18,098.50, most of which was tied up in notes and land. When the assets were distributed on 17 November 1840, Mrs. Fuller inherited a widow's share of $4,666.67, and each child received $1,333.34. At a second distribution on 19 March 1844, each child received $252.88 (Middlesex Probate, 1st ser., no. 8792).

113.   To[?]

3 November 1835
[Groton?]

I thought I should be able to write ere now, how our affairs were settled, but that time has not come yet. My father left no will, and, in
consequence, our path is hedged in by many petty difficulties. He has
left less property than we had anticipated, for he was not fortunate in
his investments in real estate. There will, however, be enough to main-
tain my mother, and educate the children decently. I have often had
reason to regret being of the softer sex, and never more than now. If
I were an eldest son, I could be guardian to my brothers and sister,
administer the estate, and really become the head of my family. As it
is, I am very ignorant of the management and value of property, and
of practical details. I always hated the din of such affairs, and hoped
to find a life-long refuge from them in the serene world of literature
and the arts. But I am now full of desire to learn them, that I may
be able to advise and act, where it is necessary. The same mind which
has made other attainments, can, in time, compass these, however uncongenial to its nature and habits.

ELfr, from *Memoirs*, 1:157.

114.   To Abraham W. Fuller

Groton 6th Novr 1835.—

My dear Uncle,

I am as sorry as you can be and ashamed to boot that I cannot acquaint you more particy with the dates of my Father's public life. But
since I am so ignorant I really have no means of becoming less so as
we find but few fragments of his journal.

The cow and two large hogs[n] hogs have been killed and the greater
part of them prepared for the use of the family. Poor Mother has had
a world of trouble with them at their death as she had all their lives;
she is but ill repaid for all her toils,[n] in having to take them at the
appraisal. Pray, my dear Uncle, make things as easy to Mother as you
can; the responsibilitie[s] and cares of her situation are very great. She
is quite ill but will write a few lines to you tomorrow, if possible.

We *do* wish to discontinue the Christian Register as, if we take but one paper, we would wish it of a more general character. We have not yet decided what to take.

As Wm told me you had sometimes opportunities to send out to Cambridge, I have taken the liberty to send two notes— I do not feel particy interested about "gay company" and should like to hear news about yourself. I am very sorry Clifford has been so sick, he must have had a sad time and Aunt Sarah too.[1] Wm told me you watched with him several nights. I hope he does not need watchers now.

Let us hear from you as often as convenient Affty your Niece.

S. M. Fuller

ALS (MH: fMS Am 1086 [9:39]). *Addressed:* A. W. Fuller Esq. / Boston / Mass. *Endorsed:* Miss Sarah M. Fuller / 7.Decr 1835 / Pr Wm H.F. / Answered Pr mail / 24 Decr 1835.

and two large hogs] and ↑ two large ↓ hogs
all her toils] all ⟨their⟩ ⟨?⟩ her toils

1. Her cousin Clifford Belcher (1819–79), son of Clifford and Deborah Fuller Belcher, was at this time a student at Harvard with R. H. Dana, Jr., John Weiss, Stearns Wheeler, and Henry David Thoreau. After becoming a lawyer, Belcher moved to New Orleans, made and lost a fortune as a plantation owner, and served as a major in the Confederate Army ("Farmington, Franklin County, Maine: Marriages—Births—Deaths. 1784–1890," NEHGS, p. 114; Henry Williams, *Memorials of the Class of 1837 of Harvard University* [Boston, 1887], pp. 64–66).

115. To Abraham W. Fuller

Groton 17th Novr 1835.

My dear Uncle,

I received your letter today and am much obliged by your remembering the book.

—This house is insured but, I presume not the barn—"at Concord. The Hopkins house was insured and Mother said Father was regretting at the time of the Charlestown fire that he had not given up the policy to Mr Livermore.[1]

It was Mr Jonathan Cobb of Canton with whom Father talked about selling the place at Easton. He put no particular confidence in him, but looked upon him as a friendly person.[2]

As Mother, in conformity with your first advice, had given up the intention of painting the house: she did not have the paints &c appraised intending to return them to the person of whom they were bought. She finds no bill of them. What is best to be done now?

I have looked in the attick but can discover no trace of the receipts of 1832.— Though there are those of so many years farther back.

With regard to the dates in Father's history I remember less and find fewer means of ascertaining than I had expected but very soon I will send you all I know.

Mr Brazer died this morning—[3] His loss is not to be compared with that of my Father or even Mrs Dana but it will be a sorrow to his family.—[4] I believe I have answered your letter as well as I can. I am very sorry now I did not lend a more heedful ear, when Father talked to me of his concerns— But I thought him so fully competent to the care of them that I felt no motive for interest except at the moment and what I was told was soon forgotten.

Mother and the children if they were here would send much love, Affectionately your niec[e]

AL (MH: fMS Am 1086 [9:36]). *Addressed:* W. Fuller Esq. / Boston / Mass. *Endorsed:* Sarah M. Fuller / 22. Nov. 1835 / Pr / Answered 1. Decr 1835 / Pr Wm. Henry / 20$ / Enclosed.

insured but, I presume not the barn] insured ↑ but, I presume not the barn ↓
The signature is cut away.

1. One of the two Cambridge Livermores, neighbors and friends of the Fullers: either Nathaniel (1772–1862), a soap manufacturer, or his son, Isaac (1797–1879), a wool merchant (Walter E. Thwing, *The Livermore Family of America* [Boston, 1902], pp. 78, 127–28).

2. Jonathan Cobb (1770?–1845), a native of Sharon, was something of an expert on the manufacture of silk (Sharon VR; Huntoon, *Town of Canton*, p. 538).

3. William Farwell Brazer, who died at fifty-three (*GVR*).

4. Rebecca Barrett Dana, wife of Judge Samuel Dana, had died on 11 May of that year (*GVR*).

116. To Eugene Fuller

[13 Dec. 1835]
[Groton]

[   ] think it can ever be but if it could" you would be very happy in the possession of a heart which you had won "in its simplicity
        "All undisguised in its young tenderness."
But you and she both will change much this coming five years. Let me know about it sometimes however.

Wm's thoughts remain fixed on E. Parker (who is now at school in Boston) though he says he would not accept her[n] if she offered herself to him. How true it is "men's love is fixed by scorning!" W. was at home Thanksgiving, 3d this month. Seems to have gotten over in [s]ome measure the deep impression [   ] Father's death made on him and showed some touch of his natural levity, yet is, on the whole, much sobered. He is not well contented at Uncle H's and wants to board somewhere else next summer.

Dr. Randall is thought to have a disease of the heart! he was seized with a palpitation last Sunday in church, fell down and was carried out. I shall not be surprized if he dies any day; he is terribly broken of late. His family would be left in a worse situation than ours as he has no near relation fit to protect them and John is nobody.[1]

Mother has had an attack of rhumatism but is now better; her spirits are much sunken this past week. Ellen Crane has left us and taken Lloyd with her for two or three weeks, which is at once a loss and gain for he is both more amusing and more troublesome than ever.

What says Col. Storrow to the Faneuil hall resolutions, to the Boston Mob, and Dr Channing's new book on slavery.[2] Miss Martineau attended a meeting of the Abolition society and expressed her concurrence in their principles and the Boston press has been at her as if[3] [   ] I think Rebecca is in a bad way. I expect she will have another paroxysm of insanity. I have been invited to pass the month of Feby in Philadelphia—if I did I suppose I could see you but I do not think of it.

ALfr (MH: fMS Am 1086 [9:246]). *Addressed:* Mr Fuller, / Farley, / Culpepper Co.— / Virginia. *Postmark:* Groton MS Dec 14. *Endorsed:* 1835 Dec 13 / going to Europe— / S.G.W.

be but if it could] be ↑ but if it could ↓
not accept her] not accept ⟨?⟩ her

1. The elder John Randall lived, however, until 27 December 1843. His son and namesake had graduated from Harvard in 1834, studied medicine and zoology, but did not embark on a career. A moody, morose young man, he was dominated by his iron-willed father (Randall, *Poems*, pp. 47–61).

2. Beginning in late summer, Boston was inflamed by a series of attacks on the abolitionists. First, on 21 August, a group of prominent Bostonians, including William and Amos Lawrence, David Henshaw, and Mayor Theodore Lyman, organized an antiabolition rally at Faneuil Hall. Lyman chaired the meeting; the principal speaker was Harrison Gray Otis. The meeting ended with the adoption of five resolutions directed against the abolitionists. Then, on 21 October, a mob that had gathered because George Thompson was rumored to be the speaker stormed a meeting of the Boston Female Anti-Slavery Society, captured William Lloyd Garrison, and would have harmed him had he not been taken to City Hall and put in protective custody. The next day the *Daily Advertiser* blamed the riot on the women, whose offense lay in having the meeting (*The Liberator*, 29 August 1835; *Boston Daily Advertiser*, 22 October 1835; Walter M. Mer-

rill, *Against the Wind and Tide* [Cambridge, Mass., 1963], pp. 103–7). Dr. Channing had published his *Slavery* on 5 December 1835.

3. At the suggestion of Ellis G. Loring, a prominent lawyer and abolitionist, Harriet Martineau had spoken at a meeting of the Female Anti-Slavery Society and declared "that in your *principles* I fully agree." This support, mild as it seems, horrified even the radical Elizabeth Peabody. Nathan Hale, editor of the *Boston Daily Advertiser*, led the attack on Martineau by reprinting a scurrilous piece from a New York paper (*Boston Daily Advertiser*, 30 November, 5 December 1835; *Liberator*, 14 and 21 November 1835; *Martineau's Autobiography*, 1:345–59).

117. To [?]

[1836?]

[   ] The occupations of the coming six months I have settled Some duties come first to parents, brothers and sister but these will not consume above one sixth of the time— The family is so small now Mother will have little need of my sewing— We shall probably receive very little company— The visits required of me by civility will be few— When the Farrars return I hope to see them frequently—and E. Woodward I may possibly know if she comes.¹ But I shall not, of free-will look out of door for a moment's pleasure— I shall have no one to stay here for a[n]y time except Eliz—² I love her and she is never in the way— All hopes of travelling I have dismissed— All youthful hopes of every kind I have pushed from my thoughts— I will not, if I can help it, lose an hour in castle-building and repining— Too much of that already! I have now a pursuit of immediate importance to the German language and literature I will give my undivided attention— I have made rapid progress for one quite unassisted— I have always hitherto been too constantly distracted by childish feelings to acquire any thing properly but have snatched a little here and there to feed my restless Fancy therewith— Please God now to keep my mind composed, that I may store it with all that may be conducive hereafter to the best good of others—

Oh! keep me steady in an honorable ambition. Favored by this calm, this obscurity of life I might learn every-thing, did not these feelings lavish away my strength— Let it be no longer thus— Teach me to think justly and act firmly— Stifle in my breast those feelings which pouring forth so aimlessly did indeed water but the desert and offend the sun's clear eye by producing weeds of rank luxuriance— Thou art my only Friend, thou has not seen fit to interpose one feeling, understanding breast between me and a rude, woful world. Vouchsafe then thy protection that I may "hold on in courage of soul."³

[   ] haughty, rigid, prudish girls, I hardly dare breathe in their presence— If I could have been easy all would have been well, but I could not— I envied M. Dana, as she called him William, and chatted so familiarly—⁴ I was silly, I would not tell him what he wished to know and made him walk next [   ]

AMsfr (MH: fMS Am 1086 [Box A]).

May not be a letter, for the manuscript is not creased.

1. The Farrars were at this time touring Europe on the trip Fuller had to forgo.
2. Elizabeth Randall.
3. Percy Bysshe Shelley: "O man! hold thee on in courage of soul" ("On Death," published in 1816 with *Alastor*).
4. Probably Mary Elizabeth Dana (1805–86), daughter of Francis and Sophia Willard Dana (*CVR*; MVR 374:250).

118. To [?]

1836

I have, for the time, laid aside *De Stael* and *Bacon*, for *Martineau* and *Southey*.¹ I find, with delight, that the former has written on the very subjects I wished most to talk out with her, and probably I shall receive more from her in this way than by personal intercourse,—for I think more of her character when with her, and am stimulated through my affections. As to Southey, I am steeped to the lips in enjoyment. I am glad I did not know this poet earlier; for I am now just ready to receive his truly exalting influences in some degree. I think, in reading, I shall place him next to Wordsworth. I have finished Herschel, and really believe I am a little wiser.² I have read, too, Heyne's letters twice, Sartor Resartus once, some of Goethe's late diaries, Coleridge's Literary Remains, and drank a great deal from Wordsworth. By the way, do you know his "Happy Warrior"?³ I find my insight of this sublime poet perpetually deepening.

ELfr, from *Memoirs*, 1:166–67.

1. Robert Southey (1774–1843), a friend of Coleridge and Wordsworth, wrote both poetry and prose and was for years a contributor to the *Quarterly Review*, where Fuller probably read his work (*DNB*).
2. Sir John Frederick William Herschel (1792–1871) had published his *Preliminary Discourse on the Study of Natural Philosophy*, the first volume of Dionysius Lardner's Cabinet Cyclopedia, in 1830 (*DNB*).
3. Most famous for his *Buch der Lieder*, Heinrich Heine (1797–1856) had published

Zur Geschichte der neueren schönen Literatur in Deutschland in 1833, and revised and expanded it under the title *Die romantische Schule* in 1836. This version was translated by G. W. Haven as *Letters Auxiliary to the History of Modern Polite Literature in Germany* (Boston, 1836) (*OCGL*). The English title suggests that Fuller read the translation in spite of her knowledge of German. Which of Goethe's diaries she read is not clear, but she may refer here to part 4 of *Aus meinem Leben, Dichtung und Warheit*, written 1824–31 but posthumously published as volume 8 of *Nachgelässene Werke*. Fuller had read *Sartor Resartus* in *Fraser's*, but she may have reread it in the Boston edition sponsored by Emerson and published by James Munroe in 1836. *The Literary Remains of Samuel Taylor Coleridge* was being edited by Henry Nelson Coleridge. Volume 1, *Uncollected Poems*, and volume 2, *Lectures and Notes on Shakespeare*, were published in 1836. Wordsworth wrote his "Character of the Happy Warrior" in late 1805 or early 1806, then published it in 1807.

119.   To Eugene Fuller

30 January 1836
[Groton?]

I was a great deal with Miss Martineau, while in Cambridge, and love her more than ever. She is to stay till August, and go to England with Mr. and Mrs. Farrar. If I should accompany them I shall be with her while in London, and see the best literary society. If I should go, you will be with mother the while, will not you? Oh, dear Eugene, you know not how I fear and tremble to come to a decision. My temporal all seems hanging upon it, and the prospect is most alluring. A few thousand dollars would make all so easy, so safe. As it is, I cannot tell what is coming to us, for the estate will not be settled when I go. I pray to God ceaselessly that I may decide wisely.

ELfr, from *Memoirs*, 1:159.

120.   To Almira P. Barlow

Groton, February 1. 1836.

I have turned over some dark pages since we met. Were I with you I could speak, but it is not easy to write of their lore. You know that I looked upon Death very near, nor at the time should I have grieved to go.[1] I thought there never could come a time when my departure would be easier to myself, or less painful to others. I felt as I thought I should feel at that awful season. It was not to be so, and I returned into life to bear a sorrow of which you know the heaviness. But my hard-won faith has not deserted me, and I have so far preserved a serenity which might seem heartlessness to a common observer. It was indeed sad when I went back, in some sort, into the world, and felt myself fatherless. Yet I gave no sign, and hope to preserve more or less fortitude. I cannot now tell you much of myself. My plans are various, but all undecided. I feel however that the crisis is approaching, and my prayer is that I may now act with wisdom and energy; and that since I *was* called back to this state of things, it may be to perform some piece of work which another could not.

Always your affectionate

M. F.—

MsC (MH: fMS Am 1086 [Works, 1:19–20]).

1. Fuller herself had been seriously ill shortly before her father died.

121. To James F. Clarke

[ca. 14 February 1836]
[Groton]

I am shocked to perceive you think I am *writing* the life of Goethe.[1] No, indeed! I shall need a great deal of preparation before I shall have it clear in my head. I have taken a great many notes; but I shall not begin to write it, till it all lies mapped out before me. I have no materials for ten years of his life, from the time he went to Weimar, up to the Italian journey. Besides, I wish to see the books that have been written about him in Germany, by friend or foe. I wish to look at the matter from all sides. New lights are constantly dawning on me; and I think it possible I shall come out from the Carlyle view, and perhaps from yours, and distaste you, which will trouble me. [   ]

I have long had a suspicion that no mind can systematize its knowledge, and carry on the concentrating processes, without some fixed opinion on the subject of metaphysics. But that indisposition, or even dread of the study, which you may remember, has kept me from meddling with it, till lately, in meditating on the life of the Goethe, I thought I must get some idea of the history of philosophical opinion in Germany, that I might be able to judge of the influence it exercised upon his mind. I think I can comprehend him every other way, and probably interpret him satisfactorily to others,—if I can get the proper materials. When I was in Cambridge, I got Fichte and Jacobi; I was much interrupted, but some time and earnest thought I devoted.[2] Fichte I could not understand at all; though the treatise which I read was one intended to be popular, and which he says must compel (*bezwingen*) to conviction. Jacobi I could understand in details, but not in system. It seemed to me that his mind must have been moulded by some other mind, with which I ought to be acquainted, in order to know him well,—perhaps Spinoza's.[3] Since I came home, I have been consulting Buhle's and Tennemann's histories of philosophy, and dipping into Brown, Stewart, and that class of books.[4]

ELfr, from *Memoirs*, 1:128–29, 127.

In his journal for 1834–36 (MHi), Clarke notes that between 22 and 25 February 1836 he had received Fuller's letter "asking for metaphysical light." Her letter thus would be ca. 14 February.

1. Her letter answers Clarke's of 7 January 1836, in which he says, "I am very glad you are going to undertake this thing. . . . [T]he public will stand ready to buy and read a good Life of the man" (*Letters of JFC*, p. 113).

2. Johann Gottlieb Fichte had published his *System der Sittenlehre nach den Principien der Wissenschaftslehre* in 1798. Friedrich Heinrich Jacobi (1743–1819) had introduced Goethe to the writing of the Dutch philosopher Benedict (Baruch) Spinoza (1632–77). Fuller probably read *Über die Lehre des Spinoza in Briefen an den herrn Moses Mendelssohn* (Breslau, 1785) (*OCGL*).

3. Fuller was attracted to Spinoza's pantheism.

4. Johann Gottlieb Buhle (1763–1821) had published *Geschichte der Philosophie* (Lemgo, 1793) and *Geschichte der neuern Philosophie seit wiederherstellung der Wissenshaften* (Göttingen, 1800–1804) (*ADB*). Fuller read either Wilhelm Gottlieb Tennemann's *Geschichte der Philosophie* (Leipzig, 1798–1819) or his *Grundriss der Geschichte der Philosophie* (Leipzig, 1812), which had appeared in two London editions and an English translation (*ADB*). Thomas Brown and Dugald Stewart (1753–1828) were leaders of the Scottish school of common-sense philosophy. Fuller must have read Stewart's *Outlines of Moral Philosophy* (Edinburgh, 1793) or his *Elements of the Philosophy of the Human Mind*, 3 vols. (Edinburgh, 1792–1827). For Brown, see letter 53, note 2.

122. To Eugene Fuller

[17 February 1836]
[Groton]

[   ] you came home—but [a] variety of circumstances make it necessary for us to get some idea of what you propose do[ing] that we may plan with reference to it— It would seem feasible on many accounts for Mother, if she could let this place, to take a small house

in the vicinity of Boston and for you and Wm to [   ] this dear
parent is worn to a shadow— Sometimes when I look on her pale face
and think of all her grief and the cares and anxieties which now beset
her I am appalled by the thought that she may not continue with us
long— God grant that you, Eugene, may return to us with the spirit
of a *man*, able and disposed to do for your mother what a daughter
cannot— Mother does not hope [   ] to begin upon the conflicts of
this world. B[ut] perhaps you are tired of school-keeping?

I have sometimes thought, dear brother, since I recovered that if I
had died when I expected to do so last autumn and you had recd the
messages I left for you then, it would have done you more good than
I can expect my life will— Nothing sustains me now but the thought
that my God who saw fit to restore me to life when I was so very,
very willing to leave it, more so, perhaps, than I shall ever be again,
must save some good [   ]

Farewell, my br[other. May God] ever bless a[nd] direct you. I am
hurt that you have never thought fit to answer me with [   ]

ALfr (MH: fMS Am 1086 [Box A]). *Addressed:* Mr. Fuller / Farley / Culpepper Co— /
Virginia. *Postmark:* [Grot]on MS 18. *Endorsed:* 1830—Feb 17.

123. To Eliza R. Farrar

17 March 1836
[Groton]

I think Herschel will be very valuable to me, from the slight glance I
have taken of it, and I thank Mr. F.; but do not let him expect any-
thing of me because I have ventured on a book so profound as the
Novum Organum.[1] I have been examining myself with severity, intellectually as well as morally, and am shocked to find how vague and
superficial is all my knowledge. I am no longer surprised that I should
have appeared harsh and arrogant in my strictures to one who, having
a better-disciplined mind, is more sensible of the difficulties in the
way of really knowing and doing anything, and who, having more
Wisdom, has more Reverence too. All that passed at your house will
prove very useful to me; and I trust that I am approximating somewhat to that genuine humility which is so indispensable to true regeneration. But do not speak of this to ———, for I am not yet sure of
the state of my mind.

ELfr, from *Memoirs*, 1:166.

1. Herschel's *Preliminary Discourse on the Study of Natural Philosophy* was a commentary on Bacon's *Novum Organum* (London, 1620).

124.   To Eliza R. Farrar

17 April 1836
[Groton]

If I am not to go with you I shall be obliged to tear my heart, by a violent effort, from its present objects and natural desires. But I shall feel the necessity, and will do it if the life-blood follows through the rent. Probably, I shall not even think it best to correspond with you at all while you are in Europe. Meanwhile, let us be friends indeed. The generous and unfailing love which you have shown me during these three years, when I could be so little to you, your indulgence for my errors and fluctuations, your steady faith in my intentions, have done more to shield and sustain me than any other earthly influence. If I must now learn to dispense with feeling them constantly near me, at least their remembrance can never, never be less dear. I suppose I ought, instead of grieving that we are soon to be separated, now to feel grateful for an intimacy of extraordinary permanence, and certainly of unstained truth and perfect freedom on both sides.

As to my feelings, I take no pleasure in speaking of them; but I know not that I could give you a truer impression of them, than by these lines which I translate from the German of Uhland. They are entitled "Justification."[1]

> Our youthful fancies, idly fired,
> > The fairest visions would embrace;
> These, with impetuous tears desired,
> > Float upward into starry space;
> Heaven, upon the suppliant wild,
> > Smiles down a gracious *No!*— In vain
> The strife! Yet be consoled, poor child,
> > For the wish passes with the pain.
>
> But when from such idolatry
> > The heart has turned, and wiser grown,
> In earnestness and purity
> > Would make a nobler plan its own,—

Yet, after all its zeal and care,
    Must of its chosen aim despair,—
Some bitter tears may be forgiven
    By *Man*, at least,— *we trust, by Heaven.*

ELfr, from *Memoirs*, 1:159–60.

1. Uhland's "Rechtfertigung" was first published in 1816.

125.   To James F. Clarke

[19 April 1836]
[Groton?]

How am I to get the information I want, unless I go to Europe? To whom shall I write to choose my materials? I have thought of Mr. Carlyle, but still more of Goethe's friend, Von Muller.[1] I dare say he would be pleased at the idea of a life of G. written in this hemisphere, and be very willing to help me. If you have anything to tell me, you will, and not mince matters. Of course, my impressions of Goethe's works cannot be influenced by information I get about his *life* but, as to this latter, I suspect I must have been hasty in my inferences. I apply to you without scruple. There are subjects on which men and women usually talk a great deal, but apart from one another.[2] You, however, are well aware that I am very destitute of what is commonly *called* modesty. With regard to this, how fine the remark of our present subject: "Courage and modesty are virtues which every sort of society reveres, because they are virtues which cannot be counterfeited; also, they are known by the *same hue*."[3] When that blush does not come naturally to my face, I do not drop a veil to make people think it is there. All this may be very unlovely, but it is *I*.

ELfr, from *Memoirs*, 1:129; also in Miller, p. 48.

1. Friedrich von Müller (1779–1849), a Weimar political figure (*ADB*).

2. Fuller obliquely refers to Goethe's life with Christiane Vulpius (1765–1816), whom he had taken as his mistress in the summer of 1788, upon his return from Italy. She was a working woman, the daughter of the official copyist in the Weimar court. In 1806 the couple married, thus legitimizing an affair that had scandalized the Weimar court and caused Goethe's name to be scorned by the righteous, especially in America (*OCGL*). In his reply Clarke observed that Goethe's "moral code was not of the strictest kind" (*Letters of JFC*, p. 119).

3. From "Maximen und Reflexionen aus Wilhelm Meisters Wanderjahren": "Mut

und Bescheidenheit sind die unzweideutigsten Tugenden; denn sie sind von der Art, dass Heuchelei sie nicht nachahmen kann. Auch haben sie die Eigenschaft gemein, sich beide durch dieselbe Farbe auszudrücken."

126. To Samuel G. Ward

Groton, 20 April 1836

You have probably just received a packet from me, (oh! what wild work makes a female pen!) yet I feel tempted to scribble to you, my fellow votary, on the subject of this morning's devotions to our common shrine.

I strolled languidly far and far over the dull-brown fields, and not an attempt at a life-like tint could I see. Some tawny evergreens and oaks, with their last year's leaves lingering, 'like unloved guests,' in vain attempted to give animation to the landscape. The sweetest southwest wind was blowing, but it did not make the heavens very blue, and was not enough for me, who wanted something to look at, and had not vital energy enough to be made happy through the pores of my skin. I was returning homeward quite comfortless and ill-paid for my time and trouble, when I suddenly came upon just what I wanted. It was a little shallow pool of the clearest amber. The afore-mentioned southwest was at work to some purpose, breaking it into exquisite wavelets, which flashed a myriad of diamonds up at each instant.

Why is it that the sight of the water stirs and fills the mind so much more than that of any other thing in nature?—why? Is it that here we see the most *subtle force* combined with the most *winning gentleness*, or the most *impetuous force* with the most *irrestible subtlety*?

I used to love, at Trenton, to go to that place where the water seemed collecting its energies so quietly, gliding on so stealthily, you could scarcely believe it was firmly resolved to display such vehemence in one more moment of time and rood of space.

I love the force of water much, but its subtlety is magic in its effects. Perfectly do I comprehend what I have heard of gazers on a riverside being tempted to drown themselves by sight of the water, and all those tales of mermaid enchantments which embody this feeling. This morning I felt a sort of timidity about standing quite at that point to which the undulatory motions (of all earthly things most lovely) seemed to tend. I felt that, unless I had an arm of flesh and blood to cling to, I should be too much seduced from humanity.

These undulations I have seen compared in poesy to the heaving of the bosom, and they do create a similar feeling,—at least, I, when I see this in the human frame, am tempted to draw near with a vague, instinctive anticipation (as far as ever I could analyze the emotion) that a heart will leap forth, and I be able to take it in my hand.

I dislike the comparison, as I always do illustrating so-called inanimate nature by man or any shape of animal life. Byron's comparisons of a mountain splendor to the "light of a dark eye in woman," the cataract to a tiger's leap, etc., displease my taste.[1] Why, again? I am not sure whether it is because man seems more than nature, or whether less, and that the whole is injured in illustrating it by a part, or whether it is that one hates to be forced back upon personalities when one is getting calmed by meditations on the elemental manifestations. Yet, though these comparisons displease my taste, they throw a light on the sympathies between the human mind and nature. I feel as if I should some time attain a precise notion of the meaning of Nature's most beautiful display, the *undulatory motion*.

ELfr, from Higginson, *MFO*, pp. 56–58.

1. *Childe Harold's Pilgrimage*, canto 3, stanza 92:

> Yet lovely in your strength, as is the light
> Of a dark eye in woman! Far along,
> From peak to peak, the rattling crags among
> Leaps the live thunder! Not from one lone cloud,
> But every mountain now hath found a tongue,
> And Jura answers, through her misty shroud,
> Back to the joyous Alps, who call to her aloud!

The second allusion is unidentified.

127.   To Ellen K. Fuller

Groton 21st April 1836.

My dear Ellen,

I think I observe notwithstanding all the kind interest you take in my affairs an affectation of coldness in your letter—[n] Why is this?— because I did not write to you as long a letter as to others. I was very weary and knew you would learn my little news from my letter to Mother. Besides I do not think you ought to dwell on every instance where I may seemingly fail to meet your feelings when you have such reason to be sure my heart is always right toward you.

I wish much to have you happy and I think you will be so. Belinda tells me you make persevering efforts to subdue your temper and I feel satisfied with what I hear of you generally.[1] I do not speak perhaps as warmly as you think I ought and it is because I have so often been deceived in judging from hearsay and should like to see with[n] my own eyes and hear with my own ears before I speak very decidedly.

Yes I do think you have been, for you, pretty deliberate about Miss Dwight.[2] I am glad she loves you and that you take pleasure in loving her— As to your making her a present, your generous feelings I dislike to check, but, really, I know nobody less able to make presents than yourself— Where are you to get money for all the necessaries you want? Summer is coming and many things must be bought. We shall not know for many months how much or how little we have to spend. Nevertheless consult Mother and if she thinks you can spare the money I should like to have you gratified.

You can give 75 cents or a dollar for my buckle. I do not know what sort would be best as I have not looked at any— Use your judgment, only let it be strong.

Give my best love to mother. Say that I recd her letter to-day and was much relieved by so doing. Nothing of importance has happened. Rebecca is still pretty well but misses her medicine. Mr Park has been here and says all is going on right. Reuben has been ploughing for two days.— I am much better and stronger in body this week. Lloyd is my chief trouble, but for him I could do a great deal and as it is I have not been idle. I do not wish her to trouble about my gown: if it is tolerably pretty I shall be content. It is not worthwhile for me to write to her again since you wished me to write to *you* but she knows I am always thinking of her.

I suppose Miss Martineau says just whatever she thinks of the Bostonians as she does of all things and persons without regard to effects. She has reason to think ill of them in some respects I daresay she adhered to justice in whatever she said. Little importance should be attached to on dits about a person like her.

I saw S. Woodbury to day: she desired her love to you and expressed impatience for your return.[3]

Now my dear Ellen I am tired and have nothing further of consequence to say. Write to me b[y] Mother give my love to E and B. and believe me always with sincere affection your Sister

M.

I am very familiar with Retsch's illustrations of Faust and admire them much.[4] See as many good pictures and engravings as you can.

ALS (MH: fMS Am 1086 [9:40]); MsC (MH: fMS Am 1086 [Works, 1:159–63]). *Addressed:* Miss E. K. Fuller. / care of Dr John Randall. / Boston, / Mass. *Postmark:* Groton MS April 22.

coldness in your letter] coldness ↑ in your letter ↓
see with] see ↑ with ↓

1. Belinda L. Randall (1816–97), third child of John and Elizabeth Wells Randall (Randall, *Poems*, p. 42).

2. Fuller probably knew four young Dwight women: Mary Ann (1816–1901) and Frances Ellen (1819–89), daughters of Dr. John Dwight and sisters of John Sullivan Dwight; and Mary Eliot (1821–79) and Sophia Dwight (1823–79), daughters of Edmund Dwight, a Boston merchant. The friendship between Margaret Fuller and John S. Dwight argues for one of the first pair (*Descendants of John Dwight*, pp. 893, 898, 1012; MVR 519:716, 402:14; Arthur W. Hodgman, "Elias Parkman of Dorchester and His Descendants," NEHGS, p. 170).

3. Possibly Sarah Lawrence Woodbury (1819–60), daughter of the Reverend Samuel and Mary Lawrence Woodbury of Groton. In 1841 she married the Reverend David Fosdick, Jr. (*GVR*; MVR 139:96).

4. In 1816 Goethe had suggested to the artist Moritz Retzsch that he do a set of illustrations for *Faust* (Ulrich Thieme and Felix Becker, eds., *Allgemeines Lexikon der Bildenden Künstler* [Leipzig, 1907–50]). Retzsch accepted the idea and that same year published *Umrisse zu Goethes Faust, gezeichnet von Retzsch* (Stuttgart and Tübingen), a work that by 1836 had appeared in at least four German editions and had been translated into English and French.

128. To Temperance H. Colburn

Groton May 8th 1836—

My dear Mrs. Colburn,

My silence has belied my feelings. Indeed I have put off writing from day to day, thinking I should be able to tell you when Mother is to come with Mrs. Park but they have not decided yet, further than that it is to be either this present or next week. Mother often expresses a wish to see you and seems to think she could *borrow courage* from you.[1] I rejoice to state that the Judge has allowed Mother the furniture, stock etc—so there is an end to *that* set of plagues.

You can have no idea how much the boys enjoyed their visit to you, nor how much they talk of the children.[2] It did them a world of good. Sister Ellen and Elizabeth Randall are coming here in a fortnight and then I want you to come and bring Mary and Jenny and, if possible, my little Sally— As for the little and great boy, if you can cram them in too, so much the better but the girls Ellen must see. I have excellent accounts of Ellen. She did not get a single bad mark all the term and Mrs. Urquhart told her she was perfectly satisfied with her. I hear you have applied to Mrs. U. for Mary—I hope it will be for Mary's good; she is a bright, observing girl and only wants the best models and generous rivals to call out her energies. I am not *sure* how she will find boarding there—about *that* I do not know but I think you will be very well pleased with the school and I should judge Mrs. U. must be trustworthy every way from all I have heard as yet.

I do not think it is worth while for Ellen to stay in Lowell on her return as we expect Eugene in a few days and she will want to see him as soon as may be. By and by I should like to have her pass a few days with you very much.

I trust that poor eye of yours has now got well and that Sarah is with you often and a pleasure to you.[3] Indeed, I am very sorry I am not where I can go in and see you frequently. It would solace me to be able to enliven some of your dark moments. But I know you are rich in friends who will help you if they can.— It troubles me much too that I cannot go to Mrs. Farrar who has been quite ill lately. If she would say she wanted me I should gratify myself by going but as it is not an extreme case I know Aunt Nancy will do for her as well as I could. So here I sit and watch for the mails to come in.

Belinda has been quite ill too with an ulcerated sore-throat. Ellen called on you in Boston: did you hear of it?

Uncle Elisha came here today and staid 30 minutes:— Uncle William is *not* engaged to Miss Livermore!

I can tell you no more of these agreeable particulars— for, in truth, I have been writing letters till I am wearied out and tis way after decent riglar bed-time but I would not fail you another day— Love to Sarah and "all your pretty ones"— My regards to Mr. Tilden. Be so good as to write this week to yours affectionately

S. M. FULLER

TC (MHarF).

1. Warren Colburn had died in 1833.

2. The Colburn children were Warren, Jr. (1824–79), who became a mathematician and engineer, like his father; Mary Ann (b. 1828?); Jane Smith (b. 1829?); Sarah Horton (b. 1832?); Theodore (1834–89), who graduated from Harvard in 1854 and became an architect; and James Henry (Lowell VR; *CVR*; *National Cyclopedia*, 10:457).

3. Mrs. Colburn's sister, Sarah Field Horton (1814–51), had the previous month married Charles Linzee Tilden (1807–62), son of Joseph and Susannah Linzee Tilden. The younger Tilden was a manufacturer in Lowell (John W. Linzee, *The Linzee Family of Great Britain and the United States of America* [Boston, 1917], pp. 803–4).

129. To [?]

23 May, 1836
[Groton?]

I have just been reading Goethe's Lebensregel.[1] It is easy to say "Do not trouble yourself with useless regrets for the past; enjoy the present, and leave the future to God." But it is *not* easy for characters, which are by nature neither *calm* nor *careless*, to act upon these rules. I am rather of the opinion of Novalis, that "Wer sich der hochsten Lieb ergeben Genest von ihnen Wunden nie."[2]

But I will endeavor to profit by the instructions of the great philosopher who teaches, I think, what Christ did, to use without overvaluing the world.

Circumstances have decided that I must not go to Europe, and shut upon me the door, as I think, forever, to the scenes I could have loved. Let me now try to forget myself, and act for others' sakes. What I can do with my pen, I know not. At present, I feel no confidence or hope. The expectations so many have been led to cherish by my conversational powers, I am disposed to deem ill-founded. I do not think I can produce a valuable work. I do not feel in my bosom that confidence necessary to sustain me in such undertakings,—the confidence of genius. But I am now but just recovered from bodily illness, and still heart-broken by sorrow and disappointment. I may be renewed again, and feel differently. If I do not soon, I will make up my mind to teach. I can thus get money, which I will use for the benefit of my dear, gentle, suffering mother,—my brothers and sister. This will be the greatest consolation to me, at all events.

ELfr, from *Memoirs*, 1:160–61.

1. From his "Epigrammatisch":

> Willst du dir ein hübsch Leben zimmern,
> Musst dich ums Vergangne nich bekümmern;
> Das Wenigste muss dich verdriessen;
> Musst stets die Gegenwart geniessen,
> Besonders keinen Menschen hassen
> Und die Zukunft Gott überlassen.

John Sullivan Dwight translates the lines (*Select Minor Poems*, p. 186):

> Wouldst make thy life go fair and square?
> For the Past, then, thou must have no care;
> Must let the very least annoy thee,
> Must in the Present still enjoy thee,
> Above all, hate no human being,
> And all the Future leave to the All-Seeing.

2. Fuller slightly misquotes the poem "Astralis," which opens the second part of *Heinrich von Ofterdingen.* The second line should read "Genest von ihren Wunden nie." John Weiss translates the lines: "Who yieldeth himself to love's deep madness, / From its wounds is never free" (*Henry of Ofterdingen* [Cambridge, Mass., 1842], p. 195).

130. To Elizabeth Hoar

Groton 14 July 1836

I will come to Concord, next week, on Friday, 22 July, if that will be agreeable to Mrs Emerson.[1]

MsCfr (MH: bMS Am 1280 [111, p. 120]). Published in *JMN*, 11:479.

Elizabeth Sherman Hoar (1814–78), daughter of Samuel Hoar of Concord, was one of Fuller's closest friends. Elizabeth had been engaged to Waldo Emerson's younger brother Charles (1808–36). After his death on 9 May she was always considered a member of the Emerson family, as though the two had married (Elizabeth Maxfield-Miller, "Emerson and Elizabeth of Concord," *Harvard Library Bulletin* 19 [July 1971]: 290–306).

1. Fuller's first meeting with the Emersons extended from 21 July to 11 August 1836. On 12 August, Emerson noted in his journal, "Yesterday Margaret Fuller returned home after making us a visit of three weeks—a very accomplished & very intelligent person." Thus began one of the most important friendships in her life (*JMN*, 5:188).

131. To A. Bronson Alcott

Groton 25th August 1836—

Dear Sir,

I am not quite sure that I understood your last words at Mr Emerson's. *As* I understood, you had applied to some other person to assist you in your school before you thought of me and would write to me after receiving an answer from that person. A letter since received from Miss Peabody leads me to think that you may on your side be expecting to hear from me and, as I find it necessary to come to some decision·about my employment for the winter, I think it best to write to you at any rate.

Will you have the kindness to answer this letter as soon as possible informing me whether you are desirous I should take Miss Peabody's place; whether, if I do take it, you expect me to reside in your family as she did; and whether any-thing would be expected from me beyond the instruction in Latin or other languages which you mentioned to me,[n] with any other circumstances which you may think proper for me to know in order to my decision. Also whether you could (if you wish me to come and I decide on doing so) dispense with my assistance till the 29th of September or the 1st of October. I could, if necessary, begin my lessons earlier, but my family affairs are so situated that it will be much more convenient to me to devote the coming month to their arrangement.

Every thing about me is in a state of uncertainty but I suppose, if I do not hear from you before Friday of next week, that I shall on that day set out on a journey which will occupy ten days or a fort-night. I should, however, leave directions for any letter from you to be forwarded to me.

My acquaintance with your views and character is not sufficiently thorough to give me a confidence that I could satisfy you. But I think as far as I understand your plan I might carry it into execution as successfully as most persons, and I should[n] like to become more conversant with your method of teaching. It would be but an experiment on both sides, for, as I have never yet been subordinate[n] to any one, I cannot tell how I should please or be pleased. But your proposal has attracted me more than any which has as yet been made to me.

If I was right in my first supposition and you did *not* make me any direct proposal but only spoke of the possibility of doing so, do not let this letter embarrass you. You have only to say how it was.—

With much regard yours

S. M. FULLER.

I am sorry that I have forgotten your first name and have no present means of ascertaining it so as to direct my letter properly. I am not usually so inaccurate; but I hope that, being directed to the street where you live, my letter will not fail to reach you.

ALS (MH:59m-312 [120]).

Amos Bronson Alcott (1799–1888) had established a school at Boston's Masonic Temple in September 1834. A master teacher, he was indifferent to the implications of his methods and ideas as they were seen by Boston's more conservative citizens. After developing a radical notion of Christ's manhood, Alcott came close to the topic of sexuality in discussing the birth of Jesus. The conversations between teacher and pupils had been recorded by Elizabeth Peabody, who served with Alcott as his assistant and secretary. Her *Record of a School* (Boston, 1835) is based on her transcriptions of the conversations. Closely identified with Alcott and his ideas, she was horrified when she recognized the scandal that would erupt should Alcott persist in publishing all the conversations. She resigned in the summer of 1836, just as Fuller began to think about taking a teaching job (Shepard, *Pedlar's Progress*, pp. 186–89; *Peabody Sisters*, pp. 93–95). Fuller became Alcott's assistant in the fall of 1836.

A. Bronson Alcott. By permission of the Louisa May Alcott Memorial Association.

to me,] to me, ⟨Also⟩
and I should] and ⟨that⟩ I should
yet been subordinate] yet been subordin⟨t⟩ate

132.   To Ellen K. Fuller

26th August [1836]
[Groton]

De[ar] Sister

I never meant that you misspelt from ignorance. What I *said* was that you were in the habit of leaving out both letters and syllables from writing in too much hurry which is the truth and which produces the effect of bad orthography. I do not remember what I said about Eliza Tenny[?] I was in jest I believe; I was not unkind, I am sure. You must not be hasty to suspect unkindness, least of all should you from me who have shown you so sincere affection,— I do *not* expect as much from you as from M. Salisbury who is several years older.[1] If you cultivate habits of industry and a cheerful, hopeful temper, I shall be well satisfied. I *am* well satisfied with you as far as I can judge from what I hear. I do not expect you to make *progress* in your Italn. If you do not lose what you have learned it is all I expect from you this summer, and I depend on your persevering in learning a little lesson every day. Do not be concerned about your faded frocks; if you are neat and lady-like in your manners they will not injure you with any person whose good opinion is worth having. Now that every one knows our circumstances it is no disgrace to us not to wear fine clothes, but a credit. I wore a "faded calico frock" in the presence of much company while at Concord, and it did not prevent my exciting respect and interest. You must, my sister, pray to our Heavenly Father to strengthen you to rise above the opinion of this world as far as vanity is concerned and only to regard it from motives of kindness and modesty. It is very difficult for young persons to do so; the lesson is long and often severe, but the acquisition is worth it all. From this source I get the little strength I have and the same will be given you if you seek it. [   ] do not suspect I think you particularly inclined to vanity. I do not by any means, but we are all in beginning life deficient in separating things of real importance from those which are not so.

Mother gives her consent to your inviting the twins, but does not think Mrs R. will let them come. She sends much love to you. Give mine to grandmother Aunt and cousin Ellen. Aunt's visit was pleasant to us and I should have liked to have had it prolonged. Mother recd yesterday a very pleasant letter from Ellen's Mr Hill.[2] Affectionately yours

M. F.

ALS (MH: fMS Am 1086 [9:43]). *Addressed:* Miss Ellen Fuller / Canton / Massts. *Postmark:* Groton MS Aug 26.

Fuller's letter is added to one from Eugene to Ellen.

1. Eugene identifies her merely as Mary Salisbury, who was soon going to St. Louis; perhaps Mary H. Salisbury of Groton, who died in 1849 (*GVR*).

2. In addition to her grandmother and her aunt Elizabeth Crane, Fuller mentions cousin Ellen Crane Hill and her husband, David.

133. To Frederic H. Hedge

Groton 31st August
1836—

Dear Henry,

I have lately been making a visit at Mr R. W. Emerson's during which you were so frequently recalled to my mind that I cannot resist the present oppory of writing you a hasty note. I have scarcely known any-thing about you since I bade you farewell at Concord last Septr.— You perhaps know that I was very ill after that and scarcely expected to recover for some time. Since then the state of our family and of my health has been such that I have not desired to tell much of myself to any one. But I do not like to be kept in utter ignorance of the estate of so good a friend as you. Pray write to me and tell me of yourself; what you are doing, what feeling and what thinking.

Let me know too whether I transgress in keeping your Eichhorn so long. You perhaps will marvel when I tell you that during the year I have had these books there has been no time when I have been well enough and free enough to use them. I hope to do so this winter, but, if I cannot, shall return them in despair of having any more hours of calm leisure. If you want them now please write and say so.

I am glad to hear your friend Mr Bradford meditates going to you.—[1] Remember me to Mrs Hedge and receive kindly this otherwise worthless note as a proof of regard[n] from your friend

MARGARET F.

ALS (MH: fMS Am 1086 [10:102]). *Addressed:* Revd F. H. Hedge, / Bangor / Maine, / politeness of Miss Brazer.

proof of regard] proof of re⟨m⟩gard

1. George P. Bradford (1807–90), Hedge's classmate at Harvard, taught in several New England towns, including Bangor. He joined George Ripley at Brook Farm in the 1840s (Harvard archives; *Boston Post*, 1 February 1890).

134. To Ralph Waldo Emerson

Groton 1st Sept 1836

I was entertained by the discussions at the Institute, particularly by Mr Frederick Emerson's horror at the idea of this common earth being peopled by gods, "an idea upon which he would not dilate—"[1]

MsCfr (MH: bMS Am 1280 [111, p. 256]). Published in *JMN*, 11:500.

1. Fuller refers to the annual meeting of the American Institute of Instruction at Worcester during the last week in August. The *Boston Daily Advertiser* published daily reports of the meetings. She refers here to a discussion on the 27th between Alcott, who was prominent among the participants, and Frederick Emerson (1788–1857), a teacher, author, and school administrator. According to the paper, Frederick Emerson and Alcott were debating the topic "Is the necessity of moral education, as the ground of all human culture, felt as it ought to be by teachers and by the community in general[?]" Alcott made his usual point that "man is a God on earth," at which Emerson "rose to express his regret that the expression, calling a man a God on earth, had been used at the Institute. He would not dilate upon it, but hoped he had misunderstood the expression" (James G. Wilson and John Fiske, eds., *Appleton's Cyclopedia of American Biography*, 6 vols. [New York, 1888], 2:341; H. E. Noyes, *A Memorial to the Town of Hampstead, New Hampshire* [Boston, 1899–1903], 1:367–69; *Boston Daily Advertiser*, 27–30 August 1836).

135. To Ralph Waldo Emerson

Boston 21st Sept 1836—

My dear friend,

I may venture to begin so since you have subscribed yourself my friend— I have just received your letter. While I was with you you very justly corrected me for using too strong expressions on some subjects. But there is no exaggeration in saying— I *must* be allowed to say that I *detest* Mr Robinson at this moment. The last thing I did was to beg that he would not invite you to preach at Groton without ascertaining that I should be there, and, if I had not, said any thing now[n] knowing how great my disappointment was on the former occasion common good nature should have prevented his doing the same thing again. Do not go, dear Sir, I intreat you, if it is possible to make any other arrangement— Is it not possible to postpone it till the third or second Sunday from this next? I fear it is not possible, but if it is I think you will do it for my sake, for I would do twenty times as much for yours. If that must not be and if I can come to Concord Saturday afternoon will you take me with you to Groton— It would be merely to spend Sunday; I should be obliged to return to Concord and come here again for I have not half-finished what I came to do— I am not sure that this would be agreeable to you, nor that I could do it at any rate, but I might try to arrange it. I should like to baffle the malice of my pastor, and hear better preaching than his own if I could.— If you were to see me just now, dear Sir, you would not like me at all for I am very far from calm and have quite forfited my placid brow but I flatter myself that my vexation will seem nothing worse than earnestness on paper.[1]

I thank you much for "Nature."[2] I hear much conversation about it that amuses me. I have it already. I gave a copy to Miss Barker and she in return gave me one accompanied by Philip van Artevelde.[3] I would not decline it lest I should not receive a copy from yourself[n] though I confess I hoped I should be so honored. I should indeed be too happy to pass a day at Concord with Miss Barker and she would have been very glad to come, but she goes to-day. Her father is with her and wishes her to go and I feel that I ought not to expect her[n] to stay; for a brother whom she loves more than all her kin, except her parents, is to leave New York in a few days for Antwerp where he is to remain as Consul and she may not see him again for years.[4] It has been both painful and gratifying to me to see her. I find her true to herself as yet, and lovely as ever but so many people have beset both of us that we have had little chance for any profitable conversation. The peace and seclusion of Concord would have been just what we wanted. But I doubt whether we could have gone even if I had received Mrs Emerson's kind invitation earlier.— Mrs Emerson does not love me more than I love her; but I am not sure how successfully our visit might have ministered to her well-being—[n] It is all over now but it is very annoying to know that you were so near us on Sunday and that nothing but my unfortunate want of eye-sight prevented my having a chance of at least showing Anna to you— If you think this ebullition worthy an answer please direct to the care of

James Dana, Charlestown.[5] I am going there to stay two or three days. respectfully and affectionately Mrs Emerson's and your friend

S. M. FULLER.

You must not make a joke of my anxiety about next Sunday, but take it seriously as I am feeling. It is a great gain to be able to address yourself directly, instead of[n] intriguing as I did last year.

ALS (MH: bMS Am 1280 [2335]); MsC (MB: Ms. Am. 1450 [62]). Published in part in Higginson, *MFO*, p. 68; published entire in Rusk, *Letters of RWE*, 2:36–37. *Addressed:* Revd R. W. Emerson. / Concord, / Mass. *Postmark:* Boston Sept 21 MS. *Endorsed:* Miss S. M. Fuller / Sept 1836.

not, said any thing now] not, ↑ said any thing now ↓
copy from yourself] copy from⟨y⟩ yourself
expect her] expect ↑ her ↓
to her well-being] to ⟨?⟩ her well-being
instead of] inste⟨d⟩ad of

1. Emerson's letter of 20 September had announced his exchange for the coming Sunday; on the twenty-second he answered Fuller saying that he would arrange a second exchange, and would indeed take her to Groton, but that, these things failing, he would be most glad to have her visit in Concord. She stayed in Charlestown with the Samuel Danas through the twenty-fifth. This was the second time Fuller would fail to hear Emerson in Groton (see letter 109) (Rusk, *Letters of RWE*, 2:36–37).

2. Emerson's *Nature* appeared on 9 September under the imprint of James Munroe of Boston. Fuller did not read the entire book until 1840, though apparently Emerson had read it to her (*Boston Daily Advertiser*, 9 September 1836).

3. Fuller had enthusiastically reviewed Henry Taylor's *Philip van Artevelde: A Dramatic Romance* in the *Western Messenger* 1 (December 1835):398–408.

4. In a letter now lost, Fuller had invited Emerson to meet Anna Barker when he was in Boston on 19 September; he missed the appointment, however, and urged Fuller to bring Anna to Concord (Rusk, *Letters of RWE*, 2:36–37). The brother mentioned here is Andrew Sigourney Barker.

5. James Dana (1811–90), son of Samuel and Rebecca Dana of Groton, graduated from Harvard in 1830, became a lawyer, and settled in Charlestown (*Dana Family*, p. 367).

136. To [?]

[ca. late 1836]
[Boston]

It was not very pleasant, for Dr. C. takes in subjects more deliberately than is conceivable to us feminine people, with our habits of ducking, diving, or flying for truth.[1] Doubtless, however, he makes better use of what he gets, and if his sympathies were livelier he would not view certain truths in so steady a light. But there is much more talking than reading; and I like talking with him. I do not feel that constraint which some persons complain of, but am perfectly free, though less called out than by other intellects of inferior power. I get too much food for thought from him, and am not bound to any tiresome formality of respect on account of his age and rank in the world of intellect. He seems desirous to meet even one young and obscure as myself on equal terms, and trusts to the elevation of his thoughts to keep him in his place.

ELfr, from *Memoirs*, 1:175–76.

1. Fuller became acquainted with Dr. William Ellery Channing (1780–1842) and went on to read German to him as an unpaid assistant. More than anyone before Emerson, Channing shaped religious thought and history in New England, for, beginning with his ordination sermon for Jared Sparks, he defined American Unitarianism. A Rhode Island man, Channing graduated from Harvard in 1798 and was installed in 1803 at the Federal Street Church in Boston, where he remained until his death (*DAB*).

137. To Jane F. Tuckerman

1837.

My beloved Child,

I was very glad to get your note. Do not think you must only write to your friends when you can tell them you are happy; they will not misunderstand you in the dark hour, nor think you *forsaken*, even if cast down. Though your letter of Wednesday was very sweet to me, I knew it could not long be as it was then. These hours of heavenly, heroic strength leave us, but they come again; their memory is with us amid after trials, and gives us a foretaste of that era when the steadfast soul shall be the only reality.

My dearest, you must suffer, but you will always be growing stronger, and with every trial nobly met, you will feel a growing assurance that nobleness is not a mere *sentiment* to you. I sympathize deeply in your anxiety about your Mother, yet I cannot but remember the bootless fear and agitation I endured about my Mother, and how strangely our destinies were guided. Take refuge in prayer when you are most troubled; the door of the sanctuary will never be shut against you. I send you a paper which is very sacred to me; bless Heaven that your heart is awakened to sacred duties before any kind of gentle ministering has become impossible, before any relation has been broken.

Ralph Waldo Emerson, ca. 1860. By permission of the Concord Free Public Library.

MsCfr (MH: fMS Am 1086 [*Works*, 1:73]). Published in *WNC*, p. 352.

Jane Francis Tuckerman (1821?–56), daughter of Gustavus (1785–1860) and Jane Francis Tuckerman (1794?–1858), was Fuller's student and later her assistant on the *Dial*. In 1843 Jane Tuckerman married John Gallison King (1819–88) (*Tuckerman Family*, pp. 61–62; MVR 103:118; *NEHGR* 5:160; Rufus King, *Pedigree of King* [n.p., 1891]).

138. To Frederic H. Hedge

Boston 6th April 1837.

Dear Henry,

I have been wishing and wishing, trying and trying to write to you this past month and after all can get no hour for the fulfilment of so good a purpose unless at the fag end of a busy eveg itself the flavorless postact to a bustling day. So please take my letter kindly and marvel not if there should be nothing in it worthy of you—or *me*!

Firstly I would scold that you are not coming here till May. Here I have been living six months and you would not come and now you must needs be planning to come just as I am going away.[1] You manage very ill, to take[n] no thought of me in any of your plans. The end of it will be that we shall not be able to talk when we do meet and that will, I think, be very grievous. For, upon the whole, I have had as satisfactory talks with you as I shall or can have in this world. And why must they end?— Just because you will not come where I am.

Secondly why is it that I hear you are writing a piece to "cut up Mr Alcott?"[2] I do not believe you are going to cut up Mr Alcott. There are plenty of fish in the net created solely for markets &c no need to try your knife on a dolphin like him.— I should be charmed if I thought you were writing a long, beautiful, wise like article showing the elevated aim and at the same time the practical defects of his system. You would do a great service to him as well as the publick and I know no one so well qualified as yourself to act as a mediator between the two and set both sides of the question in a proper light. But the phrase "cutting up" alarms me. If you were here I am sure that you would[n] feel as I do and that your wit would never lend its patronage to the ugly blinking owls who are now hooting from their snug tenements, overgown rather with nettles than with ivy, at this star of purest ray serene.[3] But you are not here, more's the pity, and perhaps do not know exactly what you are doing, do write to me and reassure me.

3dly, is it not naughty in you to throw your Bangor ice water on all the Goethero-American lyrics that were swelling into bud?—[4] Translations, as somebody printed the other day, are no better at best than an asylum for the destitute but that asylum must be provided. I dare say the public know nothing about *lyrics*. They will read the things as *verses* and be content. I hope you are not so romantic as to think of raising people up to the level of your own tastes.

4thly Why did you not send me your lecture?[5] Have not I a claim as a *literary friend*? I was obliged to *steal* it, which did not look well in me, a schoolmistress!

—These are all my quetions.— As to my biography, much of it cannot be given on a piece of paper like this. I have learned much and thought little, an assertion which seems paradoxical and *is* true. I faint with desire to think and surely shall, the first oppory, but some outward requisition is ever knocking at the door of my mind and I am as ill placed as regards a chance to think as a haberdasher's prentice or the President of Harvard University— As to study my attention has been concentrated on the subjects about which I teach. There was a time when my dearest books became detestable to me on account of the duty work I did upon them. But that bad time is passed and I think I could do what I would if I staid here.

As to reading I have read only two books, Coleridge's Literary remains and Eckermann's Conversations with Goethe, both very good!—[6]

I see many people and some of them are very pleasant but you know the best of them.

I have been very unwell all winter and am now rather worse. If May flowers and June breezes do no good I must prepare either to leave this scene or become "that extremely common character, a confirmed invalid." But I intend to get perfectly well, if possible, for Mr Carlyle says "it is wicked to be sick."— When you write tell me how you like his Mirabeau.[7] Farewell. Remember me to your wife and present my respects to your children.[8] I am sorry to hear that Mr Bradford is going to leave you, but glad you can hold converse with Mr Woods.[9]— I daresay I shall not write again, or if I do, no better a letter than this—for I write very bad letters now.

As ever your friend

S. M. Fuller.

ALS (MH-AH); MsCfr (MB: Ms. Am. 1450 [63, 79, 162]). Published in part in Higginson, *MFO*, p. 78, and Wade, pp. 547–48. *Addressed:* Revd F. H. Hedge, / Bangor, / Maine. *Postmark:* Boston 7 Apr. *Endorsed:* Boston April 1837. / Alcott.

manage very ill, to take] manage very ill, ⟨?⟩ to take
you could] you ⟨will⟩ could

1. Having quit Alcott's school because he did not pay her, Fuller was on her way to Providence, where on 5 June she became a teacher at Hiram Fuller's Greene-Street School. Hiram Fuller (1814–80) studied at Andover and taught at Plymouth before moving to Providence in 1836. Professing to imitate Alcott, he conducted a lively school. He gave up teaching for journalism in 1843, when he moved to New York to join N. P. Willis on the *New York Mirror*. Hiram Fuller's later career was contentious, for he was a Copperhead politically. In 1844 he married Emilie Louise Delaplaine, a New York heiress ("Greene-St. School," pp. 199–219).

2. In his reply of 23 May (MH-AH), Hedge confessed, "You are right about Alcott & my reputed design upon him." After declaring Alcott to be a "gentle & pious spirit," Hedge explained that he had promised a review of the *Conversations* to James Walker, editor of the *Christian Examiner*, but that after reading the book he decided it did not "come within the proper sphere of criticism, & though I had a good deal to say about Mr. A's. system I hardly knew how to handle the 'Conversations.'" Walker, Hedge said, insisted on a severe review, but Hedge was unwilling "to increase the uproar. . . . In short, I could not say what I would & I would not say what I could, & so determined to say nothing." In his 1837 journal, Alcott noted that Walker told him that Hedge was to review the book but that "Mr. H. had failed." No notice of the book appeared in the *Examiner* until an unsigned review was published in November 1837 (Carlson, "Alcott's Journal," p. 254).

3. Fuller alludes to stanzas 3 and 14 of Thomas Gray's "Elegy Written in a Country Church Yard":

> Save that from yonder ivy-mantled tow'r
> The mopeing owl does to the moon complain
> Of such, as wand'ring near her secret bow'r,
> Molest her ancient solitary reign.

> Full many a gem of purest ray serene,
> The dark unfathom'd caves of ocean bear:
> Full many a flower is born to blush unseen,
> And waste its sweetness on the desert air.

(*The Complete Poems of Thomas Gray*, ed. H. W. Starr and J. R. Hendrickson [Oxford, 1966], pp. 38–39.)

4. Hedge had refused an invitation to contribute translations to John Sullivan Dwight's anthology, *Select Minor Poems* (Hedge to Fuller, 23 May 1837, MH-AH).

5. *An Introductory Lecture Delivered at the Opening of the Bangor Lyceum. Nov. 15, 1836* ([Bangor], 1836).

6. Johann Peter Eckermann (1792–1854) served as Goethe's companion and unpaid secretary from 1823 through 1832. In 1837 Eckermann published the first two volumes of his *Gespräche mit Goethe in den letzen Jahren seines Lebens*; the third volume did not appear until 1848 (*OCGL*).

7. In his letter to Emerson of 5 November 1836, Carlyle had said, "It is a dreadful thing sickness; really a thing which I begin frequently to think *criminal*— at least in myself" (*Emerson–Carlyle Correspondence*, p. 154). Fuller refers to Carlyle's essay "Memoirs of Mirabeau," *London and Westminster Review* 26 (January 1837):382–439.

8. Three of the four Hedge children were born by 1837: Frederic Henry (1831–1918), who never married, was a librarian later in his life; Charlotte (1834–1923); and Ellen (1836–66). Caroline, who was born in 1838, died in 1876 (Mt. Auburn; Harvard archives; *CVR*; *Boston Evening Transcript*, 2 June 1923).

9. Leonard Woods (1807–78) was at this time professor of biblical literature at the Bangor Theological Seminary. The son of a prominent opponent of Unitarianism, Leonard Woods, and his wife, Abigail Wheeler, young Woods had graduated from Union College in 1827 and had translated G. C. Knapp's *Lectures on Christian Theology* (1831–33). He was soon (1839) to become president of Bowdoin College (*DAB*).

139.   To Ralph Waldo Emerson

Boston.
11th April 1837.

"Revd and dear Sir,"

I recd yesterday morng your letter in which you ask for the Necklace, and was troubling myself much to devise how I could give back what had never been in my possession, when the desired article was brought me from the Post Office where your emissary had deposited it. I was able to read it through yesty afternoon and so return it with many thanks. It is good—but not, to my mind, half *as* good as the Mirabeau.[n,1]

I think it is somewhat ungracious in you to resume your gift of the proof sheet which I was about to lay in lavender by the side of that first most appropriate token of your regard, with which you honored me during my first visit to Concord, to wit the autograph of Jeremy Bentham.[2] To me, as a lady of enthusiasm and taste, such twigs from the tree of genius, however dry, are of course inexpressibly valuable. I shall expect from you, in lieu of the proof sheet (if you *will* give it to Mrs Ripley) an autograph of Bonaparte, or Metternich, or at the very least of Grandison, Cromwell La Fayette.[3]

I send you a note from Mr R[ipley] on the subject of Eckermann as I showed him yours, thinking that the shortest way of telling the story. You see how it is. Unless he himself[n] proposed my making an arrangement to translate it for some other publishers than his, I can do nothing.[4] And I dare say it is quite as well. I have yet to see whether I shall have strength to chase butterflies, let alone edible animals, this summer. Please send me his note if you send me any thing done up in paper; if not keep it for me till that good day which shall see me at Concord.

My friend and charming pupil Jane Tuckerman is going to England the first of May and if you wished to send any thing to Mr Carlyle she would like to take it, I am sure.

I take the liberty to send Merck and the two first vols of Zelter.[5] Do not trouble yourself to send them back. All the miseries which encompass the fag end of a sojurn in a city are thick upon me. What with milliners, mantuamakers,[6] shopkeepers, notes that must be written, and calls that must be made, now or never, under penalty of general odium, (to say nothing of parting talks with sundry people I do really like) the Hand[n] of the mind has almost lost its power to grasp and the Eye of the mind is not permitted to rest in peace upon the moon or stars. But I look to Concord as my[n] Lethe and Eunoi after this purgatory of distracting, petty tasks.[7] I am sure you will purify and strengthen me to enter the Paradise of thought once more.

Last night I took my boldest[n] peep into the Gigman world of Boston.[8] I have not been to a large party before and only seen said world in half-boots, so I thought as it was an occasion in which I felt real interest, to wit, a fete given by Mrs Thorndike for my beautiful Susan, I would look at it for once in satin slippers.[9] Dr Channing meant to go but was too weary when the hour came. I spent the early part of the eveg in reading bits of Dante with him and talking about the material sublime till half past nine, when I went with Mrs C. and graceful Mary.[10] It was very pretty to look at. So many fair maidens dressed as if they had stepped out of their Grandmothers' picture frames, and youths, with their long locks, suitable to represent pages, if not nobles. Signor Figaro was there also in propria—Sa et la.— And Daniel the Great, not however, when I saw him, engaged in an operation peculiarly favorable to his style of beauty, to wit eating oysters.[11] Theodore Parker was there and introduced to me.[12] I had some pleasant talk with him but before I could get to Spinoza, somebody seized on me and carried me off to quite another S.—to Supper.— On the whole it all pleased my eye; my fashionable fellow creatures were very civil to me and I went home glad to have looked at this slide in the magic lantern also.

I prattle on to you as if you liked prattling and as if I had time. Forgive and Farewell. If it is really "wicked to be sick" I should think you might teach your own son better at so early an age.[13] Bid him get[n] quite well and strong that I may see him play *Peep* with all the vivacity which is, I hear, so much admired. Dear love to the sainted Lidian—

—yours as ever

S. M. FULLER

Miss Tuckerman's voyage is postponed in consequence of the illness of a relation. I shall know when I come to C. when she will go, if she does go.

Wednesday—

An accident prevented this packet from going today as I intended it should, but, as Thursday is the day mentioned in your note, I hope it will arrive in time.

ALS (MH: bMS Am 1280 [1236]); MsC (MB: Ms. Am. 1450 [64]). Published in part in Higginson, *MFO*, pp. 86–87, and Rusk, *Letters of RWE*, 2:64–65. *Addressed:* Revd R. W. Emerson. / Concord, / Mass. *Endorsed:* Miss S. M Fuller / April. 1837—.

as the Mirabeau] as the ⟨m⟩Mirabeau
he himself] he ↑ himself ↓
the Hand] the ⟨?⟩ Hand
as my] as ⟨?⟩ my
my boldest] my ⟨fi⟩boldest
him get] him ↑ get ↓

1. Fuller refers to two recently published Carlyle essays, "Memoirs of Mirabeau" and "The Diamond Necklace," *Fraser's Magazine* 15 (January–February 1837):1–19, 172–89. Carlyle sent bound copies of both, together with a proof sheet from his soon-to-be-published *French Revolution*, to Emerson, who received them on 1 April. The next day Emerson sent the "Mirabeau" and the proof sheet to Fuller with a promise to send the other essay "when the ladies here release it" (*Emerson–Carlyle Correspondence*, pp. 156–60; Rusk, *Letters of RWE*, 2:63). On 10 April, immediately after posting the second essay, he wrote Fuller asking for a return of "The Diamond Necklace" and the proof sheet. Fuller is responding to that request (Rusk, *Letters of RWE*, 2:65).

2. The publication in 1789 of *An Introduction to the Principles of Morals and Legislation* established Jeremy Bentham (1748–1832) as the chief philosopher of utilitarianism. In 1833 Emerson had visited Bentham's home and taken away a lock of hair and an autograph as souvenirs (Rusk, *Letters of RWE*, 1:392).

3. Emerson's letter of the previous day names "Mrs. Ripley of W," who was Sarah Alden Bradford (1793–1867), wife of the Reverend Samuel Ripley (1783–1847), Emerson's uncle. Sarah Ripley, the eldest of the nine children born to Gamaliel and Elizabeth Hickling Bradford of Boston, was perhaps the most learned woman in New England at this time. An adept scholar in Greek and Latin, she kept school at Waltham with her husband. They tutored generations of Harvard-bound and Harvard-rusticated students (Rusk, *Letters of RWE*, 2:65; *NAW*). In his "Mirabeau," Carlyle mentions "Grandison-Cromwell Lafayette" as one of Mirabeau's nicknames.

4. Soon after she read Eckermann's book, Fuller began to translate it. She sent her work to Ripley, who wrote her on 6 April, accepting her proposal that he publish her translation but saying that he could not do so for a year (MH). Fuller apparently told Emerson of Ripley's response, for he replied on 11 April, "Did you show Mr. Ripley that the translation of Eckermann could be of no mercenary value to translator or bookseller unless done now? before a British comes" (Rusk, *Letters of RWE*, 2:65). It was probably this Emerson letter that Fuller showed Ripley, and it is Ripley's letter of 6 April that she is forwarding to Emerson. Fuller and Ripley later agreed to terms, and the translation, her first major literary work, was published in July 1839 as vol. 4 of Ripley's *Specimens of Foreign Standard Literature*.

5. Johann Heinrich Merck (1741–91) was a Darmstadt literary figure who had been a severe critic of Goethe's early work but had urged the publication of *Götz von Berlichingen*. He and Goethe met often between 1777 and 1783 (*OCGL*). *Briefe an Johann Heinrich Merck von Goethe, Herder, Wieland und andern bedeutenden Zeitgenossen* was published in Darmstadt in 1835. Emerson immediately read the Merck book and told Fuller "it is inestimable to the biography of Goethe & not less for the picture it gives of the inside of Germany" (Rusk, *Letters of RWE*, 2:70–71). This exchange typifies the aid Fuller gave Emerson in his study of German. Karl Friedrich Zelter (1758–1832) was a composer of vocal music whose work so impressed Goethe that he used Zelter's music as the settings for his poetry (*OCGL*). The six-volume *Briefwechsel zwischen Goethe und Zelter in den jahren 1796 bis 1832* was published in Berlin, 1833–34.

6. Fuller's reference to "milliners" and "mantuamakers" echoes Carlyle's description of Jeanne de Saint-Remi in "The Diamond Necklace."

7. As early as 2 April the Emersons had been talking of a coming visit from Fuller, but she did not arrive in Concord until the last week in the month.

8. Carlyle used "Gig" as a metaphor for fashionable society in "The Diamond Necklace" and other essays.

9. Sarah Dana Thorndike and her niece, Susan.

Theodore Parker. Courtesy of the Boston Athenaeum.

10. Dr. Channing's wife, Ruth Gibbs Channing, and their daughter Mary (1818–91), who married Frederic Augustus Eustis (1816–71) in 1843 (*CVR*; Suffolk Probate, no. 50323; Harvard archives; *NEHGR* 32:223).

11. Daniel Webster, New England's foremost lawyer, was at this time a U.S. senator from Massachusetts (*DAB*).

12. This appears to be Fuller's first meeting with Theodore Parker (1810–60), who had recently graduated (1836) from the Divinity School at Cambridge and who was to settle at West Roxbury in June. One of the few radical Unitarians to remain in the pulpit, Parker engaged in a vigorous life of controversy and scholarship. He became Fuller's good friend and faithfully wrote for the *Dial* (he contributed twenty-one essays and reviews), but he did not wholly sympathize with her point of view and was impatient with her disdain for reform movements (*DAB*).

13. Waldo Emerson (1836–42), whose death would strike so many of Emerson's friends so hard, was a special favorite of Margaret Fuller's (*Ipswich Emersons*, p. 267).

140. To Jane F. Tuckerman

Concord, May 2. 1837.

My dear Jeanie,

I am passing happy here, except that I am not well; so unwell that I fear I must go home, and ask my good Mother to let me vegetate beneath her sunny kindness for a while. The excitement of conversation prevents my sleeping.[1] The drive here with Mr Emerson was delightful. Dear Nature and Time, often so calumniated, will take excellent care of us if we will let them. The wisdom lies in schooling the heart not to expect too much; I did that good thing when I came here, and I am rich. On Sunday I drove to Watertown with the Author of "*Nature*." The trees were still bare but the little birds care not for that; they revel, and carol, and wildly tell their hopes, while the gentle, "voluble" South wind plays with the dry leaves, and the pine-trees sign with their soul-like sounds for June. It was beauteous; and care and routine fled,—and I was as if they had never been, except that I vaguely whispered to myself that all had been well with me.

The baby here is beautiful. He looks like his father, and smiles so sweetly on all hearty, good people. I play with him a good deal, and he comes so *natural*, after Dante and other poems.

Ever faithfully your friend,

MARGARET.

MsC (MH: fMS Am 1086 [Works, 1:83]). Published in *WNC*, p. 351; published in part in Higginson, *MFO*, p. 67.

1. Fuller left Concord the following day. In his journal Emerson remarked, "Among

many things that make her visit valuable & memorable, this is not the least that she gave me five or six lessons in German pronunciation never by my offer and rather against my will, each time, so that now spite of myself I shall always have to thank her for a great convenience" (*JMN*, 5:319).

141. To Caroline Sturgis

Groton May 14th
1837.

My dear Cary,

I am disappointed that I have not heard from you. I wrote to Ellen to find out how you were but, when she came yesterday, it was to say that she had not seen you not even in the street. So I want you to write or get somebody to write, tell me how you do, and how Jane does, whether you like Mary McSellar as well as you did me, whether I am likely to see you in the course of the summer &c I think of you every day, and hope you are enjoying this lovely weather. I am better though not so *stout* yet as I had hoped I should be. I walk and ride considerably, sleep as much as I can;—for the rest *do* as much as I can with books and paper but *can* is not much yet.

I have never thanked for Herbert.[1] You could not have given me any-thing I should have liked better. I will keep and love it always.

I was very happy at Concord. It was *satisfactory*; nothing is *satisfying* in this wale of tears. The baby was beautiful to me, a perfect May morning, after regular, grown up winter people. His lovely, joyous eyes, and eager[n] maniere d'être are with me still and I see him as[n] often as St Senanus did his lovesick nymph.[2] So I am like a saint in one thing, at least.

My love to Jane, tell her I wait in hope for her Chelsea gossip about sunrises and sunsets— E. Hoar is quite in earnest for you to come to Concord, Cary, are you decided against it? Remember me to your sisters, and to Mr and Mrs Ripley, whom I should like to see.[3]

Afftly yours

S. M. FULLER.

ALS (MH: bMS Am 1221 [201]). *Addressed:* Miss Caroline Sturgis, / Summer St. / Boston.

Caroline Sturgis (1819–88), daughter of William (1782–1863) and Elizabeth M. Davis Sturgis (1789–1864), was Fuller's closest woman friend. William Sturgis was a wealthy merchant, a member of the Sturgis clan that made fortunes in the China trade. In 1847 Caroline married William Aspinwall Tappan (1819–1905), son of Lewis Aspinwall Tappan. She had a desultory writing career; several of her poems were published in the *Dial*, and she wrote children's books. Higginson once said she "was very plain but with fine eyes" (*Sturgis of Yarmouth*, p. 43; *DAB*; MVR 1905 87:49; T. W. Higginson to Franklin B. Sanborn, 10 August 1875, MHarF).

and eager] and ⟨joy⟩ eager
I see him as] I see him ↑ as ↓

1. Sturgis had probably given Fuller George Herbert's *The Temple: Sacred Poems and Private Ejaculations*.

2. Thomas Moore, "St. Senanus and the Lady," in *Irish Melodies*, which appeared in parts from 1808 to 1834.

3. Fuller refers to Caroline's two older sisters, Ellen (1812–48) and Anne (1813–84). Ellen married Dr. Robert Hooper (1810–85) the following September. Though Ellen Sturgis was a close friend, Fuller strongly disliked Hooper, possibly because he had been involved in a duel over Marian Marshall, another of her good friends, in 1834. Both Hooper and his opponent, a Captain Jones, had to leave Boston for a time (*Sturgis of Yarmouth*, p. 43; Ward Thoron, *The Letters of Mrs. Henry Adams* [Boston, 1936], pp. xiii, 463–64; Helen Davis to James Clarke, 2 February 1834, MH: bMS Am 1569 [919]).

142. To A. Bronson Alcott

Groton 18th May
1837.

Dear Sir,

I have passed many hours during" the last week in the company of your Journals, and would willingly pass many more in the same way but for the imperative call of various duties. In sending them to you I escape from temptation.

I thank you for the look you have esteemed me worthy to take into your views and feelings and trust you will never have reason to repent your confidence, as I shall always rejoice in the intercourse which has been permitted me with so fair a soul.

You will find on the first blank leaf of your journal a little poem which expresses some part of what has been suggested to me by the recor[d] of your life.[1] You will, I ho[pe,] pardon the liberty I have taken in writing it there, as the leaf may easily be cut out if the thoughts the[re] inscribed do not please yo[u.]

I should like to have y[ou] read a little piece written by me about three years since for the W. Messenger on Bulwer's novels where you will see an "*overestimate*" of his aims if not his powers" not unlike your own.[2] Perhaps this mistake made by persons of such dissimilar minds points to something real in the object which could so suggest the ideal.

274

I heard that Mr Furness, too, sympathized with my effusion which, as to manner, you will find very crude.[3] There are sad mistakes of the press such as love of *Earth* for love of *Truth*! but you will easily discriminate them.

You do me the honor to ask my correspondence— Many persons are so good as to write to me and indulge me in all manner of neglec[t] and irregularity— Neithe can I boast that my letters when they do come, (and, wi so many correspondents, they are not frequent,) are either valuable or entertaining. But yours would be very valuable to me, and if you can be as indulgent as my other friends I can promise to be as attentiv to you as I am to any of them.

I hope you are enjoying the birds, leaves and Mr Emerson[4] With great respect and friendsh believe me yours

S. M. FULLER.

ALS (MH: 59m-312 [121]); MsC (MB: Ms. Am. 1450 [180]).

many hours during] many hours ⟨?⟩ during
of his aims if not his powers] ↑ of his aims if not his powers ↓

1. The original sheet no longer exists in his journal for 1837, but Alcott copied Fuller's translation of Schiller's "Licht und Wärme" on pages 384–85, including as well the second paragraph of this letter (Carlson, "Alcott's Journal," pp. 285–86).

2. She reviewed *The Last Days of Pompeii* in her essay "The Pilgrims of the Rhine," *Western Messenger* 1 (August 1835):101–8.

3. Furness had sent his son to Alcott's school in Philadelphia.

4. Alcott had visited Emerson from Monday to Friday, 15–19 May. Though in his journal Alcott praised Emerson after the visit, he also said, "As man, however, this visit has somewhat modified my former notions of him. He seems not to be fully in earnest. He writes and speaks for effect" (Carlson, "Alcott's Journal," p. 278).

143. To Elizabeth P. Peabody

Groton 26th May—1837.

I thought this advertisement might be of some interest to you— I took it from the National Intelligencer. The last time I saw it was more than a week ago— The place may be filled, but, possibly you may think it worth your while to inquire. The name of the Edr of the Fredericsburgh Arena, my brother says, is Blackford, but I dont know that you would care— A residence in that pleasant part of Virginia would I should think have its charms—unless your brother is as great a fanatic about N. England as his sisters.[1]

I dont know that I have any matronizing to do at P. Except to let

275

my candle shine with its usual lustre, a fair ensample, to the maidens of Providence at those hours when I am with them. Further than this I shd not venture to engage not esteemed myself the most suitable material for a governess pattern or wig block. My prospectus runs thus I believe. History, *languages*, literature.— Whatever I please or whatever I think best synonymizing with this. Thus looks the Ideal held out to me— How far the real corresponds I dare say I shall write you and, if I do not see you before, may answer your questions from Providence— I dont know yet whether I shall be in town next week, but inquire of B. Randall and she will tell whether I am to be had— Hastily yours

S. M. FULLER.

There were two other advertisements in the Intelligencer for teachers—four hundred dollars salary each, not do, of course, for your brothers but might for single young men to try their teaching wings a bit.[2]

ALS (PHi). *Addressed:* Miss E. P. Peabody, / care of Dr Peabody. / Salem, / Mass. *Postmark:* Groton May 27.

1. An advertisement first appeared in the *Daily National Intelligencer* on 28 February announcing an opening for a teacher "who is well qualified to teach the Latin and Greek languages; also, all the other branches of an English education." The notice, which reappeared on 18 May, was signed "William Stephenson [and] James G. Ficklen near Winchester, Va." William Matthews Blackford (1801–64) published the *Fredericksburg Political Arena* from 1828 to 1845 (*National Cyclopedia*, 9:186; John B. Minor, *The Minor Families of Virginia* [Lynchburg, Va., 1923], p. 20).

2. The first of these advertisements sought "a gentleman of suitable attainments for the situation, and of correct moral habits and deportment," to teach at the Upper Marlborough Academy; the second wanted a language teacher for John R. Pierpoint's seminary at Alexandria, D.C. Fuller's comment refers to Nathaniel Cranch Peabody (1811–81), the only married son in the Peabody family. He eventually became a homeopathic pharmacist. The twins, George Francis (1815–39) and Wellington (1815–37), never married (*Peabody Genealogy*, p. 85).

144. To Ralph Waldo Emerson

Groton 30th May 1837.

Dear Sir,

I cannot pass *a day* at Concord, but can come on Thursday afternoon in the mail-stage and stay till the next morng, if this would be agreeable to you and yours—[1]

Mr Fuller has shown the skill of a diplomatist in baffling me.[2] Not a very promising indication with regard to future transactions! However, I think, viva voce, he could scarce elude me as he has done by letter.

Some of your books I restore. The Literary remains I have ransacked pretty thoroughly— With the Friend I should never have done therefore must get it for mine own.— I have now of yours two vols of Milton, one of Jonson, one of Plutarch's Morals, two of Degerando, with the 7th and 8th of Goethe's nachgelassene Werke.—[3] These I should like to keep this summer, if you do not want them, but, if you do, please say so—

I shall not come to Concord unless I hear from you by tomorrow's or Thursday's mail, as I shall think, in that case, the fine-weather may have tempted you to Plymouth. I do hope I may see you once more, but, in case I do not, wish to ask, that, if Carlyle's Miscellanies are to be published by subscription,[n] as, I believe, the Sartor was, you will put down my name for two copies.[4]

With love and, if need be, farewell to Lidian, your Mother[5] and your son I must now finish for I have no time to enlarge on any of the topics which present themselves— I trust, if I should not see you, you will sometimes feel inclined to write to me—

M. F.—

What do you suppose Goethe and Scougal will say to one another as they are journeying side by side?[6]

ALS (MH: bMS Am 1280 [2337]); MsC (MB: Ms. Am. 1450 [65]). Published in part in Rusk, *Letters of RWE*, 2:78. *Addressed:* R. W. Emerson.— / what shocking familiarity! *Endorsed:* Miss S. M. Fuller / May 1837.

published by subscription] published by su⟨p⟩bscription

1. She did visit Concord, though exactly when is not clear. She was probably staying with Emerson on 1 and 2 June, for he answered this letter by encouraging her to "stop on Thursday and Friday too if you can" (Rusk, *Letters of RWE*, 2:77–78).

2. Hiram Fuller in Providence.

3. Fuller mentions here Coleridge's *Literary Remains* and his *Friend: A Series of Essays to Aid in the Formation of Fixed Principles in Politics, Morals, and Religion* (London, 1818). *The Friend* had originally appeared as a periodical. Exactly what volumes Fuller borrowed from Emerson is not known, but of Milton he owned the two-volume *Poetical Works* (Boston, 1834), the two-volume *Selection from the English Prose Works* (Boston, 1826), and *Paradise Regained, Samson Agonistes, Comus, Arcades, Lycidas, etc.* (Chiswick, 1823). Emerson's Jonson was *Works* (London, 1717) in six volumes; the Plutarch was *Morals* (London, 1718); and the "Degerando" was Joseph Marie de Gerando, *Histoire comparée des systèmes de philosophie* (Paris, 1822–23) in four volumes (Walter Harding, *Emerson's Library* [Charlottesville, Va., 1967]). Fuller was requesting vols. 7 and 8 of Goethe's *Vollständige Ausgabe letzer Hand, Gedichte*, and the fourth part of *Aus meinem Leben: Dichtung und Warheit*.

4. For the third time, Emerson was having Carlyle's work published in this country; like *Sartor Resartus*, *Critical and Miscellaneous Essays* was published in America before it

appeared in book form in England. Emerson wrote the prospectus, found the publisher, and guaranteed the production costs for the book, which brought Carlyle a profit of $1 a volume. James Munroe issued the first two volumes on 14 July 1838 and the final two volumes on 1 July 1839 (*Emerson–Carlyle Correspondence*, pp. 16–22).

5. Emerson's mother, Ruth Haskins Emerson (1768–1853), lived with his family in Concord (*Ipswich Emersons*, p. 176).

6. Henry Scougal, *Life of God in the Soul of Man* (Boston, 1823).

145. To [?]

[ca. Summer 1837]
[Providence?]

I am still quite unwell, and all my pursuits and propensities have a tendency to make my head worse. It is but a bad head,—as bad as if I were a great man! I am not entitled to so bad a head by anything I have done; but I flatter myself it is very interesting to suffer so much, and a fair excuse for not writing pretty letters, and saying to my friends the good things I think about them.

I was so desirous of doing all I could, that I took a great deal more upon myself than I was able to bear. Yet now that the twenty-five weeks of incessant toil are over, I rejoice in it all, and would not have done an iota less. I have fulfilled all my engagements faithfully; have acquired more power of attention, self-command, and fortitude; have acted in life as I thought I would in my lonely meditations; and I have gained some knowledge of means. Above all,—blessed be the Father of our spirits!—my aims are the same as they were in the happiest flight of youthful fancy. I have learned too, at last, to rejoice in all past pain, and to see that my spirit has been judiciously tempered for its work. In future I may sorrow, but can I ever despair?

The beginning of the winter was forlorn. I was always ill; and often thought I might not live, though the work was but just begun. The usual disappointments, too, were about me. Those from whom aid was expected failed, and others who aided did not understand my aims. Enthusiasm for the things loved best fled when I seemed to be buying and selling them. I could not get the proper point of view, and could not keep a healthful state of mind. Mysteriously a gulf seemed to have opened between me and most intimate friends, and for the first time for many years I was entirely, absolutely, alone. Finally, my own character and designs lost all romantic interest, and I felt vulgarized, profaned, forsaken,—though obliged to smile brightly and talk wisely all the while. But these clouds at length passed away.

And now let me try to tell you what has been done. To one class I taught the German language, and thought it good success, when, at the end of three months, they could read twenty pages of German at a lesson, and very well. This class, of course, was not interesting, except in the way of observation and analysis of language.

With more advanced pupils I read, in twenty-four weeks, Schiller's Don Carlos, Artists, and Song of the Bell, besides giving a sort of general lecture on Schiller; Goethe's Hermann and Dorothea, Goetz von Berlichingen, Iphigenia, first part of Faust,—three weeks of thorough study this, as valuable to me as to them,—and Clavigo,—thus comprehending samples of all his efforts in poetry, and bringing forward some of his prominent opinions; Lessing's Nathan, Minna, Emilia Galeotti; parts of Tieck's Phantasus, and nearly the whole first volume of Richter's Titan.[1]

With the Italian class, I read parts of Tasso, Petrarch,—whom they came to almost adore,—Ariosto, Alfieri, and the whole hundred cantos of the Divina Commedia, with the aid of the fine Athenaeum copy, Flaxman's designs, and all the best commentaries.[2] This last piece of work was and will be truly valuable to myself.

I had, besides, three private pupils, Mrs. ———, who became very attractive to me, ———, and little ———, who had not the use of his eyes. I taught him Latin orally, and read the History of England and Shakespeare's historical plays in connection. This lesson was given every day for ten weeks, and was very interesting, though very fatiguing. The labor in Mr. Alcott's school was also quite exhausting. I, however, loved the children, and had many valuable thoughts suggested, and Mr. A.'s society was much to me.

As you may imagine, the Life of Goethe is not yet written; but I have studied and thought about it much. It grows in my mind with everything that does grow there. My friends in Europe have sent me the needed books on the subject, and I am now beginning to work in good earnest.[3] It is very possible that the task may be taken from me by somebody in England, or that in doing it I may find myself incompetent; but I go on in hope, secure, at all events, that it will be the means of the highest culture.

ELfr, from *Memoirs*, 1:172–75.

1. Though heavily weighted toward drama, this list suggests the breadth of Fuller's reading in late-eighteenth-century German letters when she taught for Alcott. Schiller's *Don Carlos, Infant von Spanien*, was begun in 1783 and published in 1787; *Die Künstler* (the play, not the poem of the same name) was published in 1789; "Das Lied von der Glocke" was begun in 1791 and finished in 1799. Goethe's epic poem *Hermann und Dorothea*, written in 1796–97 and published in 1797, became very popular in the nine-

teenth century. *Götz von Berlichingen mit der eisernen Hand* appeared in 1773; *Iphigenie auf Tauris: Ein Schauspiel*, a verse play, was begun in 1779 and published in 1787. *Faust* was begun on Goethe's first Italian trip, but the "Erster Teil" was not published until 1808. The tragedy *Clavigo* was published in 1774 and first performed in 1779 (*OCGL*).

2. John Flaxman (1755–1826) was famous for his illustrations for Homer and Dante. Fuller refers to *La Divina comedia di Dante Alighieri, cioé l'Inferno, il Purgatorio, ed il Paradiso. Composto da Giovanni Flaxman, scultore inglese* (Rome, 1802) (Rupert Gunnis, ed., *Dictionary of British Sculptors, 1660–1851* [London, 1968]).

3. The Farrars and Sam Ward.

146. To [?]

[Summer 1837]

The proposal is, that I shall teach the elder girls my favorite branches, for four hours a day,—choosing my own hours, and arranging the course,—for a thousand dollars a year, if, upon trial, I am well enough pleased to stay. This would be independence, and would enable me to do many slight services for my family. But, on the other hand, I am not sure that I shall like the situation, and am sanguine that, by perseverance, the plan of classes in Boston might be carried into full effect. Moreover, Mr. Ripley,—who is about publishing a series of works on Foreign Literature,—has invited me to prepare the "Life of Goethe," on very advantageous terms.[1] This I should much prefer. Yet when the thousand petty difficulties which surround us are considered, it seems unwise to relinquish immediate independence.

ELfr, from *Memoirs*, 1:176–77.

1. Fuller never completed her planned biography. In its place she translated Eckermann's *Gespräche mit Goethe*, wrote a defense of Goethe against the strictures of the critic Wolfgang Menzel, and made her most thorough analysis of the poet's work in a long essay in the July 1841 issue of the *Dial*.

147. To John S. Dwight

Groton 31st May, 1837.

Dear Sir,

Miss Tuckerman writes me that you are desirous to know what I have done in the way of translation. I am truly ashamed when I think of my large promises and small performance.

"Wie wenig, ach! hat sich entfaltet,
Diess wenige, wie klein und karg."[1]

There have, indeed, been few hours since my return home that I have felt equal to exertion of any sort, but all which I have spent in attempts at translation have made me painfully sensible of my presumptuosness in undertaking what I did. I hope you will forgive me, for I had no idea of deceiving you, but thought some good daemon would stand my friend when I should attempt to do what I so much desired; but not a breath of inspiration has been vouchsafed. My book of translations is but a sorry sight; and I never rise from it without a strong desire to wash its witness from my hand and, indeed, to wash my incompetent hands of the whole affair— Goethe's unrhimed poems are entirely beyond me. When there is no metre to guide me I can bear no words but his own and could never get beyond the first verse of "Das Göttliche"—[2] I have translated great part of Das Ideal und das Leben, and about half of die Künstler,[3] but I am altogether dispirited by the result and cannot, at present, summon courage to go on. I send you some of the poor things I have done and, I fear, the best— I fancy few so harmonious and delicately finished can have been[n] submitted to you!!—

"Die Worte des Glaubens"—"worte des Wahns," "Spiel des Lebens" —and "Hoffnung" by Schiller "Eins und Alles" and "Sehnsucht" by Goethe I have translated but still worse than what I send.[4] The little piece "To a golden heart" is done, I think, better than any of these, though translated several years ago—[5] That from Schiller "To my friends" is very bad.[6] I merely send it, because copied on the same piece of paper and I have not time to recopy.

I shall be in Boston on Friday and stay till Saty but, as I may not see you, shall leave this parcel with Mrs Ripley. I know you must be disappointed but wish to prove to you that I have, at least, not been entirely unmindful of my promises.— I do not think you will wish me to go on but, if you do, *faute de mieux*, please write to me at Providence, tell me what has been done already by yourself and others and let me know my latest day of grace, if I am to try any more. I shall make no more promises as neither time or capacity *may* be granted me to do any-thing— With best wishes for your success

S. M. FULLER.

Providence June 8th

I did not see Mrs Ripley and forgot to leave this parcel for you— Since I have looked at Dauer im Wechsel again it seems to me too unworthy; and I am inclined if time should permit to try again.[7] But I cannot tell as yet whether time will permit— I have had no moment since I came here.— I send two of Mr Clarke's translations—[8] all which I could find.—

Please say to Miss Tuckerman that I hope to write both to her and Miss Sturgis in a few days—

ALS (MB: Ms.E.4.1 [15]). *Addressed:* Revd J. S. Dwight.

John Sullivan Dwight (1813–93), the eldest child of Dr. John (1773–1852) and Mary Corey Dwight, graduated from Harvard in 1832 and pursued his interest in German literature by editing *Select Minor Poems*. He graduated from the Divinity School in 1836 and was ordained at Northampton, where he served for one year before he left the ministry. One of the Brook Farm residents, Dwight later became a noted music critic in Boston. In 1851 he married Mary Bullard (1823–60), daughter of Silas and Mary Ann Barrett Bullard of Boston (*Descendants of John Dwight*, p. 1012; *DAB*; MVR 140:98).

can have been] can have ↑ been ↓

1. From Schiller's "Die Ideale": "Ah, how little has unfolded itself, / that little, how small and mean." Dwight included in his book two Fuller translations from Goethe, "To a Golden Heart" and "Eagles and Doves."

2. "Das Göttliche" was probably written in 1783. Published in 1785 in F. H. Jacobi's *Über die Lehre des Spinoza*, Goethe's poem appeared twice in *Select Minor Poems*, translated by both Dwight and George Bancroft. Fuller published her own translation of part of the poem in her essay "Menzel's View of Goethe," *Dial* 1 (January 1841):340–47 (Gray, *Poems of Goethe*, p. 95).

3. Schiller's "Das Ideal und das Leben" was written in 1795 under the title "Das Reich der Schatten." His "Die Künstler," a philosophical poem, was written in 1788–89 and published in 1789 (Wilpert, *Schiller-Chronik*, p. 185; *OCGL*). Dwight fully sympathized with Fuller's problems, for in his notes to *Select Minor Poems* he said of "Die Künstler," "The transcendental aesthetics and the lyric inspiration do not as yet quite blend, but rather lame each other. Hence the piece is fruitful in difficulties and obscurities to the translator; while the sublimity of the conception, the depth of philosophy, the richness of imagery, and the noble, fervent aspiration which flames up in this piece to the very empyrean of the Beautiful, would not let him pass it over without an attempt to reproduce something of its warmth and sweetness" (p. 429). Dwight published his own translations of both "Die Künstler" and "Das Ideal und das Leben" in *Select Minor Poems*.

4. "Das Spiel des Lebens" was written in 1796, "Die Worte des Glaubens" and "Hoffnung" in 1797, and "Die Worte des Wahns" in 1799 (Wilpert, *Schiller-Chronik*, pp. 202, 246). Goethe's "Eins und Alles" was written in 1821 (Gray, *Poems of Goethe*, p. 186). Fuller's translation was published in Frederick Augustus Braun, *Margaret Fuller and Goethe* (New York, 1910), pp. 231–32.

5. Goethe's "An ein goldnes Herz, das er am Halse trug" was written in the winter of 1775–76 and published in 1789 (Goethe, *Gedenkausgabe*, 1:759).

6. Schiller wrote "An die Freunde" in 1802 following a visit to Goethe and his friends (Wilpert, *Schiller-Chronik*, p. 273).

7. Goethe's "Dauer im Wechsel" dates from 1803 (Goethe, *Gedenkausgabe*, 1:761). Fuller's translation, which she called an imitation, was also published by Braun (pp. 232–33).

8. Dwight published five Clarke translations in *Select Minor Poems*.

148.   To Ralph Waldo Emerson

6 June 1837
[Providence]

Dear Sir,

Every day I have mentally addressed Concord, dear Concord, haven of repose where headach—vertigo—other *sins* that flesh is heir to cannot long pursue. I willingly seize this excuse for writing to you, although it is too true that I have nothing to say which can be said in such a way— How I rejoice that you are to come on Saturday![1] I look forward to your presence as the weary traveller does to the Diamond of the Desert— Flowers will, I trust, spring up, but at present all is too new for my weak head. I think Mr Fuller has now been very precise in his indications, allow me to add one more on my own account— and remember to bring *me* a good, genial preachment full of cheer.— I saw Mr Alcott in Boston, he looked beautiful[n] and seems well prepared to be the Anaxagoras of the joiners shop.[2] I missed Henry Hedge entirely; though they said he kept coming for me all day and seven other *friends*! were in pursuit. I was very wicked to stay—yet am unrepenting.— Farewell, dear love to Lidian, and your Mother; say to Miss Bartlett that there are no muskitoes in Providence, and to little Waldo that I have thought since I came away of a hundred witty things I forgot to say to him: so he must want to see me again.[3] Please bring my chain which I left at your house and do come to see me, if possible, as soon as you arrive—

M. F.

This is not the *smart letter* which is to be lent to Miss Whiting &c—[4]

ALS (MH: bMS Am 1280 [2338]); MsC (MB: Ms. Am. 1450 [19, 66]). *Addressed:* Mr. R. Waldo Emerson / Concord / Mss— *Postmark:* Providence RI Jun 6. *Endorsed:* Mr Fuller / Miss Fuller / June 1837.

Fuller added her letter to that of Hiram Fuller to Emerson.

he looked beautiful] he looked ⟨ver⟩ beautiful

1. Emerson gave the dedicatory address at the opening of the Greene-Street School in Providence on 10 June 1837 (*Emerson Lectures*, 2:191–204).

2. Alcott had declined an invitation to attend the Providence ceremony, probably to spare Hiram Fuller any embarrassment, for the controversy over Alcott's *Conversations* was increasing almost daily (Shepard, *Pedlar's Progress*, p. 204). Fuller's phrase "Anaxagoras of the joiner's shop" compares Alcott, who had moved his school from the spacious room 5 to the much smaller basement room 3 in the Masonic Temple, with the Greek philosopher Anaxagoras (ca. 500–ca. 428 B.C.), a pre-Socratic idealist who was prosecuted for impiety.

3. Miss Bartlett is unidentified, though perhaps she is the friend of Lidian's by that name mentioned in several of Emerson's letters (Rusk, *Letters of RWE*, 2:10).

4. Probably Anna Maria Whiting (1814–67), daughter of William and Hannah Conant Whiting of Concord (Whiting, *Memoir*, p. 255).

149. To Jane F. Tuckerman

Providence, June 16. 1837.

My dear Jeanie,

I pray you amid all your duties, to keep some hours for yourself. Do not let my example lead you into excessive exertions. I pay dear for extravagance of this sort. Five years ago, I had no idea of the languor and want of animal spirits which torment me now. Animal Spirits are not to be despised. An earnest mind and seeking heart will not often often be troubled by despondency; but unless the blood can dance at proper times, the lighter passages of life lose all their refreshment and suggestion.

I wish you and Cary could have been here last Saturday. Our school-house was dedicated and Mr Emerson made the address; it was a noble appeal in behalf of the best interests of culture, and seemingly here was fit occasion. The building was beautiful, and furnished with an even elegant propriety. I am at perfect liberty to do what I please, and there are apparently the best dispositions if not the best preparation, on the part of the hundred and fifty young minds with whom I am to be brought in contact.

I sigh for the country; trees, birds and flowers assure me that June is here, but I must walk through streets many and long, to get sight of any expanse of green. I had no fine weather while at home, though the quiet and rest were delightful to me; the sun did not shine once really warm, nor did the apple-trees put on their blossoms till the very day I came away.

MsCfr (MH: fMS Am 1086 [Works, 1:85–87]). Published in *WNC*, pp. 357–58.

150. To Caroline Sturgis

18 June 1837
[Providence]

[   ] hold forth, as the large room is too much for my vision— Below on the ground floor are rooms for the "tender juvenals."ⁿ I am only there in the morng—and flatter myself, if I can only get settled with having lovelyⁿ quiet aftns here at home. I have not been able to get really pleasant rooms for myself but those with whom I live are very neat, seem kind and disposed to leave me free.— I think I shall do very well—

I had a grand reading time at home—my Groton homeⁿ I only wished it had been ten times as long. I was in a state of extreme exhaustion and langour, quite unfit to write or talk but reading suited me exactly— I was in a more receptive state than I have been for years.— I think the air of *this* place will suit me— I have been unusually well and strong this past week.

I do not want to tell you any more now both because my attention is much dissipated and because my impressions are ill-arranged as yet— I write principally to assure you of my love and mindfulness and to make you write to me. Since I have given you nothing good of my own I will bestow on you two verses written by a better person than myself— See if you think them pretty. The title is Compensation. Do not show it unless to Janeⁿ

> Why should I keep holiday
>   When other men have none?
> Why but because when these are gay
>   I sit and mourn alone.
>
> And why, when Mirth unseals all to tongue
>   Must mine alone be dumb?
> Ah late I spoke to the silent throngs
>   And now their turn has come.[1]

Will you present my respects to your father and ask him if I may have some books which are to be sent me from Europe directed to his care. I suppose he is constantly sending hisⁿ clerks to the custom house and would, perhaps, have the kindness to let me trouble him thus far.

Is not Jane doing nicely?— Does she "look and act as she did?"— Write me all about her Thomas a Kempis and George Herbert are constantly at my elbow and remind me[2] [   ]

ALfr (MH: bMS Am 1221 [202]). *Addressed:* Miss Caroline Sturgis, / care of William Sturgis Esq. / Boston, / Mass. *Postmark:* Providence R.I. Jun 18.

Below on the ground floor are rooms for the "tender juvenals."] ↑ Below on the ground floor are rooms for the "tender juvenals." ↓

with having lovely] with ↑ having ↓ lovely
my Groton home] ↑ my Groton home ↓
Do not show it unless to Jane] ↑ Do not show it unless to Jane ↓
constantly sending his] constantly send ↑ ing ↓ his

1. An early version of Emerson's "Compensation." The poem was first written in his journal "A" for 1834 (now *JMN*, 4:347) and was published in *Poems* (Boston, 1847). Fuller's transcription matches both the early and the published Emerson versions from lines 1 to 4, but her copy differs somewhat from his in lines 5 to 8.

2. Thomas a Kempis (Thomas Hamerken von Kempen [1380–1471]) wrote *De Imitatione Christi.*

151. To A. Bronson Alcott

Providence 27th June, 1837.

Dear Sir,

I had flattered myself that you would have been in haste to begin our correspondence since you disappointed me of the expected oppory of conversing with you at the time of the dedication of the school— But since you will neither come nor write my desire to hear from you is so strong that I must do something on my side—

I am sorry you were not here to listen to Mr Emerson's "good words" which fell, if I may judge from the remarks they called forth, on stony soil—[1] Yet there is always comfort in the thought that, if such seed must not fertilize the spot for which it was intended, the fowl of the air may carry it away to some more propitious clime. And I myself—who was much cheered and instructed on the occasion, may be that bird if there should be none other, which I may not think. For here also the Sun speaks, and the Moon smiles, and here also human souls must be alive to their vocation and some must know how truth and knowledge are to be wooed and won—

I am much pleased with my new haunt as far as the eye is concerned— I believe you have never seen the building—it is in excellent taste[n] and all the arrangements speak of comfort quiet and even elegance. Nothing is wanting to make it look the home of thought except more books, a few casts and a picture or two which will be added in due time.— As to the occupants of this fair abode I have not yet seen them through and through but feel now able to form a tolerably fair estimate of the state of the children and from their state can infer that of the families to which they belong. It is low compared with Boston and even with villages in its vicinity, for here is the hostile element of money getting with but little counterpoise— Yet there is an affectionate, if not an intelligent sympathy in this community with Mr Fuller and his undertaking which will not, I trust, be felt in vain. Mr Fuller is in many respects particularly suited to this business. His ready sympathy, his active eye, and pious, tender turn[n] of thought are so adapted to all the practical part; The danger arising from that sort of education which has unfolded there is that he may not be sufficiently systematic[n] and not observe due gradation and completeness in his plans. However all is tentative that is doing yet and those Powers who have so [favored] him[n] will now, it is to be hoped, turn a [fairer] side[n] to the light— I often think, dear Sir, with pleasure on the roundness (as Mr Emerson perhaps would express it) of your world— There were details in which I thought your plan imperfect, but it only needs to compare pupils who have been treated as many of these have with those who have been under your care to sympathize with your creed that those who would reform the world should begin with the[n] beginning of life—[2] Particularly do I feel the importance of your attempts to teach the uses of language and cultivate the imagination in dealing with young persons who have had no faculties exercised except the memory and the common,[n] practical understanding. In *your* children I found an impatience of labor but a liveliness of mind, in many of *these* with well-disposed hearts, [the] mind has been absolutely torpid. Those who have been under Mr F's care are in far better state than the rest.—

I hope you will write soon and let me know as much of your thoughts and affairs as you can. Please give my regards to Mrs Alcott and believe me always sincerely your friend.[3]

S. M. FULLER.

ALS (MH: 59m-312 [122]); MsC (MB: Ms. Am. 1450 [1b, 181]). Published in part in *The Critic* 43 (October 1903):340–41. *Addressed:* A. Bronson Alcott, / Boston, / Mass— *Postmark:* Providence R.I. Jun 29.

excellent taste] excellent taste⟨s⟩
tender turn] tender ⟨?⟩ turn
sufficiently systematic] sufficiently syst⟨m⟩ematic
so [favored] him] *added from copy 1b.*
[fairer] side] *added from copy 1b.*
should begin with the] should ↑ begin with the ↓
and the common,] and the ⟨gra⟩ common,

1. Matt. 13:5.
2. In her journal Fuller recorded Alcott's attitude: "I understand what is meant by a Redeemer. I preferred this to all savants and unifiers. I thought I too would be a Redeemer. . . . And, seeing that all other Redeemers had so imperfectly performed their tasks, I sought a new way. . . . They began with men, I will begin with babes" (Fuller journal fragment, MH: Os 735 M.800[1]).

3. On 23 May 1830 Alcott had married Abigail May (1800–1877), daughter of Colonel Joseph and Dorothy Sewall May (William Dawson Bridge, *Genealogy of the John Bridge Family in America, 1632–1924* [Cambridge, Mass., 1924], p. 107; *DAB*).

152. To [Ralph Waldo Emerson?]

Providence R I July 3d 1837

I was fully persuaded in my own mind that I shld never recover, and was only kept up by the conviction that till it was time for me to die, I ought to act as if I hoped to live.

I cannot yet say whether I shall stay here, at first I was much disappointed on examining my field of action. It seemed to me that I could not work at all on subjects so unprepared as I found here. However I tried and think I already perceive that it is not in vain. There is room here, if I mistake not, for a great move in the cause of education, but whether it is I who am to help move, I cannot yet tell. I some times think *yes*, because the plan is becoming so complete in my mind, ways and means are continually occurring to me, and so far as I have tried them, they seem to succeed. I am left almost as much at liberty as if no other person were concerned with me. The arrangements I have made in the school are satisfactory to me for the present. I am sure I shall do good in the way of clearing the ground either for myself or somebody else. About sixty pupils, I should think, are under my care more or less, and they many of them begin already to attempt to walk in the ways I point but which are unknown indeed to most of them. Activity of mind, accuracy in processes, constant looking for principles, and search after the good and beautiful, "that's the ground I go upon" as Mr S says in Vivian Gray, and many of those who have never studied any thing but words seem much pleased with their new prospects—[1] However I am aware that if there is difficulty, there is charm too to them in all this novelty, and am prepared to see new obstacles constantly rising up. Besides, my own progress in any of those acquirements, whh I have most loved will be no wise aided by staying here. I must work years to get ready a hill side for my vineyard [   ] As to Goethe I scarce know how to answer you. I should think after hearing me say so much about him, you wld be aware that I do not consider him from that point of view you wish me to take.[2] I do not go to him as a guide or friend but as a great thinker, who makes me think, a wonderful artist who gratifies my tastes— As far as he had religion or morality, I shld say they were expressed in this poem of his "Eins und Alles," of whh I send you a rude translation

MsCfr (MB: Ms. Am. 1450 [160]). Published in part in *The Critic* 43 (October 1903):343.

1. *Vivian Grey* (London, 1826), published anonymously, was the first novel by Benjamin Disraeli (1804–81).

2. No surviving letters or journal entries shed light on Emerson's "point of view" toward Goethe at this time. In his letter to Fuller of 18 July (which probably answers this Fuller letter), Emerson said, "If the soul of Goethe shines also with unabated light & attraction before you, who is happy but you?" (Rusk, *Letters of RWE*, 2:88).

153.   To Arthur B. Fuller

Providence 5th July, 1837—

My dear Arthur—

I was glad to get a few lines from you, but I wish you to study the art of saying more in your epistles and saying it well. Nothing [but] practice is necessary for this I know, as you have plenty of thoughts in your mind. Many boys in our school of ten or eleven, inferior to you in natural capacity,[n] write better. They have acquired some power of expression and a neat hand by the practice of keeping a journal for Mr Fuller and some of their intimate friends to read. *All* the scholars in the upper department of our school are now to do this. Each has been provided with a book, neatly bound in morrocco, and lettered on the back "School journal." I, too, have one of these books, but do not write in it[n] as much as my pupils do in theirs— They are very anxious to know if they shall ever be permitted to read mine— I tell them; perhaps so, if I am able to speak well of them in it.— Last week some of theirs were read aloud to the school, though without mentioning the names of the writers. The journal of one boy who spoke of the girls as "sweet sisters" and "fair *as Eden's garden birds*" excited a general *smile*. We are too refined to laugh loud at the Greene St School!!

I will now tell you how I pass my time and give some idea of our school. I am, (bid Mother[n] marvel,) almost always up at 5 and sometimes at half past 4 in the morning. I am completely dressed by 6 and then devote myself to my own studies till half past 7 when we breakfast. My school lessons require no preparation and I have got them nicely arranged now. They are in composition, elocution, histy, three classes in Latin, one of boys, several of whom I am much interested in and will describe them when I write to Richard, two classes in Natural philosophy, and one in Ethics. These are so distributed as not to fatigue me at all. At half past 8 I go to the school. You enter through a wide, gate, a piazza, and a pretty, wide door into a small entry on each side of which is a dressing room, one for the girls and one for the boys. Each dressing room is furnished with looking glasses,[n] pegs for each scholar's hat, or bonnet, and places for overshoes if they wear them. There are two doors into the great hall one for the girls, one for the boys, so they need never and do never romp or interfere. This hall is thickly carpeted, the walls are white, finished with pink, the ceiling arched with a place in the centre for a chandelier, if it should be needed. We talk of having eveg conversations or dances, or musical parties for scholars next winter—but nothing is decided about that. Between the doors stands the piano with a neat French cloak upon it. The principal color of the carpet is orange which harmonizes very well with the black and brown desks and chairs. There are on[n] each side of this hall two rows of boys and girls, *all* neatly dressed, indeed, some people object to us that rather too much ambition about appearance is encouraged, but if they lived there they would like the comfort of dealing with neat well dressed people as well as we do. At the upper end on a platform raised two steps from the floor stand Mr F's chair and study table with shelves and drawers for books and papers. On it stand two vases for flowers wh are filled by the children; (tell Mother we had two blossoms from a tulip tree to day and they are beautiful,) and four glass goblets from wh the children drink water wh is kept for[n] them in a handsome urn before the platform. On the right hand is a sofa for visitors and where I too sit when I am not in one of the recitation rooms. Mrs Nias and Miss Aborn are generally in the morng[n] down stairs where is the schoolroom for the little children, with the[n] washroom &c—[1] I see I shall not have time to describe them particularly as I could wish

All these young people look healthy and *excessively* happy. They seem enchanted with the school. Almost all are docile, many eager in improvement. I have already become attached to individuals. I find all very easy to manage and feel as if they were beginning to understand what I want of them. As I said before I will describe some of my favorites a week or two hence when I write to Richard. I shall write to Mother next. Perhaps, too, I shall tell him about the procession and the fireworks wh I saw yesterday from the roof of the mansion House.

I did not receive the books till day before yesterday and then not without a deal of trouble and vexation. But I deserved it for my carelessness in omitting my direction I suppose I thought I had given it and, being in haste, did not read the letter over. Ellen's roses were mouldy, but I thank her as much as if they were fresh. I generally have bouquets from the school girls every fair day— I see I did not tell what I did with the rest of my day after school. I get home when I do not go to walk, a little before one, dine at half-past, lie down till three, then write or study till tea time. After tea walk or make visits till ten,—to bed about eleven. So I live very rationally—

Dear Mother must not make herself sick, unless she wants to make me miserable.— Love to All the family and Rebecca. If Miss Tilden is with you give my regards to her and say I am glad she is with you for Mother and Ellen's sake.[2] Eugene must write me about his journey to Boston" &c— Has John Randall gone? very afftly your Sister

M..

ALS (MH: fMS Am 1086 [9:44]); MsC (MH: fMS Am 1086 [Works, 1:613–21]). Published in part, though misdated, in *The Critic* 43 (October 1903):342–43. *Addressed:* Arthur Buckminster Fuller. / Groton, / Mass. *Postmark:* Providence RI Jul 6.

in natural capacity,] in natural ⟨pra⟩ ↑ capacity ↓ ,
write in it] write in ⟨?⟩ it
(bid Mother] (bi⟨?⟩d Mother
with looking glasses] with ↑ looking ↓ glasses
There are on] There are ⟨?⟩ on
is kept for them] is kept ⟨from⟩ ↑ for ↓ them
are generally in the morng] are ↑ generally in the morng ↓
children, with the] children, ↑ with the ↓
journey to Boston] journey ↑ to Boston ↓

1. Georgianna Nias, the dancing teacher, was an Englishwoman who separated from her husband and emigrated to America. She later opened a school for girls in Providence before returning to England ("Greene-St. School," p. 216). Frances Aborn (1816–90), another teacher, was the daughter of Edward (1776–1815) and Susan Potter Aborn (1780–1869) of Providence. At one time during her stay, Fuller lived with the Aborns (*Potter Families*, pt. 2, p. 18; James N. Arnold, ed., *Vital Records of Rhode Island, 1636–1850* [Providence, 1891], vol. 8).

2. The Fuller family correspondence identifies Mary Parker Tilden (1793–1879), daughter of Joseph and Sarah Tilden, as a longtime friend of Mrs. Fuller (*Boston Births*; MVR 312:39).

154. To Elizabeth[?] P. Peabody

8 July 1837
[Providence]

Mr. Fuller is as unlike as possible to Mr. Alcott. He has neither his poetic beauty nor his practical defects. [   ]

As to the school, [   ] I believe I do very well there. I am in it four hours every morning, five days in the week; thus you see I can have much time, notwithstanding many casual interruptions. All Saturday and Sunday to myself. I rise so early that I often get an hour and a half before breakfast, besides two or three hours in the afternoon on school days. This is quite enough for health, and the time is good time, for the school rarely tires me at all. I feel so perfectly equal to all I do there, without any effort; my pupils, although miserably prepared, are very docile, their hearts are right, and I already perceive that I am producing some effect on their heads. My plan grows quietly and easily in my mind; this experience here will be useful to me, if not to Providence, for I am bringing my opinions to the test, and thus far have reason to be satisfied.

ELfr, from Higginson, *MFO*, pp. 80–81.

Two excerpts are joined on the assumption that Fuller completely described the school in one letter to Peabody, who was not a frequent correspondent.

155. To Frederic H. Hedge

Providence July 12th
1837.

Dear Henry—

Mr Angier came to our temple this morng just as I had completed my *sacrifices* for the day and offers to take a note for me to you. So I think I will scribble a line for I suspect my letter to Miss P. was very unsatisfactory in that part which was intended for you and Lucy as there was a person in my room at the time, talking to me, or looking *at* me wh is as bad.— However I cannot remember what I *did* say, so please to imagine I said every thing pretty— I assure you I intended so to do.

I cannot but laugh when I think of your former way of talking about "Dr Channing's women" to hear of Miss P. as domesticated with you—[1] And I too whose youth you misled by your jibes and jeers am now quite under Miss P's wing and in this region of (*entre nous*) as complete Philistency as can exist at Bangor am received as a *"female whom that truly eminent divine"* delighteth to honor. That ever such should be my pass-port!!

But what I most want to say is this— Will you, Henry, can you tell me all the scandal about Goethe—about his marriage and so forth?[2] I have asked Mr Emerson and others whom I thought might know, but the little they can tell only puzzles and disturbs me. In all the books I have had sent me there is nothing which enables me to know what I am about on this subject and I ought, before I go any further, in my business— Will you write me in a few days any thing you know of his first residence at Weimar and about his living so many years with the person he afterwards married— How could that be at so decorous a court and under the eye of the Grand Duchess—[n3] I hope you will be able to give me light, but, if not, I intend writing to Madame Jameson—[4] Say nothing to Miss P. if she is with you or, indeed, to any one— Write when you can to a poor, lonely *"female"*— Afftly

M. F.

ALS (MH: fMS Am 1086 [10:102]). *Addressed:* Revd F. H. Hedge, / Bangor, / Maine, / Politeness Mr Angier.

the Grand Duchess] the ⟨?⟩ Grand Duchess

1. In his reply of 2 August 1837 (MH-AH), Hedge reported that Elizabeth Peabody had visited him in Bangor as she looked for a teaching job for her brother. Defensive about Fuller's jibe, Hedge said, "I cannot sympathise in her enthusiasm or her personalities, but these things are so balanced by other qualities that they trouble me much less than I had supposed they would."

2. Hedge replied that he had no knowledge of Goethe's "liaisons," but urged her to try Carlyle or Francis Lieber, who was then in Philadelphia.

3. Though she objected to the affair, Anna Amalia, Herzogin von Sachsen-Weimar, was unable to alter its course (*OCGL*).

4. Fuller waited until December to write Anna Jameson (see letter 168).

156.   To Caroline Sturgis

Providence July 15th
1837.

My very dear Cary,

I have deferred answering your letter because I have constantly been expecting to go to Boston and I thought I could say the needful so much better than write it— I think now I shall come to Boston on Friday next in the afternoon and stay till the afternoon of the next day, or possibly, though not probably, till Monday morng— If I return on Saty I may have no time to see you except Friday eveg, so I would like you to leave a note at my uncle's saying whether you will come there, or go to walk with me, or whether I shall have an oppory to talk with you if I come to your house.

I would like very much to see Jane, too, but I fear there is no chance of her being in town. I wish you would, if possible, let Mrs Ripley know that I shall try to come to her house that I may have a chance of finding her at home. If you are out of town and cannot see me then, or any thing should happen to prevent my going I want you to come here the first fine Saturday. You can come alone without any impropriety. Come here in the early cars and you will arrive at nine. I will be at the depot to receive you if you write before and let me know that you will come,[n] and will see you safe home in the same way that afternoon or the following Monday—

I want very much to talk to you about many things beginning with your poor head. Mine is doing finely. I am very well at present. Farewell— In the hope of meeting yours faithfully and affectionately

S. M. FULLER.

ALS (MH: bMS Am 1221 [203]). *Addressed:* Miss Caroline Sturgis, / care of William Sturgis Esq. / Boston—Mass. *Postmark:* Providence R.I. Jul 17.

if you write before and let me know that you will come] ↑ if you write before and let me know that you will come ↓

157.   To Ralph Waldo Emerson

Providence 14th August
1837.

Dear Sir,

I suppose that, if you have esteemed[n] the subject worthy of any thought, you expected to hear from me before this. I might assign small reasons in abundance for not writing, but I will not, for, though I have made use of them to myself, I believe the true cause of my not writing has been that I have not wished to write. For I have been in an irreligious state of mind, a little misanthropic and sceptical about the existence of any real communication between human beings. I bear constantly in heart that text of yours "*O my friends*, there are no friends" but to me it is a paralyzing conviction.[1] Surely, we are very unlike the Gods in "their seats of eternal tranquility" that we need illusions so much to keep us in action.

However, I must say I feel a desire, now that my vacation really is coming, to see my dear *no friends*, Mr and Mrs Emerson, and since you say you wish me to come I would arrange the time with you.— Vacation begins on Saty next, the 19th and continues three weeks.—[n] At present my plan is to go to Kingston, near Plymouth, on that day and stay till the following Wednesday or Thursday. I shall then go to Boston and stay a day. I suppose you will not want me at Concord till you are rid of your oration.[2] I shall therefore go home by the way of Lowell where I shall stay a few hours, probably, as the people express a desire to see me. I then propose to go home but the next week to come to Cambridge and hear your speech. Caroline Sturgis will meet me there and wishes me to return to Newbury[n] with her, there to be silent and enjoy daily woodwalks or boat excursions with her. But as I cannot come to Concord and do this, I shall, if it be your wish, return from Cambridge to Concord for two or three days. Perhaps you will take me back with you, but do not trouble yourself in any way to do this; my brother will be with me at Cambridge and in point of convenience I could quite as well go with him. I only should like to be with you that I might see you more. But perhaps you would rather go to Cambridge in your stage coach, or perhaps you will not want to talk to a poor private person after addressing the public; do not violate your slightest feeling because I have made this suggestion, but arrange it all to suit yourself. Or, if a visit from me would not be hailed with *positive pleasure* at that time, please say so, and I shall go to Newbury with Cary.—

Will you write to me about this as soon as possible?[3] I shall not receive a letter here after Friday, so if you cannot write to reach me by that time direct to me at Plymouth.

—I fear I have not much to tell that will amuse you. With books and pens I have, maugre my best efforts been able to do miserably little If I cannot be differently situated I *must* leave Providence at the end of another term. My time here has been full of petty annoyances, but I regret none of them; they have so enlarged my practical knowledge. I now begin really to feel myself a citizen of the world— My plan lies clearer before my mind, and I have examined almost all my materials, but beyond this I have done nothing. I shall, however, have so soon an oppory to tell you all, that I will not now take time and paper.—

I attended last week, somewhat to the horror of Mr Fuller, the Whig Caucus here and heard Tristram Burgis.[4] It is rather the best thing I have done.

Farewell, good love to Mrs Emerson. I hope the baby has not grown too large for me to hold for my heart is much *set* upon that pleasure. I am very strong now: have lately been again troubled by my head, but I shall be perfectly well after my excursion to Plymouth, that good place which cured you!—

S. M. FULLER.

ALS (MH: bMS Am 1280 [2339]); MsCfr (MB: Ms. Am. 1450 [161]). Published in part in Higginson, *MFO*, p. 87, and Rusk, *Letters of RWE*, 2:94–95. *Addressed:* Revd R. W. Emerson. / Concord, / Mass. *Postmark:* Providence RI Aug 15. *Endorsed:* Margaret Fuller / Aug. 1837.

if you have esteemed] if you have e⟨t⟩steemed

the 19th and continues three weeks.—] the 19th ↑ and continues three weeks.— ↓

return to Newbury] return ⟨on the⟩ to Newbury

1. In his quotation book "Encyclopedia," Emerson wrote, "'O my friends, there is no friend,' said Aristotle" (*JMN*, 6:161). Emerson probably found the quotation in Montaigne's "On Friendship." Montaigne had the aphorism from Diogenes Laertius: "He who has friends can have no true friend" (Diogenes Laertius, *Lives and Opinions of Eminent Philosophers*, trans. R. D. Hicks [Cambridge, Mass., 1959], 1:465). Diogenes Laertius apparently had two sources in Aristotle: *Ethica Eudemia* and *Ethica Nicomachea*.

2. Emerson gave the annual Phi Beta Kappa address at Harvard on 31 August.

3. Apologizing for his slowness, Emerson replied on the 17th, directing the letter to Fuller in care of George Bradford at Plymouth, and invited her to return with him from Cambridge to Concord after the address and to "give us what time you can afford. Our plan is now to have a meeting of Mr Hedges Club." The club did meet on 1 September, and Fuller attended (Rusk, *Letters of RWE*, 2:95).

4. Hiram Fuller, a Democrat, surely scorned Tristam Burges (1770–1853), the accomplished orator who addressed the Whig caucus on 9 August on behalf of their nominees for Congress. Burges had been professor of oratory at Brown, a state and national representative, and a chief justice of the Rhode Island Supreme Court (*Biographical Directory*).

158. To Caroline Sturgis

Providence 16th August
1837.

My dearest Cary,

I should like very much to have a quiet week with you at Newbury and thank your cousin for her invitation,[n] but I fear I cannot manage it; my time seems to be so appropriated.[1] If any thing should occur to render it possible I will let you know when we meet at Cambridge and go with you then.

I expect to go to Plymouth next Saty and from there to Boston Wednesday[n] or Thursday. From Boston I shall go home and return to Cambridge with my brother for Phi Beta— I wish you and Jane and I could go to Phi-Beta together; could not it be arranged?— After Phi Beta I, at present, expect to go to Concord, but this is not quite certain.— I am glad you think you love Jane as well as you did— I fear you do not, but cultivate in yourself a tender state of feeling towards her. If a real disunion has commenced, if your characters have had upon one another all the action they were by Nature intended to have, all the trouble you could take would be useless, for, as S. T. C. says, "The love is o'er / Which must *resolve to do* what *did itself* of yore."[2] But if interest only flagged a little because you were in a morbid state &c you can do a great deal towards keeping affection alive. Jane has faults but she is a noble girl, with a lively mind, a deep heart, perfect ingenuousness, and a considerably extended knowledge of your character. You will scarce be able to fill her place.— I had a letter from her lately. She told me Robert Waterston had gone to see you— did he at all edify your spirit?—[3]

You must not die, my Cary,—you must keep on bearing nobly; by and by you shall go to Europe; meanwhile you must come here and live with me in November.—

I know little about *new* books. I have read only two English books this summer, Miss Martineau "America," and the "Letters from Palmyra."[4] This last book disappointed me a little yet pleased me much. I think it is less of a failure in[n] the difficult task of fixing up the beautiful antique for modern use than such books as Moore's "Epicurean," or, if my memory play me true, than Lockhart's "Valerias," and rises immeasurably above Philothea, a Romance, by Mrs Child.[5] It has no creative genius, nothing of that spontaneousness which R. H. Dana talks so much about, but shows uncommon cultivation, much ardour of spirit and love of the Beautiful.

Such books as Carlyle's life of Schiller, or Mrs Jameson's Visits and Sketches you know of course. The Memoirs of Alfieri or Benvenuto Cellini, or among fictions Lockhart's "Reginald Dalton" Hope's "Anastasius" or Beckford's "Caliph Vathek" are very good. Beckford's "Italy" or "Portugal" would interest you very much but I do not think you can get them. I have never heard you mention the travels of the German Prince if you have never read them I will bring them you; the book is one of my especial favorites and would last you a long while.[6]

Yes! John Dwight's translations are beautiful—wonderful even!—[7]

I said I had read only two Engh books, but I have one other curious[n] and interesting, lent me by Mr Greene who has many good things "Gaudentio di Lucca" by Bishop Berkley; did you ever hear of it?—[8] I never had!— I am finishing the last of my Gn books. I give to them all the time I have.—

My friend, Mr Hedge, was here last night.— I went last week to the

Whig Caucus and heard Tristram Burges. Other things have been done or thought, but I cannot tell them now.— A note for me left at my uncle's would be recd next Thursday, but do not write much to hurt your poor eyes. Let Jane know, if you communicate with her, that I hope to see her this vacation, if not, shall write, but am just now very busy and very languid. If you were to be in town next week I would go with you to see Jane but I fear I shall not find my way to Chelsea alone.

Adieu; I have written on the gallop—so forgive all that needs forgiveness. Heaven keep you—

M. F.—

ALS (MH: bMS Am 1221 [204]). *Addressed:* Miss Caroline Sturgis, / ⟨Wm Sturgis Esq. / Boston,⟩ / Saml Curzon Esqe. / Newburyport. *Postmarks:* Providence R.I. Aug 17. Boston Mas. Aug 21.

thank your cousin for her invitation] thank ⟨you⟩ ↑ your cousin ↓ for ⟨your⟩ her invitation

Boston Wednesday] Boston ⟨?⟩ Wednesday

of a failure in] of a failure ⟨at⟩ in

one other curious] one ↑ other ↓ curious

1. The cousin is unidentified but is probably one of the Curzon children.

2. From Coleridge's "Love's Apparition and Evanishment," published in *STC Letters*, Letter XXXIX.

3. Robert C. Waterston (1812–93) graduated from the Divinity School in 1837 and became minister at large for the Pitts Street Chapel in Boston (1839–45). In 1840 he married Josiah Quincy's daughter Anna (*CC*, 18 April 1840; *DivCat*; *Proceedings of the Massachusetts Historical Society*, 2d ser. 8:292–302).

4. Harriet Martineau, *Society in America* (London, 1837); William Ware, *Letters of Lucius M. Piso from Palmyra, to His Friend Marcus Curtius, at Rome* (New York, 1837). Fuller reviewed Ware's book in the *Western Messenger* 5 (April 1838):24–29.

5. Thomas Moore, *The Epicurean* (London, 1827); John Gibson Lockhart, *Valerius: A Roman Story* (Edinburgh, 1821); and Lydia Maria Francis Child, *Philothea: A Romance* (Boston, 1836) were all novels.

6. Fuller's catalogue includes Carlyle's *Life of Friedrich Schiller*, Anna Jameson's *Visits and Sketches at Home and Abroad*, Vittorio Alfieri's *Vita di Vittorio Alfieri da Asti* (London, 1804), Benvenuto Cellini's *La Vita di Benvenuto Cellini* (Naples, 1728), John Gibson Lockhart's *Reginald Dalton* (London, 1823), and Thomas Hope's *Anastasius: or, Memoirs of a Greek* (London, 1819). William Beckford's *Vathek* (Lausanne, 1787 [1786]) had been published in French but translated into English by Samuel Henley as *The History of the Caliph Vathek* (London, 1786) and had appeared in numerous English and American editions before 1838. Beckford's *Italy: with Sketches of Spain and Portugal* (London, 1834) was also published in America (Philadelphia, 1834). The German Prince is Pückler-Muskau.

7. Dwight was still preparing his *Select Minor Poems*. Fuller had no doubt read his translations in manuscript, though he had by this time published his English version of Schiller's "Das Lied von der Glocke" in *American Monthly Magazine*, n.s. 3 (January 1837):33–40.

8. Albert Gorton Greene (1802–68), a prominent man of letters in Providence, named his fourth daughter Sarah Margaret Fuller Greene (Clarke, *Greenes*, pp. 587–88). *Memoirs of Sigr. Gaudentio di Lucca* (London, 1737) was for many years attributed to

The Greene-Street School, Providence. Courtesy of the Rhode Island Historical Society.

George Berkeley, but the romance was probably the work of the Reverend Simon Berington, a Roman Catholic priest (T. E. Jessop, *Bibliography of George Berkeley* [London, 1934], pp. 24–25).

159.   To [?]

Sepr 2d Providence [1837]

Mr Dwight's translations from Goethe are very beautiful, if for those alone, the little volume he is editing for Mr Ripley will be valuable to the public. They make me despair of success, indeed all the translations I have done are, compared with his, so pitiful and so clumsy that I do not think I shall give one to his volume.

While at Concord I read the first vol of Carlyle's French Revolution which he sent to Mr Emerson.[1] I know not when before, I had read a book which I could strictly term fascinating, certainly not since the two first years of my acquaintance with the Germans; but this was so indeed. I could not turn my thoughts from it when obliged to lay it down, and leaving it made me quite forlorn It is written in the same style as the Mirabeau; the same clear and wide view, the same pictorial power and sparkling wit, and is animated by the same energy of faith— Mr E has sent for twenty copies, it is a dear book, but paper and print are very fine.

MsCfr (MB: Ms. Am. 1450 [160]).
1. Thomas Carlyle, *The French Revolution* (London, 1837). Emerson was the first American to see the book, for Carlyle sent a copy that arrived at Emerson's house on 22 August 1837. By 31 October, Emerson had arranged for Little and Brown to publish it in Boston. The edition appeared on Christmas Day 1837, sold well, and earned Carlyle fifty pounds (*JMN*, 5:372; *Emerson–Carlyle Correspondence*, pp. 18–19, 166–68).

160.   To Margarett C. Fuller

Concord 5th Septr 1837—

My very dear Mother,

Do not suffer the remarks of that sordid man to give you any uneasiness— Proceed to act as we agreed when I was with you. It is perfectly clear to my mind that the arrangements we then made are the right ones and I do not fear to hold myself responsible for the consequences.

If Abraham Fuller continues to annoy you in this manner I am decidedly of opinion that the management of our affairs had better be transferred to someother lawyer. I think Hillard and Sumner would give us satisfaction; their reputation stands very fair:[1] They arranged Mr Tuckerman's affairs at the time of his failure; both would be interested in me.[2] If you preferred an older man we can find such an one. We pay Abraham and we could as well pay another man who would confine himself to his proper post of managing the money. You must, my dear Mother, steadily consider yourself as the guardian of the children. You must not let his vulgar insults make you waver as to giving the children advantages to which they would be well entitled if the property were only a third of what it now is. I cannot like you think that feelings of kindness, however narrow the mind of the writer, could induce him to taunt you or Eugene or say things which he knows to be false. Do not suffer yourself to be puzzled or scared by such stuff. No Judge in the world will ever interfere with your management of the minor children unless we who are of age request it, as you are well aware we never shall.

Fit out the children for school, and let not Lloyd be forgotten. You incur an awful responsibility by letting him go so neglected any longer. I shall get Ellen a place at Mrs Urquhart's, if possible; if not, I may take her to Providence, for I hear of no better place. She shall not be treated in this shameful way, bereft of proper advantages and plagued and cramped in the May of life. If I stay at Providence and Abraham manages to trouble you about money before we can get other arrangements made I will pay her bills, if I do not stay there,[n] I will put the affair into the hands of a lawyer: we will see if she is not to have "a year's schooling from twelve to eighteen. I am not angry but I am determined. I am sure that my Father, if he could see me, would approve the view[n] I take. If means are wanting I am sure I could find them. If I stay in Providence and more is wanting than can otherwise be furnished I will take a private class which is ready for me and by which, even if I reduced my terms to suit the place, I can earn the four hundred dollars that Ellen will need. If I do not stay I will let her have my portion of our income with her own, or even capital which I have a right to take up and come into this or some economical place and live at the cheapest rate. It will not even be a sacrifice to me to do so for I am sated and weary of society; and long for the[n] oppory for solitary concentration of thought for my book. I know what I say— if I live you may rely on me.

Nothing will grieve me so as to know that you have given up the plans we arranged. My only regret is that you are to give that sum of eighty dollars to a member of our family whom it will in nowise benefit. I advise you to sell as much of the stock as you can and use the money for fitting out the children and paying up your house bills. The school bills may be sent to A.W.[n] So soon as I receive money at P and have a safe oppory I will send you some. Be firm, and pay no attention to the thoughts[n] of your low-minded brother in law.

Ellen must take great care not to take cold, now that she has the eruption on her. I should be very sad, if any ill should come to my good little sister. Write to me on Saturday, direct to Providence let me know how she is and how Frances Shattuck is.[3] God be with you, my dear Mother, be sure he will prosper the doings of so excellent a woman if you will only keep your mind calm, and be firm. Trust your daughter too— I feel increasing trust in mine own good mind; we will take good care of the children and, one another. My best love to Eugene, love to the boys and Rebecca. Never fear to trouble me with your perplexities I can never be situated so that I do not earnestly wish to know them. Besides things do not trouble me as they did for I feel within myself the power to aid—to serve. Mention the Tildens when you write. I do hope the journey will benefit poor Maria.[4]

Most afftly your[n]

S. M. F.

Wednesday morng— I feel so anxious about Ellen that I wish you would write directly you receive this—direct to Boston instead of Providence, care of H.H. Fuller, post paid—

I will take Eugene's letter from the P. Office in Boston and send it to Groton. He will probably get it Saturday or Sunday.

ALS (MH: fMS Am 1086 [9:45]); MsCfr (MH: fMS Am 1086 [Works, 1:163–69]). Published in part in *WNC*, pp. 344–45, and Chevigny, pp. 119–20. *Addressed:* Mrs Margaret Fuller. / Groton, / Mass. *Postmark:* Concord MS Sept 7[?].

do not stay there,] do not ↑ stay there, ↓
approve the view] approve the ⟨means⟩ ↑ view ↓
and long for the] and ↑ long for ↓ the
The school bills may be sent to A.W.] ↑ The school bills may be sent to A.W. ↓
to the thoughts] to the ⟨?⟩ thoughts
Most afftly your] Most afftly your ⟨daughter M.⟩

1. Abraham W. Fuller had been appointed executor of his brother's estate. George Hillard and Charles Sumner were law partners at this time in Boston. Hillard (1808–79) graduated from Harvard in 1828 and entered the bar. A man of many talents, he was a friend to several writers, including Fuller, Emerson, and Hawthorne (*DAB*). Sumner (1811–74), who graduated from Harvard in 1830 and from the law school in

1833, became one of the most prominent antislavery men in America. A powerful orator, he distinguished himself in the U.S. Senate (*DAB*).

2. Gustavus Tuckerman, Jane's father.

3. Frances Jane Shattuck (1829–1913), daughter of Colonel Daniel and Sarah Edwards Shattuck. In 1849 she married Louis A. Surette (1819–97) (Lemuel Shattuck, *Memorials of the Descendants of William Shattuck* [Boston, 1855], p. 301; MVR 473:176, 1913 32:468).

4. Maria Dall Tilden (1813–89), daughter of Bryant Parrott (1781–1851) and Zebiah Brown Tilden (1784?–1842) (Linzee ms. genealogy, NEHGS, box 1, sec. 1; MVR 401:69). Bryant Tilden, a Boston merchant, was Mary Parker Tilden's brother.

161. To Caroline Sturgis

Providence 14th Octr 1837.

My dear Cary,

I had been quite distressed at not hearing from you, fearing you were ill.— I was so anxious that I should have written, if I had not been too miserably unwell myself to make any exertion[n] beyond giving my lessons and reading a little— I have been bled and am better now. I rejoice to think from the tone of your letter and still more the appearance of your hand-writing that *you* must be better.

This is to be a business epistle, so I will dispatch all that part first and, if there should be room, say a word or two extra.

I have now made up my mind to stay in Providence and am desirous you should be with me if you still wish it and you say you do in yr letter.[n] But as *I* must make the arrangements for our establishment *in the body* and they ought to be made now we must come to understanding thereabout.

I see you speak of teaching Susy drawing this winter—how is that?[1] I had supposed that you meant, if you could be content, to pass at least the three winter months with me.

The time at which I should like you to come would be at the beginning of my next term which will be eight weeks from Monday next—

I want you to look forward to staying here[n] as much as three months for several reasons. I cannot hope to do much for you, if I have not time to do it in.— I do not intend to sacrifice my writing to you; my teaching, I cannot, of course. But I propose reading with you some part of each day. Carlyle's French Revolution I hope to have for you then. Plenty of other good books are to be had here, and if you are with me so long and can be patient, I think you will have a chance to follow out a good many topicks in a more satisfactory way than you have ever yet done. There are some people here whom I think you will like. I do not know how much we shall see of them, however, in the depth of winter. I can promise for nobody but myself, and not for myself with absolute certainty because my health is so frail. In coming to me you know what you give up; your old friends, your old resources, and, perhaps, what I mourn so much for myself, a new course of lectures from Mr Emerson. Those lectures, however, will sometime be printed in a book and I doubt what you may get from me will not be put into books.[2] At least for four weeks past it has seemed as if there were no great stock of oil to feed my wick. Perhaps the cruise[n] may be filled again by some prophet before thou comest.[3]

Then be it known to thee, O Cary, inexperienced in the vulgar arrangements of a pence-saving, pence paying world, that one makes bargains with boarding house men and women and that, if I take rooms or a room, I must take them for the winter and that I must know before hand whether they are to be for thee and me or for me alone. And if thou hast wishes about them *I* would wish to know those wishes although no ways sure that it would be in my power to fulfil them. For in sooth I have but little power over the material of life.

Be it also understood that, if you be not happy, you need not stay a day. I could break up and make new arrangements, no doubt. But in order to making them now[n] I must know thy intent. And do not defer but answer me[n] forthwith for I must see about my future in a few days. When I know your feelings I shall, probably, write to your father as I told him I would.— The reason I defer your coming to me so long is that my sister is to be with me a while next month. I supposed too that you might not wish to come earlier

I have only space for a few words more. I hope my dear Jane is with you. If so say to her that I should be happier to hear how she fares. I hope she will not pay too dear for her discoveries in the land of Story!—[n] Ellery Channing I never talked with but once.[4] He has been an intimate of S. Ward's who had a great opinion of his talents and individuality of character; and he and you are not like to be wrong in your judgement of people— Mr Emerson's child is one of Raphael's cherubs.—[5] I did not say I was *crazy* about Mr Loring.—[6] I never talk, much less *write*, so. I suppose I said I liked him *much* as that was the case.

I wish I had room to tell you about some of my late experiences Deleuze's history of Prevision— six sermons from James Clarke— W. Simmons's recitation and what I thought. Russell's songs and what I thought, my visit to the blind somnambulist her pity for my head and what she said and what I thought[7] but here is no room for any thing except ys afftly

S. M. F.

ALS (MH: bMS Am 1221 [205]). *Addressed:* Miss Caroline Sturgis / ⟨care Wm Sturgis Esq. / Boston⟩ / Mass— ⟨to be forwarded immedy.—⟩ Saml Curson Esqe. / Newburyport. *Postmark:* Boston MS Oct 16.

make any exertion] make any ⟨a⟩exertion
and you say you do in yr letter] ↑ and you say you do in yr letter ↓
to staying here] to ↑ staying here ↓
Perhaps the cruise] p⟨?⟩erhaps the cruise
to making them now] to ⟨choo⟩ making them ↑ now ↓
not defer but answer me] not defer ↑ but ↓ answer⟨ing⟩ me
I hope she will not pay too dear for her discoveries in the land of Story!—] ↑ I hope she will not pay too dear for her discoveries in the land of Story!— ↓

1. Caroline's sister Susan Sturgis (1825–53) married Henry Jacob Bigelow (1818–90), a Boston doctor and teacher (*Sturgis of Yarmouth*, p. 43; Arthur W. Hodgman, "Elias Parkman of Dorchester and His Descendants," NEHGS, p. 94; Harvard archives).

2. Emerson delivered the ten lectures in his "Human Culture" series at the Boston Masonic Temple from 6 December 1837 to 7 February 1838. While the series did not appear in book form as such, many of the passages in the lectures appeared in *Essays: First Series* and *Essays: Second Series*, most notably "Heroism" and the first half of "Prudence," which were published in the former (*Emerson Lectures*, 2:205–364).

3. The prophet Elijah, after condemning King Ahab's land to drought, went to Zarephath, where he was supported by a widow whose cruse of oil was continually replenished by God (1 Kings 17:12–16).

4. William Ellery Channing (1817–1901), son of Dr. Walter Channing, was an acquaintance since at least 1836, according to an entry in Fuller's journal. He was a moody, spoiled, captivating young man who became a poet, married Margaret's sister Ellen, and settled at Concord to be near Emerson. In later years Margaret Fuller greatly disliked his treatment of Ellen (*DAB*; Robert N. Hudspeth, *Ellery Channing* [New York, 1973]).

5. Possibly the two angels with upturned eyes in Raphael's Sistine Madonna, painted in 1513 for the bier of Pope Julius II.

6. Ellis Gray Loring (1803–58), a Boston lawyer and one of the founders of the New England Anti-Slavery Society, became Fuller's close friend. The wealthy, socially prominent Loring married Louisa Gilman (1797–1868) in 1827 (*DAB*; Charles H. Pope and Katherine P. Loring, *Loring Genealogy* [Cambridge, Mass., 1917], p. 255).

7. Joseph Philippe François Deleuze, *Mémoire sur la faculté de prévision* (Paris, 1836). For some time before this letter was written, Providence had been a center of activity among the mesmerists. Charles Poyen of the University of Paris had lectured on Franz Mesmer's work in the fall and winter of 1836; Thomas Hartshorn translated Deleuze's earlier work, *Instruction pratique sur le magnétisme animal* (Paris, 1825), into English (Eric J. Dingwall, ed., *Abnormal Hypnotic Phenomena* [New York, 1968], 4:2–78). William Hammatt Simmons (1812–41), a Harvard graduate (1831), was a professional lecturer who spoke in Providence (Harvard archives). The *Providence Journal* for 10 October advertised "Mr. H. Russell in concert this evening at City Hotel." Henry Russell (1812–1900), an English composer and singer, toured the United States from 1833 to 1841. His extremely popular performances included "Woodman, Spare That Tree" (*Grove's Dictionary*). In his journal of 1836–39 (MHi), Clarke describes Fuller's reactions to his preaching ("She said I wanted pathos in delivery commonly—it was rather strong & empathetic than touching") and some of his topics—"Utilitarianism," "Social Distinctions," and "Resurrection." He goes on to describe their visit to Miss Loraina Brackett,

a blind somnambulist. First a Dr. Capron put her to sleep. "She was put in communication with S.M.F. and discovered the point in her head where she suffered from violent pain, and after some rubbing this pain was relieved."

162. To Caroline Sturgis

Providence 17th Octr 1837.

My dear Caroline,

I must confess I had supposed you had attached more importance to the plan of being with me and would not relinquish it so lightly— I think your first duty till you recover your health is to yourself.— Your Father not only consented but seemed to receive the idea of your being with me with pleasure, as likely to be of advantage as well as pleasure to you, and I, myself, had the vanity to take the same view of it.—

If you are not well, you will do no good at home, but rather[n] be a burden to your family. You would not be so to me, if you were content, because I understand you. I should hope to give you back to them, renewed.

However, though I do not coincide with those reasons, you may have decided wisely for others. It is however far from being my wish to give up your visit if you will not come to stay— If it were for the winter I should want to make pleasant arrangements that we might both enjoy. But for a month or six weeks it will not signify. I can make you tolerably comfortable wherever I am—do not fail to come, my dear.

You can come in Novr, after my sister goes away, or return with me after my vacation in Decr,[n] whichever you prefer; write me word when you are to leave Newbury and which time you had rather come and then we will settle the rest.

I have no more time now

S. M. F.

Eveg— This aftn I have been to the Hotel and I find it is doubtful whether I could get pleasant rooms for us there at any rate— Such accomodations as I now have I suppose I can promise you whenever you come.

I have also looked into the almanac and thence ascertained the following important facts. My vacation is to come six weeks from next Saty— The 2d Decr. It will last only a week— My sister will not leave me till the 18th or 20th Novr. So if you came to me in Novr you would have only a fortnight to stay. Therefore I hope, instead, you will return with me when *I* return and stay as long as you wish or think best. But if you have reasons for preferring Novr, come then; I shall be glad to see you any-time. Take good care of your health and be sure not lose any little you may have gained. Write only a few lines in answer to this if writing hurts your eyes.

   in great haste yours

                                   M. F.

ALS (MH: bMS Am 1221 [206]). *Addressed:* Miss Caroline Sturgis, / ⟨care of Wm Sturgis Esq. / Boston⟩ / Saml Curson Esqe, / Newburyport Mass. *Postmarks:* Providence R.I. Oct 20. Boston Mas Oct 21.

  but rather] but ⟨may⟩ ↑ rather ↓
  my vacation in Decr] my vacation in ⟨Septr⟩ ↑ Decr ↓

163. To Harriet Martineau

                             [ca. November 1837]
                                   [Providence?]

On its first appearance, the book was greeted by a volley of coarse and outrageous abuse, and the nine days' wonder was followed by a nine days' hue-and-cry. It was garbled, misrepresented, scandalously ill-treated. This was all of no consequence. The opinion of the majority you will find expressed in a late number of the North American Review.[1] I should think the article, though ungenerous, not more so than great part of the critiques upon your book.

   The minority may be divided into two classes: The one, consisting of those who knew you but slightly, either personally, or in your writings. These have now read your book; and, seeing in it your high ideal standard, genuine independence, noble tone of sentiment, vigor of mind and powers of picturesque description, they value your book very much, and rate you higher for it.

   The other comprises those who were previously aware of these high qualities, and who, seeing in a book to which they had looked for a lasting monument to your fame, a degree of presumptuousness, irreverence, inaccuracy, hasty generalization, and ultraism on many points, which they did not expect, lament the haste in which you have written, and the injustice which you have consequently done to so

                                   307

Harriet Martineau. Oil painting by Charles Osgood. Courtesy of the Essex Institute, Salem, Massachusetts.

important a task, and to your own powers of being and doing. To this class I belong.

I got the book as soon as it came out,—long before I received the copy endeared by your handwriting,—and devoted myself to reading it. I gave myself up to my natural impressions, without seeking to ascertain those of others. Frequently I felt pleasure and admiration, but more frequently disappointment, sometimes positive distaste.

There are many topics treated of in this book of which I am not a judge; but I do pretend, even where I cannot criticize in detail, to have an opinion as to the general tone of thought. When Herschel writes his Introduction to Natural Philosophy, I cannot test all he says, but I cannot err about his fairness, his manliness, and wide range of knowledge. When Jouffroy writes his lectures, I am not conversant with all his topics of thought, but I can appreciate his lucid style and admirable method.[2] When Webster speaks on the currency, I do not understand the subject, but I do understand his mode of treating it, and can see what a blaze of light streams from his torch.[3] When Harriet Martineau writes about America, I often cannot test that rashness and inaccuracy of which I hear so much, but I can feel that they exist. A want of soundness, of habits of patient investigation, of completeness, of arrangement, are felt throughout the book; and, for all its fine descriptions of scenery, breadth of reasoning, and generous daring, I cannot be happy in it, because it is not worthy of my friend, and I think a few months given to ripen it, to balance, compare, and mellow, would have made it so. [   ]

Certainly you show no spirit of harshness towards this country in general. I think your tone most kindly. But many passages are deformed by intemperance of epithet. [   ] Would your heart, could you but investigate the matter, approve such overstatement, such a crude, intemperate tirade as you have been guilty of about Mr. Alcott,—a true and noble man, a philanthropist, whom a true and noble woman, also a philanthropist, should have delighted to honor; whose disinterested and resolute efforts, for the redemption of poor humanity, all independent and faithful minds should sustain, since the "broadcloth" vulgar will be sure to assail them; a philosopher, worthy of the palmy times of ancient Greece; a man whom Carlyle and Berkeley, whom you so uphold, would delight to honor; a man whom the worldlings of Boston hold in as much horror as the worldlings of ancient Athens did Socrates. They smile to hear their verdict confirmed from the other side of the Atlantic, by their censor, Harriet Martineau.[4]

I do not like that your book should be an abolition book. You might have borne your testimony as decidedly as you pleased; but why leaven the whole book with it? This subject haunts us on almost every page. It *is* a great subject, but your book had other purposes to fulfil.

I have thought it right to say all this to you, since I felt it. I have shrunk from the effort, for I fear that I must lose you. Not that I think all authors are like Gil Blas' archbishop.[5] No; if your heart turns from me, I shall still love you, still think you noble. I know it must be so trying to fail of sympathy, at such a time, where we expect it. And, besides, I felt from the book that the sympathy between us is less general than I had supposed, it was so strong on several points. It is strong enough for me to love you ever, and I could no more have been happy in your friendship, if I had not spoken out now.

ELfr, from *Memoirs*, 1:192–94; MsCfr (MH: 59m-308 [13], pp. 410–11). Also in Higginson, *MFO*, pp. 123–24, and Chevigny, pp. 117–18.

Alcott says in his 1839 journal that the letter was to Martineau and that he copied part of it from Fuller's journal. Presumably that Fuller copy (now lost) served as the text for the Memoirs *editors.*

1. Typical of the reaction to Martineau's *Society in America* was John Gorham Palfrey's review in the *North American Review* 45 (October 1837):418–60: "In short, Miss Martineau's rash and worthless judgments are too often expressed in terms, having an unpleasant character of rude assumption" (p. 424).

2. Théodore Simon Jouffroy had published several volumes of his lectures, including the first volume of *Cours de droit naturel* (Paris, 1834–35) and *Cours d'histoire de la philosophie moderne* (Paris, 1831).

3. Daniel Webster's two most recent speeches on the bank controversy (28 September and 3 October 1837) were summarized in the *Boston Daily Advertiser*.

4. Without naming Alcott, Martineau attacked him at length in her book. Among other things, she said, "His system can be beneficial to none, and must be ruinous to many" (*Society in America* [London, 1837], 2:278).

5. In *The History and Adventures of Gil Blas of Santillane*, the archbishop of Grenada instructs the hero to read and improve the prelate's prose. Faithfully executing his duties, Gil Blas offends the archbishop and is discharged.

164. To Caroline Sturgis

Providence 2d Novr 1837.

My dear Cary—

'Tis more than a week since I recd your letter and I am very sorry not to have answered it sooner. But, last week I was very unwell and could attend to nothing that was not absolutely necessary from day to day and this I have been engaged every moment—

I *do* think you had best come to me. I feel as if I might be of use to you *now*, more use than any other person. I do not think you can be of use at home in your present state. If it should prove that I am mistaken, if my health be too weak or my time too much engrossed, or my resources less than I suppose, or any reason should make it desirable for you to return,—you can.

I could not but laugh at your catalogue of the things you must not have—nothing striped diamonded or (above all things) *square*, that is driving me to close quarters I think. However I believe nothing that is to be appropriated to you will offend your eye. There is nothing too *bright*, certainly, on the contrary every thing is *dingy* and the figures are nondescript.

I found no rooms at the City Hotel which would suit us and, besides, if Iⁿ had gone there I shd have been troubled by the intimacy of some people whom I do not want. There is no better boarding house in this part of the city than this where I am, so I have engaged a room for you here if you will come. The house is small and, as I said, dingy but very clean. There will be no boarders except ourselves. We shall have the whole of the second floor to ourselves including my parlor and a very small room where I sleep and one for you of good size and decently furnished. I think it comfortable for you in every respect except that it has only a straw carpet— If I find that, in consequence of this, you suffer from cold, I shall change rooms with you, as I do not, I believe, feel cold as much as you do.

There will be wood-fires—yours will be made for you to dress by and undress, if you please but you will, probably, prefer passing your *day* in my parlor.

The family is composed of Mrs Aborn, her two daughters and three grand children.[1] They are kindhearted but ordinary people. Probably some of their ways may not be agreeable to you as they are not to my ladyship, but they are quiet, unobtrusive, and you will only see them at meals.

They offer you such accommodations as I have described for four dollars and a half a week, unless it should be extremely cold, when, if large fires are required, they will ask a little more.

Elizh Channing is to pass the winter with the Farleys, who are my near and kind neighbors.[2] She was your fellow pupil at Dolly's (she tells me) and is desirous of reading to you morngs for a while when I am in the school.[3] You will do about this, as you please. I shall read to you but little, as I am weak and busy, but that little will be from good books— I want you now to give me your final answer as soon as you can, as the important question of whether Mistress Aborn is to engage "a boy to wait and tend" hangs upon your decision.

Present my respects to your father and mother[n] and say that, if they commit you to my keeping, I will do for your well being both of body and mind whatever is in my power as I would for a sister.

I have no time for more now except God bless you, my dear Cary and make your decision right and best both for you and me. Affetly your friend

S. M. FULLER—

ALS (MH: bMS Am 1221 [207]). Published in part in *JMN*, 11:377. *Addressed:* Miss Caroline Sturgis / care of Wm Sturgis Esq. / Boston.— Mass.— *Postmark:* Providence R.I. Nov 3.

besides, if I] besides, ↑ if ↓ I
father and mother] father and ⟨?⟩ mother

1. Susan Potter Aborn and her family. Which two of the three daughters were at home is unclear: Hannah (1807–58), Elizabeth (1813–44), or Frances Mary, Margaret's colleague at the Greene-Street School. Among the grandchildren were surely John Farnum and Edward Amory Chapin, sons of Sarah Ann Aborn (1811–31) and her husband, Amory Chapin (W. W. Chapin, "The Aborn Family of Rhode Island," 1913, RHi, p. 19; *Potter Families*, pt. 2, p. 18; Snow et al., *Alphabetical Index*).

2. Elizabeth Parsons Channing (1818–1906) was the daughter of George Gibbs (1789–1881) and Elizabeth Sigourney Channing (MVR 1906 64:126; *NEHGR* 8:319; *CVR*; Norfolk Probate, nos. 22243 and 52368). Frederick Augustus Farley (1800–1892) graduated from Harvard in 1818 and from the Divinity School in 1828. He was ordained that year at the Second Unitarian Church in Providence, where he served until 1841. In 1830 he married Elizabeth Channing's cousin Jane Carter Sigourney (1803–90), daughter of Charles and Mary Greenleaf Sigourney (*Heralds*, 3:109–12).

3. Dorothea Lynde Dix (1802–87), later to become famous as a reformer on behalf of the insane, had been a tutor for Dr. Channing's children before she conducted her own school in Boston from 1831 to 1836 (*DAB*; *NAW*; Helen E. Marshall, *Dorothea Dix* [Chapel Hill, N.C., 1937]).

165.   To Caroline Sturgis

Providence Novr 10th
1837—

My dear Cary,

I was surprized and sorry when I received your letter, for I had not anticipated any further obstacles, but had made up my mind to read to you Bancrofts History and Carlyle, and take care of you in all peace and quietness—[1] I am quite clear I am not mistaken as to what your father said to me in September.— There was no talk of a *visit*: it was of your boarding here with me and all that he said gave me the impression that he wished it and thought it would be good for you. He has changed, I suppose, and we must change with him, for "parents and guardians are the representatives of the divine authority &c—

My Cary, too, is somewhat inconsistent; In two of her letters she has said that she wished to come if only for a fortnight, in two others, that she did not wish to come at all, if only for a fortnight. But if she be disposed to come when my sister goes, (a week from next Monday) and stay with me the remainder of my term, I shall be glad to see her, very glad, and able to devote myself a good deal to her. As to a later visit I do not know— Mrs Aborn will probably let her room to some one else since you are not to come. Besides I should think a later visit would interfere with your arrangements, Mr Emerson's lectures &c—

I think Mr Alcott would be glad to read to you, but I do not know; I have not heard from him since I saw him in Boston last Septr—

—I cannot tell you now the little I know about Magtism, or any thing else that requires detail. I am tired and busy; besides I shall soon see you and be able to communicate in a less laborious manner—

The blind girl said my head would never be better while I read so much.— She has almost entirely lost the gift of clairvoyance (if she ever possessed it,) and is good for nothing.

Farewell, my dear Cary. Heaven keep and cure you! Very faithfully your friend

S. M. Fuller—

ALS (MH: bMS Am 1221 [208]). *Addressed:* Miss. Caroline Sturgis, / care of Wm Sturgis Esq. / Boston / Mass. *Postmark:* Providence R.I. Nov 10.

1. George Bancroft, *The History of the United States from the Discovery of the Continent* (Boston, 1834–75). The first three volumes, which Bancroft intended to be a unit, carried the history to the French and Indian Wars. Vol. 1 appeared in 1834, 2 in 1837, and 3 in 1839.

166. To Caroline Sturgis

Providence Rhode Island
16th Novr 1837—

My dear Caroline,

When I saw your Father in September[n] I felt a natural delicacy about interfering in your affairs, (although conscious of very pure and kind motives) and apologized, to which he replied by begging me not, and saying that he must always consider any manifestation of interest from me in your behalf as a *kindness and a favor*—

When I spoke of your coming here and asked if it would be agreeable to him, he replied *it would extremely so*; that *he could have no objection except from the fear that I might be taking too much care upon myself.*— When I asked if he would *object to your boarding at the City Hotel* with me, and gave some reasons for fearing he might, he said that he had *perfect confidence in your discretion*, and that any *arrangement I might think proper for myself he should also esteem proper for you*, and left me, requesting *to hear from me on the subject as soon as I should decidedly know what arrangements I could make.*

Remembering all this distinctly (for I was much pleased by your father's manner and spoke of it to several of our mutual friends and by repetition even his words were impressed on my memory,) I cannot but feel strong indignation at the statements contained in your letter, at the levity and discourtesy with which I *seem* to be treated, and at the unnecessary trouble which has been given me.

I have nothing to say as to what you shall do. My feelings towards you are unchanged. They are those of warm affection and interest for your welfare. I know not of another young person of whom, under my present circumstances, I would have taken similar charge. I have avoided taking one into the house who would have given me very little trouble, and whose friends were earnestly desirous of having her under my influence— I may venture to say that my motives with regard to you[n] were those of disinterested,[n] and uncommon kindness, and ought to have been met in a very different manner.

The question as to whether you shall come rests with yourself and your family. Here or any-where I shall be glad to receive you. I might cease *to visit you* but should always be happy to have you v[is]it me. I live at Mrs Susan Aborn's,[n] Aborn St.— Any hackman when[n] you leave the cars would know where it is. I should not wish to receive you before Tuesday unless you can mail a letter so that I can get it on Saty to tell me that you can come on Monday. We have no Sunday mail, I believe. And this much ceremony, at least, is due me and quite necessary as I must inform my hostess about your coming.—

As to transcendentalism and the nonsense[n] which is talked by so many about it—I do not know what is meant. For myself I should say that if it is meant that I have an active mind frequently[n] busy with large topics I hope it is so— If it is meant that I am honored by the friendship of such men as Mr Emerson, Mr Ripley, or Mr Alcott, I hope it is so—[1] *But* if it is meant that I cherish any opinions which interfere with domestic duties, cheerful courage and judgement in the practical affairs of life, I challenge any or all in the little world which knows me to prove such deficiency from any acts of mine since I came to woman's estate.—

You are at liberty to show this letter if you please to your parents. I permit but do not *require* it, because I think as your letter was written in haste some expressions may have given me exaggerated notions— You are on the spot, and can judge; do as you think proper.

Let me once more, before I close, repeat to you the assurances of my affection. If you have dallied with me, I know it is not your fault— You would never wilfully interfere with my comfort or feelings in any way[n] and are incapable of treating[n] me in an indelicate manner. But at the same time, if you do not come, I shall not write again. I do not wish to be needlessly agitated by exchanging another letter on this topic— I will let you know when I am in Boston and see you there at least once— Sincerely your friend

S. M. FULLER.

ALS (MH: bMS Am 1221 [209]). *Addressed:* Miss Caroline Sturgis, / Care of Wm Sturgis Esq. / Boston / Mass— *Postmark:* Providence R I.

Father in September] Father in ⟨Ma⟩ September
motives with regard to you] motives ↑ with regard to you ↓
those of disinterested] those of ⟨a⟩ disinterested
Mrs Susan Aborn's] Mrs Susan ⟨Ab⟩ Aborn's
Any hackman when] Any hackman ⟨before you⟩ when
and the nonsense] and ⟨other⟩ ↑ the ↓ nonsense
mind frequently] mind ↑ frequently ↓
feelings in any way] feelings in any ⟨?⟩ way
incapable of treating] incapable of ⟨?⟩ treating

1. The cautious William Sturgis undoubtedly distrusted all the writers Fuller mentions.

167. To Margarett C. Fuller

Providence 18th Novr 1837.

My dear Mother,

As I am just this moment at leisure, I think I will begin a letter to you although uncertain whether I shall be able to finish it.

I am sorry Ellen's reports should have occasioned you so much alarm about my health. As to what I said about the probability of never being perfectly well again; it is, you know, my disposition always to prefer being prepared for the worst— I do not trouble myself

315

about it or look gloomily forward to a future which lies in the hand of God. I am cheerful, steadfast; if I should never be well I yet trust to do well. The only part of it I regret is that nothing but dissipation agrees with me. You need not be afraid of my exerting my mind too much. It is no longer in my power to write or study much. I cannot bear it and do not attempt it. Heaven, I believe, had no will that I should accomplish any-thing great or beautiful. Yet I do not dispair, daily I do a little and leave the result to a higher power. As to my writing constant bulletins of my health; it is impossible— I cannot; it would be too irksome; even disgusting to me, and quite like our old acquaintances the Misses Williams;[1] besides my feelings vary so much from day to day that I should probably be feeling well and bright by the time[n] you had my letter and were mourning over my ill health. If I am seriously unwell I will certainly let you know— I do not wish to write a minute account of my circumstances, but I shall see you in Boston in about three weeks, and then, if I am not better, you can talk with a physician and I will take tonics—[n] I feel much better these last few days, Ellen fixes eggs with wine and they do me a great deal of good.

I think Ellen very much improved both in mind and manners. I take pleasure in her society and should like to have her remain with me, if it were best for her, but I am satisfied it would not be. She has, I believe, enjoyed herself here very much. All her things are nicely made up and she looks very pretty in them.[n] She has been about here a good deal and seen some of the best people who are pleased with her. Mr Fowler the phrenologist, has been here, and examined both our heads.[2] His sketch of her was excellent. She will tell it you when you meet.

Mr Hastings, (Fanny's father) has been here this afternoon.[3] He is a droll man.

My love to Eugene— Tell him I hav had two letters from Thesta, the last of which I have not yet answered. She wishes to come here awhile, and board this winter. Said "she was very triste at Kingston, she scarce knew why" but I do—she is too fond of the excitement of society.[4]

I believe, when I wrote, we had not seen Ellen Tree.[5] She passed a day in Providence with some parishoners of Mr Farley's and Mr F. took Ellen and myself, with Elizh Channing, to see her. We had a very agreeable eveg. She is very pleasing in her manners, talks very intelligently and read to us some of the last scenes in Ion.[6] I forgot to ask her how she liked Uncle Abraham!

I shall write to Richard next time. Do not urge me to write more frequently; once a fortnight is as much as I can. I pay like attention to no one else. Nothing disagrees with me so much as writing, and I avoid it when possible. Letters from those in whom I am most interested, from Mr Emerson, M. Channing, S. Ward have been lying[n] for many weeks unanswered in my desk.[7]

I hope you have of late been undisturbed and that every thing goes on smoothly. Love to the boys and Rebecca. I am so glad Lloyd is fairly at school, a weight is lifted from my conscience. Heaven bless you, dearest Mother, your and Eugene's affectionate letter was very grateful to me.

In all love and duty yours

S. M. FULLER.

Tell Eugene I am charmed with Ernest Maltravers and think it Bulwer's best.[8]

ALS (MH: fMS Am 1086 [9:56]). *Addressed:* Mrs Margaret Fuller, / Groton / Mass— *Postmark:* Providence R.I. Nov 18.

by the time] by the ⟨had⟩ time
I will take tonics—] I will take ⟨?⟩ tonics—
pretty in them] pretty ⟨o⟩in them
have been lying] have been ⟨?⟩ lying

1. Sophia and Eliza, daughters of Dr. John Williams in Cambridgeport.
2. Orson Fowler (1809–87) had visited the school. He and his brother Lorenzo (1811–96) lectured frequently on phrenology to large audiences. Throughout her life Fuller was fascinated with phrenology, animal magnetism, and mesmerism (Stern, "Phrenologist-Publishers," pp. 229–37).
3. William Henry Fuller's father-in-law, Daniel Hastings.
4. Thesta Dorcas Dana (1816–1907), daughter of Samuel and Rebecca Barrett Dana of Groton. In 1849 she married her cousin James Jackson Dana (*Dana Family*, p. 41). She had been visiting her sister, Ann Dana Sever, at Kingston.
5. Ellen Tree (1805–80) was an English actress touring America. She made her debut at Covent Garden in 1823 and in America in 1836. In 1842 she married Charles Kean (William C. Young, *Famous Actors and Actresses on the American Stage* [New York, 1975], 2:1080).
6. While Euripides wrote an *Ion* (ca. 417 B.C.), the reference here is to Thomas Noon Talfourd's *Ion* (London, 1835).
7. Emerson had written her on 24 October announcing his plans to publish Carlyle's *History of the French Revolution* (Rusk, *Letters of RWE*, 2:98–100).
8. Edward Bulwer Lytton, *Ernest Maltravers* (London, 1837).

168. To Anna Jameson

Providence Rhode Island
22d Decr 1837

Dear Madam

The enclosed is a copy of a letter which I addressed to you some weeks since, supposing you to have returned to England.

How great was my mortification on a late visit to Boston to find that you had just left that city, and that, as you had passed much of your time with persons whom I know well, I too should have enjoyed your society if I had gone thither a little earlier.

But all this pain was increased when I was told by Dr Channing that you had lived so long in the family of Goethe's daughter in law and were consequently the very person in the world who could best aid me.[1] He added that you seemed to feel a natural delicacy about any new disclosures. But oh! if I could but see you I am persuaded that you would tell me all I wish to know— Is it quite impossible for me to see you? How I wish I was famous or could paint beautiful pictures and then you would not be willing to go without seeing me. But now—I know not how to interest you,—the miserable frigid letter within will not interest you— Yet I am worthy to know you, and be known by you, and if you could see me you would soon believe it, and now I need you so very much. I would come to New York and see you if it were possible, but I fear it is not. I have no days to myself except Saturday and Sunday. I teach in the mornings in a school the other five days in the week— You must not get an ugly picture of me because I am a schoolmistress. I have not yet acquired that "strong mental odour" that Coleridge speaks of.[2] I am only teaching for a little while and I want to *learn* of you.

I had quite given you up, for Mr Dwight told me you were to sail in a few days and I saw no means of getting at you, but Mr Thompson, an artist, who was here today, tells me you are still expected in New York and that he hopes to see you there.[3] May I request th[at] you will write me a line and say [how] long you shall be there although I fear, I fear I cannot come. And when a few hours talk with you would do me so much good—*are* there not hard things to bear in life?—

Be so good as not to speak of my intended work—it is known only to a few persons. Precarious health, the pressure of many ties make me fearful of promising what I will do.— I may die soon—you may never more hear my name. But the earnest aspiration, the sympathy with greatness never dies— Es lebt im Asche—[4]

Respectfully

S. M. FULLER.

ALS (CtY). *Addressed:* Mrs Jameson, / New York, Politeness Mr C. G. Thompson.

1. Ottilie von Pogwisch (1796–1872) married Julius August von Goethe (1789–1830) in 1817 (*OCGL*). After meeting Frau Goethe in 1833, Mrs. Jameson recorded her impressions of the Goethe family in *Visits and Sketches at Home and Abroad*.

2. "Has any one known a teacher of youth who, having attained any repute as

such, has also retained any place in society as an individual? Are not all such men 'Dominie Sampsons' in what relates to their duties, interests, and feelings as citizens; and, with respect to females, do they not all possess a sort of *mental* odour?" (*STC Letters*, p. 206).

3. Cephas Giovanni Thompson (1809–88)—who carried this letter to Jameson—was a portrait painter who had recently been working in Providence but who now lived in New York City. Though he came from a family of painters and was popular with the literary set in New York, Thompson's work was undistinguished (*DAB*).

4. "It lives in ashes."

169. To Arthur B. Fuller

Providence 31st Decr 1837,—

My dear Arthur,

I wish I were near enough to send you some new year's gift tomorrow, but, since I am not, you shall, at least, have a letter.

I thought you would like to have a picture of the house where I pass so many hours and have, therefore, taken one of the bills to write upon. I sent one to Richard and intend writing to Lloyd in the same way by and by.

I was very glad to get your letter, but very sorry it was so short. I want my brother, who can talk so fluently, and who has many thoughts which *I* should think worth knowing to learn to express them in writing. It is the more important to me as I may, probably, be very little with you the remainder of my life, and, if you do not learn to write, you and I, who have been such good friends, may become as strangers to one another. It is more desirable that you should write than I, both because you are changing more than I shall change, and because I have many occupations and many claims on my feelings and attention; you, comparatively, few. I wish you would begin a letter to me as soon as you receive this, write in it from time[n] to time as things occur worth telling and whenever the sheet is full send it me. I will not fail to answer it as soon as I can. You need not pay postage when you write to me, but I will pay when I write to you as I suppose you want all your pocket money.

You express gratitude for what I have taught you. It is in your power to repay me a hundred fold by making every exertion now to improve. I did not teach you as I would, yet I think the confinement and care I took of you children, at a time when my mind was much excited by many painful feelings, have had a very bad effect upon my health. I do not say this to pain you or make you more grateful to me, (for, probably if I had been aware at the time what I was doing, I might not have sacrificed myself so,) but I say it that you may feel it your duty to fill my place and do what I may never be permitted to do. Three precious years at the best period of life I gave all my best hours to you children—let me not see you idle away time which I have always[n] valued so, let me not find you unworthy of the love I felt for you. Those three years would have enabled me to make great attainments which now I never may. Do you make them in my stead that I may not remember that time with sadness.—

I hope you are fully aware of the great importance of your conduct this year. It will decide your fate. You are now fifteen and if, at the end of the year, we have not reason to be satisfied that you have a decided taste for study and ambition to make a figure in one of the professions, you will be consigned to some other walk in life. For you are aware that there is no money to be wasted on any one of us, though, if I live and thrive, and you deserve my sympathy, you shall not want means and teaching to follow out any honorable path—

With your sister Ellen's[n] improvement and desire to do right and perseverance in overcoming obstacles I am well satisfied. I feel pretty sure Richard will do well, but I feel greater anxiety about you, my dear Arthur. I know you have both heart and head, but you have always been deficient in earnestness and forethought May God bless you, may I assist you to conquer these faults and make this coming year a prelude to many honorable years!

If Mr Haven is still at Leicester I wish you to present my compliments to him and say that I much regret never having had an opportunity to thank him for his kind care of you when you were there before[1] Next time I write, I will not fill the whole sheet with advice. Advice, generally, does little good, but I will not believe I shall speak in vain to my dear Arthur.—

Very affectionately your sister

S. M. FULLER.

ALS (MH: fMS Am 1086 [9:46]); MsC (MH: fMS Am 1086 [Works, 1:621–27]). Published in part in Higginson, *MFO*, p. 59; published entire in Wade, pp. 549–50, and Chevigny, p. 120. *Addressed:* Arthur B. Fuller. / Leicester / Mass. *Postmark:* Providence R.I. Jan 1.

from time] from ↑ time ↓
have always] have ⟨?⟩ always
sister Ellen's] sister('s) ↑ Ellen's ↓

1. Luther Haven (1806–66), son of Luther and Experience Parker Haven of Framingham, was assistant preceptor of the Leicester Academy from 1834 until 1845. He then went to Chicago and became superintendent of schools there (Theodore Parker,

Genealogy and Biographical Notes of John Parker of Lexington [Worcester, Mass., 1893], pp. 167–68; *The Centenary of Leicester Academy* [Worcester, Mass., 1884], p. 11).

170.   To Albert G. Greene

[ca. 1838]
Thursday—
[Providence]

My dear Mr Greene,

I see you are no practical man after all, or you would have more tact than to have the headach when the occasion is approaching sacred to eating.— However I did not think of coming to your house this eveg—for I am too busy to spend hours in libraries full of novels and the armour of carpet knights.— I suppose you have not got Mr Whipple's piece for me; as gentlemen never pay proper attention to ladies behests in modern times.[1] You must get it tonight, if you do not wish to see me much out of temper, for I shall come to your door tomorrow before breakfast and wo be unto the peace of the family if I dont find it!— Tell Mrs Greene I take it particularly unkind that she should refuse to let me come tonight when there are so many attractive circumstances, a supper, twenty gentlemen, and novels in the library![2] Perhaps I should have staid away but I gloried in the invitation. I suppose now I shall be invited some Sunday eveg^{n} to talk over the old Testament instead.

S. M. F.

ALS (RPB). *Addressed:* Mr Greene.

Sunday eveg] Sunday ↑ eveg ↓

1. Probably John Whipple (1794–1866), a well-known lawyer and member of the Rhode Island Legislature (Henry E. Whipple, *Brief Genealogy of the Whipple Families* [Providence, 1873], pp. 42–44; *Rhode Island Biographical Cyclopedia*, pp. 216–17).

2. In 1824 Greene had married Mary Ann Clifford (1797–1865) (Clarke, *Greenes*, p. 587).

171.   To Caroline Sturgis

Providence 3d Jany 1838.^{n}

My dear Cary,

For I really cannot comply with your request and drop that which has become almost a household name to me.— I thank you for taking so much pains about Mrs Jameson— Mr Thompson, the Artist, was here a few days since and, as he said he should see her if she came to N. York, I gave him a letter for her and, having now done mon possible, have abandoned the whole affair to its fate.

I am much grieved, my Cary, at all you tell me of yourself; but it skills not for me to say any-thing now. From your own self[?] must come the[?] [   ] you, if you persevering [   ] resist.

You would have done no hurt if you had come to bid me goodbye that morng, for there were people with me all the time up to the very last minute and I should never have got back here, if Mother had not packed my clothes— I had hoped to rest in the cars, but a gentleman, who sat by me, talked to me almost all the way. Next day I found it was very fortunate I did not stay even for Mr Alcott and Dr Channing, for I was so tired I could hardly sit up.— If I had not had that day's rest I never could have gone into school. Brother Eugene did not go till Tuesday and I did not get refreshed till the next Saturday[n] I seemed to need absolute silence and Saty and Sunday I staid at home all day and wrote and sewed. Christmas day I was ill and, as it was holy day) lay on the sofa and read the Music of Nature—[1] Ah!—then I was happy indeed. I read it completely through from ten in the morng to twelve at night, reading leisurely and calmly too. I was only interrupted by visits about an hour in the afternoon. It is a most fascinating book, has solved for me many doubts and confirmed many cherished opinions— How I envy you[n] Caradori!—[2] It will be one of the mistakes in the administration of this world if I do not hear her. She could be so much to me! Her voice and Mr Emerson's lectures—surely I have much to regret in Boston this winter. Yet [   ] full of my natural energy. I dare not hope this will last but have availed myself of the halcyon moments and accomplished much for the time.— I have got the school into beautiful order and Mr F. has done his part like a man. It is very full, only one vacancy. Five or six maidens, from eighteen to twenty, intelligent and earnest, attracted by our renown have joined the school for more advanced culture. This was just what I wanted. Add to this that my old birds seem really to appreciate the value of what is doing for them. They express a great deal of gratitude and eagerness and act upon it. I cannot but feel with a happy glow, that many minds are wakened to know the beauty of the life of thought. My own thoughts have been flowing clear and bright as amber. I have now formed a large class in Rhetoric and been very successful in setting afloat in their minds a subject so interesting to me. Whately's Rhetoric is what I use.[3] I have been reading it and[n] thinking it over with great profit to myself.— I am *sure* I shall never regret coming into this school; if I could devote all my energies to it I should be overpaid by the unfolding of powers which lay comparatively dormant in me— Besides the school, I am to take a German class— There are ten members engaged, six of them gentlemen. Mr Hague, of whom I have talked to you, is one. Whitaker whose poem we heard at the Exhibition and Mr Gammell, one of the professors whom we saw there, are members. The others you do not know except Mrs Whitman and Mr Fuller. M. Channing's friend, Miss Tillinghast is one.[4] I am a little afraid of so many grown men, but I trust inspiration will be given at the time and that I shall not *seem* abashed at lecturing to so many of our natural lords and masters!!!—

President Wayland has called on me at last, charmed I presume by my assurance not appearance, mind![n] that day at the Exhibition but I was not at home—[5] I have also been studying most happily on Goethe's Propylea—and reading also with delight the book on Language which I was inclined to scout—[6] But I will talk of these when I have more room.

I have been out very little, three parties and one Coliseum meeting is all! If I can be but well and bear application I shall go out very little.

Yes I should like the critique on Vandenhoff.[7] I have not seen it and dont know where to find it I have a leaf on the same subject in my journal. I expect Mother to come here, perhaps in a few days[n] will thou not find out when she is coming, and send me the Bell, and also, if possible, get from J. Dwight Tennyson's 2d vol and the Lives of Hayden and Mozart for me.[8] Any letters too from good people would be to me most welcome to me, an exile!

I do not remember what novels I mentioned, but will mention "De Lisle" and "Village Belles" as excellent in their different ways.[9] You must not expect another like St Leon such do not grow on every bush.—[10]

Give my love to "Aunt Cary" and let me know how she doeth.[11] Farewell! I shall not write again for two or three weeks— I oug[ht] not, but do you write to me whenever yo[u] feel like it and your eyes permit. I tht your first letter quite eloquent. I[n] what is J. Dwights review?— Remember [me] to Mr and Mrs Ripley, Mr and Mrs Loring and [m]y dear Jeannie.[12] Always your friend

M. F—

I am sorry had no chance of reading you part of Anna Barker's delicious letter from Switzerland.

ALS (MH: bMS Am 1221 [210]). *Addressed:* Miss Caroline Sturgis / care of William Sturgis Esq. / Boston. *Postmark:* Providence R Jan 3. *Endorsed:* 1838.

1838] 183⟨7⟩8
till the next Saturday] till ↑ the next ↓ Saturday
I envy you] I envy ⟨ho⟩ you
reading it and] reading it ⟨through⟩ and
assurance not appearance, mind!] assurance ↑ not appearance, mind! ↓
perhaps in a few days] ↑ perhaps in a few days ↓

1. William Gardiner's *Music of Nature* (London, 1832) was published in Boston in 1838.

2. Maria Caterina Rosalbina Caradori-Allan (1800–1865), daughter of an Alsatian nobleman, made her debut in *Le nozze di Figaro* in 1822. Madame Caradori had her greatest successes as a concert singer, though she did continue to sing operatic works. The Boston newspapers announced her "final concert" for 2 January 1838 (*Grove's Dictionary*; *Quarterly Magazine of Music* 7 [September 1825]:347–50).

3. Richard Whately's *Elements of Rhetoric* (London, 1828) had been published in Boston in 1832. Whately (1787–1863), formerly professor of political economy at Oxford, was appointed archbishop of Dublin in 1831 (*DNB*).

4. Her students are William Hague (1808–87), a Baptist minister; Henry Clay Whitaker (1818–87), a Brown graduate in 1838 (he read his poem "The Spirit of Romance" at the Brown University Exhibition on 2 December 1837); William Gammell (1812–89), assistant professor of rhetoric and English literature at Brown; Sarah Helen Power Whitman (1803–78), a poet who later was engaged to Edgar Allan Poe; and Rebecca Tillinghast (d. 1889), daughter of Joseph L. Tillinghast (1791–1844), a member of Congress (Hague and Whitaker: *Brown Historical Catalogue*; Whitaker: *Providence Journal*, 2 December 1837; Gammell: *Rhode Island Biographical Cyclopedia*, pp. 378–79; Snow et al., *Alphabetical Index*, vol. 8; Whitman: *NAW*; Tillinghast: Philadelphia Probate, 1889, no. 1365; *Rhode Island Biographical Cyclopedia*, p. 236).

5. Francis Wayland (1796–1865) was president of Brown from 1827 to 1855 (*DAB*).

6. From 1798 to 1800 Goethe collaborated with Hans Heinrich Meyer in publishing *Die Propyläen*, a periodical devoted to a classical point of view (*OCGL*). The book on language is unidentified.

7. John M. Vandenhoff (1790–1861), an English actor, was on an American tour (*DNB*). The critique Fuller mentions is probably the review in *Knickerbocker* 10 (December 1837):556, which praised Vandenhoff's performances in Shakespearian roles. Fuller's own notes on Vandenhoff were not published during her lifetime but appear in *Memoirs*, 1:187. She observed that he had "no inspiration, yet much taste."

8. Fuller refers to John Sullivan Dwight's translation of Schiller's "Lied von der Glocke." Dwight had reviewed Tennyson's *Poems* for the *Christian Examiner* 23 (January 1838):305–27. Fuller knew Alexandre Cesar Bombet's *Vies de Hayden, de Mozart, et de Métastase* in an English translation, *The Lives of Hayden and Mozart*, first published in London in 1818 and then in Providence in 1820. Bombet was one of the pseudonyms (Stendhal being the more famous) of Marie Henri Beyle (1783–1842). Fuller discussed the book at length in the *Dial* 2 (October 1841):148–203, observing that "though superficial, and in its attempts at criticism totally wanting in that precision which can only be given by a philosophical view of the subject, [it] is lively, informed by a true love for beauty, and free from exaggeration as to the traits of life which we must care for" (p. 154).

9. Elizabeth Caroline Grey, *De Lisle: or, the Distrustful Man* (London, 1828). *Village Belles* (London, 1833) was written anonymously by Anne Manning.

10. William Godwin, *St. Leon* (London, 1799).

11. Probably Mary Ann Perkins Cary (1798–1880), wife of Thomas Graves Cary (1791–1859), a lawyer, businessman, and man of letters (*CC*, 3 June 1820; Harvard archives; Mt. Auburn).

12. Jane Tuckerman.

172. To Caroline Sturgis

[14 February? 1838]
[Providence]

[   ] How flat, stale, and unprofitable are the Morisons &c^n near these really living beings?[1] I am not sure I should have behaved well the Bliss anti Holiness evening. I grow impatient and domineering— my liberty here will spoil my tact for the primmer timider sphere. 'Tis but a few evegs since I read the most daring passages in Faust to a coterie of Hannah Mores[2] who dared [   ] Mr Ripley gave me a most amusing acct in his letter of your beautiful courteous manners á present. I hope they will be in full bloom when I come. I shall write to Mrs R. when [   ] at present I do nothing [   ] [r]ather unwell, tired to death [   ]ing sparkling and frivolous— I am very glad nothing will interfere with my Jeanie's coming. I will write a letter to her about it when I get hers. [   ]

ALfr (MH: bMS Am 1221 [211]). *Addressed:* Miss Caroline / Care of W. *Postmark:* Providence R.I. Feb 14. *Endorsed:* Feb 1838.

Morisons &c] Morisons ↑ &c ↓

1. *Hamlet*, I.ii.133–34: "How [weary], stale, flat, and unprofitable / Seem to me all the uses of this world!" Morison is probably John Hopkins Morison (1808–96), who had graduated from Harvard in 1831 and from the Divinity School in 1835. Early in 1838 he was a private tutor in the New Bedford family of Robert Swain, who often entertained Sturgis on her vacation visits. In May 1838 Morison became minister at New Bedford (*Heralds*, 3:256–58).

2. Hannah More (1745–1833) was an English religious writer (*DNB*).

173. To Arthur B. Fuller

Providence 19th Feby 1838

My dear Arthur,

I was very glad to get your letter and meant to have answered it long since, but a press (*alas, not un*usual) of engagements has prevented. I have been the more sorry as it was, by far, the best letter I ever received from you. It really gave me a picture of your mind, and was every way gratifying to me, except in the penmanship, which is not yet what I would wish and that you had sealed it so that I lost a considerable part of it. You never need seal letters containing your most *awful secrets* at the sides: a letter, if properly folded is made perfectly secure by *one seal*, and those at the sides oblige the receiver to tear it all to bits before he or she can get at one line—

I wish you could see the journals of two dear little girls eleven years old[n] in my school. Their names are Ann Brown and Harriet Paine; they love one another like Bessie Bell and Mary Gray in the ballad.[1] They are just of a size, both lively as birds, affectionate gentle, ambitious in good works and knowledge. They encourage one another constantly to do right; they are rivals, but never jealous of one another. Harriet has the quickest intellect, Anna is the prettiest I have never had occasion to find fault with either and the forwardness of their minds has induced me to take both into my own reading class where they are associated with girls many years their elders. Particular pains do they take with their journals: these are written daily in a beautiful fair, round hand well composed, showing attention and memory well trained, and with many pleasing sallies of playfulness and some very interesting thoughts. Do thou likewise, my dear Arthur.

I rely with confidence on your assurances about yourself and venture to think of you always as going on in the way you think I would approve. You well know how much this must tend to make me happy. Perfect yourself as much as possible in Greek and Latin. They will be valuable to you[n] not less as a means than an end. But I hope you are receiving instruction in Arithmetic, Geography, and English composition, although you do not mention it.

Mother has been here more than a fortnight; her presence has, as you may well suppose been most agreeable to me. She says Lloyd is behaving (according to the report of his master) extremely well and appears as demure as possible. I have not heard from Richard lately. Eugene is well, by the way I hope you have recd some money sent you via him,[n] nearly a fortnight since. Ellen has been quite unwell with a cold. She studies hard and seems to have no time to write to you or to any one.

Let me hear from you soon. Adieu, my dear, and believe me always your very affectionate sister

S. M. FULLER.

ALS (MH: fMS Am 1086 [9:47]); MsC (MH: fMS Am 1086 [Works, 1:627–31]). Published in part in *WNC*, pp. 347–48. *Addressed:* Master Arthur B. Fuller / Leicester Academy, / Mass. *Postmark:* Providence R.I. Feb 20.

The address is not in Fuller's hand.
girls eleven years old] girls ↑ eleven years old ↓
valuable to you] valuable to ⟨them⟩ you
sent you via him] sent you ⟨by⟩ ↑ via ↓ him

1. "The Twa Lasses," a popular seventeenth-century Scottish ballad that tells of the deaths of two young women by the plague, appears in Charles Kirkpatrick Sharpe's *A Ballad Book* (Edinburgh, 1824). Ann Frances Brown (b. 1825), daughter of Hugh H. Brown, married the Reverend Darwin B. Cooley in 1857 ("The School Journal of Ann Frances Brown, 1836–39," RPB). Harriet Paine is not identified.

174. To Ralph Waldo Emerson

Providence 1st March 1838—

My dear friend,

Many a Zelterian epistle have I mentally addressed to you full of sprightly scraps about the books I have read,[n] the spectacles I have seen, and the attempts at men and women with whom I have come in contact. But I have not been able to put them on paper, for even when I have attempted it, you have seemed so busy and noble, and I so poor and dissipated that I have not felt worthy to address you.

At present I am not at all Zelterian in my mood but very sombre and sullen. I have shut the door for a few days and tried to do something— You have *really* been doing something! And that is why I write— I want to see you and still more to hear you. I must kindle my torch again. Why have I not heard you this winter? I feel very humble just now yet I dare to say that being lives not who would have received from your lectures as much as I should. There are noble books but one wants the breath of life sometimes. And I see no divine person. I myself am more divine than any I see— I think that is enough to say about them— I know Dr Wayland now, but I shall not care for him. He would never understand me, and, if I met him, it must be by those means of suppression and accommodation which I at present hate to my hearts core. I hate every-thing that is reasonable just now, "wise limitations" and all. I have behaved much too well for some time past; it has spoiled my peace. What grieves me too is to find or fear[n] my theory a cheat— I cannot serve two masters, and I fear all the hope of being a worldling and a literary existence also must be resigned— Isolation is necessary to me as to others. Yet I keep on "fulfilling all my duties" as the technical phrase is except to myself.— But why do I write thus to you who like nothing but what is good i e cheerfulness and fortitude? It is partly because yours is an image of my oratory. I suppose you will not know what this means. and if I do not jest when I write to you I must *pray*. And partly as a preliminary to asking you, unsympathizing, unhelpful, wise good

327

man that you are to do several things for me. I hear you are to deliver one of your lectures again in Boston. I would have you do it while I am there. I shall come on Wednesday next and stay till the following Monda Perhaps you will come to see me, fo though I am not as good as I was, yet as I said before, I am better than most persons *I* see and, I dare say, better than most persons *you* see. But perhaps you do not need to see anybody, for you are acting and nobly— If so you need not come yourself, but send me your two lectures on Holiness and Heroism to read while in Boston. Let me have these two lectures to read *at any rate*, whether you come or no. Do not disappoint me. I will treat them well and return them safe. I shall be at Mr Sturgis's all the time. I shall come out on Thursday to hear you at Cambridge, but they wrote me that lecture would be on the Heart and not so fine as some of yours.[1]

I have not read any books except what every body reads, Gardiner on Music (thank *you* for that; it was a great deal to me.) Carlyle as noble as I hoped, absorbing me quite for a fortnight, Lamb's letters, Whately's Rhetoric.[2]

Lately I have been amusing myself with looking at you through two pair of spectacles of very dissimilar construction in Brownson's review and the Democratic.[3] I have a disciple of yours in my German class— a very lovely young man. He has never seen you but gets regular bulletins of you from some friend in Boston— I suppose I could get them animated into inviting you to speak to the Larvae here if you would come. Several gentlemen promised me their aid, if there was a chance of getting you. Adieu Sanctissime. Tell Lidian that the thought of her holiness is very fragrant to me. Tell your son that if he has grown less like Raphael's cherubs I will never forgive him. Tell my dear Elizabeth that I love her just as I did last August, but shall probably never write to her—

Devoutly if not worthily yours

S. M. FULLER.

ALS (MH: bMS Am 1280 [2341]); MsCfr (MB: Ms. Am. 1450 [76]). Published in part in Higginson, *MFO*, pp. 89–91. *Addressed:* Revd. R. W. Emerson, / Concord / Mass. *Postmark:* Providence R I Mar 2. *Endorsed:* Miss S. M. Fuller / Feb. 1838.

I have read] I ↑ have ↓ read
find or fear] find ↑ or fear ↓
in my German] in my ↑ German ↓

1. Emerson's lecture in Boston was "War," read before the American Peace Society on Wednesday, 12 March, the day Fuller had planned to leave, but in his journal Emerson mentions a meeting with her on the thirteenth (*JMN*, 5:462; William Charvat, "A Chronological List of Emerson's American Lecture Engagements," *Bulletin of the*

New York Public Library 64 [September 1960]:502). Emerson's "Heart," originally the fifth lecture of his "Human Culture" series, opened the Cambridge lectures on 8 March. "Heroism" and "Holiness" were the eighth and ninth, respectively, of the series (*Emerson Lectures*, 2:204–364).

2. Emerson had been quite taken with William Gardiner's *Music of Nature* (*JMN*, 5:421, 432–33). Presumably Fuller was still reading Carlyle's *French Revolution*. Thomas Noon Talfourd edited *The Letters of Charles Lamb* (London, 1837).

3. Orestes Brownson (1803–76) was a mercurial intellectual whose religious beliefs began in Universalism and ended in Catholicism; his early radical politics gave way to a pronounced conservatism. In the fall of 1837 he laid plans for a magazine, *The Boston Quarterly Review*, which he edited from January 1838 to October 1842 (*DAB*). In the first issue of the magazine he reviewed Emerson's Phi Beta Kappa address, praising the "manly spirit" but deploring the style that kept Emerson aloof from the common people. The second review Fuller mentions, "Nature—A Prose Poem," *United States Magazine and Democratic Review* 1 (February 1838):319–29, called Emerson's book "a divine Thought, borne on a stream of 'English undefiled.'" Margaret Neussendorfer has conclusively identified this review as being by Elizabeth Peabody.

175. To Abraham W. Fuller

Providence 26th March
1838—

A. W. Fuller Esq.

Dear Sir,

A sudden emergency induces me to apply to you for money, although it had not been my intention to take money at present from the family fund.

When I last recd money from you, you told me, I think, that I had recd 600$ and— from my patrimony. I did not at that time take a note of the precise sum. I wish now that you would advance as much as makes my receipt amount to 700$

I cannot give an order for the sum as I do not know exactly what it is but my brother will give his note for me and I will settle with him.

That there may be no misunderstanding, I wish to say that it is not my intention to replace this money, but that it is my hope not to need more, while in health to take care of myself. I shall, however, make no promises, as accidents, like the present, may occur again.

Let me entreat you, by the warm love my father bore you, to smooth as much as possible the way for my mother now in the step she contemplates.[n] I know you are not partial to us children (though I have heard you showed the kindest sympathy for my brother William in the difficulties he brought upon himself) but my Mother deserves your regard for the light in which she has always viewed you. If you had left one dear to you to my Father's care, he would not merely have managed her affairs honorably, but acted the part of a sympathizing friend. Perhaps our affairs will be less troublesome to you after the family are removed hither. If I live and am well I assure you I will try to make them so— With much respect your Niece

S. M. FULLER—

ALS (MH: fMS Am 1086 [9:48]). *Endorsed:* Sarah M. Fuller / 29. March 1838 / Pr Eugene Fuller / Former letter / 20. March 1837.

now in the step she contemplates] now ↑ in the step she contemplates ↓

176.   To Caroline Sturgis

Providence 17th April [1838]

My dear Cary,

I suppose you have never read Goethe's Prometheus[1] Here is a bit of it— You will see how the old Greeks felt sometimes, for even they knew the agonies of blight and imperfect development.

> I know nothing poorer
> Under the sun than you, ye Gods,
> You pitifully nourish
>   Your majesty
> With hecatombs of victims
> And the breath of prayers,
> And would perish were not
> Children and beggars
> Fools full of hope.
>
> When I was a child,
> Knew not my way out or in,
> Perplexed I turned my eye
> To the Sun, as if there would be
> An Ear to hear my moans,
> A Heart such as mine is
> Ready to pity those who suffer.
>
> Who was it that helped one
> Against the arrogant fury of the Titans,
> Who saved me from death

330

From Slavery?
Didst thou not all thyself accomplish
My religious-glowing heart?
And in thy youthful glow of goodness
Didst thou not, cheated, offer thanks
To the sleepers there above.

I honor *Thee*, Zeus!— Why?—
Hast thou ever softened the pangs
Of the heavy-laden?
Hast thou ever[n] dried the tears
Of the sorrowing?
Has not to manhood forged me
Allpowerful Time,
And eternal Destiny,
My lords and thine?—

And didst thou dream, perhaps
I would hate[n] life,
Fly to the desert
Because not all
Flower-dreams bore fruit.

Here I sit, form men
In mine own image,
A race who shall be like me
To suffer, to weep
To enjoy, and to rejoice
And heed Thy power as little
As I.—

Which of us has not felt the questionings expressed in this bold[n] fragment— Does it not seem, were we Gods or could[n] steal their fire! we
would make men not only happier, *so* much happier, but "free, glorious"— Yes, my life is "strange" thine is strange.— We are, we shall be
in this life mutilated beings, but there is in my bosom a faith that I
shall sometime see the reason. There is in my bosom a glory that I can
endure to be so imperfect, (God forbid that I should ever sink into
the stupid blindness of so many as to the imperfections) the hateful
imperfections of our lot.) And there is a motive, a feeling ever elastic
that Fate and Time shall have all the shame and all the blame if I am
mutilated. I will do all *I* can— will not you?— And if one cannot
succeed, there is a beauty in martyrdom.—

331

Poor Sue— Since she has a "change of heart" how I do wish I could take her for one year.[2] But it may not be—

I thank you for the acct of your visit. It gave me much pleasure. Never fear to write too long letters for me. I did not like your letters always; they were too unnatural; but now they are excellent.— I did not feel so much that you *expected* confidence as that you might *wish* it; and a wish from you is a claim.— and I could not begin anew and write at my ease till I had put in a protest. I did not know I had repaired from you; But I take my natural position always, and the more I see, the more I feel that it is regal.— Without throne, sceptre, or guards, still a queen!— I shall not, of course, think about it, but let things take their natural course. You need not know the works of Alfieri to enjoy such a character. His works are only the ebb to the flow of his life. Cellini was a statuary and carver in gems. I mentioned them both as being great and strong natures who swept away life with the force of the cataract [   ]

The Titans are the lower passions— They dared to attempt to scale with ladders those serene heights where dwell the gods. But they are crushed, scathed with thunderbolts, and lie imprisoned beneath mountains of *matter*. Still they have power to cause volcanoes in the fairest scenes.— [   ]

ALfr (ViU); MsC (MH: fMS Am 1086 [Works, 3:253–61]). Published in part in *Memoirs*, 1:235, and *Jahrbuch für Amerikastudien* 12 (1967):240–45. *Endorsed:* 12th April 1838.

thou ever] thou ↑ever↓
I would hate] I would ⟨have⟩ hate
in this bold] in ⟨these⟩ this bold
Gods or could] Gods ⟨and⟩ or could

1. Written in 1774, Goethe's poem "Prometheus" was published without permission by F. H. Jacobi in *Über die Lehre des Spinoza* (Breslau, 1785). Goethe's fragmentary drama "Prometheus" was published in 1830 (*OCGL*). Fuller here translates all but the opening and closing stanzas of the poem.
2. Probably Susan Sturgis, Caroline's sister.

177. To Thesta Dana

Providence May 30th 1838—

My dear Thesta,

I must scribble a few lines in reply to your affectionate letter recd yesterday, though this is the last day of my term, and I have every thing to do as I go to Boston early tomorrow morng.— It will not be possible for me to come to Plymouth. I shd like it much especially when the Ripleys are added to the other attractions, but my short vacation is all portioned out.— If Martha is at Warwick I hope you will come here this summer and give me a chance to talk with you.[1] Without knowing more fully your situation and feelings at present, I cannot judge of your plans; but as far as I do know I should say the one you mention (of going to the South) was not desirable or necessary— I hope you will take a journey and under favorable auspices.— Niagara *I* shd prefer to all others— I had a very good time at N. Bedford the last day and eveg when I was a little better, and the journey has done me good.— My health, however, is in a bad state.— Mother will not come to me till autumn, if she can then.— The Grinnells will tell you all about me which I have not time to write.—[2] Any attention you may have it in your power to show them, while in Plymouth, would oblige me as much as if paid to myself.— Mrs G. is one of the most amiable beings I have ever known and Ellen is one of my favorites— Mary Manton, too, may go with them; she is a pretty girl and one whom I love.—[3]

I thank you, dear Thesta; for the book you promise which is one I should particularly like— Please give my best regards to your sister, Miss Russell, and Mr Sever, I wish you would write me some acct of the girls who are coming to our school.[4] Is this letter worse or better than nothing?—

Yours with unchanged affection

S. M. FULLER—

ALS (CtY). *Addressed:* Miss Thesta Dana, / Kingston near Plymouth. / Mass— / Miss Grinnell.

1. Martha Barrett Dana, Thesta's sister, who had married George S. Greene in 1837 (*GVR; Dana Family*, p. 309).

2. Perhaps William Taylor (1815–81) and Abigail Barrell Grinnell (1817–50) of Providence, but the reference to Ellen suggests another Grinnell family (Charles H. Farnam, *History of the Descendants of John Whitman of Weymouth, Massachusetts* [New Haven, 1889], p. 363; *Boston Evening Transcript*, 12 July 1881).

3. Perhaps Mary W. Manton (b. 1822), daughter of Joseph and Mary Whipple Manton (William W. Chapin, "The Descendants of Daniel Manton," RHi, p. 6).

4. Ann Dana Sever; Miss Russell may be Lydia Cushing Russell (1817–81), daughter of the Honorable Thomas Russell (1788–1854) and Mary Ann Goodwin Russell of Plymouth. Lydia married Thomas Whiting (1813–73) of Concord in 1840. Mr. Sever is John Sever, Thesta Dana's brother-in-law (Davis, *Ancient Landmarks*, pp. 223–24; *Plymouth Church Records*, pp. 614, 692, 702; Waldo Higginson, *Memorials of the Class of 1833 of Harvard College* [Cambridge, Mass., 1883], p. 57; Whiting, *Memoir*, p. 247; *GVR*).

178. To Arthur B., Richard F., and Lloyd Fuller

Providence 28th[n] June
1838—

To Arthur, Richard and Lloyd,

Dear Boys,

I thought I would try and write you some account of the French frigate before the picture faded in my memory though both my head and hand are rather tired tonight.[1]

We set out at eight in the morng in the Kingston, a small steamer. There had been a sham-fight the day before at Newport which had attracted crowds so[n] we were less troubled this day[n] than we otherwise should have been.— When we came in sight the vessels looked finely as they lay full rigged and mounted between us and the bright blue sky.— The Fallriver steamer had just drawn up on the other side of the Hercules as the big ship was named (this steamer is called the King Philip, after the famous sachem of Mount Hope)[2] The sail boats and barges flew about merrily. One of the barges with sixteen rowers looked so pretty moving as regularly as if it had really been a fish. The men took in the ladies with the utmost care and then sat, waving their oars in the air with a regular pulsation like that of the heart, till the word was given. Allons—[n] then a simultaneous dash of the oars followed of exquisite[n] precision— Usually ladies are taken up in chairs[n] from these barges into the ship, whose sides are as high out of the water as the house at Groton. The[n] French had regular stairs but as these were very steep, they were manned with sailors who passed along each lady with airs[n] and graces *beautious* to behold and not less *wondrous* to one accustomed to the simple American Jack Tar.

The Hercules is, I believe pierced for a hundred and twelve guns and carries eighty. Many who liked were allowed to try how easily they may be fired; a mere[n] touch does it. On the upper deck are the apartments[n] of the prince and officers. The prince is the third son of Louis Philippe and now about nineteen.[3] He has served regularly as a midshipman and has lately been promoted.

His apartments consist of[n] a quite large parlour prettily furnished, a dressing room; the apparatus all white china with the crown gilt, and cut glass, elegant but very simple, and a bed-room just large eno' for a French bedstead and a case for wearing apparel, or papers.

Close to his is the officers dining room a tolerably handsome room. Their dinner service was neat, no more— A balcony runs about these rooms. I think the prince must greatly enjoy going out at sunset or on beautiful moonlight evegs and standing or walking there alone, while this mighty vessel is dashing through the waters leaving a broad[n] and sparkling wake for him to watch. I thought I should much like to command such a vessel, despite all the hardships and privations of such a situation. We visited three decks below where we saw the officers bedrooms, the kitchen where every thing is cooked with great convenience on furnaces, the sailors dining room. Their little tables are fastened up to the roof when they are not using them,—the magazine, the armoury where was a brilliant display of boarding cutlasses; and many things I have not room I see to detail.

The crew is a picked one of near a thousand men, and they are, indeed a fine-looking set of men, and so polite I wish you could take lessons from them. The fencing master and the dancing master were giving lessons on deck though the crowd was immense. Forty little boys, I understood were there receiving a naval education. One, about nine, is the prince's page.

They had on board a tame lion, a tame bear, parroquets and a fawn, a most lovely little creature.

I have not had room to say half I intended, but shall expect a letter from one of you in answer.

    your affectionate sister

S. M. FULLER.

ALS (MH: fMS Am 1086 [9:49]); MsC (MH: fMS Am 1086 [Works, 1:631–37]). *Addressed:* Arthur B. Fuller. / Groton. / Mass. *Postmark:* Providence R.I. Jun 29.

    Providence 28th] Providence 2⟨9⟩8th
crowds so] crowds ⟨the day b⟩ so
troubled this day] troubled ↑ this day ↓
Allons] Allo⟨?⟩ns
of exquisite] of exq⟨?⟩uisite
taken up in chairs] taken up ↑ in chairs ↓
Groton. The] Groton.⟨but⟩ The
each lady with airs] each lady⟨s⟩ with airs
a mere] a ↑ mere ↓
are the apartments] are the ap⟨p⟩artments
apartments consist of] apartments ⟨are⟩ ↑ consist of ↓
leaving a broad] leaving a bro⟨d⟩ad

1. The French ship *Hercule* arrived at Newport on 8 June and remained until the twenty-second. It was a popular attraction, drawing an excursion boat up from New York to participate in the "entertainment given on board," according to a contemporary newspaper account (*Providence Journal*, 23 June 1838).

2. King Philip, son of Massassoit, assumed leadership of the Wampanoag tribe in 1662 and began to fight the English in 1675. After initial successes, he was driven back to Bristol's Mount Hope, where he was killed (*DAB*).

3. François, duc de Joinville (1818–1900), later became rear admiral in the French navy. He fled to England after the revolution of 1848, then served on the staff of General George McClellan in the American Civil War (T. E. B. Howarth, *Citizen-King: The Life of Louis-Philippe, King of the French* [London, 1961], pp. 134, 276, 336).

179. To Ralph Waldo Emerson

[July? 1838?]
[Providence?]

Mr Alcott's thoughts

There is no God except Spirit. Most men consider this belief impious and worship a mangod whom they can press to "the bosom of daily experience" Yet God, heaven are independent of space and time, and if they be discerned at all must be spiritually discerned.

The Soul also is spirit and its[n] health or salvation lies in its power of discernment.

All spirit is subject to law which only spirit can apprehend. And why the gropings of earthly experience were ever substituted for the natural mode of intuition I, for one, do not perceive. Yet, seeing that thought is for some reason expressed emblematically, I pay the debt of humanity and strive to read the emblems.

The workings of Divinity in human nature correspond with its manifestations in external nature. But man understands best when spoken to directly and has called that kind of communication which he has had through other men Revelation, though in fact it is no more so than the lowest whisper of Thought in the moving leaf.

Matter as far as I can perceive is an accident. I do not like it and always put it out of my way as much as possible. Historically I admit its existence. But it surely cannot be a necessary means of education to the soul. Let the soul cast aside this film as early as possible.

The idea of Father, Mother, Child, I comprehend. I do not indeed see the aim of this trinitarianism and my own nature is always leading me back to unity. Yet I see and enjoy the *mode of its operation*. In like manner, though theoretically nothing suits me but the Holy Ghost, yet practically I find the idea[n] of a Redeemer or Reformer very significant and should like to express it in action.—
My dear Friend,

Although I cannot recall any valuable thoughts of Mr Alcott's except those I have here noted down, yet I see that this is a very unfair mode of stating them.[1] Such a paper should be headed Confession of Faith or Plan of the Universe and should stretch out to a much greater extent. For, as you will say—nothing here is distinctive of Mr A.; and his lively perception of spiritual[n] existences and the piety of renunciation deserve to be sharply marked.

I see I have been impertinent (as I so often am,) in saying I would put his thoughts on a page— I wrote a long paper about them and[n] this is only the summing up.

—By and by I will give his synthesis in such shape as shall grow out of the occasion and not out of a pledge and then I shall be fair. Meanwhile, please tell me what you find to add to the indications in this paper.

Far more impertinent was I in promising a schedule[n] of your mental furniture. For though you do not take a more elevated view of Man and his destiny than Mr A. as, indeed, who could?— You have a thousandfold more organs by which to make acquaintance with the subject. I should divide my inventory in this way.

> Truth the primary law.—
> The Universal Mind the only legitimate existence
> Love of the intellect for dualism and
> Desire of the spirit to suppress it.

But I should need to make a very ample sketch to give any idea how the lesser thoughts radiate from these points

—If you are not ashamed of me for writing this letter I may attempt it some good day like this breezy one, only more leisurely, for I am threatened with an engagement in a quarter of an hour.

Have you read our friend Mr Bowen's Berkeley?— Dont you think Mr Bartold's Carlyle much better than yours?[2]

Give my love to the ladies and the cherub. Be kind and write to me, indeed—indeed I will try not to be impertinent about philosophers again. I send some of Cary's letters but[n] they must be kept for your own reading *exclusively* and returned when I see you next—

Always yours

S. M. F.—

ALS (MH: bMS Am 1280 [2340]). *Addressed:* Rev. R. W. Emerson.

and its] and ⟨her⟩ ↑ its ↓
I find the idea] I find ⟨that⟩ ↑ the idea ↓
perception of spiritual] perception of ⟨of⟩ spiritual
about them and] about ⟨it⟩ ↑ them ↓ and
promising a schedule] promising a ⟨?⟩schedule
Cary's letters but] Cary's ↑ letters ↓ but

1. Fuller is responding to Emerson's letter of 28 June, in which he said, "Send me I entreat you Mr Alcotts List of thoughts; and mine: Our *Thus far no farther*" (Rusk, *Letters of RWE*, 2:143).

2. "The Works of George Berkeley, D.D., Bishop of Cloyne," *Christian Examiner* 24 (July 1838):310–45, was signed "F.B." Francis Bowen (1811–90) later published his essay as *Berkeley and His Philosophy* (Cambridge, Mass., 1838). Bowen graduated from Harvard in 1833, taught there, and edited the *North American Review* from 1843 to 1853. A conservative student of philosophy, he frequently attacked the Transcendentalists (*DAB*). Cyrus Augustus Bartol (1813–1900), however, was a follower of Emerson. He was graduated from Bowdoin in 1832 and from the Harvard Divinity School in

1835, and served as minister at Boston's West Church from 1837 to 1889 (*DAB*). The same issue of the *Examiner* (pp. 342–62) carried his review of Carlyle's *French Revolution.*

180. To Caroline Sturgis

Providence—[24?] July 1838—

Your letter, my dear Cary, deserved an immediate answer, but I can hardly prevail on myself to write even at this late date. In that cool place where you have been so fortunate as to pass this excessively hot weather you can have no idea how I have suffered. The thermometer has been at ninety and ninety three many days when I have walked a mile and a half from my school home. And I walk in same distance in morng[n] Repeatedly I have been wrought up almost to frenzy by the heat— I have been obliged to sit down and cry a long while after I got there to relieve myself and repeat the process on returning home.

Home! Oh Cary, my extreme weakness has made me feel so homeless, so forlorn! at such times I have felt so much the need of somebody to bring me strengthening drinks, or to bathe my head. However I shall drag through somehow,[n] I suppose.— In many respects I am more fortunate than heretofore. I suffer no violent pain, I have an appetite— the country is very lovely round me and though I rarely feel able to take walks, I look out of my window with great satisfaction and watch the afternoon lights and shades. I do not attempt to do any thing unless I am obliged. I know what a terrible weight of business must come on me by and by to pay[n] for all this inertia, but I cannot help it. This is the first time I have really felt so utterly incompetent to do any thing. I do wish I could yield entirely to this languour. I wish I could lean on some friendly arm for a while It cannot be. I cannot even neglect my friends with impunity, for, if I do they will not write to me.— You have not written again, though you have nothing to do, and are in a cool atmosphere. I had, some fortnight since a long letter from Mr Emerson I will show it you sometime. He says he had some two hours or more of good talk with you "*which is much.*" The address is to be printed— I did not go down to hear.[1] I could not have made such an exertion at any rate, but Mrs Cumming was with me then.[2] She plays with as much genius as ever. I will take you to hear her if I have an oppory. But shall you not stay in your fairy home through August. I do not think I shall go to New-bury with you, though I often long to see that river. But I do not need beauty so much now for I have had it this summer. And I may have no more days at Groton. W. Channing (Revd) is staying at Moth-er's now but I suppose he will be gone long[n] before I return.

There is a seat on the top of this house and I was very happy there last moon. I used to go up there and watch the sunset, and the moon till twelve o'clock It lights up the distant river here and there. One night was magnifique thunder clouds in the west rent every moment by the most Pandemonic lightning I ever saw, and the moon riding opposite on her car of clouds, with the full look of peace and love. Then sailed immense black clouds, fishshaped, portentous, slowly over to her,[n] but she quenched their ill intent and made them pearly and lustrous by her glance.— I wish you had been here. I wish you were here to night. I could talk. But you see I cannot write letters. Thank me for this nothing and write to me dear Cary. O—if you knew how I have been perplexed worldly ways. I sometimes think I will not kill myself in Providence at any rate— does not Mr Morrison want somebody to help him "do good" at N. B. I should like to do good and stay at Nashon too. Or if I had one friend here to me like what I suppose Mr Swain is to Mr M. it were well for me.[3] Write soon again, thy last letter was good. S. W. has returned to Boston.[4] I do not like to write even to him; think how indolent I must be.

M.

ALS (MH: bMS Am 1221 [212]). *Addressed:* Miss Caroline Sturgis, / care of Wm Swain Esq. / New Bedford / Mass— *Postmark:* Providence R.I. Jul 25. *Endorsed:* July 1838.

school home. And I walk in same distance in morng] school ↑ home. And I walk in same distance in morng ↓

drag through somehow] drag through some⟨w⟩how

by and by to pay] by and by ↑ to pay ↓

he will be gone long] he will be gone ⟨when⟩ long

slowly over to her] slowly over to ⟨you⟩ her

1. Emerson's letter of 28 June mentions his visit with Sturgis (Rusk, *Letters of RWE*, 2:143). The address probably was "Heroism," the concluding lecture in the "Human Culture" series Emerson gave in Concord from 18 April to 13 June. If Fuller, who was in the Boston area on that date, had been with her family in Groton, she declined the chance to go "down" to Concord to hear the lecture, which presumably she had already read in manuscript (see letter 174).

2. Elizabeth Randall Cumming.

3. Robert Swain (1819–44), son of William Swain of New Bedford (New Bedford VR). Lying off the coast at New Bedford, Naushon Island was owned by the Bowdoin family. In 1843 William Sturgis, acting as the purchasing agent, bought it for William Swain and John Murray Forbes (Amelia Forbes Emerson, *Early History of Naushon Island* [Boston, 1935], p. 82).

4. Samuel G. Ward.

181.   To Ralph Waldo Emerson

[13 August 1838]
Monday—
[Boston]

My dear friend,

If I should pass through Concord, would it be agreeable to Lidian and yourself that I shd come on Wednesday P. M. stay at your mansion that night and go on to Groton Thursday morng.— Say just as it is, for if not convenient I shall go by the way of Lowell, and perhaps I shall not be able to come at any rate, but I suppose your Concord stage man will bring a note tomorrow aftn to say whether you will let me come if I can. I am staying at my uncle's No. 2. Avon place but shall be out at Brookline during the day—¹ (tomorrow)ⁿ

In real haste

S. M. FULLER.

ALS (TxU). *Addressed:* Revd R. W. Emerson. / Concord. / Mass. *Endorsed:* Miss Margaret Fuller / Aug 1838 / Medford / [?] / Aug 13.

the day—(tomorrow)] the day— ↑ (tomorrow) ↓

1. Fuller, who was staying with her uncle Henry H. Fuller, visited the Emersons on 15 and 16 August on her way from Boston to Groton.

182.   To Lidian J. Emerson

[19 August 1838]
Sunday morng—
[Groton]

Dear Lidian,

Fret not that kindest heart because of my evil doing. Your remark was rather the occasion than the cause for any pain I felt. I was in a state of weak sensitiveness while at your house, which I probably shall not get free from till I have enjoyed for some time the benefits of seclusion and repose.

I trust and believe that you will always show your esteem for me by the same freedom you have formerly used. I, on my side, should cease to come, if I could not speak and act as naturally as I always have. But there is no fear of that, I think.

I shall write to Mr F. and will make the desired inquiries about

Sophia—[1] I shall, however, probably leave Providence at the end of next term.— I wish I could feel more joy at the prospect of escape from uncongenial pursuits and the oppressive intercourse with vulgar minds. But I cease[n] from a noble effort to consult my own health and feelings. I have done[n] and suffered much without attaining my object, or removing one evil which formerly afflicted me, and I cannot be joyful.

I hope the little charmer is better It was sad to see a cloud on him. With affectionate remembrance to your goodly company I am yours as ever

S. M. Fuller.

ALS (MH: bMS Am 1280.226 [3909]). *Addressed:* Mrs Lidian Emerson, / care of R. W. Emerson / Concord, / Mass. *Postmark:* Groton MS Aug 19.

But I cease] But ⟨I feel that⟩ I cease
I have done] ⟨that⟩ I have done

1. Sophia Brown (1821–42), daughter of Charles and Lucy Jackson Brown of Plymouth, was Lidian Emerson's niece. Fuller was clearly trying to arrange a position for Sophia at Hiram Fuller's school, but in a letter of 1 September, Lidian reported that her niece would not be able to go to Providence (Davis, *Ancient Landmarks*, p. 45; *Plymouth Church Records*; Rusk, *Letters of RWE*, 2:155).

183. To Jane F. Tuckerman

Providence, September 21. 1838.

I have more beautiful letters from Cary. This summer has indeed been halcyon, and will be hallowed to her. The Swains must be the most rational people in existence.

I had excellent times at home, with my own soul, and excellent times with Mr Emerson, seeing his shine out through all this fog. I have fine friends certainly; how dignified they look, while dirt is being thrown at them![1]

I staid with Mrs Ripley at Waltham.[2] I admire her. So womanly, so manly, so childlike, so human! She is as unfettered as we, yet very *wise*.

That day at Brookline was very pleasant. Frank was highly ornamental.[3] By sunset light weaving oak garlands beneath an old tree, and in the morning before breakfast, glittering in the purple bloom of youth, he was a sight for sair een.

I have found a new young man, very interesting, a character of monastic beauty, a religious love for what is best in Nature and books.[4]

And I have a new friend, a gentleman not young, but noble in form and mind, and more rich in intellect than any person I have known since Mr Emerson.

I had a most delightful time on the Island.[5] Such cloudless sunsets, with floods of rose and amber light; such overpowering moonlight, such wood walks, such beach walks, and all with proper people. Are you not glad? I leave Providence in December.

MsCfr (MH: fMS Am 1086 [Works, 1:89–91]).

1. On 15 July, when Emerson addressed the senior class of the Divinity School, he made his most famous and controversial public statement about historical Christianity. The ensuing controversy continued for months in the press and among the Boston clergy. The published address was advertised for sale on 25 August 1838.

2. Sarah Alden Bradford Ripley.

3. Probably Jane's brother John Francis Tuckerman (1817–85), a Harvard graduate in 1837. In 1847 he married Lucy Saltonstall (*Tuckerman Family*, pp. 61–62).

4. Almost certainly Charles King Newcomb (1820–94), son of Henry Stearns (1788?–1825?) and Rhoda Mardenbrough Newcomb (1791–1865) of Providence. Young Newcomb graduated from Brown in 1837, tried his hand at writing, and spent some time at Brook Farm, where he was noted for his love of incense and ritualistic devotions. Later he became a businessman in Providence. He published "The Two Dolons" in the *Dial*, but despite the support of both Fuller and Emerson, he never became a serious writer. George Curtis gave an unflattering picture of him to George Willis Cooke: "He was slight in person, awkward, and slouchy in gait, and was never taken very seriously by any body [at Brook Farm]" (John Bearse Newcomb, *Genealogical Memoir of the Newcomb Family* [Elgin, Ill., 1874], p. 490; *Brown Historical Catalogue*; Curtis to Cooke, 9 June 1882, MHarF).

5. The "island" is Newport.

184. To Charles K. Newcomb

Sept 27th Eveg [1838?]

Dear Charles,

I received your letter so full of affection and faith. I am not indeed unmindful as I seem. But at Newport, I could not, and since I would not write, for all the little imps of care are round me and I must catch and cage them, before I can feel ready to meet you again Yet I think it will not now be many days before you get a full utterance from your friend

MARGARET.

Write to me, if you will; it gives pleasure.

ALS (MH: fMS Am 1086 [10:130]). *Addressed:* Charles K. Newcomb / Providence / R.I.

185. To Almira P. Barlow

Providence, October 1838.

I have four maidens in the house now under my care, and have, and shall have till December, when I go away, a crowd of engagements, or perhaps I should have written to you sooner; but now I pen no superfluous line.

MsCfr (MH: fMS Am 1086 [Works, 1:23]).

186. To Caroline Sturgis

Oct. 1838
[Providence]

My museum is so well-furnished that I grow lazy about collecting new specimens of human nature.

MsCfr (MH: bMS Am 1280 [111, p. 16]). Published in *Memoirs*, 1:286, and *JMN*, 11:461.

187. To Mary ———

Sunday—
Providence 7th Octr 1838—

My Mary;

Your birth-day comes tomorrow, but lest I should not have time *then*, I write today.

And first about Lilly. Please say to your Aunt that she is to be transferred to a larger room in a day or two. I believe she is comfortable, and she has been well, but at present she has a bad cold. I would not have your Mother sanguine as to what I can do for her.[1] She is a pleasant child whom all common people like, and with their approbation she is content. She is, I think, peculiarly callous and self-satisfied. I never saw a child whom it was so difficult to put to the blush. I have acquired no real influence over her, for there seems to be neither enthusiasm nor sense[n] of shame to address one'self to. But she is perfectly docile and amiable. She tries to please me, but that is all; she has no earnestness in her about improving herself. Her music lessons are a fair sample of her proceedings. She sits at the piano just as long as I bid her, and no moment longer, and practices in an indolent way that does her no good. I suppose all she learns is while the music master is with her. If I said the word she would practice four times as much and with no more results. I think your mother undervalued her habits of observation. She sees and has seen every thing before her, but there is no depth in her observations, she looks at the outside of things, and never inquires into their causes or connection. My present impression is that she will never excel in any thing or think and feel deeply, but may be formed into an amiable domestic woman. New sides may turn up, but all I have yet seen is of a piece. However she is as well situated here as any where and at the end of the autumn I shall be able to pronounce upon her more decidedly.— I believe her father need not be afraid of her getting excited. She likes S. Whipple because she is pretty, and I fancy that is all she thinks about her.[2] But I will take care of her, in these respects—

For yourself, dear Mary, you have indeed attained an important age. No plan is desirable for you which is to be pursued with precision. The world, the events of every day which no one can predict are to be your teachers, and you must in some degree give yourself up and submit to be led captive if you would learn from them. Principle must be at the helm but thought must shift its direction with the winds and the waves.

Happy as you are thus far in worthy friends, you are not in much danger of rash intimacies or great errors. I think, upon the whole, quite highly of your judgement about people and conduct; though your first feelings are often extravagant, they are soon balanced.

I do not know other faults in you beside that want of retirement of mind which I have before spoken of If Marianne and Caroline want too much seclusion, and are too severe in their views of life and man, I think you are too little so.[3] There is nothing so fatal to the finer faculties as too ready or too extended a publicity, there is danger lest there be no real religion in the heart which craves too much of daily sympathy. Through your mind the stream of life has coursed with

344

such rapidity that it often swept away the seed, or loosened the roots of the young plants before they had ripened any fruit.—

I should think writing would be very good for you. A journal of your thoughts and analyses[n] of your thoughts would teach you how to generalize, and give firmness to your conclusions. Do not write down merely your impressions that things are beautiful or the reverse, but what they are and why they are. And show these papers at least at present to nobody. Be your own judge and your own helper. Do not go soon to any one with your difficu[l]ties Try to clear them up for yourself.

I think the course of reading you have fallen upon of[n] late will be better for you than such books as you have read addressed rather to the taste and the imagination than the judgement. The love of beauty has rather an undue development in your mind See now what is and has been, sift the Real, then return to the Ideal.

I should think two or three hours a day were quite enough at present for you to give to books. Now learn buying and selling, keeping the house, managing the servants, all that will bring you worlds of wisdom if you will only keep it subordinate to the one grand [ai]m of perfecting the whole being. And let your self respect forbid you to do imperfectly any thing that you do at all.

I always feel ashamed when I write with this air of wisdom, but you see, my Mary, by these hints what I think. Your mind wants depth and precision, your character condensation. Keep your high aim steadily in view, life will open, the paths to reach it I think Marianne even if she be in excess is an excellent friend for you. Her character seems to have what yours wants, and her aim, whether she has found the way or not the true one.

My plans for the winter are yet undecided, perhaps I shall be in Boston, if so, and you choose me for one of your preachers, I dare say I shall find texts every now and then, which will give room for more valuable discourses than those like this, so general.— I do not understand what your Father wished to know about the translation, please ask again. Adieu, dear Mary. Heaven bless you and make you all that liberal Nature meant, very affely your friend

S. M. FULLER.

ALS (MH: fMS Am 1086 [9:50]); MsC (MH: fMS Am 1086 [Works, 1:171–77]). Published in *WNC*, pp. 345–47.

nor sense] nor ⟨nor⟩ sense
thoughts and analyses] thoughts and ⟨the⟩ analyses
fallen upon of] fallen upon ⟨naturally⟩ of

1. Neither Mary, Lilly, the mother, nor the aunt is identified.

2. Possibly Sarah Whipple (1817–95), daughter of John and Maria Bowen Whipple of Providence. Sarah married William H. Potter (F. T. Calef, "Whipple" [genealogy], RHi, pp. 468–69; Snow et al., *Alphabetical Index*).

3. Marianne Jackson (1820–46), daughter of Judge Charles Jackson (1775–1855) and his second wife, Frances Cabot, was Fuller's close friend (*CVR*; Mt. Auburn; James J. Putnam, *A Memoir of Dr. James Jackson* [Boston, 1905], p. 96). Caroline is Caroline Sturgis.

188. To John S. Dwight

Providence 9th Octr 1838—

Dear Sir,

You are at liberty to put my name to the translations as S. M. Fuller.[1] They are not of such distinguished beauty that I shall incur the charge of vanity thereby!

I rejoice that you have been able to do something for Mr Alcott.[2] Would that I had such a claim to self-complacency!

I think, perhaps, I shall pass my winter with the wise and excellent people of Boston. If Mr and Mrs Ripley have returned please give them my love and say that I have become acquainted with Mr Calvert, and that I[n] shall write to them when any one will tell me whether they are yet in Boston or no—[3]

Yours with much regard

S. M. FULLER.

ALS (MHarF). *Addressed:* Revd J. S. Dwight / Boston / Mass. *Postmark:* Providence / Oct 4. *Endorsed:* S. M. Fuller—Oct. 1838— / (1).

and that I] and ↑ that I ↓

1. Fuller's translations were so identified in Dwight's *Select Minor Poems.*

2. After closing his Temple School in June, Alcott planned to hold conversations in Lexington, Hingham, and Waltham. During the summer he became increasingly close to Dwight, who apparently encouraged him to lecture. In September Alcott did hold a conversation in Lexington, where Dwight was preaching. Fuller probably alludes to the support Dwight gave Alcott in this new venture (Alcott journal for 1838, MH: 59m-308 [11], pp. 303–5).

3. Henry Calvert (1803–89) of Baltimore was an author, poet, and translator of German. In 1829 he married Elizabeth Steuart (1802–97), daughter of Dr. James and Rebecca Sprigg Steuart (*DAB*; George N. Mackenzie, *Colonial Families of the United States of America* [New York, 1907]).

189.   To Jane F. Tuckerman

Providence, October 21. 1838.

I am reminded by what you say, of an era in my own existence; it is seven years bygone.[1] For bitter months a treble weight had been pressing on me; the weight of deceived friendship, domestic discontent, and bootless love. I could not be much alone; a great burden of family cares pressed upon me; I was in the midst of society, and obliged to act my part there as well as I could. It was at the time I took up the study of German, and my progress was like the rebound of a string pressed almost to bursting. My mind being then in the highest state of action, heightened by intellectual appreciation, every pang, and Imagination, by prophetic power, gave to the painful present, all the weight of as painful a future.

At this time I never had any consolation, except in long, solitary walks, and my meditations then were so far aloof from common life that on my return, my fall was like that of the eagle which the sportsman's hand calls bleeding from his lofty flight to stain the earth with his blood.

In such hours we feel so noble, so full of love and bounty that we cannot conceive that any pain should have been needed to teach us. It then seems we are so born for good, that such means of leading us to it were wholly unnecessary. But I have lived to know that the secret of all things is pain and that Nature travaileth most painfully with her noblest product. I was not without hours of deep spiritual insight, and consciousness of the inheritance of vast powers. I touched the secret of the universe, and by that touch was invested with talismanic power which has never left me, though it sometimes lies dormant for a long while.

One day lives always in my memory; one chastest, heavenliest day of communion with the soul of things. It was Thanksgiving-Day. I was free to be alone; in the meditative woods, by the choked-up fountain I passed its hours, each of which contained ages of thought and emotion. I saw then how idle were my griefs; that I had acquired *the thought* of each object which had been taken from me, that more extended personal relations would only have given me pleasures which then seemed not worth my care, and which would surely have dimmed my sense of the spiritual meaning of all which had passed. I felt how true it was that nothing in any being which was fit for me, could long be kept from me, and that if separation could be, real intimacy had never been. All the films seemed to drop from my existence, and I

347

was sure that I should never starve in this desert world, but that manna would drop from heaven, if I would but rise with every rising sun to gather it.

In the evening I went into the church-yard; the moon sailed above the rosy clouds. That cresent moon rose above the heavenward-pointing spire. At that hour a vision came upon my soul, whose final scene last month interpreted. The rosy clouds of illusion are all vanished, the moon has waxed to full. May my life be a church, full of devout thoughts, and solemn music. I pray thus, my dearest child: "Our Father, let not the heaviest shower be spared, let not the gardener forbear his knife, till the fair hopeful tree of existence be brought to its fullest blossom and fruit!"

MsCfr (MH: fMS Am 1086 [Works, 1:91–95]). Published in *WNC*, pp. 358–60.

1. Fuller probably refers to her unhappy experiences with George Davis.

190. To Charles K. Newcomb

[22? October 1838]
Monday eveg—
[Providence]

Dear Charles,

I went to see the sun set from those heights where you went with me one moonlight evening, and never did I behold more beauty. The woods are so rich and soft, and catch the light so exquisitely just before the sun drops;—do go there tomorrow; there is nothing like it on the other side of the bridge. Be sure and get there at least 15 minutes before sunset and look through every gap as you go up the hill that you may miss nothing of that rapturous mellowness of hue. I am unhappy that I cannot pass my days in the woods now they are in such perfection. Surely the limes and birches never looked so lovely as now. But there are no words for this intoxicating state of colour. The pity is that it can only last two or three days. I have repented ever since that I talked in the woods last Saturday morning instead of looking at the trees. And in the afternoon I w[as too] tired to go out again. Bu[t] while *you* are free to look, beauty does not smile here in vain. Be sure and see my sunset, if it is fair tomorrow. I wish I could be there too, but fear I cannot.

M. F.

ALS (MH: fMS Am 1086 [10:126]). *Addressed:* Mr Charles Newcomb. / Providence. *Endorsed:* From Miss Fuller—Oct. 23. '38.

191. To Richard F. Fuller

Providence, 30th [27?]ⁿ Octr 1838—

My dear Richard,

Your letter was duly received and I was pleased both by the manliness of thought it showed and by the care with which it was written. There are some mistakes and one or two slight improprieties which I shall point out to you when I see you. These are in the style and handwriting.

As to the subject of your letter, it has not changed my opinion except in this respect. I think that Lloyd had best go to Stoughton the first Decr. Will you say to our Mother that I think he will in many respects be more favorably situated there than at home. If he does not learn much in lessons the influence on his character and manners is better. And peace at home is all important to me. I earnestly hope she will send him.

I am equally clear that you had best remain at home till we leave Groton. I know that Mother wishes it strongly, and her wish should be law, not only to your conduct but your feelings. There is no hurry about you. You can undoubtedly go away to school by the first of May and in May you will only be fifteen. After that time you will be able to pursue your education uninterruptedly as our dear Mother will no longer need that aid, which you have been so fortunate as to render,ⁿ and I believe so far with truly dutifulⁿ good will. It is extravagant to send every boy from home while we still have a home. I admit that you have a better claim than others, but Arthur is too old to wait, and Lloyd unfortunately is unfit to take your place. Rely upon me, your faithful friend, that, if you make up your mind to pass this winter at home and do every thing in your power to assist, you shall not in after life have the least occasion to regret it.

With regard to your studies I am no longer situated as I was when I devoted all my mornings to you, Ellen and Arthur. My time is very valuable, even in a pecuniary point of view. While at Groton I must devote to writing all the time that I am well and bright, and after two years incessant teaching should prefer an absolute respite from that occupation. But I have engaged to give your sister lessons in German twice a week and will give you lessons in Latin and composition the same days. That is I will hear all the Latin you can prepare between whiles, and your sister Ellen will give you daily lessons in French. If your brother Eugene will do the same for you in Greek and writing I shall be very glad. The other branches you name I think you had best defer till you go to school. Mr Haven is fond of mathematics and offered to give Arthur extra lessons, if he[n] should take such interest in you, I think you would be grateful[1]

I do not wish you to make me any compensation in money. I receive from private pupils at the rate of half a dollar for a quarter of an hour lesson. But you cannot pay me at that rate, nor would I take a private pupil this winter for *any money*. Compensate me by willingness to take my advice and by that neatness in your dress, politeness in your manners, and devotion to the wishes of our Mother which will tend to make my home happy this winter.

I trust you will acquiese in my opinion. I think you must feel that your honor and happiness is one of my chief objects in life and that I would not sacrifice your good to my own convenience With love to the family and to Fanny I am your affectionate sister

S. M. FULLER.

Tell Fanny that her father made us a short visit a day or two since.[2]

Tell Eugene I shall send the paper to Uncle A. today, but that no newspaper came with it. Ellen has a bad cold, but seems stronger and in better spirits.

ALS (MH: fMS Am 1086 [9:51]); MsC (MH: fMS Am 1086 [Works, 2:615–23]). *Addressed:* Richard F. Fuller. / Groton, / Mass. *Postmark:* Providence R.I. Oct 28.

Though Fuller dates the letter 30th Octr, the postmark is clearly "28."
as to render,] as to render ⟨it⟩,
truly dutiful] truly dutiful⟨l⟩
if he] if ⟨s⟩ he
1. Luther Haven at Leicester Academy.
2. Frances Fuller and her father, Daniel Hastings.

192. To Charles K. Newcomb

[ca. November? 1838]
[Providence?]

Dear Charles,

You can keep these a week. Read Thoughts and Images by Archaeus, as well as the[n] poem.[1] Please be very careful that they get no dust or other soil. I feel at perfect liberty to lend any thing of Mr E's but I would not to any one but you, because, I always so much wish to return books in good order.

M. F.

ALS (MH: fMS Am 1086 [9:125]).

The holograph is inside an envelope addressed to Newcomb at Brook Farm and endorsed "Oct 30. 45." The contents suggest that it was written shortly after Fuller received the August number of Blackwood's *from Emerson, who sent it to her, with some letters, on 23 October (Rusk, Letters of RWE, 2:169–70).*

as the] as the ⟨other⟩

1. "Archaeus" was the pen name of John Sterling (1806–44), who contributed to various periodicals, but who was best known as the center of a literary group named after him. His associates were Carlyle, Tennyson, John Stuart Mill, and Lord Houghton (*DNB*). The reference is to his "Thoughts and Images," *Blackwood's Edinburgh Magazine* 44 (August 1838):197–207.

193. To Almira P. Barlow

Providence, Nov 8. 1838.

I am sorry on some accounts you will not come to Groton, yet I fear the seclusion of the place would be too much for you. For me, it is what I most covet. I shall go home about Christmas and stay till April, and never set foot out of doors unless to take exercise; and see no human face, divine or otherwise, out of my own family. But I am wearied out; I have gabbled and simpered, and given my mind to the public view these two years back, till there seems to be no good left in me.

Pray Heaven I may find some in those vestal solitudes.

M. F.—

MsCfr (MH: fMS Am 1086 [Works, 1:21–23]). Published in part in Higginson, *MFO*, p. 94.

194. To Elizabeth S. Calvert

Providence 16th Novr 1838—

My dear Mrs Calvert,

Miss Whipple brought me a message from you more than a week since, but I have not earlier been at leisure to write.[1] I sincerely thank you for your kind interest in my behalf, but my health is so much improved that I think it will be quite safe for me to stay in New England this winter.

I heard with unspeakable pain Dr Channing's opinion that I must go away. I was so wearied out with this public life I have led two years, and had so ardent a desire to return at least for a short time to the quiet of home, and the care of my mother, that no change of the sort could have been agreeable to me. I shall not feel so long. I am by nature energetick and fearless; if I should recover my natural tone of health and spirits, I[n] shall not dread labor nor shrink from meeting a circle of strangers as I do now. Should it then be necessary for me to recommence my exertions,[n] I may perhaps again appeal to your kindness.— If I had come to Baltimore this winter, I should have had not only to meet a class, but to prepare a course for it, as nothing that I had arranged for Boston would have suited your city according to your own acct.[n] I have[n] a half sketched plan which, if it ripen in solitude, I may perhaps state to you by and by, and you will judge whether it be suited to your meridian.

At present I hope to go home the 1st Jany and pass three months with my own family. Then 1st April[n] my Mother gives up her place in the country and I do not know what we shall do. But I do not look beyond. These three months of peace and seclusion after three years of toil, restraint and perpetual excitement, which my very bad health has made so hard to bear, wear to my fancy an Elysian brightness, of which you who have been more happily situated can scarce form an idea.

While I release you, dear Madam, from all present trouble on this[n] account, I would fain impose one of another kind. A letter from you would give me much pleasure. May I not[n] hope that you will write to me in the course of the winter? My brief acquaintance with yourself and Mr Calvert is very sweet to my memory. It turned my thoughts from painful subjects at a period of great anxiety, and antedated (I would hope) a more peaceful season[.] I would not be forgotten. Yet do not write, if other engagements and interests so absorb you as to make it a task. Mr Calvert, I suppose, is engaged in some turret chamber of the baronial castle, now you have finished furnishing *your own drawing room*. In the hope, however, that I shall not beg in vain, I would say that I shall remain here till the 20th Decr, then make a short visit to Boston. Any time after the 1st Jany a letter directed to me at Groton, Mass would reach me and "make a sunshine in the shady place."[2]

With renewed thanks for your remembrance[n] of my wishes (and in

especial of my desire for a pleasant *home*) and with best respects to
Mr Calvert I am very truly yours

S. M. FULLER.

ALS (MHi). *Addressed:* Mrs Calvert, / Care of George H. Calvert Esq. / Baltimore /
Maryland. *Postmark:* Providence R.I. Nov 19. *Endorsed:* Miss Fuller / 38.
and spirits, I] and spirits, ⟨as⟩ I
recommence my exertions] recommence my ⟨l⟩exertions
according to your own acct] ↑ according to your own acct ↓
I have] ⟨At present⟩ I have
Then 1st April] Then ↑ 1st April ↓
trouble on this] trouble on ⟨my⟩ ↑ this ↓
May I not] May I ⟨h⟩not
for your remembrance] for your ⟨m⟩remembrance
    1. Probably Frances Harriet Whipple (1805–78), daughter of Samuel Whipple. She
was a poet, a reformer, and an abolitionist. She married Charles C. Green, an artist, in
1842, divorced him in 1847, and married William C. McDougall in 1861 (*DAB*).
    2. Edmund Spenser, *The Faerie Queene*, bk. 1, canto 3, stanza 6:

> Her angel's face,
> As the great eye of heaven, shyned bright,
> And made a sunshine in the shady place;
> Did never mortall eye behold such heavenly grace.

195. To William H. Channing

Providence, 9th Decr 1838—

My dear Mr Channing
or may I just rather begin with My dear friend,
    Mary Channing gave me some message from you which I could not
understand about writing to you at Cincinnati—[1] Although I do not
know *what* was desired yet I may suppose that, if you wished a letter,
it was in the hope of getting from it entertainment or other good
cheer. As nothing of that kind will be afforded by this document, I
will not make the imperfectly understood invitation my excuse but
beg you to kindly receive a letter written about my own plans, written
to you because you can give me light—for mercy's sake.ⁿ
    I am on the point of leaving Providence, and I do so with un-
feigned delight, not only because I am weary and want rest, because
my mind has so long been turned outward and long[s] for concentration and leisure for tranquil thought, but because I have here been
always in a false position and my energies been consequently much

353

repressed. To common observers I seem well placed here, but I know that it is not so, and that I have had more than average difficulties to encounter, some of them insurmountable. But from these difficulties I have learned so much that I cannot but suppose my experience is to be of further use.

I do not wish to teach again at all. If I consult my own wishes I shall employ the remainder of my life in quite a different manner. But I forsee circumstances that may make it wrong for me to obey my wishes.

Mother has sold her place at Groton, and as she is to leave it in April, I shall go home and stay three months with her. These three months at least I dream of Elysian peace, of quiet growth and other benefits no doubt well known to your imagination

Then I hope to prevail on her to board with Ellen and me, and send the boys to school for some months. But after that we must find a sure foothold on the earth somewhere and plan anew a home.

But this leaves me nearly a year for my own inventions. If at the end of that time, it should seem necessary for the good of all concerned that I should teach again I wish to do it, and by the success I have already attained and by the confidence I now feel in my powers both of arrangement of a whole and action on parts feel myself justified in thinking I may do it to much greater pecuniary advantage and with much more extensive good results to others than I have yet done.

I am not without my dreams and hopes as to the education of women. They are not at all of the Martineau class, but, though brilliant, such, I think, as you, or any spiritual thinker however soberminded[n] would sympathize in. I have not space for any detail, but, should this prove at last my vocation, I do believe you would think them entitled to your aid.

Several lures have been already held out to me in case I should return to an occupation in which few persons of ability are at present engaged. But each of these plans seems[n] to me in some respect ineligible for my family if not for myself.

Two years since Mr J. Walker[n] was in Boston and left this message, (as I understood it) with a friend for me "that such a school as I could keep is much wanted in Cincinnati and that if I could make up my mind to be transplanted thither, I need only write to him, and he could make arrangements."[2]

I have always had some desire to be meddling with the West, and have only been checked in my tendencies thitherward by the mode[s]t

354

fancy that the *East* was not at a sufficiently advanced step of culture for my plans, how then should her younger sister be!!!

This message turned my thoughts towards Cincinnati. I have made many enquiries about the place and the result is that I think that place would, on the whole, suit me better than any other I have in view.

It would be an excellent starting point for my brothers, and I could, I suppose, be more independent of *aristocratic patrona[ge]* than in any of the great Eastern cities.

If you should remain there it would be a very strong additional inducement to come. Mother, as you saw, is both naturally and professionally a *parishioner*. She would want a clergyman whom she could respect, aid, and love." You so completely won her heart and Ellen's that I think your pastoral care would make them contented with any decent fold. To me your sympathy and the cooperation to which" you would, I believe, be inclined would be most valuable.

I should be *near?*" my friend's James, and Mr Eliot or at least within sympathizing distance which I am not now.[3] James says somewhat of Louisville, but I do not think I should like that place except for his friendly and intelligent aid.

Do not think I should not expect many dangers and difficulties. I should so, and have confidence in my own energy and *external* patience. As to *patience of the spirit*, I have laid to heart your wise reproof and I hope, not without some profit.

But, as my plan would be for an expensive establishment of which I should have the sole responsibility, because I should want absolute power, as it" would be a very important move for my family, and as, if I again undertake any plan, it will be laid for years that I may not only sow but reap, I wish to have it long under consideration, and that I may also have" all proper means for this you, who are on the spot, can be of the greatest advantage to me, if you will not esteem it a trouble and I think you will not.

You may not stay and I may never be obliged to teach again but if you" should and if I should I only want you to keep the project in your eye. See whether you think I could have sixty girls on the same terms as in Boston or Philadelphia. Whether I can have some three or four intelligent men and as many as even one woman who will steadily and understandingly aid and abet me. Whether the influences around you are such as would suit Mother and improve my sister and brothers. The rest you know.—

If I do something of this kind it will not be before Jany 1840—
What hostile or friendly star may not take the ascendant before that

time?ⁿ But you will be at Cincinnati till spring at all events.— A letter will reach me at Groton any time from Jany to April.

James will convey to you much gas and some small drop of essential fragrance from Boston. I have had some pleasant hours [   ]

ALfr (MB: Ms. Am. 1450 [35]). Published in part in Higginson, *MFO*, pp. 91–92.

mercy's sake.] *The salutation and opening paragraph have been heavily canceled by a later hand.*

thinker however sober-minded] thinker ↑ however sober-minded ↓

these plans seems] these ↑ plans ↓ seems

Mr J. Walker] Mr ↑ J. ↓ Walker

and love.] *The remainder of the paragraph has been heavily canceled by a later hand.*

cooperation to which] cooperation ↑ to ↓ which

be *near?*] be *near* ↑ ? ↓

power, as it] power, ⟨and⟩ as it

that I may also have] that I may ↑ also ↓ have

but if you] but ⟨y⟩ if you

that time?] *The remainder of the sheet has been heavily canceled by a later hand.*

1. Probably Dr. William Ellery Channing's daughter.

2. James Barr Walker (1805–87), an antislavery man, had been ordained as a Presbyterian minister in 1837. He moved from Hudson, Ohio, to Akron and then in 1839 to Cincinnati (*DAB*).

3. James Clarke and William Greenleaf Eliot (1811–87). Ordained in 1834, Eliot organized the First Congregational Society of St. Louis in 1835. Both Clarke and Eliot were instrumental in the founding and success of the *Western Messenger* (Heralds, 3:90–97).

INDEX

Library of Congress Cataloging in Publication Data

FULLER, MARGARET, 1810–1850.
   The letters of Margaret Fuller.

   Bibliography: p.
   Includes indexes.
   Contents: v. 1. 1817–38 — v. 2. 1839–41.
      1. Fuller, Margaret, 1810–1850—Correspondence.
2. Authors, American—19th century— Correspondence.
I. Hudspeth, Robert N.   II. Title.
PS2506.A4   1983   818'.309 [B]   82-22098
ISBN 0-8014-1386-9 (v. 1)